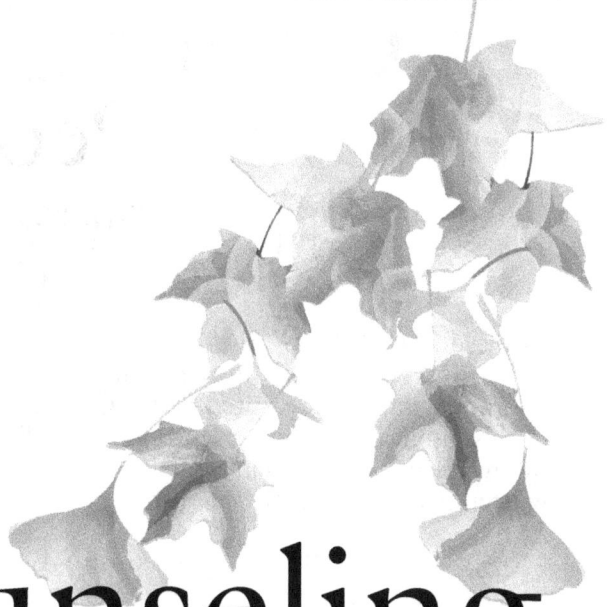

Counseling
Older People
opportunities
and challenges

Charlene M. Kampfe

AMERICAN COUNSELING
ASSOCIATION
6101 Stevenson Avenue, Suite 600 • Alexandria, VA 22304 • www.counseling.org

Counseling Older People

opportunities and challenges

10   9   8   7   6   5   4   3   2   1

American Counseling Association
6101 Stevenson Avenue, Suite 600 • Alexandria, VA 22304

Associate Publisher • Carolyn C. Baker

Digital and Print Development Editor • Nancy Driver

Production Manager • Bonny E. Gaston

Copy Editor • Kimberly W. Kinne

Cover design by Bonny E. Gaston

Library of Congress Cataloging-in-Publication Data
Kampfe, Charlene M.
    Counseling older people: opportunities and challenges/Charlene M. Kampfe.
      pages cm
    Includes bibliographical references and index.
    ISBN 978-1-55620-323-7 (pbk. : alk. paper)
1. Older people—Counseling of. 2. Older people—Psychology.
3. Older people—Social conditions.   4. Older people—Mental health. I. Title.
    HV1451.K356 2015
    362.6'6—dc23   2014038869

Table of Contents

Preface

The older population is one of the fastest growing groups in the United States (Administration on Aging, 2007). The growth of this population can be both an opportunity and a challenge for professional counselors, including general counselors as well as those who specialize in group work, employment, rehabilitation, multicultural issues, gerontology, substance abuse, grief and loss, mental health, spirituality, assessment, military, family, and forensics.

With the growth of the older population, we counselors will have the exciting opportunity to carve a place for our profession in those systems that serve older people. Currently in those systems, older people are often disempowered, and there are few programs and resources that provide gerontological counseling. Although some counselors may not have worked with older consumers in the past, they already have many of the skills necessary to do so. Counselors understand and support the concept of empowerment. They know how to provide a safe, respectful, and challenging environment in which individuals can explore their thoughts, feelings, and behaviors. They have been trained to be good listeners, advocates, problem solvers, and case managers.

The challenge for counselors is to become informed about the characteristics of the older population, specific issues faced by this group and their families and friends, services and benefits available to them, advocacy issues associated with aging, vocational interests and concerns of older people, family dynamics that may influence older people and their adult children, assessment issues associated with older people, attitudes toward older people, death and dying perspectives, systems in which older people are served, laws and regulations that apply to the older population, and specific counseling techniques that are effective for individuals who are experiencing certain conditions associated with being older. Learning about these topics will extend the boundaries of counselors' competence and will take them closer to meeting the recommendations of both the American Counseling Association (ACA) and the Council on Rehabilitation Education (CORE) codes of ethics that counselors practice in specialty areas only if they have appropriate education, training, and supervised experience.

The purpose of this book is to provide practical, anecdotal, and research-based information and perspectives to counselors who wish to work with the older population. Personal experiences, case studies, practical suggestions, and various exercises and activities are included to help the reader analyze, incorporate, and assimilate the material. The book is based on the concepts of personal power, personal choice, variability, and the dignity of older persons who counselors serve. In writing this book, I have relied on many resources: (a) my professional experience in working with older consumers and their families; (b) scholarly study of this population, including writing about this group; (c) membership in the Association for Adult Development and Aging; (d) consultation with agencies and programs that provide services to older people; (e) discussions with colleagues and professors who provided information, wisdom, perspective, practicality, and philosophy regarding aging; (f) presentations to various audiences regarding the aging process; (g) years of experience teaching about and being actively involved in advocacy issues; (h) experience with my own family members' aging process; (i) interaction with agencies, programs, and individuals that have provided services to my older relatives; and (j) my own personal journey through the aging process.

About the Author

Charlene M. Kampfe, PhD, is a professor emeritus of rehabilitation counseling at the University of Arizona, Tucson, and has also taught in the School of Medicine at the University of North Carolina, Chapel Hill. She received her doctorate from the Department of Rehabilitation Counseling at the University of Arizona and is a national certified counselor, a nationally certified gerontological counselor, and a national certified rehabilitation counselor.

Dr. Kampfe has served as a governing council member of the ACA, president of the Association for Adult Development and Aging (AADA), and board member for both the American Rehabilitation Counseling Association (ARCA) and the National Council on Rehabilitation Education (NCRE). She has served on and chaired many committees of these associations and has received numerous awards for her service (e.g., Outstanding Contributions in the Field of Government Relations from ARCA, Government Relations Award from AADA, Distinguished Service Award from the AADA, President's Award from the Arizona AADA, and Outstanding Member Award from the Arizona Counselors Association). She has also been involved in international consultation and capacity building with Mexico, Kenya, and Afghanistan, and she has served on local advisory committees for various projects of the Tucson Botanical Gardens Horticulture Therapy program, which focuses on aging issues.

Dr. Kampfe has published 11 chapters, 65 journal articles, and one group-written book, *The Aging Workforce,* for which she was a group editor. She has given more than 100 presentations at the local, national, and international levels regarding various aspects of counseling and the human condition, and she has been a keynote speaker or panel facilitator of opening/closing sessions for 10 national meetings or conferences. She has served on numerous editorial review boards and received several national awards for her scholarship (e.g., Outstanding Research Award from the Counseling Academic and Professional Honor Society International, Outstanding JADARA Article from the American Deafness and Rehabilitation Association, Ralph F. Berdie Memorial Research Award from ACA, and Best Practices Faculty Research Award from ACA).

Acknowledged as an exceptional teacher and mentor, Dr. Kampfe has received numerous awards for this aspect of her professional life. Her awards include Honored Faculty Member at the First Annual Learning Disability Gala, University of North Carolina; Faculty in Models of Teaching Excellence, University of Arizona; Mentor of the Year Award, AADA; Outstanding Teacher, College of Education, University of Arizona; Outstanding Faculty Member, Disability Resource Center, University of Arizona; Sarah Folsom Memorial Award, Arizona Rehabilitation Counseling Association; Extraordinary Faculty Award, University of Arizona Alumni Association; Counselor Education Advocacy Award, ACA; and Rehabilitation Educator of the Year, NCRE. Furthermore, a student fund was established in her name by the ARCA Student Task Force. Since her retirement, she has continued to teach or act as a mentor with the Rehabilitation Counseling Program, Auburn University, Auburn, Alabama; and the Humanities Seminars Program, University of Arizona.

Dr. Kampfe is a creative dancer, singer, and drummer. She belongs to the International Association for Creative Dance and dances regularly at the Tucson Creative Dance Center and at national conferences. She has incorporated creative dance philosophy into the counseling process and has given several presentations at national conferences regarding the parallels between creative dance and creative counseling.

Acknowledgments

I wish to thank Carolyn Baker, Nancy Driver, Dr. S. Mae Smith, Dr. John Wadsworth, Dr. Jane Myers, Dr. Juliette Neihaus, Dr. Larry Burlew, Richard Helling, Dr. Phil Johnson, Dr. Manley Begay Jr., Dr. Linda Shaw, Art Terrazas, Dr. Will Stroble, Holly Clubb, Dr. Michelle Wade, Jennifer Fowler, Caroline Chilewski, Dr. Catherine Roland, Sandy Durazo, Kimberly Kinne, and all of my teachers, students, friends, and members of the AADA for their wisdom, practical advice, challenges, insights, and scholarship in the field of counseling with older adults. I want to thank all the older people with whom I have lived and worked for sharing their stories with me and for informing me of the potential life experiences and perspectives an older person can have.

I give special thanks to my parents (Royce and Vivian Chipps), my grandparents (Paul and Mattie Chipps, Fred and Eva Robinson), and my great-grandparents (Frank and Emma Chipps, Little Grandma Wilhemina Robinson) for all their lessons about love, honor, kindness, and follow-through and for sharing their experiences in the aging process. I also want to thank my husband (Ron Kampfe) and his family, my sister (Tami Jonak) and her family, my aunts and uncles (Mildred, Bernie, Bob, Doris, Jack) and their children, and my friends (from childhood to the present) who are, happily, too numerous to mention. I also want to express my admiration for the ancestors who I never knew. They have all shaped my life and my opinions about older people. I also want to thank my dog, Buddy, who sat under my chair as I wrote and occasionally reminded me that it is time to play.

Chapter 1

The Increasing Older Population and Its Characteristics

The purpose of this chapter is to provide an overview of the aging population in the United States. The chapter includes discussions of the levels, classifications, and definitions of old age; the growth in the older population; the diversity among this group; and attitudes toward aging and older people. In addition, there is an acknowledgment that the older population is composed of the strong ones, that is, the ones who survived.

Levels, Classifications, and Definitions of Old Age

There are many classifications or categories of old age. Although these classifications may have little practical or meaningful significance to counselors or their clients, counselors should be aware of them in order to understand and evaluate the literature, research, laws, regulations, and attitudes that exist about aging. Counselors should also be aware that the classification systems can be confusing and should be viewed with caution. One problem with age classifications is that writers define them differently or provide different birth dates for the same classification title.

The most often used classification is *chronological age* (i.e., the number of years that a person has lived, such as age 65, age 85, age 105). This classification is typically used in literature, legislation, policies, research, and reports. Age 65 is the age by which the general public typically defines "old" (Wadsworth, Smith, & Kampfe, 2006).

Examples of chronological age classifications include the *young-old* (age 65 to age 74 or 75), the *old-old* (age 75 to age 84), the *oldest-old* or *very-old* (approximately 85 years or older), the *centenarians* (age 100 years or older), and the *super centenarians* (age 110 years or older; Chatters & Zalaquett, 2013; Lehembre, 2012; Schaie & Willis, 2002; Whitbourne & Whitbourne, 2011). Yet another term for the very old is *nonagenarians* (Lehembre, 2012).

Other classifications are based on actual dates that individuals were born (*age cohort*). Age cohort is much different than chronological age and often reflects the experiences that a group of people have in common. People who were born in 1925 will have very different experiential backgrounds than people who were born in 1945. For example, the cohort of people born in 1925 likely experienced the Great Depression and thus learned to live in moderation. They may, therefore, have a different perspective of life than the cohort of people who were born in 1945 (Loe, 2011).

There is some danger in classification systems for older people because people vary widely within each age group and because the definition of "old" is evolving. Because of the variability among people who have reached a particular chronological age, gerontologists have encouraged the use of new classification systems that are based on functional age. Three of these classifications systems are biological age (based on quality of bodily systems), psychological age (based on memory, intelligence, and learning abilities), and social age (based on social roles; Whitbourne & Whitbourne, 2011).

Another term that has been used to refer to older people is *the elderly*. It has been suggested that this term is a subtle form of ageism because it connotes many images and behaviors that are thought to be common among older people (e.g., frailness, forgetfulness). Because the term *the elderly* broadly categorizes people as objects, the American Psychological Association (APA) has indicated in its popular style manual that it should not be used; instead, APA advocates using terms such as *older adults*. Therefore, counselors may want to avoid using the term *the elderly* in their work with older people (J. E. Myers & Shannonhouse, 2013).

Projections of Growth of the Older Population

The older population is one of the fastest growing groups in the United States (Dixon, Richard, & Rollins, 2003). In 2000, at least 35 million U.S. citizens were age 65 or older (U.S. Census Bureau, 2000). It has been projected that by 2030, 71 million Americans will be age 65 or older, and by 2040, 80 million Americans will be this age. The increase in the older population is primarily attributable to increased life expectancy and the large number of Baby Boomers who are aging (Administration on Aging, 2007).

Life expectancy in the United States has increased in recent years. According to the Administration on Aging (2007), life expectancy increased by 2.5 years from 1900 to 1960 and by 4.3 years from 1960 to 2004. Persons who were age 65 in 2007 were expected to live another 18 years, and those who were age 85 were expected to live an additional 6 to 7 years (Federal Interagency Forum on Aging, 2006). Increased life expectancy is primarily attributable to improvements in health care practices for the general public (Devino, Petrucci, & Snider, 2004; Hogg, Lucchino, Wang, & Janicki, 2001) and preventive practices with regard to onset or progression of disabling conditions among older people (Fried & Guralnik, 1997). Life expectancy has also increased for people who have had lifelong disabling conditions (Mitchell, Adkins, & Kemp, 2006), such as amputations (Briggs, 2006), traumatic brain injury (Weintraub & Ashley, 2004), multiple sclerosis (DeVivo, 2004), and developmental disabilities (Hogg et al., 2001).

Baby Boomers are those people who were born from 1946 through 1964, and there are approximately 72 to 79 million of them (Haaga, 2011). The first of these individuals reached age 65 in 2011; over the next two decades, the remainder of the group will reach this age (U.S. Census Bureau, 2006). Many of these individuals are considered to lead more productive lives and to be healthier than earlier groups at their age (Institute on Rehabilitation Issues, 2009).

This growing population provides an opportunity for counselors to infuse themselves into the systems that serve older people. Counselors have the basic and important skills to assist this group. They are good listeners, facilitators of empowerment and problem solving, and advocates who provide a respectful, safe, yet challenging environment that encourages clients to explore their thoughts, feelings, and behaviors and to effectively cope with the multiple issues that older people face.

Diversity of the Older Population

The older population is very heterogeneous. Indeed, the term *diversity* has been used in discussions of their characteristics (Larkin, Alston, Middleton, & Wilson, 2003). Although members of this population share the descriptive term *older*, they vary widely with regard to gender, race, ethnicity, culture, education, employment, occupation, socioeconomic status, religion, immigration and migration patterns, personality development, life experiences, family constellation, health status, disability status, and functional level (Kampfe, Harley, Wadsworth, & Smith, 2007; Middleton, 2005; S. M. Smith & Kampfe, 2000). This diversity is expected to increase in coming years as the current younger population becomes older (Dixon et al., 2003). One of the core professional values of the *ACA Code of Ethics* (ACA, 2014) is to honor and embrace "a multicultural approach in support of the worth, dignity, potential, and uniqueness of people within their social and cultural contexts" (Preamble). This value certainly applies to the widely diverse group of older people.

The older population is composed of a large percentage of females. In 2007, the overall ratio of men to women among older people was approximately 100 to 138. This ratio continues to change with age. For example, the ratio of men to women among the population age 65 to 69 was 100 to 114, whereas the ratio among the population age 85 or older was 100 to 213 (Administration on Aging, 2007). Because older women outnumber older men, counselors will need to become aware of the situations faced by women and develop effective counseling strategies to work with them (Choate, 2008). Counselors also need to be aware that males are, essentially, a minority group among the older population and may require unique counseling strategies designed for them.

The fastest growing subgroup of older people is composed of those from minority backgrounds. In 2000, the minority subgroup represented 16.4% of the older population, but this proportion is projected to rise to 23.6% by 2020 (Administration on Aging, 2007). Older individuals from minority groups have been reported to have low economic status and limited access to health care, both of which interact to result in the highest incidence of chronic disabling conditions among that older population (Larkin et al., 2003). Counselors should be familiar with health care and rehabilitation services that are available to this population and determine the degree to which individuals need or want assistance in identifying and accessing these services. Counselors should be mindful of the type of services that older minority clients may prefer. For example, they may wish to use indigenous healers or informal networks rather than the systems used by the current majority population (Harley, 2005; Kampfe, Wadsworth, Smith, & Harley, 2005).

The older population is also diverse because of the multiple age cohorts it represents (i.e., ages ranging from 65 to 105+ years). These ages represent at least four decades and several generations. People from each age cohort will have experienced unique life events and environmental conditions that have shaped their perceptions of the world, sense of autonomy, sense of security, views of spending and saving, values, spirituality, definitions of oldness, and other aspects of their lives (Kampfe et al., 2007). Counselors should not, therefore, assume that all older people belong to one group of individuals with similar histories, values, and behaviors.

There is also broad variation within each age cohort. Variables such as urban versus rural lifestyles; geographical location (e.g., East, Midwest, West, South); natural surroundings (e.g., mountains, flatlands); personal, racial, ethnic, and cultural backgrounds; past and current cultures experienced as an outsider; family composition and atmosphere; socioeconomic status; gender; religious background; disability status; and individual personality styles will all contribute to the variation among people within each age cohort (Institute on Rehabilitation Issues, 2009; Kampfe & Dennis, 2000).

Because each person will have his or her own broad combination of group or cultural backgrounds that may influence thoughts, feelings, and behaviors, counselors cannot assume that individuals from a particular age cohort or cultural group will share all the same beliefs and practices of that particular group. In other words, counselors will need to be open to a variety of individual client styles and needs while being sensitive to the specific cultures that are important to each consumer. It is particularly important for counselors to be aware of and respectful of the various views of aging that individuals have and to take these into account when considering therapeutic interventions and client decisions (Kampfe et al., 2007). The implication of the wide diversity among the older population is that counselors must continue to develop cultural competency.

Negative Attitudes Toward Aging and Older People

Unfortunately, our society has typically devalued older people. This devaluation has been characterized by negative stereotypes about this population (i.e., ageism/prejudice against older people), fear of aging (gerontophobia), and misconceptions about what it means to be old (Saucier, 2004; Shmotkin & Eyal, 2003; Wadsworth et al., 2006). Furthermore, our society typically holds negative attitudes toward disability (Gordon, Feldman, Tantillo, & Perrone, 2004). Because older people are likely to have one or more disabling conditions, they may have two risk factors for being devalued.

Negative attitudes can, and do, influence behaviors toward an individual or a group of people (McCarthy & Light, 2005). For example, older people have often been discouraged from making their own life decisions or doing things for themselves, forced to make unnecessary residential relocations, and discriminated against in the workplace. They are sometimes spoken to disrespectfully or as if they were children; they are called "honey"; they are addressed using the "royal we," as in "How are we today?"; and they are spoken "about" in front of them, as in "Has he taken his meds today?" Other inappropriate behaviors include ignoring older people's perspective or concerns and using degrading body language (e.g., rolling eyes, knowing smiles; Doyle, Dixon, & Moore, 2003; Kampfe et al., 2005; J. E. Myers & Schwiebert, 1996).

In addition to direct behaviors that show devaluation, indirect and systemic messages of low value are given. For example, older people are sometimes excluded from various epidemiological studies, which may be a subtle and perhaps unconscious statement by researchers that the older population does not matter or is inappropriate for a particular study, simply by virtue of advanced age (Kampfe et al., 2005; Wadsworth et al., 2006). Other examples of devaluation can be seen in advertising and in television programming. One only needs to watch television to see the large number of devaluing statements that are made regarding older people or aging, especially for women (Choate, 2008). I invite you, the reader, to partake of the following exercise.

Media and Advertising Activity

1. At any time during the day or night, turn the television on for 1 to 4 hours.
2. List all items having to do with age (both positive and negative). Items may include physical appearance (e.g., hiding the gray, reducing wrinkles, etc.); depictions of older people as weak, slow, or with memory loss; portrayals of older people as wise; and depictions of interactions between younger and older people.
3. Tabulate the number of positive messages versus negative messages about aging.
4. After completing this list, consider how these messages (a) reflect the general population's perceptions of aging and older people, (b) influence the general population's perception of aging and older people, (c) influence counselors' perceptions of aging and older people, and (d) influence your own perceptions of aging and older people.
5. Brainstorm strategies that you can use to counteract the potential negative attitudes that exist in the media, in the public, in older people (themselves), in the counseling profession, and in yourself.

Because counselors are a part of this society, they, themselves, may have fears, stereotypes, and general negative views of aging and older people. They may unconsciously associate aging with decline, disability, death, weakness, dependence, inability to make decisions, disinterest in learning new things, and inability to contribute to society (Kampfe et al., 2005; Kimmel, 2012; Shannonhouse & Myers, in press; Wadsworth et al., 2006). In contrast, believing that all older people are sweet, kind, or wise may also be a form of ageism because these views indicate the belief that all older people are the same and perhaps one-dimensional (Kampfe, 1990b). These thoughts and feelings may limit counselors' openness, understanding, and expectations of older clients (J. E. Myers & Schwiebert, 1996; Shallcross, 2012c). Counselors will, therefore, need to examine their own attitudes about aging and challenge any negative perceptions that they have about older people.

Counselors' self-evaluations of their attitudes toward aging and older people are likely to be a lifelong endeavor that will require considerable introspection, supervision, training, and perhaps personal counseling.

Counselors can benefit by participating in training sessions or graduate courses regarding this issue (e.g., dignity vs. dehumanization training, values clarification workshops). They can join the AADA, attend AADA annual conferences, or attend AADA-sponsored training at the ACA World Conference. They can engage in personal exploration of their attitudes through individual or group counseling or discussions with colleagues or supervisors; they can refer to their professional code of ethics and professional philosophy, which promote the right to productivity, dignity, independence, and self-determination (Kampfe et al., 2005); and they can read information about ageism such as that provided by J. E. Myers and Shannonhouse (2013).

Individual Exercise: Counselors' Perceptions of Aging

1. Make a list of all the descriptors of older people. When doing this, try to be as honest as you can with yourself about your current perceptions of this population. Start with physical descriptors then move to mental, spiritual, emotional, and other descriptors. Describe their energy levels, work tolerance, personal power, desire to work, level of independence, types of skills, and type of disabilities you are aware of. List both positive and negative attributes.
2. For each of these, reflect back to the source of these perceptions or attitudes. How accurate are these perceptions? What has contributed to your views of older people? What is there about you, personally, that has resulted in these views?
3. Discuss your answers with a group or with another person. These discussions may provide additional insight.
4. As you read the book and as you do further study of the older population, return to your list and examine any changes you make regarding your opinions.

Group Exercise: Influence of Stereotypes

The purpose of this group exercise is to encourage counselors to consider how stereotypes or prejudices can interfere with the counseling process (Kampfe et al., 2007). It can also be used with family members and community service providers.

1. Two people sit or stand facing each other approximately 15 feet apart. One of these people will be the counselor, and the other will be an older consumer.
2. One at a time, the group members will call out negative stereotypes that society may have about older people.
3. As each stereotype is called out, that person stands between the counselor and the consumer. Continue this process until at least four or five people are standing between the counselor and the consumer.

4. At the end of the process, the question is raised, "Can the counselor see the consumer?"
5. Discuss the implications of this exercise in the counseling process.

This exercise can be repeated, with the counselor being an older person and the consumer being the younger person. Again, stereotypes about older people are called out, and people stand between the younger consumer and the older counselor. The question can be asked, "Can the consumer be open to the older counselor?" As typically happens, it becomes clear that negative stereotypes and attitudes about older people may impede the counseling process.

Older people, themselves, may have internalized societal ageist concepts. They may demonstrate these concepts by avoiding other older people, developing low self-concepts or self-efficacy, feeling vulnerable, questioning their abilities and worth, lying about their age, and getting facelifts or makeup to disguise their age. Furthermore, they may believe that older people should behave in certain ways and therefore restrict their activities to what they consider to be age-appropriate behaviors. In other words, internalized societal ageist concepts may affect their thoughts, feelings, and behaviors. Counselors need to be alert to these ageist attitudes, challenge them, and help clients work through negative self-perceptions associated with aging (Edmondson & Kondratowitz, 2009; J. E. Myers & Schwiebert, 1996).

Counselors can do much to change the attitudes of the community, family members, other service providers, and older people themselves. One of the most effective strategies in changing attitudes is to model appropriate behaviors and language. For example, when a counselor observes family members or others making decisions for the client, the counselor can stop the conversation and ask the client what he or she wants. If someone asks a family member or the counselor what they want to do about the client, the counselor can say, "Let's ask him." When a client is present but someone speaks about that client rather than to that client, the counselor can face the client and speak directly to him or her about the topic. When a service worker speaks to the client with the sticky sweet voice, as if speaking to a child, the counselor can model direct adult-to-adult communication with the client. Counselors can also provide training to family members and service providers regarding attitudes and behaviors. For example, they can use the above exercises with these individuals or other training resources described throughout this book. In addition, counselors may benefit by having more detailed information about healthy aging. An entire chapter focuses on this topic.

They Are the Survivors: The Strong Ones

An important point for counselors to remember is that older people are the survivors. Regardless of their current physical and mental functioning, they are the strong ones. They are the ones who lived to be older people. They are the ones who learned to adjust and to make it beyond age 65 or age 85 or age 100, when others did not. I have found that when older people hear that I perceive that they are the strong ones (e.g., that they have survived when others have not) and that they have wisdom and information to impart, their eyes brighten because this seems to be a new concept (even a revelation) to them. They sometimes indicate surprise that anyone has thought this. Such communication often leads to very strong counseling relationships that can support the counseling process. I do not remember which wise friend, teacher, or scholar taught me this concept, but it has stayed with me, and it has become my own. I have assimilated it. I own it. I hope that you, the reader, can also make it your own belief.

A relatively recent movement has been underway to recognize the strengths of older individuals (Choate, 2008). Various positive characteristics have been associated with people who have had long and successful lives. These attributes include optimism, adaptability, resilience, a sense of responsibility for oneself, belief in personal power, healthy self-esteem, involvement in meaningful relationships and projects, a history of work habits and skills, and potential for leadership and mentoring (Borman & Henderson, 2001; Institute on Rehabilitation Issues, 2009; Kampfe, Wadsworth, Mamboleo, & Schonbrun, 2008).

A variable that will strengthen the shift toward positive attitudes about older people is the aging of the Baby Boomers. This group is bringing a new definition to the terms *older* and *aging*. Furthermore, the shift in improved health among the older population appears to have resulted in a concomitant positive shift in attitudes toward aging (J. E. Myers & Degges-White, 2007). This change in attitudes is reflected in the terms *healthy aging, resourceful aging, positive aging,* and *successful aging* (Angus & Reeve, 2006). These terms are examples of how attitudes can change the language being used to describe someone as well as how changing the language can be used to change attitudes.

Although attitudes are beginning to shift from negative to positive, stereotypical views of older people and dehumanizing behaviors are still displayed throughout our culture. Fortunately, counselors, at their basic core, have been trained to support the independence, respect the opinions, and promote the integrity of the people they serve; therefore, they are well-suited to serve people who are older (Doyle et al., 2003; Finch & Robinson, 2003; Kampfe, 1994; Kampfe et al., 2005).

Summary

The older population is one of the fastest growing groups in the United States. This group is widely diverse; consequently, counselors cannot expect that one older person will be the same as another. Our society has traditionally had an ageist attitude. Counselors will need to examine their own attitudes toward aging and older people and take steps to ensure that these attitudes are appropriate. They can also encourage older clients and their communities to develop and maintain positive attitudes toward aging. An underlying belief that can support counselors in this process is that older people are the strong ones. They are the survivors.

Chapter 2
Counselor Considerations When Working With Older People

The purpose of this chapter is to provide information that is specific to gerontological counselors. Topics include counselor education program standards; other professionals who work with older people; responsibilities mandated by the Health Insurance Portability and Accountability Act (HIPAA); evidence-based practice and programming; the dangers of transference; the concepts of autonomy, personal control, independence, and empowerment; multicultural issues associated with aging and the need for counselor cultural competency; therapies used with older people; case management; assessment; and assistive technology.

Counselor Education Program Standards

The *ACA Code of Ethics* (ACA, 2014) reiterates the importance of appropriate training for and competence of counselors who work with special populations (Standards A.11.b., C.2.a., C.2.b., and E.2.a.). Individuals who wish to become gerontological counselors must seek appropriate graduate counselor training (i.e., from an accredited counselor education program) to ensure both that they have basic counseling skills and that they will be able to obtain certification and licensure to practice. At the present time, there are three important bodies or organizations from which counselor education programs can obtain accreditation: the Council for Accreditation of Counseling and Related Educational Programs (CACREP), the Council on Rehabilitation Education (CORE), and the Master's in Psychology and Counseling Accreditation Council (MPCAC). Furthermore, as of 2013, CACREP and CORE offer dual CACREP/CORE accreditation standards (i.e., Clinical Rehabilitation Counseling Standards).

Counselors need to "engage in ongoing professional development regarding current topics" (ACA, 2014, Introduction) associated with the older population in order to keep themselves up-to-date regarding this diverse population and "to ensure the competence of their work and protect others from possible harm" (ACA, 2014, Standard C.2.b.; also see Standard C.2.f.). With knowledge, counselors will be likely to have an accurate understanding of their clients' experiences and an arsenal of resources to help them deal with these experiences. To gain knowledge, counselors can read textbooks and journal articles about counseling older people, contact the resources suggested in this book, partake in continuing education options that focus on aging, seek supervision to evaluate their efficacy, obtain an additional gerontology certificate from a college or university, study the newer concepts about human growth and development, and do an internship in a program that serves older people (ACA, 2014; Shallcross, 2012c).

A major concern is that the term *gerontological counselor* currently has varying definitions. For example, a general term used for many types of professionals who specialize in working with older people is *gerontologist*. According to some sources, one group of gerontologists is composed of *gerontological counselors*, broadly defined as "applied gerontologists," who work directly with older people and their families to provide materials and education. Requirements for gerontological counselors can range from a bachelor's degree with special training in counseling, to professional counseling certification plus training in gerontological issues, to a master's degree in mental health counseling, to a doctorate in psychology. Furthermore, the definition for gerontological counselor varies from state to state. Such broad and varying definitions of gerontological counselor are of great concern because there is no guarantee of specific, consistent training or skills in counseling or in working with older people. In order to maintain control over the qualifications for gerontological counselors, the counseling profession may wish to advocate for national certification and educational program accreditation for this specialty, similar to that which existed in the past (see J. E. Myers & Schwiebert, 1996).

Other Professionals Who Work With the Older Population

According to the *ACA Code of Ethics*, counselors "work to become knowledgeable about colleagues within and outside the field of counseling . . . and develop positive working relationships and systems of communications with colleagues to enhance services to clients" (ACA, 2014, Section D, Introduction). Hence, counselors should be aware of the many specialists who are qualified to work with older people.

Professionals who specialize in mental health and aging include psychologists who focus on the older population (*geropsychologists*), social workers who focus on gerontological issues, and horticultural therapists who focus on aging issues (Casciani, 2012a, 2012b; Crawford & Walker, 2004; J. Neihause, personal communication, December 8, 2013; Weinstein, 2008). Counselors may find that working as a team member with these professionals can enhance services for their older clients.

Physicians who specialize in aging issues are called *geriatricians*. These individuals have skills and knowledge to recognize and treat the multiple physical conditions associated with aging; be aware of the unique effects, side effects, and interactions of medications on older people; understand how older bodies differ from younger bodies; and be familiar with other geriatric issues and needs. Unfortunately, there is a shortage in geriatricians, and this shortage is projected to increase as the Baby Boomers continue to reach age 65. Furthermore, in many cases, medical students have not had clinical rotations in geriatrics and therefore have not received even the basics in geriatrics during their training (Butterfield, 2007; Kimmel, 2012). Other medical specialists who may treat older people are neurologists, who focus on nerves and the brain; physiatrists, who focus on physical medicine and rehabilitation; and geriatric psychiatrists, who focus on mental disorders. Because of the unique nature of medical issues associated with older people, general doctors may miss important diagnostic clues, prescribe inappropriate or excessive medications, and have limited knowledge of cutting-edge medical treatments for older people. Counselors need to be aware of these potential problems and encourage older people and their families to seek medical advice and treatment from geriatricians if possible. Counselors can help clients find geriatricians or other medical specialists using the websites of the following organizations: the American Medical Association (https://apps.ama-assn.org/doctorfinder/html/patient. jsp), WebMD (http://doctor.webmd.com/), Find a Doc (http:// www.findadoc.com/), and the American Geriatric Society (http:// www.americangeriatrics.org).

Geriatric care managers (GCMs) provide geriatric care management and case management regarding a variety of topics (e.g., banking, accounting, trust departments, elder law, senior real estate, assisted living, medical care systems). GCMs represent a wide range of educational backgrounds (e.g., nursing, social work, gerontology, occupational therapy, and physical therapy) and a synthesis of theory and knowledge from each of these professions. Geriatric care management has become a professional business field with its own certificates and academic degrees. GCMs help older people and their families solve problems using client assessment, service coordination, nursing and social work tools, care planning, referral, monitoring, and help in time of crisis. In other words, they are case managers who provide a personal, individualized service on a 24-hour-a-day, 7-days-a-week basis. Furthermore, they act as surrogate family members who develop a long-term relationship with the older people they serve (Cress, 2007). Although counselors have not traditionally been listed as potential GCMs, they are very appropriate candidates because they often function as case managers (L. Shaw, personal communication, November 3, 2013). It might, therefore, be helpful for counselors to explore the certification, licensure, and training process for GCMs in their states.

HIPAA

Counselors who are working with clients of any age must be knowledgeable about HIPAA, which is designed to protect the privacy of their clients. Because counselors often work with various professionals, programs, family members, and friends of older people, it is vital that they are totally familiar with the HIPAA rules and that they follow them carefully. A discussion of these rules is beyond the scope of this book; however, counselors should find ways to update themselves regarding HIPAA and how to apply it to the type of work that they are doing.

Evidence-Based Programming and Practice

Evidenced-based programming and counseling practices are important in providing optimal services to clients. In other words, counselors should use programming and techniques that have been shown to be effective via well-designed research (ACA, 2014, Standard C.7.a.). Counselors would do well to read data-based, refereed articles to determine whether the counseling strategies or specific programming they use have been studied for their effectiveness with older populations (ACA, 2014, Standard C.7.a.). Thus, counselors need to have the ability to judge the quality of the research being described. As mentioned elsewhere in this book, the National Council on Aging's Center for Healthy Aging (see http://www.ncoa.org/improve-health/center-for-healthy-aging) helps community organizations identify and put into place evidence-based practices; however, they focus only on depression, physical activity, and fall prevention. This center and perhaps other similar organizations would likely be good resources for information regarding successful counseling strategies and programs. Furthermore, counselors can contribute to the development of evidence-based practice by collaborating with researchers who are conducting studies of this nature.

Unfortunately, many of the programs and practices designed for older people have yet to be examined for their effectiveness using data-based research designs; therefore, many of the suggestions made in this current book are anecdotal rather than data-based. It will be important for current and future researchers to apply rigorous methodology to study any and all techniques and concepts suggested in the literature and in this book.

Potential Dangers of Transference Among Counselors and Older People

Counselors must be cautious about interacting with older clients in a manner that could lead to transference (e.g., older clients remind them of relatives and situations that may or may not have been resolved in their own lives; Kimmel, 2012; J. E. Myers & Shannonhouse, 2013). This potential transference may influence their interactions with, understanding of, and openness to older clients. Counselors may remember their elders as strong or weak, kind or irritable, supportive or demanding, loving or cold, involved or uninvolved. They may have feelings of pity, deference, love, guilt, worship, anger, or sadness associated with their elders. These old memories and feelings may influence their thoughts and feelings about their current clients. Thus, it is important that counselors understand themselves and work through any old issues associated with their own elders or with societal ageist perspectives to ensure that these issues do not influence their current interactions with older clients. If counselors are unable to work through their unresolved thoughts or feelings about older people, they should probably not work with this population until these issues are resolved (Shallcross, 2012c).

Autonomy, Personal Control, Independence, and Empowerment

The concepts of autonomy, personal control, independence, and self-determination are often used interchangeably and are rooted deeply in our counselor codes of ethics, beliefs, and practices (ACA, 2014; Kampfe et al., 2007). A sense of personal autonomy (i.e., the perception that one has control over his or her environment and choices) has been shown to be positively related to physical well-being, psychological well-being, and health-promoting coping strategies. Conversely, lack of personal control has been found to relate negatively to psychological well-being (Kampfe, 1994, 1995, 1999, 2002; Kampfe & Mitchell, 1991; Trouillet, Gana, Lourel, & Fort, 2009). An AARP survey (L. L. Fisher, 2010) provided strong support for this notion. Among respondents age 60–69, 99% of men and 98% of women stated that independence was important to their quality of life. Among those age 70 or older, 99% of the men and 93% of the women indicated it was important.

The concept of empowerment is closely related to autonomy. Perhaps the best definitions of empowerment are those of J. E. Myers and Shannonhouse (2013) and Sales (2007). According to J. E. Myers and Shannonhouse (2013), "Empowerment refers to actions intended to help people help themselves or to create personal power" (p. 159). According to Sales (2007), "Empowerment is the process of supporting an individual in learning how to and becoming able to gain more control over himself or herself in the environment" (p. 81). Both of these definitions focus on the power of the person rather than the counselor's ability to give them power (a very important distinction). E. B. Waters and Goodman (1990) also focused on the power of the client rather than the ability of the counselor to give power. The following books can provide in-depth considerations of the concepts and practices associated with empowerment: *Empowering Older Adults: Practical Strategies for Counselors* (E. B. Waters & Goodman, 1990); *Rehabilitation Counseling: An Empowerment Perspective* (Sales, 2007); and *Empowerment for Later Life* (J. E. Myers, 1990).

For people to make choices, they must be aware of and understand their options; however, older people are sometimes either not informed of their options, not included in making choices, or discouraged from making choices about issues that strongly affect their lives. Because our society often discourages older people from making their own choices and because some disabling conditions experienced by older people narrow their opportunities for choice, it is especially important for counselors to support and advocate for client choice. First and foremost, this support involves respecting and honoring clients' autonomy. It might also involve supporting older people as they identify, evaluate, and make decisions about their options. Furthermore, it may involve advocacy for client choice and independence among significant others and institutions (Institute on Rehabilitation Issues, 2009; Kampfe et al., 2005). See Chapter 3 for additional discussions of autonomy and the benefits and dangers of advocacy.

Multicultural Issues Associated With Older People and the Need for Counselor Cultural Competency

As indicated in Chapter 1, the older population is widely heterogeneous. For this reason, counselors need to be informed of the social norms (e.g., status, roles, expectations, issues of respect, views of death, appropriate communication styles, spirituality) that are associated with older people from different cultures and be mindful and respectful of these norms during the counseling process (ACA, 2014, Standards A.4.b. and A.11.b.; Harley, Jolivette, McCormick, & Tice, 2002; Nelson, 2004). For example, older people in one particular culture might be viewed as the most valuable members of the family and community, whereas older people in another culture might be perceived to have lost their value. These perspectives would influence the older person's own view of himself or herself, and they would also influence the views of the older person's family, friends, and service providers.

Cultural groups have official and unofficial rules and practices of communication and courtesy. Some groups believe in letting a short time pass before responding to a statement in order to allow the speaker to finish his or her thought, whereas others believe they need to give immediate feedback; some feel that a certain amount of physical space between people is important, whereas others feel comfortable with physical closeness; some may feel very uncomfortable expressing feelings, and others may be very expressive; and some may believe that punctuality is very important, whereas others may not have this perception of time. Furthermore, some may think that saying "no" or refusing to do something is rude and may therefore consent to something that they do not wish to do. In the end, they may simply not follow through or they may find excuses for not doing what they had agreed to do (e.g., didn't feel well, forgot; Ivers & Veach, 2012). By not knowing or following these rules or practices, counselors can either misunderstand or damage the relationship between themselves and their older clients.

Cultural groups may have unique ways of communicating. Some cultures may be more sensitive to and aware of verbal communication and focus on the actual words that are being said, whereas other cultures (e.g., some ethnic minorities) may be more attune to nonverbal, contextual communication (Ivers & Veach, 2012). For example, some groups may use their lips or hand signals to signify certain concepts, whereas others may avoid body language; in addition, some believe that direct eye contact is important, whereas others believe it is not appropriate. Because communication is central to the counseling process, it is essential for counselors to understand and feel comfortable with any nonverbal messages and nuances that clients use to communicate. It is also important to be aware of one's own means of communication (both verbal and nonverbal).

Another multicultural issue that might influence the counselor–client relationship has to do with the client's desire (or lack of desire) to develop an interpersonal relationship with the counselor that involves a mutual sharing of information. In most situations, counselors refrain from providing their own personal information; however, when working with people from cultures that value this type of interaction, counselors can consider sharing peripheral information about themselves (e.g., a favorite sport or hobby) in order to develop a trusting relationship with the client (Ivers & Veach, 2012).

Counselors should choose treatment strategies that will validate clients' cultural identities (Corey, Haynes, Moulton, & Muratori, 2010). One important concern is that the majority of counseling theories and practices are based on individualistic, Eurocentric perspectives. Individualism typically involves the belief that individuals have a sense of worth and meaning for themselves, make decisions for themselves, proceed alone to accomplish their goals, and control their own lives. Collectivism involves the importance of the group with regard to value and worth, decision making, goal setting, and goal accomplishment. In these cases, the group may be defined as family, but it can also be a larger group. Obviously, it is very important for counselors to determine the client's perspectives with regard to individualism or collectivism and to tailor their counseling approaches to these perspectives (Ivers & Veach, 2012).

The *ACA Code of Ethics* (ACA, 2014, Standard A.4.b.) states that "counselors are aware of—and avoid imposing—their own values, attitudes, beliefs, and behaviors." Although counselors may know that it is inappropriate to impose their own values or beliefs on a client, they may convey their values and beliefs in subtle ways (Corey et al., 2010; P. Richards & Bergin, 2005). The counselor's tone of voice, facial expressions, body language, choice of which issues to reflect back to the client, and words used to paraphrase content or reflect feelings can all demonstrate the counselor's perspective to the client. Although subtle, these messages can influence the client's own thoughts, beliefs, and feelings about a situation (Corey et al., 2010); therefore, counselors must be cautious about their verbal and nonverbal messages to consumers.

Although it is very important to be aware of and respectful of cultural norms, it is also important for counselors to realize that people will have varying degrees of acculturation. In other words, clients may follow the beliefs and practices of their culture; they may hold some of these beliefs and practices, but not others; or they may not hold to their culture's beliefs and practices. For this reason, counselors cannot make assumptions about an individual client's beliefs and practices just because he or she was born into a particular culture or ethnic group. Related to this issue is the reality that people can belong to many groups on the basis of gender, religion, race, ethnicity, socioeconomic level, and so forth. Because of these multiple group connections, counselors cannot automatically assume that a person from a particular culture will ascribe to that culture's traditional perspectives and practices.

Counselors should also be aware of the potential damage that cultural or other kinds of bias can have on individuals. The Minority Stress Model (Meyer, 2003) suggests that people with minority status experience stressors on a daily basis that exceed those experienced by people with majority status. Such stressors can include *microaggressions* (e.g., derogatory remarks, brief indignities, and hostile/negative insults), threats, actual violence, or even death. These stressors are theorized to result in higher overall stress levels for people who have a minority status (Meyer, 2003; Sue, 2010; Sue et al., 2007). Counselors may, therefore, wish to evaluate the stress levels of older minority clients and use stress-reduction strategies with these individuals.

Counselors who are not culturally competent may fail to consider the social forces that can affect clients, make inaccurate assessments, make incorrect assumptions regarding clients' perspectives or identities, engage in inaccurate case conceptualization, focus only on visible racial or ethnic backgrounds, and provide inappropriate treatment (Corey et al., 2010). It is therefore vital that counselors work toward cultural competency.

There are many ways to develop cultural competency, and it can be a lifelong process. One important aspect of cultural competency is to be aware of one's own culture or cultures and how these might influence interactions with clients of other cultures (ACA, 2014, Section E, Introduction; Bellini, 2002; Moore et al., 2008). Several years ago, I taught a course in which students were asked to examine and describe their own cultures. In some cases, people from the majority culture (i.e., Caucasian) indicated that they did not have a culture. After careful examination of their lives, however, they could identify their culture, how it had helped shape them, and how it might affect their interactions with clients from other cultures. I invite you to engage in the following exercise.

Cultural Awareness Exercise (Who Am I?)

The purpose of this exercise is to help you understand your own culture and how it might influence your interactions with older people of other cultures.

1. Write a one- to five-page description of your own culture. Focus on your own culture's meanings, customs, rules of communication, conception of time, spirituality, traditions, understanding of healing, and collectivism versus individualism. Include your culture's view of older people (status, roles, expectations, respect) and the kinds of things that happen to older people that might be unique to your culture.
2. Consider how these aspects of your culture might, in some ways, influence your response to, and understanding of, older people of another culture.
3. List strategies that you can use to help you become more aware of your own culture and of the cultures of the older consumers you will likely serve.
4. If you have the opportunity, discuss the results of this activity with fellow counselors, friends, family, or people from other cultures.

Multicultural Case Study

Counselor X first came to the Southwest as a professional counselor. He was not familiar with many of the beliefs of various American

Indian tribes who lived in the area. His earlier professional experience had been in psychiatric rehabilitation while working in psychiatric centers in the Midwest. Through these experiences, he learned much about serious mental illness that he was able to apply in subsequent employment.

One of his first experiences with the Southwest perspective began when one of his older Native American clients came for her sixth appointment. Until this session, she had said very little. The counselor had kept the sessions short, had not pushed her to talk about personal things, and had tried to be comfortable with long silences. He did this, initially, because he had been told of the need to wait until some Native American clients were ready to talk.

But this day, the client sat down and said, "I am ready for you to know me" and proceeded to tell him about her life. She talked for 2 hours and would have stayed longer if the building had not been closing down. She told him of *shape-shifters* (her mother, who could change from being a coyote to a human and back), *brujas* (her sister, who was a witch and who practiced many types of magic), *chindis* (malicious spirits who remained near where they died), her desire not to speak of the dead after this session (speaking of the dead would invite them into her life), her fear that spirits would remain in the counselor's office, and her need to return to the reservation to partake in a *sweat* or other ceremony to regain balance.

During and after the counseling session, the counselor became concerned that this client may have serious psychiatric issues. On the basis of his earlier experiences and training in psychiatric rehabilitation, he recognized many of the thoughts and behaviors that had been markers of mental illness in the Midwest. Fortunately, he was also aware that he had no knowledge of the culture from which his client came. Instead of looking in the *Diagnostic and Statistical Manual of Mental Disorders (DSM)* for advice, he sought the advice of a Native Healer who was familiar with this particular person's tribal beliefs. In doing so, he learned that all the client's concerns were legitimate from her cultural perspective. Discovering this helped him (a) avoid a misdiagnosis, (b) take steps to clean his office of spirits (the healer cleansed the area with a ceremony), (c) be open to the client's concerns, (d) not press the client to speak of her dead relatives, and (e) be able to problem solve with her regarding her need for a ceremony to help her achieve balance, as defined by her culture.

From a broader cultural perspective, he learned that (a) counselors sometimes have to wait a long time until they are trusted and before a client will begin to discuss important issues; (b) when clients are ready to talk, they might want to talk for several hours; (c) counselors need to listen respectfully and quietly once the client begins to talk; (d) counselors should not draw conclusions about the client if they do not understand that person's culture; and (e) it is important to obtain consultation from someone who understands specific aspects of a culture before drawing inaccurate conclusions or making a tentative diagnosis.

Therapies Used With Older People

It is important to note that individual counseling techniques or therapies (e.g., person-centered, cognitive behavioral, Gestalt, interpersonal, etc.) are appropriate for older people, and that a genuine nonjudgmental relationship that is based on trust, unconditional positive regard, respect, and safety forms the basis for counseling with older people (Hazler, cited in Shallcross, 2012a; J. E. Myers & Schwiebert, 1996). Additional therapies that may be helpful include group work, creative problem solving, bibliotherapy, life review work, pet therapy, relaxation therapy, dance/movement/music therapy, and horticultural therapy.

Group Work

Group work has been used a great deal with older people. Group principles, processes, and dynamics are basically the same for all ages; therefore, counselors who graduate from CACREP- or CORE-accredited graduate counselor education programs will have the basic training and supervision to lead groups. Because of the special issues experienced by older people, however, counselors will need additional knowledge, training, and supervision to develop expertise in this important aspect of counseling.

Group work may be especially important for older people both because this population often experiences loneliness and isolation and because interpersonal interaction is vital for physical and psychological well-being. In addition to facilitating social interaction, group work can provide opportunities to share information and feelings with others who are experiencing similar situations, grieve openly with group support, do problem solving regarding a particular issue, meet role models, renew former interests or develop new ones, help other people, develop new coping skills, and become more active (L. L. Fisher, 2010; J. Golden et al., 2009; Hawkley, Thisted, Masi, & Cacioppo, 2010; P. Martin, Hagberg, & Poon, 1997; J. E. Myers & Schwiebert, 1996).

Therapeutic group work can involve counseling, psychoeducation, therapeutic techniques, and support, with the goal of growth and healing in an environment that is confidential (Riordan & Beggs, 1988). This type of group can be helpful to older people in developing coping skills, relieving feelings of isolation, and expressing feelings in a safe environment (Thomas & Martin, 2010). When selecting and recruiting older group participants, counselors will need to be mindful of the purposes of the group and make certain to select group members "whose needs and goals are compatible with the goals of the group, who will not impede the group process, and whose well-being will not be jeopardized by the group experience" (ACA, 2014, Standard A.9.a.; also see J. E. Myers & Schwiebert, 1996).

Other types of groups (e.g., self-help groups or support groups) are usually open to the public and are run by members of the group itself. Their purpose is to provide information, advocacy, and support (Riordan & Beggs, 1988). These groups can be very helpful to older individuals because they typically include people who come together to share feelings, thoughts, and information about a particular situation or problem and sometimes to give physical assistance, such as help with caregiving, transportation, and so forth (e.g., Lotsa Helping Hands, available at http://www.lotsahelpinghands.com).

Regardless of whether groups are led by counselors or are self-help groups, it might be helpful if they are composed of people of similar ages because of their many common experiences. For example, a group of older people may focus on multiple losses, retirement, grief, widowhood, multiple or specific medical problems, the aging process, grandparenthood, life review, residential relocation, leisure activities, or caregiving (J. E. Myers & Schwiebert, 1996). On the other hand, there are benefits to having group members of various ages, especially for older people who do not have the opportunity to interact with younger people (and vice versa).

Additional information about group work with older people can be found in Erwin's (2013) book on group techniques for older people, Thomas and Martin's (2010) chapter on group work with older people and their caregivers, and Salizar's (2009) book on multicultural group work practices. Another resource is ACA's Association for Specialists in Group Work.

Creative Problem Solving

Counselors can use creative problem solving in situations that require decisions and actions by clients and/or their families. The following steps are sometimes helpful in this process. These steps come from a lifetime of working with students and clients and from mentoring from Dr. Nancy Eldredge, University of Arizona, in the 1990s.

The first step involves understanding the problem. To do this, counselors and clients need to (a) identify the problem (this can take some time and involve one or more sessions), (b) describe the problem (what, where, when), (c) describe the intensity of the problem (degree of feelings, frequency, and duration), and (d) identify the consequences of the problem (feelings, thoughts, and other consequences of the problem).

The second step involves exploring alternative actions by using brainstorming. Brainstorming can be either a very positive and exciting process or it can be frustrating, depending upon the situation. The goal is for the client to explore as many alternatives as he or she can think of (note that the counselor should avoid suggesting alternatives or evaluating the alternatives). The process is dynamic, and it involves many open-ended questions and a great deal of support for the hard work the client is doing. Following are some questions and comments that can facilitate brainstorming: "If you could do it another way, what would you do?" or "So, you could . . . or you could . . . Is there anything else you could do?" If clients are unable to think of ideas, counselors can ask additional questions, such as, "How have other people done this?" "What would you tell me to do if I were in this situation?" "Is there anyone else you can ask about this situation?" "Are there any situations in your past that you can draw from?" and "I have a couple of books and pamphlets about this kind of situation . . . Would you like to take a look at those?"

The third step involves inviting the client to evaluate the potential consequences of one or more alternatives. Counselors can say the following: "Now let's look at some of these ideas, one at a time," "What do you think would happen if you . . .?" "How would you feel about this?" "Let's say you . . . What would you gain?" "Anything else?" "What would you lose?" "What else?" and "What would happen if you don't do this?"

The fourth step in the process is to compare the alternatives and to ask clients to choose one. "Now, let's compare these ideas. Do any of them seem better or worse than the others?" "Which of these seem like something you really can do?" "Now that we have looked at all these alternatives, which one do you want to try?" and "Which one are you willing to do?" The client's final decision can be stated verbally by the client, paraphrased by the counselor, and perhaps written down.

The final step involves making a plan. At this stage, the client is encouraged to state and perhaps write out the plan. The process is similar to the earlier steps, but this time the client is asked to be specific about how he or she will follow through with the decision. Statements or questions from the counselor can include, "Where do you need to start?" "Do we need to break this down into smaller steps?" "What are you willing to do for starters?" "Is there anyone else who can help you?" and "Let's write this down."

Throughout this process, it is important for counselors to maintain a positive and supporting attitude and to paraphrase each of the client's ideas. Paraphrasing will help the client know that the counselor is really listening, and it will help the counselor be sure he or she understands what the client is saying. Paraphrasing also helps clients hear what they have said and may encourage them to be more specific, alter their ideas, be more firm in their ideas, or discover that they do not like the idea.

Bibliotherapy and the Use of Other Media in Therapy

Bibliotherapy can be an excellent tool when counseling older people. It involves the use of materials (e.g., texts, novels, biographies, autobiographies, talking books, short stories, poems, television programs, films, plays, pamphlets) in the therapeutic process (J. E. Myers & Harper, 2004; J. E. Myers & Schwiebert, 1996). Counselors can use these materials to give clients insight into other people's feelings, thoughts, beliefs, and actions associated with similar situations that they are facing. Bibliotherapy can also be used to open up issues that clients may not have been able to discuss or face, elicit feelings that have not yet been expressed, normalize a situation that seems far from normal to the client, encourage reevaluation of perceptions of or actions related to a specific situation, provide important information about a topic, offer alternatives to a specific situation that the client may not have considered, and work through unfinished business.

An important aspect of bibliotherapy is processing what clients have read or seen (Hynes & Wedl, 1990; J. E. Myers & Schwiebert, 1996). Counselors can begin by asking clients to describe their reactions to the materials. The following types of questions can encourage processing of the materials: "What did you think of this movie?" "What important message did you receive from this book?" "How did this story relate to your situation?" "If this had been you, how would you have responded?" "Are there any important points that you think you disagree/agree with in this material?" and "How did this book make you feel?" Counselors can reflect both the content and the feelings of clients' answers to these questions. Clients' responses can then be further explored with regard to thoughts, feelings, and actions they might want to take.

Throughout this book, various materials have been suggested for bibliotherapy. In some cases, detailed examples of how to use these materials are given, whereas in other cases the materials are simply listed. One final and important point regarding bibliotherapy is that counselors should have read or viewed the material prior to giving it to clients and perhaps have asked themselves the same questions that they invite the client to consider.

Life Review/Reminiscence Work

Life review (i.e., the tendency of older people to look back over their past and to examine the meaning of their lives) is considered to be an important life task (Erikson, 1982). Life review work, therefore, is a therapeutic technique that is very appropriate for this population (J. E. Myers & Harper, 2004). The terms *life review work* and *reminiscence therapy* are both used to describe a similar therapeutic approach. These terms, therefore, are used interchangeably in this book.

Although life review work is based on an activity that older people do naturally, when it is done within a counseling environment it is more structured, it is done with purpose, and it includes an evaluative component (Molinari, 1999). The various purposes of life review work include integrating various aspects of clients' lives, identifying and/or resolving unfinished business, expressing feelings that may have been bottled up, reviewing or reestablishing old personal relationships, mending old hurts or broken relationships, bringing about resolution of various other issues, describing activities that were once enjoyed while identifying new related activities to engage in, identifying life-time themes and patterns, recognizing sources of motivations, and deciding upon a legacy to leave. Life review work can also be used to encourage clients to identify their lifelong strengths and accomplish-ments, to describe how these have worked for them, and to consider how they can use these strengths in current and new experiences. Focusing on positive aspects of clients' lives may encourage them to maintain or enhance a positive self-image and counteract depression or other negative feelings associated with their current lives (J. E. Myers & Harper, 2004; Shallcross, 2012c).

Life review work/reminiscence can also be used to discuss the grief associated with various losses. Using time-limited small reminiscence groups for older people who had experienced various losses (e.g., pets, homes, health, loved ones), Gibson (1992) found that participants perceived that they received support and strength for expressing their feelings. Some participants indicated that this was the first time they had been given the opportunity to discuss their feelings and losses and that they had gained a sense of self-esteem because their issues were affirmed to be important.

Life review can be used to help people remember experiences that contributed to their past physical and psychological well-being and to apply this information to their current lives. When clients have identified activities that they enjoyed or for which they were particu-larly talented, counselors can use open-ended questions and reflective listening to help them further identify the qualities of these activities and to discover new activities that might have the same qualities. For example, if a client loved playing baseball but can no longer play the game, his counselor can ask him to describe the aspects of the game that he enjoyed (e.g., team membership, demonstration of personal leadership or skills, enjoyment of the season when games were played, sounds and smells of the game or the crowd, other people's responses to his skills, the challenge, winning, interaction with a coach, eating hot dogs). His counselor can then use creative problem solving to identify other activities that would meet some of these needs. For example, the client might want to get a large-screen television or join a group that meets regularly to watch games, identify other sports that he can participate in (e.g., if blind, play "beep" baseball; if in a wheelchair, play wheelchair baseball), ask local senior programs to organize a group with similar interests, and invite family members or friends to attend a game. The client can also consider engaging in other activities that do not involve baseball but provide similar satisfaction (e.g., collecting cards, doing activities that involve the same type of challenge, eating hot dogs with all the fixings). The point is to find ways to meet the needs and passions that were met by a previous activity.

Past orientations (i.e., positive recollections vs. negative recollections) have been found to be related to present well-being. For example, older cardiac patients who had more positive past orientation used more health-promoting activities and showed higher levels of spiritual growth than those who had more negative past orientations (Hamilton, Kives, Micevski & Grace, 2003). Other studies have also shown that people with positive past orientation had more positive psychological adjustment and less anxiety, anger, depression (Livneh & Martz, 2007), and distress than people with negative past orientation (Holman & Silver, 1998). The implication of these findings is that counselors may be able to use past orientations, as identified in life review work, as predictors of anxiety, depression, anger, and health-promoting activities.

Life review work can be done individually or in a group setting; however, small groups are especially effective for this activity (Molinari, 1999). Regardless of which format is used, counselors can activate reminiscence by introducing a topic or asking open-ended questions about the past, such as, "What is the most important thing you accomplished in your life?" "If you had your life to live over, what would you change?" "What did you like most/least about your childhood?" "What was your greatest loss/disappointment?" "Who was the most important person to you?" and "What part of your life did you enjoy/dislike most?" Counselors can also ask clients to reflect back to their very first memory, special songs, dances, poems, previous employment, significant others, or meaningful events. They can ask clients to remember the significance of their first car, their first job, their first kiss, their first love, and their biggest life transitions. Counselors can be creative regarding the type of questions they ask, tailoring these to focus on issues that their clients may have and then using their listening skills to delve deeper into their clients' answers.

Another way to initiate life review is to ask clients to bring meaningful objects, such as photo albums, family videos, family tree information, quilts, award certificates, memorabilia, and hand-made objects, to the counseling session. Autobiographical writing and reminiscence can be helpful in life review, especially among well-educated individuals (Kenyon, Ruth, & Mader, 1999). This type of life review may require considerable introspection, and when shared with the counselor, it can provide topics to discuss.

Music can activate significant memories and elicit feelings, perhaps because it can be associated with various cultures, religions, time periods, topics, or people. Specific musical entertainers (e.g., Rudy Vallee, Spike Jones, Jimmy or Tommy Dorsey, Bing Crosby, Rosemary Clooney, Doris Day, Elvis Presley, The Doors, Eric Clapton, Dionne

Warwick) or specific dances (e.g., the Lindy Hop, Jitterbug, waltz, tango, country western, rock and roll) are often strongly connected to past feelings. Counselors can, therefore, use this music to activate life review work.

In summary, life review has both a backward and a forward focus. Even though life review starts with a focus on the past, it is primarily used to help people adjust to the present and prepare for the future. Without this present and future orientation, life review work may not be effective and may even be counterproductive. For example, some studies have found that past orientation is an ineffective coping strategy, whereas present and future orientation is most often effective (Alberts & Dunton, 2008; Anubhiti, 2008; Holman & Silver, 1998; Livneh, 2013; Nolen-Hoeksema & Larson, 1999). Because of the wide range of temporal coping, perhaps counselors can help individuals integrate their past, present, and future. In other words, clients can be helped to remain present and future oriented while taking into account their past.

Pet Therapy—Assistive Animals

It has long been acknowledged that pets contribute to older people's lives. Some of the reasons for the positive influences of pets include (a) receiving therapeutic sensory stimulation through touching, stroking, cuddling, or holding another living thing; (b) engaging in physical exercise (e.g., taking walks); (c) having fun, playing, and laughing; (d) finding meaning or purpose in life; (e) taking responsibility for another living being; (f) staying connected with another living thing, which reduces loneliness; (g) meeting other people who might be interested in the pet; (h) experiencing unconditional affection and companionship; (i) feeling safer because of the pet; and (j) adding structure to everyday life (AARP, 2012a; J. E. Myers & Schwiebert, 1996; L. Robinson & Segal, 2012).

Many of these benefits can reduce stress and anxiety, boost the immune system, and contribute to one's sense of well-being. Research has shown that pet owners have lower blood pressure during stressful situations, less depression, lower cholesterol, and lower triglyceride levels. They have been found to survive longer after a heart attack and make 30% fewer doctor visits than those who do not have pets. Furthermore, serotonin and dopamine (calming and relaxing secretions) may increase when playing with pets. Even watching a fish can reduce pulse rate and muscle tension (L. Robinson & Segal, 2012).

When older people are thinking about acquiring a pet, they need to consider several issues. For example, if people need or prefer to stay indoors most of the time, they may want to choose a pet that would also be somewhat comfortable indoors (e.g., cat, bunny, fish, bird, reptile). If people prefer walking, jogging, being outdoors, or working in the yard, they may prefer a dog. If people are frail, unsteady, or have activities-of-daily-living (ADL) issues, they may need to avoid pets that might get underfoot, jump on them, or require a great deal of physical care (L. Robinson & Segal, 2012).

Potentially negative issues associated with pet ownership have to do with the costs associated with veterinary care, pet food, licensing, grooming, boarding fees, bedding, toys, and general upkeep. Other issues may include allergic reactions to pets, being injured by the pet, or deciding to stay at home to be with the pet rather than engaging in outside social activities or making a much-needed move to assisted living. It is also important to consider the lifetime commitment that one gives to a pet. Pets can live from 5 to 20 years or more, which may have implications for pet care as the person ages or dies. Furthermore, the death of a pet may be a major loss for an older person (AARP, 2012a; J. E. Myers & Schwiebert, 1996; L. Robinson & Segal, 2012).

In cases where it is not feasible to own a pet, there are ways to facilitate animal–human interaction. For example, some animal shelters appreciate volunteers who spend time with animals who have not yet found homes (AARP, 2012a; L. Robinson & Seagal, 2012), wildlife rehabilitation centers may need volunteers to help feed the animals (J. Roberts, personal communication, September 15, 2012), and neighbors or children may have pets that enjoy a visit with a caring person who has lots of time for them.

Counselors can use creative problem solving with clients to ensure that they have given sufficient forethought to decisions about pet ownership and, once they have a pet, to discuss their options for caring for it. Counselors, as case managers, can help clients find financial assistance for their pets' needs (e.g., food, veterinary care). The Humane Society website (http://www.humanesociety.org) provides information on this topic. Other ways to save money are to purchase generic pet medications and larger boxes of pet food (AARP, 2012a). Ways to ensure that people can control their pets include having smaller animals and/or obtaining pet training. Often people do not wish to travel without their pets, both for their own needs and the pet's needs. In this case, counselors can use problem solving to help them find resources for ways to do this (e.g., see http://www.tripswithpets.com).

Animal-assisted therapy (pet therapy) involves the introduction of animals (e.g., dogs, rabbits, cats, birds, horses, fish) to patients or residents of health care facilities, hospice programs, nursing homes, or long-term care settings. During these visits, people are invited to touch, talk to, groom, hold, or pet the animals. If residents are unable to interact with animal visitors, they can allow them to sit on their laps or their beds. This therapy has been shown to reduce anxiety and improve mood (L. Robinson & Segal, 2012). One example of this type of program is PAWS, a nonprofit organization that coordinates personal pet visits to local hospitals and hospices (AARP, 2012a).

Other examples include allowing people in nursing homes to keep their pets in their rooms during a portion of the day, especially those who have newly transferred into such a setting; having permanent pets who live in the facility and belong to everyone; or inviting friends and family members to bring their pets when they come to see residents (e.g., Rose Lane Home in Loup City, Nebraska).

In addition to providing companionship, pets can act as service animals. Seeing-eye dogs are perhaps the most common example of this kind of animal. Other types of service animals include companion dogs who recognize blood sugar problems or who give emotional support to people who have posttraumatic stress disorder (PTSD). Counselors need to be aware of the rules associated with service dogs. For example, outsiders should not typically touch or talk to the animal. Doing so can distract the animal and perhaps interrupt the relationship that exists between the animal and its owner. A good rule of thumb is to ensure that there is plenty of room for the service animal in your office and to ignore him or her unless the owner gives permission to talk to or touch it. A resource associated with the therapeutic aspects of pets is ACA's Animal Assisted Therapy in Mental Health Interest Network (see http://www.counseling.org/aca-community/aca-groups/interest-networks).

Relaxation Training and Other Related Modalities

Because older people are likely to experience multiple stressors, sleep disturbance, and conditions that may involve muscle tension, counselors may wish to develop skills in relaxation training techniques. Relaxation training—in which the client is trained in relaxation strategies—has been used by a variety of therapists, especially those who specialize in cognitive behavioral therapy (Bernstein, Borkovec, & Hazlett-Stevens, 2000). There are many related techniques that can help clients relax, some of which counselors can provide and some of which they cannot. These techniques include progressive relaxation training, behavioral relaxation, electromyography, biofeedback, structured and unstructured meditation, autogenic training, visualization, guided imagery, self-hypnosis, therapeutic touch, acupuncture, therapeutic massage, confession, healing prayer, and other spiritual rituals associated with various cultures (J. E. Myers & Schwiebert, 1996; Nelson, 2004).

Relaxation training can be used by counselors to help people relax muscle parts, facilitate discussions of emotionally charged issues, encourage a positive relationship between the therapist and the client, reduce chronic tension that may be affecting other body systems (e.g., digestive system), provide tools for the client to use in stressful situations, decrease insomnia, lessen irritability, reduce anxiety, and alleviate or reduce many medical and emotional problems (e.g., hypertension, headaches, chronic pain, irritable bowel syndrome, PTSD). Counselors should be aware of the research findings associated with the use of relaxation training for any of the above issues prior to using this strategy with clients (Bernstein et al., 2000; Johnson, 2011). Although findings have been mixed and studies are sometimes less than rigorous, a recent well-designed study by Johnson (2011) found that progressive relaxation training for older individuals with neuroleptic-induced orofacial tardive dyskinesia (i.e., abnormal involuntary movement disorder of the face muscles caused by neuroleptic medications) may be helpful in reducing involuntary facial movements, either as an adjunct or alternative to surgical or pharmacological management of this disorder.

When determining whether relaxation training can be helpful, it is important to know the cause of the client's tension, whether relaxation techniques are appropriate, and whether relaxation training should be accompanied by other forms of treatment (e.g., counseling regarding stress or anxiety, desensitization, etc.). It is also important to determine whether the client's complaints are attributable to other medically treatable conditions, whether there are contraindications for the use of relaxation training, whether there are certain muscles that need strengthening rather than relaxing, and whether there is a need to adjust drugs (e.g., tranquilizers) for muscle or other relaxation. For these reasons, counselors should obtain medical clearance from the client's physician to ensure that relaxation treatment is appropriate (Bernstein et al., 2000).

Many books are available for professionals who wish to incorporate relaxation into their practice; however, reading books is not enough. It is very important to receive one-on-one training and supervision from professionals who have expertise in relaxation techniques. At this time, there are no formal certifications or licensures for many of these practices; therefore, counselors must be very cautious when learning, using, or recommending these techniques.

One free resource for guided meditation as well as other techniques to manage stress can be found in helpguide.org (Segal, Smith, & Robinson, 2013), which offers a meditation experience titled "Ride the Wild Horse." The purpose of this particular exercise is to teach caregivers (e.g., family members) one form of progressive relaxation to help them work toward minimizing bothersome anxieties and to bring their lives into balance. The exercise, however, can be used for other purposes. Another resource for relaxation exercise is a CD entitled *Stressbuster Relaxation Exercise, Volume 1* (Erford, n.d.), which provides guided relaxation exercises and is available through ACA.

Dance and Music Therapies

Dance and music can be used in the therapeutic process (J. E. Myers & Schwiebert, 1996) either passively (watching or listening) or actively (music making or dancing). As indicated above, these media can be powerful tools in life review work because they typically stimulate older memories as well as elicit emotional responses to those memories. Conversely, dance and music can encourage a focus on the here and now, that is, being in the moment; in addition, they can contribute to growth, socialization, insights, creativity, and the development and use of the kinesthetic sense (e.g., awareness of placement in space and time). Furthermore, dance and music can encourage people to express their unique thoughts, feelings, and insights through a creative process (Brehm & Kampfe, 1998; Kampfe, 2003; Kampfe, Brehm, Pohanic, & Grayson, 1998–1999).

One example of the use of dance to enhance older people's lives is depicted in the classic photograph/poster titled *Dancers of the Third Age* (DeLoria, 1981), which demonstrates a multigenerational working dance group (i.e., Liz Lerman Dance Exchange). Another example of the use of creative dance and music making is Pohanic's work with older people in retirement communities, special arts programs, and workshops where she invited participants to interactively stretch, bend, drum, and dance. Participants who were unable to walk could dance in their chairs. Furthermore, Pohanic emphasized the need for awareness of pain or balance problems on the part of the participants (N. Pohanic, personal communication, August 19, 2013). Texts that focus on movement exploration are *Materials of Dance: A Creative Art Activity* (Mettler, 1989) and *Creative Dance for Learning: The Kinesthetic Link* (Brehm & McNett, 2008).

Horticulture Therapy

Horticulture therapy is considered to be a process through which gardening and the innate connection between nature and human beings can be used to conduct therapy and rehabilitation (S. Davis, 1998). Horticulture therapy can take many forms, for example, giving a person a plant to take care of, sponsoring accessible gardens in nursing homes or senior centers, visiting senior centers with plant projects, inviting seniors to public gardens to partake in gardening, visiting seniors' homes to see their gardens, and sponsoring multigenerational projects. Horticulture therapists use client-centered therapeutic techniques that include respecting client individuality and desires, encouraging creativity, allowing for mistakes, believing in client autonomy and control, listening actively, and attempting to understand the whole person. The emphasis is on process (interaction with people and plants) versus product (a finished garden; Haller, 1998; J. Neihause, personal communication, December 8, 2013). The underlying purposes of horticulture therapy include improved physical function, increased self-esteem, increased interpersonal interaction, reduced stress, the sense that one is doing something worthwhile, and positive feedback from others (J. E. Myers & Schwiebert, 1996).

Case Management

Case management typically involves coordination of both short-term and long-term activities and services in the community or institutions to promote cost-effective use of various programs, quality of care, and functional independence. Case management can focus on home care, skilled nursing care, hospital care, hospice, Medicare and Medicaid, supplemental insurance, finances, and so forth (Lamb, 2005).

Primary goals of case management are to help older individuals stay in the community, improve their functional levels, obtain the cost-effective services they need, and maintain quality of life. Case managers can have many roles, including assessing clients' risks for various conditions, identifying needs for specific services, developing a plan, finding resources for special equipment, identifying community-based programs that can meet clients' needs, providing client counseling and education, evaluating services, coordinating services, advocating for the client, and monitoring the entire system. Case managers also identify gaps in the system and make recommendations for improved services. Filling these roles requires that the case manager has extensive knowledge of each of these areas (Lamb, 2005). Additional and practical information regarding case management can be found in Cress's (2007) *Handbook of Geriatric Care Management.*

An underlying aspect of case management is the importance of the client–counselor relationship that emphasizes respect, empowerment, self-care, choice, independence, collaboration, interaction of various aspects of life, and consistency with the client's values and goals. In this relationship, case managers can encourage clients to develop realistic objectives; provide clients with information about resources and options; and help clients and significant others evaluate the costs, benefits, and quality of their options (Lamb, 2005). Given counselors' skills and attitudes, they are ideally suited to provide gerontological case management.

Assessment, Evaluation, and Testing

Counselors may or may not engage in formal assessment; however, they often request testing, use tests results for case planning, and explain test results to clients. Furthermore, their clients may be tested by other professionals for other purposes (e.g., diagnostics for a medical condition). The *ACA Code of Ethics* states that "Counselors are responsible for appropriate application, scoring, interpretation, and use of assessment instruments relevant to the needs of the client" (ACA, 2014, Standard E.2.b.). Regardless of who is doing the testing, "At all times counselors maintain their ethical responsibility to those being assessed" (Standard E.9.c.). Counselors must, therefore, be aware of the issues associated with testing older people so that the results of assessments can be meaningful and valid.

As indicated earlier, the older population is one of the most diverse groups in the United States. Because culture affects the way problems are defined and experienced, counselors will need to take into account their clients' personal, cultural, and socioeconomic contexts in the assessment process (ACA, 2014, Section E, Introduction, and Standard E.5.b.). Counselors need to "recognize the effects of age, color, culture, disability, ethnic group, gender, race, language preference, religion, spirituality, sexual orientation, and socioeconomic status on test administration and interpretation, and they place test results in proper perspective with other relevant factors" (Standard E.8.). Another issue associated with assessment is that the age range for older people can be from 65 to 105+ years. This age range spans the same number of years as the age range of 20 to 60+ years. With this perspective, counselors can be aware of the broad range of needs, functional levels, and norms of older clients who are being evaluated and take these into consideration when reviewing the results (Kampfe et al., 2005; S. M. Smith & Kampfe, 2000).

The *ACA Code of Ethics* (ACA, 2014) indicates that counselors need to "carefully consider the validity, reliability, psychometric limitations, and appropriateness of instruments when selecting assessments and, when possible, use multiple forms of assessment, data, and/or instruments in forming conclusions, diagnoses, or recommendations" (Standard E.6.a.). In order to be valid, instruments need to be appropriate for the population on which they are being used (ACA, 2014, Standards E.8. and E.9.b.; Powers, 2013). Unfortunately, relevant norms for older people may not exist (Uriri & Thatcher-Winger, 1995). For example, some instruments have not been normed for populations of ages 60 to 65 or older, and even instruments that include norms for older age groups typically do not include participants who are beyond age 89 or 90. Because many instruments have not been developed or normed for the older population, test administrators need to recognize their limitations and select other more appropriate instruments or at least analyze the results with the recognition that they may not be valid.

Some testing instruments and practices may be inappropriate for older people because testing may require unique approaches and instruments for this group. For example, certain conditions exist that may skew test results. People with low energy levels, low endurance levels, slow reflexes, sensory loss, or other disabilities may require testing accommodations (Fried & Guralnik, 1997; Kampfe et al., 2005; S. M. Smith & Kampfe, 2000). Tests that require speed and endurance may not be appropriate, especially if the test is not espoused to test these qualities. For example, shortened screening instruments for depression may be more useful than, and as effective as, full-length instruments (Schade, Jones, & Wittlin, 1998). Likewise, a short form of the Wechsler Adult Intelligence Scale (WAIS; Wechsler, 1955) has been found to be as effective in analyzing intellectual functioning as the full WAIS for people over age 65 (Clara & Huynh, 2003). If a timed test is required, test administrators can note the results when the time limit is reached but allow individuals to continue until they have completed the instrument in order to obtain a picture of their capacities without the need for speed. Because reaction time and processing speed are reduced when clients repeat familiar tasks, it might be appropriate to allow the person to take a timed test twice in order to obtain richer results. Because many older people have a hearing loss, it is important that the test administrator ensure that clients understand oral directions or questions. If not, they may be inaccurately perceived as having a mental deficit or medical condition (Kampfe et al., 2008). As the *ACA Code of Ethics* states, "When assessments are not administered under standard conditions, as may be necessary to accommodate clients with disabilities, or when unusual behavior or irregularities occur during the administration, those conditions are noted in interpretation, and the results may be designated as invalid or of questionable validity" (ACA, 2014, Standard E.7.a.).

Counselors must also be aware that being tested may be threatening to older people who have not had recent testing experiences, and the client's emotional reaction to a "test" may result in invalid results. Prior to testing, older individuals may, therefore, need more information about the process, the benefits of testing, and the degree to which the tests are relevant to them (Kampfe et al., 2005; S. M. Smith & Kampfe, 2000). Furthermore, computerized testing may create a validity problem for older people who are not familiar, comfortable, or skilled with the use of computers; therefore, such testing approaches may need to be avoided with some older individuals (Institute on Rehabilitation Issues, 2009).

For older people who wish to continue to work in a new job or or return to work, tests of functional level can assist in career planning. Perhaps one of the most important tools for this type of assessment is an interview that reviews all previous jobs and an exploration of the skills and responsibilities involved in these. Such an interview can help the client and counselor identify transferrable skills and strengths. Other relevant methods of assessing job skills are situational assessments or job trials. These types of assessments may be more meaningful and may reflect skills and potentials better than paper-and-pencil tests (Institute on Rehabilitation Issues, 2009; Kampfe et al., 2005).

A number of instruments have been developed to measure older people's functional status (Hoenig, Nusbaum, & Brummel-Smith, 1997). For people who need a functional assessment of independent living or daily living skills, the Instrumental Activities of Daily Living Scale can be useful (Nourhashemi et al., 2001). This instrument is considered to be an effective tool in determining present functioning as well as predicting frailty of older women.

Assessment for physical and mental conditions can be complicated by many variables, which may lead to misdiagnosis. As indicated in Chapter 5, individuals might be diagnosed as having Alzheimer's disease when there may be some other treatable reason for a temporary cognitive dysfunction (e.g., a physical condition, reaction to multiple medications, extreme isolation). These assessment errors may sometimes be the result of a diagnostician's preconceived ageist notions about older people. For this reason, counselors need to "recognize historical and social prejudices in the misdiagnosis and pathologizing of certain individuals and groups and strive to become aware of and address such biases in themselves and others" (ACA, 2014, Standard E.5.c.).

Assistive Technology (AT)

As people age, the need for assistive technology (AT) may increase because of one or more disabling conditions (Agee, Freedman, & Cornman, 2005). The goal of AT is to support people as they engage in ADLs, employment, and leisure activities. AT can involve many types of technology, from changes in the height of a chair or a walker to very sophisticated and specially designed pieces of equipment. Depending upon clients' limitations and residual abilities, the following basic types of aids, technology, or modifications may be helpful: raised toilet seats, electric razors and toothbrushes, bathtub benches, walk-in/roll-in bathtubs or showers, washing mitts with soap pockets, appropriately placed grab bars, and specially designed utensils and cups. Mobility aids can include wheelchairs, scooters, braces, and so forth (National Stroke Association, 2012b; Rubin & Roessler, 2008). More complex AT can include sophisticated bionics, robotics, human augmentation, nanotechnology, and computers (A. N. Lewis, Cooper, Seelman, Cooper, & Schein, 2012).

If clients can no longer talk, there are many types of technological devices that can be used for communication. Such tools are wonderful because they can open up verbal interaction between the client and other significant individuals, such as family members, caregivers, friends, and counselors. These devices must be carefully selected to meet the specific needs and abilities of the individual (e.g., ability to use hands, fingers, or lips to manipulate keyboards or point to objects/pictures; ability to recognize letters and numbers; etc.).

Appropriate assessment of an individual's needs prior to obtaining an assistive device is vital (Finch & Robinson, 2003). This assessment should be done by a qualified, impartial professional who is able to evaluate the need for AT and make recommendations for what kind of AT is best. There are several types of professionals who can conduct an evaluation, and it is sometimes important to have an assessment team composed of several well-trained members. Members of the team can include physical therapists, occupational therapists, speech/language therapists, rehabilitation engineering technologists, otologists, audiologists, physiatrists, rehabilitation counselors, personal care assistants, family members, nurses, and qualified suppliers (A. N. Lewis et al., 2012). The person being evaluated should be involved in the entire process and included in any final decisions that are made regarding the AT he or she plans to use.

Once an assistive device is decided upon, it is vital that clients receive sufficient training and follow-up in order to ensure that the AT will work for them, that they will not be injured from it, that they are satisfied with it, and that they will continue to use it. This training and follow-up can be done by one or more members of the evaluation team or other technicians associated with these professionals, depending upon the type of device that is being used and the expertise of the trainer. Recently, virtual training devices (virtual coaches) have been developed for certain types of AT. These devices can track both the proper use of the AT and the amount of time that the client uses the AT (A. N. Lewis et al., 2012).

Counselors can use nonjudgmental, empathetic listening and open- and closed-ended questions to determine the degree to which clients want, are willing to use, and are having problems with assistive devices. Counselors can also help clients through the transition stages of use of these devices. For example, counselors can encourage clients to (a) make informed decision in the selection of devices, (b) obtain appropriate training in the use of devices, (c) follow instructions regarding fitting and maintaining devices, (d) seek additional advice if a device or technique is not working, and (e) schedule follow-up visits to be certain that the devices or strategies are working properly and are a good fit for the client's needs (National Stroke Association, 2012b). Counselors can also advocate for each of these steps to be a part of the process.

One important legislative act associated with AT is the Technology-Related Assistance for Individuals with Disabilities Act of 1988 (Pub. L. No. 100-407), with subsequent reauthorizations (e.g., Pub. L. No. 111-260, Twenty-First Century Communications and Video Accessibility Act of 2010). This law requires that states develop and monitor policies and strategies that address barriers of various types, empower people with disabilities to have access and control of assistive devices, provide outreach to rural and underrepresented populations, and earmark at least 60% of their AT dollars for loan programs or alternative financing for assistive devices (A. N. Lewis et al., 2012). Counselors, as case managers, will want to identify which state agency or agencies are responsible for administering the provisions of this act and encourage consumers to work with them.

There are many resources to help with the evaluation and selection of an appropriate assistive device. Two of these are the Job Accommodation Network (JAN) and AbleData. JAN offers direct one-on-one consultation regarding specific situations via e-mail, live-chat, or an

800 number. Advisors are well trained, creative, good listeners, and have access to multiple resources for accommodation. JAN also offers a computer bulletin board that lists information about technology resources. JAN can be contacted via the Internet at https://askjan. org or via phone at 800-JAN-PCEH. AbleData provides information regarding the costs, types, functions and sources of assistive techno-logical devices. It can be accessed at http://www.abledata.com or at 800-227-0216. A useful text that provides detailed information about AT and resources is *Foundations of the Vocational Rehabilitation Process* (Rubin & Roessler, 2008). This text is updated regularly, so counselors will want to watch for the most recent edition.

Summary

There are many things to consider when counselors decide to work with the older population. One of the most important is for counselors to ensure that they have had the training to do so. This training involves obtaining a master's degree in counseling from an accredited program and then developing expertise in gerontology. Because the term *gerontological counselor* has devolved to many definitions, counselors need to advocate for both educational and certification standards for this profession. Counselors working with older people need to be aware of other professionals who are work-ing with older people; the HIPAA requirements; evidence-based research findings; the potential for transference; the importance of autonomy for older people; multicultural issues associated with the older population; the variety of therapies that can be used with older people; and the need for case management, appropriate assessment, and AT among older individuals.

Chapter 3
Advocacy and Aging Issues

One important task for counselors is to provide advocacy at individual, group, institutional, systemic, and societal levels to remove potential obstacles that inhibit clients' growth, development, and quality of life. Advocacy also involves efforts to make programs and services accessible to clients (ACA, 2014, Standard A.7.a. and Section C, Introduction). The purpose of this chapter is to provide an overview of various types of advocacy and to provide practical, specific suggestions for each of these. This chapter focuses on legislative/public policy advocacy, systems/systemic advocacy, and individual client advocacy.

To be an effective advocate, one must be aware of and practice the ACA Advocacy Competencies (J. A. Lewis, Arnold, House, & Toporek, 2002). These competencies were endorsed by the ACA Governing Council in 2003 and are available on the ACA's website (www.counseling.org). Furthermore, these competencies are discussed in various publications (e.g., Corey et al., 2010; Ratts & Hutchins, 2009; Ratts, Toporek, & Lewis, 2010) and have been used in developing this chapter.

Legislative/Public Policy Advocacy

Legislation is a fundamental basis for system development (A. N. Lewis, 2008). Legislative advocacy involves working with state and national legislators on laws that affect clients and the counseling profession. It is vital that all counselors recognize the importance of this type of advocacy and understand the legislative process so that they feel comfortable advocating at this level. The topic is so important that the Association for Adult Development and Aging (AADA, a division of ACA) held its 2014 conference in Washington, DC, where the focus was on legislative advocacy.

One of the counselor's greatest legislative advocacy tools is his or her own knowledge of clients' issues and needs. Legislators are always seeking good information about their district and constituents. Counselors who work with older individuals are among the most knowledgeable experts and can provide important information regarding the needs of older people and the type of legislation that meets these needs. Counselors are also in a good position to inform legislators of problems associated with current or pending legislation.

Case Example of Legislative/Public Policy Advocacy

Years ago, when I was president of the AADA, I visited with Representative Roe's staff (with the help of the ACA Public Policy and Legislation staff) to assist in writing a mental health section of a bill for older Americans. We were successful in ensuring that counselors were listed as "billable" service providers in the proposed bill; however, the bill was not passed. At the time, I knew very little about the legislative process and felt frightened about visiting with Representative Roe's staff. I discovered, however, that they were respectful, gracious, knowledgeable, open to new ideas, thankful for the information, and appreciative of ACA's and AADA's support in helping them with the bill that Representative Roe was sponsoring. I found that although I knew very little about the legislative process, I did know a great deal about aging and counseling—information that Representative Roe's staff needed in order to introduce the bill. I learned that counselors have valuable knowledge that they can share with their legislators even if they do not understand or are uncomfortable with the legislative process.

Becoming an Advocate for Public Policy Issues

There are many ways to become an advocate for public policy issues. With the support of associations such as ACA and AARP, counselors can become quite adept at legislative advocacy. For example, ACA has a long and distinguished record of working with Congress and offers training in working with legislators. This training involves practical suggestions regarding contacting legislators, updates on critical issues or bills being considered by Congress, and mentoring regarding legislative advocacy. Counselors who wish to receive such training can visit www.counseling.org/publicpolicy. At the time that I am writing this chapter (i.e., 2014), ACA offers continuing education credit for viewing a webinar at this address and provides many materials that describe the legislative process. Furthermore, ACA offers an annual

Institute for Leadership Training that involves hands-on training in Washington, DC, where participants visit and lobby their legislators.

There are other fun ways to become informed about the legislative process. One way is to watch movies, DVDs, or other media programs that focus on lawmaking activities. For example, Disney's Special 30th Anniversary DVD edition of *School House Rock* features "I'm Just a Bill" (Newall, Eisner, & Warburton, 2002), a short animated film that shows the rudimentary steps necessary for a bill to become a law. The movie *The Distinguished Gentleman* (Kaplan, Goldberg, Peyser, & Lynn, 1992) demonstrates how a single sincere constituent can influence a legislator's perspective, how lobbyists or interested parties can have a strong influence on some decisions, and how the Rules Committee of the House of Representatives influences the processes of reviewing a bill. Other movies such as *Mr. Smith Goes to Washington* (Cohn & Capra, 1939) offer insight into the legislative process, with a dynamic description of committee work. Counselors can also learn a great deal about the process and the status of specific current bills by watching either of the two CSPAN channels, which televise Congress daily. One channel focuses on the activities of the U.S. Senate and the other on the U.S. House of Representatives.

Perhaps one of the best ways to learn about the legislative process and to empower oneself is to simply jump in and advocate. Meeting with legislators and their aides, writing letters, joining legislative advocacy groups, attending hearings, and making mistakes (yes, making mistakes) can all result in understanding of and working with the legislative process. Counselors and their clients can also stay abreast of the latest legislation and regulations by subscribing to the *Aging News Alert* (http://www.cdpublications.com), which is an independent electronic news service that posts daily and weekly updates of relevant issues as well as funding resources for senior services. Counselors can learn about current counseling-related bills that are being reviewed by Congress by visiting www.counseling.org/publicpolicy or by directly contacting the ACA public policy staff. They can also join Counselors for Social Justice, a division of ACA.

Legislative Advocacy Activity

As indicated above, one of the best ways to learn about the legislative process is to become involved. This activity will give you the opportunity to jump in and try your hand at communicating with your legislators.

1. Identify a bill associated with an aging issue that is being considered by either the House or Senate. You will be surprised at how many bills exist that, in some way, meet this one criterion. Because ACA and/or AARP may be working on issues or bills associated with aging issues, they will be appropriate resources for topics.

2. Find out who your member of Congress is and how he or she can be contacted.
3. Prepare and send an individually written letter or e-mail to this person.
4. Wait for a response. If you do not receive a reply, follow up with a positively stated request for a response.

One note of caution regarding legislative advocacy is that counselors need to be aware of their employers' policies regarding this activity. In most cases, counselors need to advocate on their own time, avoid acting as representatives of their employers or agencies, and avoid using the employers' stationary.

Systems/Systemic Advocacy

The *ACA Code of Ethics* indicates that counselors should engage in *pro bono publico* (no fee) service activities that will contribute to the community (ACA, 2014, Section A, Introduction; Section C, Introduction; and Standard C.6.e.). This type of activity can take place at local, state, or national levels and can involve systems/systemic advocacy.

Systems/systemic advocacy is similar to legislative advocacy in that it involves working with systems, communities, and agencies to change rules, regulations, policies, and practices that influence a body of clients. This type of advocacy can include individual communication with (i.e., presenting to, visiting with, writing to) city offices or city councils, city transit services, county offices and officials, state agencies or officials, and federal agencies and programs that make decisions about large systems that affect the older population. Systems advocacy can also involve requesting special programming from Area Agencies on Aging, serving on boards of programs that serve clients in order to advocate for important issues, providing direct consultation to programs serving older individuals, and preparing and submitting written and multimedia materials regarding systems and issues that affect the older population.

Systems advocacy can also involve joining organizations, a group of individuals, or committees that are trying to make changes in various systems. This type of advocacy is often more powerful than acting on one's own because a larger body of people or organizations may be more likely to make an impression than a single counselor. Examples of this kind of advocacy would be joining with the Area Agency on Aging to change certain city or county practices (e.g., transportation or other services); joining with an independent living center to promote independent living opportunities in the community; serving on a Statewide Independent Living Council; or participating in large-scale meetings, events, or projects of groups who are trying to change a system.

Training Module That Can Be Used for Systemic/Systems Advocacy

Systems advocacy can involve providing direct training to staff and administrators of specific programs, facilities, or systems that offer services to older clients. For example, over the years, I have provided training to administrators and staff of nursing homes regarding dignity versus dehumanization in long-term care settings. I did this through an Area Agencies on Aging whose administrators wanted to change practices among nursing homes in their state. This training outline, *Dignity Versus Dehumanization in Long-Term Care Settings for Older Persons: A Training Outline* (Kampfe, 1990b), can be obtained from the ERIC Education Resource Center.

Dignity Versus Dehumanization Activity

1. Obtain a copy of the *Dignity Versus Dehumanization Training Outline*.
2. Identify a program that serves older individuals and ask them if they would like free training regarding this topic.
3. Provide the training, either in one 3-hour session or over three longer sessions.
4. After the training, consider which parts worked and which did not work.
5. Adjust the training outline to meet your feelings, thoughts, and comfort level.
6. Try doing it again with a different group of people.

Advocacy for Social Justice and Against Ageism

Advocacy involves the promotion of social justice for all clients, a core professional value and principle of the *ACA Code of Ethics* (ACA, 2014, Preamble). Advocacy for social justice is based on respect for diversity, equality, and human rights; it typically involves working with oppressive systems that do not support social justice. Counselors should embrace the concept and actions associated with social justice because of their professional values and because they are in a unique position to work toward justice, both individually and systemically (Branfield & Xiong, 2012). Advocacy for social justice is similar to the concept of advocacy against *ageism*, which has been defined as "an unreasonable prejudice against persons based on chronological age" (J. E. Myers & Shannonhouse, 2013, p. 151). Perhaps one of the most important aspects of advocacy for older people is, therefore, the effort to combat ageism or negative attitudes toward aging.

Counselors must dispel myths associated with the negative attitudes toward aging and advocate for the concept that older people can adapt, thrive, and maintain a sense of achievement and life satisfaction as they face the multiple changes associated with aging (Chatters & Zalaquett, 2013). Extended discussions of ageism and related concepts can be found throughout this book; in *Counseling for Multiculturalism and Social Justice: Integration, Theory, and Application* (Ratts & Pedersen, 2014); and in *Counseling for Social Justice* (Lee, 2007).

Advocacy for Individual Clients

Individual client advocacy is different from legislative and systems advocacy because it deals with specific issues of a specific client. It is also the type of advocacy that may illicit more feelings on the part of the counselor, family, community, and service providers because it involves a particular and immediate situation and people. For this reason, it is important for the counselor to develop a climate of understanding among the people involved.

A variety of instances exist in which counselors find themselves acting as an individual client's advocate. For example, a counselor may become aware of situations in which a client has been treated unfairly, is not receiving quality services, is in danger of mental or physical deterioration because of the care he or she is receiving, is being abused, is being treated with disrespect, appears to be overmedicated, is being discriminated against with regard to employment, or is being devalued. In these cases, counselors can use various methods to advocate for the client. These methods can include involvement in team meetings, individual visits with administrators or caregivers within a program, consultations with pharmacists, meeting with employers, role-modeling appropriate behavior or communication, meeting with family members, and reporting abuse to the appropriate authorities. It is important to obtain the client's written consent before engaging in most of these types of advocacy and to inform the client of the purpose of sharing information, the people the counselor will be communicating with, and the information being shared (ACA, 2014, Standards A.7.b., B.2.e., and B.3.b.). For clients who lack the capacity to give such consent, counselors can seek permission from the appropriate third party (ACA, 2014, Standards A.2.e. and B.5.c.). If counselors are unsure about which situations need client consent, they can seek consultation from a colleague, supervisor, appropriate authorities, or the ACA Ethics and Professional Standards Department (ACA, 2014, Standard I.2.c.).

When advocating for an individual during a staffing or group meeting, it is often helpful to enter these meetings with a nonadversarial perspective and to preface one's concerns with a statement such as, "I know that everyone is wanting to do the best for the client and that we can work as a team to resolve any issues." Being open to the wisdom, knowledge, experiences, values, and perspectives of other members of an interdisciplinary group is important because collectively they can contribute to a client's well-being (ACA, 2014, Section D, Introduction, and Standards D.1.a. and D.1.c.). It is also important to be prepared for these meetings (e.g., have a list of concerns and ideas about how these can be resolved) and to be assertive in the process. After the group has identified strategies or practices that can resolve the issues at hand, it is helpful to restate these and to add timelines and names of people who will be responsible to carry out any decisions that have been made during the meeting. It is also helpful to follow up with a written list of concerns along with the action items, time frames, and names of responsible people. This list can be provided to all participants, the department head, or an administrator; however, it will be important to ensure that only the appropriate individuals (i.e., only those who are authorized) receive a copy of this report and that clients or their official representatives have given written permission to share this report (ACA, 2014, Standards B.6.b. and B.6.g.). Counselors can contact the program and group at a later date to review progress toward making changes. See Chapter 12 for application of these strategies within a long-term care setting.

Another more subtle way to advocate for an individual client is to act as a role model. For example, a counselor may observe dehumanizing behaviors on the part of service providers, community members, or family members. In these cases, the counselor can model appropriate behavior. If subtlety does not work, counselors can speak directly to the staff person or significant other to explain how certain behaviors can be dehumanizing and to suggest other behaviors.

Individual client advocacy can also involve helping clients communicate with friends, family, or service providers. Counselors can do this by asking clients to describe the situation, identify coping strategies they have used in dealing with significant others, brainstorm new strategies that they might use, and practice these new strategies (i.e., role play) before trying them out. This strategy is perhaps the best and first strategy to use rather than advocating directly for the client because advocating for the client may result in disenfranchisement or disempowerment of that client.

As indicated in Chapter 2, it is vital to recognize that different cultures have different perspectives on aging and on what it means to be a family member or friend of an elder. What may seem inappropriate in one culture may be the norm in other cultures; therefore, counselors must attempt to understand the cultural context of the individual and significant others when they are advocating for clients.

Advocacy: Elder Abuse

One important aspect of advocacy involves elder abuse. An extended discussion of elder abuse can be found in Chapter 7. Unfortunately, it has been estimated that nearly 85% of elder abuses are never reported to Adult Protective Services (APS) agencies (O'Neill & Vermeal, 2013). Financial abuse is thought to be the most unreported form of elder abuse, perhaps because it is often done by caregivers or family members. When financial abuse occurs, older individuals may not report it because they do not want to "get someone into trouble," have diminished mental capacity, are ashamed or embarrassed, blame themselves, or are afraid of retaliation (O'Neill, n.d.).

There are many reasons for underreported elder abuse by professionals. For example, APS agencies are governed and funded by states; therefore, regulations and statutes regarding elder abuse vary across states. In addition, there are multiple definitions and perspectives of elder abuse, a lack of knowledge about the warning signs or reporting procedures of elder abuse or neglect, concerns that reporting a situation may make it worse, an assumption that the abused or the abuser will deny the allegation, a desire to remain "loyal" to clients/ families, concerns about damaging client–family–provider rapport, and the belief that reporting is not worth the effort because clients and family members are adults and can refuse intervention. Other reasons for lack of reporting include views that elder abuse is a private family matter, clients' concerns about the impact on their relationship with the abuser, and clients' fears of reprisal (Lawson, 2013; National Center on Elder Abuse, 2005; O'Neill & Vermeal, 2013).

In contrast, the *ACA Code of Ethics* (ACA, 2014) clearly states, "The general requirement that counselors keep information confidential does not apply when disclosure is required to protect clients or identified others from serious and foreseeable harm or when legal requirements demand that confidential information must be revealed" (Standard B.2.a.). The *Code* also indicates that "counselors, acting in the best interest of the client, may adhere to the requirements of the law, regulations, and/or other governing legal authority" (Standard I.1.c.), and that "when counselors are required by law, institutional policy, or extraordinary circumstances to serve in more than one role in judicial or administrative proceedings, they clarify role expectations and parameters of confidentiality with their colleagues" (Standard D.1.e.).

Related to this issue is the concept of the ethical dilemma, which may involve a conflict between two different aspects of the *ACA Code of Ethics* (e.g., confidentiality vs. protection of client). Counselors who feel they are experiencing an ethical dilemma need to follow guidelines for making a decision of this kind. A primary aspect of this process is to obtain input from "other counselors who are knowledgeable about ethics and the *ACA Code of Ethics*, with colleagues, or with appropriate authorities, such as the ACA Ethics and Professional Standards Department" (ACA, 2014, Standard I.2.c.).

Another aspect of the 2014 *ACA Code of Ethics* that applies to this situation is the importance of maintaining paperwork. The *Code* states, "At initiation and throughout the counseling process, counselors inform clients of the limitations of confidentiality" (Standard B.1.d.); in addition, it states, "Counselors have an obligation to review in writing and verbally with clients the right and responsibilities of both counselors and clients" (Standard A.2.a.). In other words, it is vital to inform clients, at the beginning of a counseling relationship, of situations in which confidentiality does not apply (e.g., elder abuse). The *Code* further states, "Counselors are accurate, honest, and objective in reporting their professional activities and judgments to appropriate third parties" (Standard C.6.b.), and "counselors apply careful discretion and deliberation before destroying records that may be needed by a court of law, such as notes on child abuse, suicide, sexual harassment, or violence" (Standard B.6.h.). Other documents that should be maintained are the notes and written strategies used by the counselor in making a decision regarding the report of abuse. For example, Standard I.1.b. indicates that

> when counselors are faced with an ethical dilemma, they use and document, as appropriate, an ethical decision-making model that may include, but is not limited to consultation; consideration of relevant ethical standards, principles, and laws; generation of potential courses of action; deliberation of risks and benefits; and selection of an objective decision based on the circumstances and welfare of all involved.

Counselors also need to know that the authorities, not the counselor, will follow up on any reported concerns and decide what needs to occur, and that APS laws, regulations, and ethics typically prevent investigators from sharing any information about an investigation after they receive reports of possible elder abuse (O'Neill & Vermeal, 2013). Because of these regulations, people who report abuse are not considered to be responsible for the situation once it has been reported. Neither will they be told of any actions taken or outcomes of these actions.

Danger of Client Disempowerment in Advocacy

A very important point when discussing advocacy is that although counselors are expected to advocate for their clients, there is a danger of disempowering these people in the process. In other words, there is danger in being too much of an advocate. Counselors must therefore watch for cues, such as the following, that their advocacy may actually be destructive:

- Counselor feels like a "knight in shining armor."
- Counselor senses that he or she did something wonderful.
- Clients or outsiders indicate that the client could not have accomplished something without the counselor.
- Counselor feels concern that the client will not be able to do things without them.

- Clients continue to ask for assistance in working with others or agencies when they could do it themselves.

As indicated above, it is important to avoid being the "savior" in advocating for specific individuals. Taking on too much responsibility for anyone can be dehumanizing and may be feeding into one's own need to be the leader or to be in charge. When counselors do too much for the client, they may be robbing them of their dignity. Because respecting and promoting the dignity of clients is the primary counselor value (ACA, 2014, Preamble), this issue is of utmost importance.

Laws Designed to Protect the Rights of Older People

In advocacy, it is important to be knowledgeable about the laws or programs designed to protect or to provide services for clients. Several federal laws are associated with consumer protection; however, each state also has its own laws and regulations. Following are some examples of federal laws to protect the rights of older people.

The Age Discrimination in Employment Act (ADEA) of 1967 prohibits discrimination in employment (hiring, benefits, pay, promotions, layoffs or firings, job duties, training, apprenticeship opportunities) on the basis of age (ages 40 or older). Information about and charges can be filed with the Equal Employment Opportunity Commission (EEOC) at http://www.eeoc.gov or 800-669-4000.

The Americans with Disabilities Act of 1990 (ADA) prohibits discrimination on the basis of disability. Information about and charges can be filed with the EEOC at http://www.eeoc.gov or 800-669-4000.

The Civil Rights Act of 1964 (Titles VI and VII) prohibits discrimination on the basis of race, religion, sex, national origin, age, and disability.

The Elder Justice Act of 2010, located within the Patient Protection and Affordable Care Act of 2010, is a comprehensive federal elder abuse prevention law that provides funds to state APS agencies to protect elders from abuse (Blancato & Donahue, 2012).

Nursing home and other program regulations are unique to each state; therefore, counselors will need to identify which state department is responsible.

The Rehabilitation Act of 1973 (Section 504) prohibits discrimination against persons with disabilities and sets no age limit for rehabilitation services. The State Client Assistance Project is designed to help individuals who believe they have not been given the services they deserve from a state rehabilitation agency.

Resources Regarding Advocacy

Administration on Aging, http://www.aoa.gov

Centers for Disability Law (one or more of these centers can be located in each state)

Clearinghouse on Abuse and Neglect of the Elderly, http://www.cane.udel.edu

Counselors for Social Justice, http://www.counselorsforsocialjustice.net

Eldercare Locator, http://www.eldercare.gov or 800-677-1116

Elder Justice Coalition, http://www.elderjusticecoalition.com

ElderLawAnswers, http://www.elderlawanswers.com or 866-267-0947

National Academy of Elder Law Attorneys, http://www.naela.com or 703-942-5711

National Adult Protective Services Association, http://www.apsnetwork.org

National Association of State Units on Aging, ncea@nasua.org or 202-898-2586

National Center on Elder Abuse (NCEA), http://www.ncea.aoa.gov/ncearoot or 855-500-3537

National Committee for the Prevention of Elder Abuse, http://www.preventelderabuse.org

National Consumer Voice for Quality Long-Term Care, http://www.theconsumervoice.org

National Council on Aging (NCOA), http://www.ncoa.org or 202-479-1200

National Disability Rights Network, http://www.NDRN.org

National Long Term Care Ombudsmen Resource Center, http://www.ltombusdmen.org

Office for Older Americans, Consumer Financial Protection Bureau (CFPB), http://www.consumerfinance.gov or 855-411-2372

SCAN Foundation, http://www.thescanfoundation.org

State Adult Protective Services (find at state level)

Summary

Advocacy comes in many forms. It can be legislative, systemic, and individual. It can focus on attitude change, behavior change, systems change, and client protection from ageism or abuse. When advocating for clients, it is vital that counselors avoid disempowering them. It is also important for counselors to realize that clients can advocate for themselves and to support this endeavor to the degree possible.

Chapter 4
Aging Well/ Successful Aging

One of the core professional values of the counseling profession is to enhance human development throughout the life span (ACA, 2014, Preamble). The purpose of this chapter is to focus on adult development and aging, successful aging, and the individual practices that contribute to aging well.

As indicated in Chapter 1, people who have achieved old age have been successful in survival. They have special qualities that have enabled them to avoid or survive threats associated with illness, accident, violent acts, and so forth. Perhaps these qualities have to do with genetics, social support, lifestyle, choices, vocational background, or psychological status. The key is that older people have already achieved longevity, and something about them has supported this achievement. The second and related major concept has to do with thriving, productivity, creativity, and growth in older adulthood. Older adults not only can survive, but they can live well during the latter part of their lives.

Adult Development and Aging

Aging, as a developmental process, has long been a part of the literature. So much so that several excellent books have focused on this issue. Among the more recent of these are Hoyer and Roodin's (2009) *Adult Development and Aging*, Cavanaugh and Blanchard-Fields's (2006) *Adult Development and Aging*, Schaie and Willis's (2002)

Adult Development and Aging, and Whitbourne and Whitbourne's (2011) *Adult Development and Aging: Biopsychosocial Perspectives.* Counselors can gain a deep understanding of adult development by reading one or more of these books.

Several theories of adult development have been postulated. Counselors can use these theories to obtain insight or guidance in the counseling process. Following are brief descriptions of some of these theories.

Erik Erikson, in the 1960s–1980s, classified people according to expected psychological development and the conflicts (or extremes) that can occur at different stages of life (i.e., Erikson's Theory of Psychological Development). He classified late-adulthood as a time when people become more aware of their death and also look back over their lives in an evaluation of their worth. At this stage, the conflict involves *ego integrity* (i.e., they perceive they did a good job and had a meaningful and significant life, are satisfied with themselves, and have a high sense of self-worth) versus *despair* (i.e., they have unresolved or negatively resolved issues; they perceive that they made poor decisions; they feel that have no control over their lives; they have low self-esteem; and they experience gloom, doubt, and low self-worth). The process involves reviewing one's life (i.e., life review), tying up loose ends, making sense of it all, and integrating its elements. Positive resolution of this conflict may result in wisdom, a quality often associated with aging (J. E. Myers & Schwiebert, 1996; Rybash, Roodin, & Hoyer, 1995; Schaie & Willis, 2002). As Erikson, himself, aged he and others began to note that perhaps the struggle for integrity may be resolved when people are in their 60s and 70s and that the very old may be facing new conflicts regarding autonomy, especially for those who have new physical issues (J. E. Myers & Shannonhouse, 2013).

Donald Super also changed his theory of career development as he aged. Originally, he speculated that people underwent career development stages (i.e., fantasy, exploration, establishment, maintenance, and decline). In his later years, however, he developed a life-career rainbow that focused on life roles that people hold throughout their lives. Some of these roles include being a student, a parent, a leisurite, and a worker (J. E. Myers & Shannonhouse, 2013).

Robert Havinghurst, a pioneer in social gerontology, indicated that older people must face the following developmental tasks:

> a. adjusting to decreasing physical strength and health, b. adjusting to retirement and reduced income, c. adjusting to death of a spouse, d. establishing an explicit association with one's age group, e. adopting and adapting societal roles in a flexible way, and f. establishing satisfactory physical living arrangements. (J. E. Myers & Schwiebert, 1996, p. 31; Schaie & Willis, 2002)

Havinghurst developed these tasks some time ago (e.g., 1972) and did not take into account the wide age range and diversity of older people. Regardless of this issue, counselors can consider whether these tasks are appropriate topics to be discussed and perhaps resolved.

Riker and Myers (1989) developed the Theory of Later Life Development, which focused on life stages and tasks that may occur at age 60 or over. The assumption was that people of all ages experience frequent changes that require adaptation (tasks), and that some of these tasks may be repeated/required throughout the life span. The focus is on the process of coping with transitions rather than outcome. In other words, active involvement in life tasks represents a healthy approach to life. Although people experience similar life tasks across a lifetime, tasks may evolve from focus on relationships with others to focus on relationships with oneself and one's god. People may also face particular tasks at various decades in their lives. The tasks one faces in one's 60s may include reviewing life habits, helping others, seeking new meanings, and developing personal capacities. In one's 70s, tasks may focus on leisure activities, family, friends, and meaning of life. The tasks one faces in one's 80s may include strengthening the sense of self and personal power. In one's 90s, tasks may include building a sense of spiritual wholeness, putting aside past issues, focusing on present relationships and present activities, and facing future insecurities with composure (J. E. Myers & Schwiebert, 1996).

Successful Aging

There are many perspectives about what constitutes successful aging. These include (a) having good health, a strong body, and high levels of physical functioning, vigor, and activity (L. L. Fisher, 2010; Rowe & Kahn, 1998; Saisan, Smith, Segal, & White, 2012; Schaie & Willis, 2002); (b) being able to adjust to, cope with, and thrive during multiple life events (Saisan, Smith, et al., 2012); (c) being able to avoid negative life events (Schaie & Willis, 2002); (d) being productive and creative (L. L. Fisher, 2010; Rowe & Kahn, 1998; Whitbourne & Whitbourne, 2011); (e) having high levels of cognitive functioning (Rowe & Kahn, 1998; Schaie & Willis, 2002); (f) being socially engaged and connected in truly meaningful relationships (L. L. Fisher, 2010; Kissane & McLaren, 2006; Rowe & Kahn, 1998; Saisan, Smith, et al., 2012; Schaie & Willis, 2002); (g) having a sexually satisfying relationship (L. L. Fisher, 2010); (h) contributing to, being concerned about, or being responsible for others (L. L. Fisher, 2010; Kissane & McLaren, 2006; Whitbourne & Whitbourne, 2011); (i) sharing wisdom with the younger generation (Saisan, Smith, et al., 2012); (j) having fun and a sense of humor (Ryff, 1989); (k) having confidence, possessing a positive self-concept, and recognizing one's wisdom (Saisan, Smith, et al., 2012; Schaie & Willis, 2002); (l) having personal independence and autonomy (L. L. Fisher, 2010); (m) having spiritual well-being (L. L. Fisher, 2010); and (n) having financial security (L. L. Fisher, 2010). These elements of successful aging are thought to relate to and/or reinforce each other (Whitbourne & Whitbourne, 2011). For example, people who have maintained their cognitive abilities may be more likely to be socially engaged, productive, and independent. People who have maintained social contacts may be more physically able to interact and may have more positive self-concepts.

Contrary to the negative perspectives and myths about aging, older people generally age well. It has been suggested that between 33% (Whitbourne & Whitbourne, 2011) and 95% (Depp & Jeste, 2006) of older people have met many of the above subjective criteria for aging well. For example, a survey of 3,000 Americans showed that among people age 65 and older, 91% felt they were needed, 90% did not view themselves as a burden, 86% were able to drive, 84% were able to pay their bills, 83% were not lonely, 80% did not indicate that they were sad or depressed, 79% did not have serious illness, 79% reported being sexually active, and 75% did not have memory loss. This high level of subjective well-being extended to the older group in this survey, too. Among those age 75 years or older, 81% indicated that they were "pretty" or "very happy" about their lives (Pew Research Center, 2009). An AARP survey of quality of life did not result in such high ratings, but it showed that about half of their respondents indicated that their quality of life was high. On a scale of 1 (*very low*) to 10 (*very high*), 53% of the men and 48% of women age 60 through 69 gave a rating of 8 to 10 (high quality of life), and 40% of men and 48% of women age 70 or older also gave these high ratings (L. L. Fisher, 2010). So, although older people may experience many negatively charged conditions and events, researchers have found that many of them maintain high levels of well-being. Furthermore, they tend to exhibit lower levels of depression than those age 40 to 59 years (Chatters & Zalaquett, 2013). Other studies have also found that older people tend to have a positive perspective on life (Gomez, Krings, Bangerter, & Grob, 2009; Werngren-Elgstrolm, Carlsson, & Iwarsson, 2009). This ability to maintain a positive perspective in spite of negative objective circumstances has been called the *paradox of well-being* (Mroczek & Kolarz, 1998).

Personal variables that seem to contribute to older people's positive subjective well-being are their abilities to adapt or habituate to negative situations, to compare themselves to others who have much worse situations or conditions (*positive social comparison*), and to emphasize the positive versus the negative aspects of their lives. High levels of well-being, in the face of many negative past circumstances, may also be attributable to *identity assimilation*, which involves giving a positive spin to aspects of one's life that might otherwise be viewed negatively. Because of this process, people can look back at their life stories and see them in a positive light, even when their actual experiences did not support this. Doing so can help them maintain their self-esteem and maintain a positive sense of subjective well-being (Whitbourne & Sherry, 1991; Whitbourne, Sneed, & Skultety, 2002; Whitbourne & Whitbourne, 2011).

Having a positive perspective in later adulthood is also thought to relate to certain lifetime personal qualities and temperaments. For example, extroverts are more likely than introverts to have a positive perspective of events, which allows them to maintain high levels of psychological well-being (Mroczek & Spiro, 2005; Whitbourne & Whitbourne, 2011). People who had high levels of childhood self-esteem seem to have high levels of self-esteem in adulthood (Robins & Trzesniewski, 2005). Those who set high goals for themselves in midlife tend to do the same in later adulthood. This is particularly true of those who valued an active cultural life and contribution to the community (Holahan & Chapman, 2002).

Other more objective contributors to subjective well-being are education level (Jang, Choi, & Kim, 2009) and sufficient financial support or higher socioeconomic status (Deacon, 2008; Rostad, Deeg, & Schei, 2009). There is some concern, therefore, that because many older people do not have sufficient funds to retire comfortably, they may have a lower sense of well-being (see Chapter 7).

Clients can be asked to consider the possibility that it is never too late to begin positive aging practices. Many of the practices discussed in this book can help maintain or sharpen mental processes, boost the immune system, help people stay active and positive, increase energy, and improve mental and physical health. Saisan, Smith, et al. (2012) indicated that older people report that they simply feel better when they are making an effort to improve their health and other aspects of their lives. This comment makes sense, because such activities are essentially problem-focused coping (i.e., facing the problem, making a plan, and following through with the plan) and have been found to have a positive relationship to a variety of outcome variables.

Resilience

Resilience is important to successful aging and can be defined as the ability to adjust well to one or more changes. People who are resilient are able to maintain a positive self-image, good health, and/or good psychological well-being in spite of their situations (Chatters & Zalequett, 2013; Reid & Kampfe, 2000). In other words, resilience helps people thrive in difficult times.

Personal characteristics that may contribute to resilience closely parallel descriptors of successful aging and include the following: having a good self-concept; allowing for diverse perspectives while maintaining one's own ideas or boundaries; having the ability to integrate new situations and concepts into one's life; being flexible and adaptable; being or becoming self-aware and self-accepting; having a sense of humor; and maintaining balance between the spiritual, intellectual, emotional, and physical self. Those who are resilient typically plan ahead but are not "thrown" when these plans are not possible; seek social support; practice problem-solving, problem-focused coping, such as brainstorming and implementing; find time to relax and be alone; have strong social support; use "I" statements when expressing desires, thoughts, and feelings; reframe potentially stressful events; and use stress management strategies such as meditation and relaxation (Furr & Carroll, 2003; Kampfe, 1999; Reid & Kampfe, 2000; Saisan, Smith, et al., 2012; Sturges, 2012; Trouillet et al., 2009).

Counselors can use this information to encourage clients to engage in practices and develop attitudes that will help them maintain, regain, and/or develop their resilience. For example, counselors might ask clients to find ways to face a problem rather than avoid it; brainstorm regarding solutions to a problem; take things one step at a time in order to avoid feeling overwhelmed or helpless in difficult situations; focus on the things that can be controlled or changed and accept things that cannot; plan ahead, when possible; and reframe problems as opportunities for personal growth and learning. Counselors can also invite clients to acknowledge, express, and process their feelings; use "I statements" to make their needs and feelings known; learn and practice various methods of relaxation; interact with others; find time to be alone; accept diverse opinions while maintaining their own; and accept themselves for who they are (Chatters & Zalequett, 2013; Furr & Carroll, 2003; Saisan, Smith, et al., 2012).

Counselors can use a strength-based perspective (e.g., developmental counseling/therapy, therapeutic lifestyle changes) in which they encourage clients to focus on the positive aspects of aging and decrease the focus on problems they are experiencing (Chatters & Zalequett, 2013; Loe, 2011). Furthermore, counselors can help clients recognize, believe in, and have confidence in the strengths that they have. For example, counselors can help clients identify their effective coping skills, healthy lifestyle choices, spirituality, culture, and community (Daniel-Burke, 2012). To do this, counselors can remind clients that they have demonstrated resiliency by doing a number of things in their lives (e.g., living a long life, remaining actively sober, raising a family in spite of difficulties, surviving specific events). Leading statements can include one or more of the following: "I noticed something, and I wonder if you noticed it too. In spite of X, you were able to achieve X"; "Even though things have been difficult, you have X"; "You have survived to age X, which shows me that you are one of the strong ones"; and "You have showed me that you are a resilient person; tell me more about your strengths and how you use them to adjust to life events." Counselors will be able to make these statements if they have been listening for both client problems and the methods they have used to effectively overcome them. Clients are often surprised to hear these positive reflections of content and are able to begin to see some of their own qualities of resiliency. Once clients begin to see that they have resiliency, counselors can invite them to apply the same skills to current difficult situations.

As stated in other sections of this book, counselors' attitudes can influence their methods and effectiveness. Counselors will, therefore, want to trust and believe in their clients' resilience, powers to overcome challenges, abilities to create meaningful lives, and abilities to avoid being victims of circumstances (Shallcross, 2012c).

Wisdom

Wisdom is often associated with successful aging. According to Erickson's theory, wisdom is thought to be the result of the resolution of the conflict between ego integrity and despair, in which individuals tie up loose ends and review and make sense of their lives (J. E. Myers & Schwiebert, 1996; Rybash et al., 1995; Schaie & Willis, 2002). Wisdom is also thought to be the result of having had many past positive and negative experiences to draw from and being able to integrate these experiences and observations when making current decisions. In other words, older people have learned from the past and can use these lessons in the present. For example, older people may have learned that bad situations typically end or improve and that really good times are also short-lived. These two perspectives can help older people endure rough situations and cherish or fully enjoy the fleeting good times (Howard, 2012b, referring to Carstensen and the Stanford Center on Longevity). Counselors can use life review work to support this process.

It is thought that both older and younger people can benefit when older people share their wisdom and experience (Saisan, Smith, et al., 2012); however, in today's ageist society, wisdom may not be expected or recognized in older people. Counselors can work with clients and their families to consider the value of and access to the older person's wisdom (Rybash et al., 1995) and perhaps use creative problem solving to find ways to use their wisdom.

Maintaining a Healthy Body: Physical Fitness/Physical Activity

An AADA survey found that older people indicated that being vigorous, healthy, and physically active are important to quality of life and aging well. Among those who were age 60 through 69 years old, 100% of males and 96% of females rated this variable as important. Among those who were age 70 and older, 99% of males and 97% of females also indicated such. Their reports of actual engagement in moderate to vigorous exercise were somewhat less than their rating of importance of physical well-being. Among this group, 64% of men age 60 through 69 and 66% of men age 70 or older engaged in moderate or vigorous exercise, but 27% of men age 60 through 69 and 23% of men age 70 or older did not exercise. Women were less involved in exercise than men, with 61% of women age 60 through 69 and 49% of those age 70 or older engaging in moderate to vigorous exercise. Furthermore, 28% of women who were age 60 to 69 and 44% of women who were age 70 or older did not engage in moderate or vigorous exercise (L. L. Fisher, 2010).

Regular exercise of all types is important in maintaining and improving physical health and vigor as well as overall mental health. Exercise and other physical activity can reduce stress, improve flexibility, reduce risk of type 2 diabetes and cardiovascular disease, strengthen bones and muscles, improve balance and prevent falls, help maintain or lose weight, reduce visceral fat, ease aches and pains, improve memory and brain health, maintain vitamin B12, reduce depression, maintain aerobic capacity, and support a restful nighttime sleep (Agnvall, 2012; American Health Assistance Foundation, 2012a; Center for Healthy Aging, National Council on Aging, 2012; Healthways SilverSneakers Fitness Program, 2012; Reynolds, 2011; L. Robinson, Boose, & Segal, 2013).

A combination of exercises can be used that focus on aerobics, strength building, flexibility building, and balance enhancement. Recommendations vary regarding amount of exercise needed; however, it is thought that older individuals can benefit from 2.5 hours of activity at least twice a week or from 30 to 40 minutes four to five times a week (Center for Healthy Aging, National Council on Aging, 2012; Centers for Disease Control and Prevention [CDC], 2012; L. Robinson et al., 2013). Furthermore, there are many exercise programs designed to meet the needs of people who have specific limiting conditions. For example, the PACE (People with Arthritis Can Exercise) program is designed for those with arthritis.

Exercise does not have to be strenuous or done at the gym to be effective. In fact, beginners should start slowly and gradually increase the intensity and amount of time doing exercise in order to avoid injury or other negative results. Furthermore, walking is an excellent way to stay fit, and it can be done anywhere without equipment, training, or experience. Even people who have not exercised in the past can start doing so when they are older (Reynolds, 2011; Saisan, Smith, et al., 2012).

Exercise is so important that the CDC (2012) has recommended that counselors discuss this need with older clients and ask them to determine the degree to which they wish to engage in physical exercise, the methods they can use to do this, and whether they will make a commitment to follow through with their decisions. Counselors can use creative problem-solving strategies in this process. They can start by asking clients to consider the positives and negatives of physical exercise and make a decision about whether or not they wish to become involved in a physical activity. Counselors can then invite clients to review the types of activities that best suit their interests, abilities, and limitations. Some individuals may enjoy competitive sports, whereas others dislike these kinds of activities. Some may like taking guided classes, whereas others prefer to engage in their own private exercises. Some may have little or no physical limitations, whereas others may have major limitations. For clients with physical limitations, counselors can help them identify programs that take these limitations into account (e.g., PACE).

Once clients decide about the type of activity they wish to engage in, the counselor can help them identify programs or places that best suit their exercise needs and can ask them for a commitment to their plan. One very important issue that counselors will need to discuss with their clients is the need for outside consultation (e.g., physician, physical therapist, coach) to ensure that the exercise they choose is compatible with their medical conditions or medications and to obtain guidance and learn appropriate safety practices. It is also important to remind clients that it is best to start slowly and with less intensity and then increase exercise as one's body becomes stronger (Reynolds, 2011; Saisan, Smith, et al., 2012).

Community organizations, senior centers, and other local organizations often offer programs to help older individuals stay physically and mentally active. For example, senior centers often include (free of charge or at a nominal fee) programs that focus on physical fitness/wellness, weight lifting, yoga, tai chi, fall prevention, and self-management (e.g., disease, medication, depression). The National Council on Aging's Center for Healthy Aging offers information, assistance, and tools to these organizations to set up evidence-based programs that encourage personal health promotion. Locations of these programs can be found at the Center for Healthy Aging's website (http://www.ncoa.org/improve-health/center-for-healthy-aging) or at the local Area Agency on Aging. Other resources include the SilverSneakers Fitness Program, a national fitness program for older individuals that may be offered free of charge by their supplemental health insurance companies. Local SilverSneakers facilities can be found at http://www.silversneakers.com or at 888-423-4632. Other programs or guides can be found at http://www.helpguide.org, http://www.yogahealthfoundation.org/yoga_month, http://www.arp.org/walking, and http://www.nihseniorhealth.gov/exercise/oc.html.

Maintaining a Healthy Brain

The human brain is able to produce new brain cells at any age. Practices that contribute to a healthy brain include physical exercise, regular mental and intellectual stimulation, social interaction, a healthy diet, vitamin B12, plenty of restful sleep, stress management, low alcohol intake, and absence of smoking (Howard, 2012b; M. Smith, Robinson, & Segal, 2012). Simply walking can contribute to a healthy brain.

M. Smith et al. (2012) cited a statement by the American Academy of Neurology that walking from six to nine miles per week can prevent memory loss and brain shrinkage and that those who walk can cut their risk of memory loss by up to half versus those who do not walk.

Challenging intellectual and mental activities are thought to preserve or improve cognitive functioning because such activities stimulate neural connections. Examples of these activities include learning to play a new musical instrument; learning a new language, game, recipe, or driving route; reading challenging books, newspapers, or magazines; singing alone or in a choir; playing chess, bridge, scrabble, or other games that involve strategy; playing memory games and computer or video games designed to challenge memory or logic skills; creating art; doing challenging crossword or number puzzles; meeting new people; conversing with others face to face or via writing, e-mailing, skyping, or texting; taking a course on something unfamiliar; starting a project that involves planning and design (e.g., a quilt, a garden, a koi pond); doing something new; doing new versions of old things; and moving beyond one's comfort zone. The key is finding activities that are enjoyable so that they maintain a person's interest and involvement. Other strategies that can be used to encourage mental exercise are to pair it with other enjoyable things, such as playing favorite music or giving oneself a reward after doing so (Budd, 2012; Saisan, Smith, et al., 2012; M. Smith et al., 2012).

Several of the above activities not only challenge the brain, but also provide the opportunity for social interaction and physical activity, which contribute to mind and body health (American Health Assistance Foundation, 2012a). Conversely, several of the above activities can be done by oneself, which may decrease loneliness and boredom when clients have no options for social interaction.

Although there are mixed findings, memory training programs seem to have a durable effect, lasting at least 6 months and longer. The most effective training seems to be associated with participants' knowledge, in advance, about what to expect in the training. There are many types of memory training, and they all seem to be equally effective. For example, Rasmusson, Rebok, Bylsma, and Brandt (1999) found no difference in outcome between an audiotape memory improvement program, a microcomputer-based memory training program, and a group memory course. It is important to note that different programs focus on different specific aspects of memory, and that the skills learned in one program may not generalize to other memory functions (Hoyer & Roodin, 2009).

A discussion of each of these activities is beyond the scope of this chapter; however, counselors need to be aware of the possibilities and use this information to do brainstorming with their clients to identify activities they might be interested in trying.

Healthy Diet/Nutrition

Older people can benefit from good nutrition. A healthy diet can help build muscles and energy levels (Pennar, 2012a, 2012b), improve brain function (Alzheimer's Disease Education and Referral Center, 2012a), reduce some pain (Howard, 2011), maintain appropriate vitamin B12 levels (M. Smith et al., 2012), and maintain or improve mental and physical health. These benefits are discussed in other chapters.

There are many foods that are especially nutritious. These include legumes (e.g., beans, peas), green leafy vegetables, cauliflower, broccoli, tomatoes, whole grains, carrots, red grapes, red and blue berries, foods rich in omega-e fatty acids (such as "oily" fish like salmon and tuna), olive and canola oils, seeds, and nuts (American Health Assistance Foundation, 2012a; Bhide, 2011a, 2011b; Saisan, Smith, et al., 2012). For example, deep red or blue berries contain polyphenols that activate proteins that break down and recycle toxic chemicals that are associated with age-related mental deterioration. Strawberries are strong in vitamin C, and acai berries have a high degree of omega-6 and omega-9 fatty acids, which are thought to support the cardiovascular system (Bhide, 2011a). It is also important to eat foods that are rich in vitamin B12 and to take B12 supplements (M. Smith et al., 2012). Conversely, diets should exclude saturated fat and added sugar (American Health Assistance Foundation, 2012a; Bhide, 2011a, 2011b; Saisan, Smith, et al., 2012).

Following are some examples of issues that clients may have and possible solutions to these issues. People who live alone and who do not have an appetite may benefit from eating with other people (Saisan, Smith, et al., 2012). As with all suggestions, however, eating with others may not be appropriate for everyone. Some may find that they are less likely to eat when they are with others because they prefer to talk, they are concerned about their teeth, or they are worried that they may spill food on themselves. Again, it is important for counselors not to make suggestions but rather to brainstorm with clients about ways to regain an appetite. Counselors might also wish to make a referral to a nutritionist who can help clients understand their alternatives.

If clients are on a low budget, counselors can use brainstorming to encourage them to identify various ways they can obtain healthy and affordable food. Older people may be eligible for the Supplemental Nutrition Assistance Program (SNAP; formerly food stamps) and for 10% grocery store senior discounts on certain days of the week or month. Joining a neighborhood community garden group can also save a great deal of money while providing the opportunity to socialize and eat healthy food (AARP, 2012b). Other strategies to save money are getting a group together to buy in bulk, cooking from scratch rather than buying premade items, purchasing from community-supported agricultural programs, cooking perishable food first, cooking larger quantities and freezing leftovers, and buying seasonal food (Denn & Park, 2012). For those who prefer not to cook or who cannot cook, senior centers almost always offer low-cost lunches that can be eaten at the center or be delivered to the home. Many restaurants offer senior menus and special coupons, and some (e.g., Ikea restaurants) offer free or very low cost breakfasts on certain days or at certain times (AARP, 2012b).

Religion and Spirituality

As indicated throughout this book, religion and spirituality are important to older people. An AARP survey, for example, showed that among individuals age 60 to 69, 84% of the men and 94% of the women indicated that spirituality was important to quality of life. Likewise, 86% of men and 94% of women who were age 70 or older indicated the same (L. L. Fisher, 2010). Another study of older hospitalized individuals found that 86% used religion and 98% used prayer to cope with their medical or disabling conditions (Reyes-Ortiz, 2006). These findings are consistent with a Pew study in which older individuals were more likely than younger individuals to indicate that religion was important to them (Salman, 2009).

The Association for Spiritual, Ethical, and Religious Values (ASERVIC, 2009), a division of the ACA, has developed Competencies for Addressing Spiritual and Religious Issues in Counseling (available at http://www.aservic.org/resources/spiritual-competencies/). According to these competencies and the *ACA Code of Ethics* (ACA, 2014, Standards A.4.b. and A.11.b.), it is essential that counselors understand their own beliefs, attitudes, and values; are careful not to impose their own perspectives about religion and spirituality on their clients; are sensitive, respectful, and accepting of their clients' beliefs; recognize spiritual and religious themes and incorporate them into the counseling process when beneficial; and recognize that an individual's religious/spiritual beliefs can contribute to both their well-being or their problems, depending upon the situation.

Religion has been defined as a person's identification with an organized belief system (Whitbourne & Whitbourne, 2011). *Spirituality* has been defined as a belief set that is not necessarily associated with a specific organized religion but involves transcendence, meaning, hope (Hoyer & Roodin, 2009), awareness of a higher order or a higher purpose (Klass, Silverman, & Nickman, 1996), a connectedness to the universe and to others (Hoyer & Roodin, 2009; Jacobs, 2004), and a sense of purpose and power (Aldredge, 2000). Religion and spirituality are strongly interrelated and can both provide meaning to many aspects of life (Atchley, 2000; Hospice and Palliative Nurses Association, 2009a; Wadsworth, Harley, Smith, & Kampfe, 2008; Whitbourne & Whitbourne, 2011).

Religion and spirituality are particularly important to older people because they can provide support and perspective when people are dealing with multiple challenges and losses. For example, religion and spirituality give people grounding, comfort, strength, and coping strategies that they can use to understand, interpret, and adapt to various stressful situations (Kampfe & Kampfe, 1992; Klemmack et al., 2007; Shallcross, 2012c; Wadsworth, Harley, et al., 2008). People who are going through stressful transitions can use prayers (Kampfe & Kampfe, 1992; Rodriguez, Glover-Graf, & Blanko, 2013), religion-based rites and ceremonies (Nelson, 2004), and fellowship/ social support (Klemmack et al., 2007). Furthermore, research has shown that religious and spiritual beliefs have positive effects on coping, adjusting, and healing (Breslin & Lewis, 2008).

Conversely, loss of a close friend or family member may cause people to question their faith and put them into "spiritual distress" (Lynch, 1998). They may feel angry with a higher power (Kübler-Ross & Kessler, 2005) and be unable to understand the meaning of the death. On the other hand, people experiencing a crisis or illness may have an awakening of spirituality (Nelson, 2004) and a strengthening of faith (Lynch, 1998). In either case, counselors will need to be sensitive to these situations and be willing listeners. These issues are further discussed in Chapter 13.

Spirituality issues are strongly related to multicultural issues (Corey et al., 2010; Nelson, 2004). African Americans, Native Americans (American Indians), and Latinos tend to have strong religious and spiritual convictions (Longshore, Grills, Annon, & Grady, 1998; Reid & Kampfe, 2000; Rodriquez et al., 2013). These values and convictions should be respected in the counseling process and can sometimes be used to gain perspective about particular issues. One spiritual practice that counselors may not be familiar with, but is used in many cultures, is Shamanism or some similar type of healing practice. A shaman is typically thought of as a medicine man or priest who can help people in difficult times. This person uses powers and knowledge that are considered to be helpful in bringing people into a state of harmony, wholeness, or balance. The shaman may use rituals that focus on specific issues. He or she may help clients reach an altered state of consciousness in which they are more receptive to change and healing and have an expectancy that healing will take place (Nelson, 2004). Other cultures may rely on curanderas for some aspect of their spirituality and healing. These women use similar age-old practices to bring believers into balance and health (I. Marinez, personal communication, November 19, 2013). Additional discussion of spirituality, as it relates to culture, can be found in Nelson's (2004) book on senior spirituality and in Cashwell and Young's (2011) book on integrating spirituality and religion into counseling.

Productivity and Creativity in Older Individuals

Many older people want to be productive. An AARP survey showed that among a group of older individuals age 60 to 69, 87% of men and 89% of women indicated that contributing and being productive was important to their overall quality of life. Those who were age 70 or older also rated productivity and contribution as important, with 82% of both men and women indicating this was so (L. L. Fisher, 2010).

Older people can remain productive in many ways. Their work may be reflective, subjective, and introspective (Lubart & Sternberg; 1998) and may represent an integration and synthesis of the vast amount of information and insights that they have acquired over a lifetime (Schaie & Willis, 2002). For example, Simonton (1989) found that the last works of older classical composers (e.g., Verdi, Wagner) appeared to reflect creative wisdom and a sort of life review that may have substantiated a so-called swan song phenomenon. Examples of other individuals who produced synthesized works in their later adulthood are Wilhelm Wundt, the father of modern psychology, who finished his 10-volume work at the age of 88; Asa Gray, who wrote *Elements of Botany* at age 77; and John Henry Comstock, who wrote *An Introduction to Entomology* at age 71. Examples of older scholars who published integrated works about aging are G. Stanley Hall, who wrote *Senescence: The Last Half of Life* when he was age 75; B. F. Skinner and a colleague, who wrote *Enjoy Old Age: A Practical Guide* when Skinner was in his late 70s; and Sir John Floyer, who wrote the first book on geriatrics when he was age 75 (Schaie & Willis, 2002).

Although older people can and want to be productive, our ageist society may have taught them that productivity is not appropriate or possible. One way to challenge the concept that older people are no longer capable of producing at high levels is to recognize many older scholars, musicians, actors, artists, public figures, and so forth who have been productive in their older years. Put another way, the recognition of these individuals may contribute to people's positive attitudes toward the capabilities of older individuals.

Examples of the many musical performers from the 1960s and 1970s who have remained productive are Mick Jagger, Cher, Paul McCartney, Aretha Franklin, and Robbie Shankar. Counselors or their clients can attend, or watch recordings of, these musicians' later performances (or the performances of other older musicians) to experience the strength, vigor, beauty, skill, enthusiasm, and thoughtfulness that they carried forward into their older years. These performances will illuminate the ability of older people to continue to be productive and strengthen counselors' and clients' positive attitudes toward aging. Counselors might also wish to use these types of performances with appropriately aged clients to stimulate life review and to encourage them to consider their own productivity. Many of these performances can be found on the public broadcasting system website (http://www.pbs.org) on programs such as *Live at Lincoln Center*.

Classical musicians, artists and architects, writers, scholars, sports figures, performers, and public figures have also remained productive in their older years. For example, the pianist Rubenstein gave advice about how to maintain high quality during a performance, even with some limitations associated with aging. Public leaders or activists who continued to be active are Nelson Mandela and Russell Means. Artists and architects who remained productive include O'Keefe, Picasso, Monet, Niemeyer, and Gehry. Writers who remained productive are John G. Neihard, John Irving, and Stephen King. Scholars/researchers who remained active include Jane Goodall and Jane Myers. Athletes and fitness specialists who continued to be competitive or active include Joan Campbell, Bob Heins, and Richard Simmons. Performers/public figures who remained productive include George Burns, Della Reese, Regis Philbin, Betty White, Samuel L. Jackson, Dustin Hoffman, Robert Duval, Bill Cosby, Cecily Tyson, Catherine Hepburn, Hal Holbrook, William Shatner, Phyllis Diller, Dick Van Dyke, Christopher Walken, Morgan Freeman, Yoko Ono, Robert Redford, Maya Angelou, Richard Roundtree, Tommy Lee Jones, Clint Eastwood, Jack Nicholson, Shirley MacLaine, Harrison Ford, Donald Sutherland, Maggie Smith, Linda Hunter, and Buzz Aldren.

Discussions of any these people's later productivity may add richness to individual or group counseling sessions. Furthermore, counselors can ask clients to identify other older people who are continuing to be productive in their own vocation, avocation, community, or family. Such discussions may introduce the idea that just because people are older, they do not need to stop being productive; this idea may therefore provide the impetus for clients to consider ways that they, themselves, can remain productive. On the other hand, discussions of other people's productivity may elicit sorrow, guilt, anger, and frustration for people who are no longer able to be productive or who wish not to be as productive as they have been in the past.

Counselors will need to be sensitive to all types of responses and use their counseling skills to understand clients' perspectives and to help them work through and resolve issues they might have about their own productivity. For example, although older people may wish to remain productive, researchers have found that they typically are not as productive as they had been in their youth (Whitbourne & Whitbourne, 2011). It may, therefore, be unrealistic for them to expect themselves to be as productive as when they were younger. For this reason, counselors will need to provide a balanced and rational approach to discussions of older client's productivity levels.

The concept of *trying another way* may apply to many of the markers of successful aging mentioned above and especially to productivity.

Try another way was first introduced in the 1960s by Marc W. Gold. Essentially, this concept suggests that if people are unable to accomplish a particular task or achieve a particular goal, they need not give up. They can simply find another way to accomplish that task, achieve that goal, or change the focus. Examples of trying another way can be found in the arts. The old age style (Lindauer, 1998), which is considered to be simpler and more powerful than other styles, sometimes occurs because of physical limitations such as reduced ability to see color and fine lines. This style, therefore, deemphasizes the fine details and focuses on the intended meaning, form, and subjective/affective aspects of the piece. It is an example of the combination of a lifetime of experience, highly developed skills, and adjustment to potentially disabling conditions. Other examples of trying another way in the arts are Henri Matisse, who because he could no longer paint began to make paper sculptures as his art form, and Georgia O'Keeffe, who moved from painting to sculpture as her eyesight decreased (Whitbourne & Whitbourne, 2011).

The concept of trying another way can be applied to many aspects of aging. For example, social support and interpersonal relationships are very important; however, clients might not be able to spend quality time with their own family members for various reasons. If this is the case, they can develop extended family ties in which the client is valued, supported, and supportive of the members. Applying this concept to productivity, clients who are no longer physically able to engage in specific activities that they did in the past can identify other types of related activities or perhaps new activities that they value and can achieve. Counselors can use creative problem solving to help clients find other ways to continue to be productive.

Joy, Satisfaction, and Fun

A part of aging well is achieving a sense of joy, satisfaction, and fun. Counselors can encourage clients to identify activities that support these important aspects of life (Davidson, 2011; Saisan, Smith, et al., 2012). One way to identify activities that clients might enjoy is to ask them about the things that they would like to have done in their lives and then follow up with creative problem solving to determine whether these can be done. The use of poems, movies, short stories, and so forth can facilitate this process. For example, counselors can invite clients to read books such as Martz's (1992) anthology *If I Had My Life to Live Over I Would Pick More Daisies*, in which women review the choices they have made in their lives. After clients read this book, counselors can ask them to describe the fun things they would do if they had their lives to live over. Then the counselor could ask questions such as, "Would you still like to do these things?" If the answer is affirmative, counselors can use creative problem solving to encourage clients to make a plan for doing so (e.g., "How can you do these now?").

Another way to identify possible fun activities is to ask clients about the things they used to enjoy but are no longer doing (an aspect of reminiscence therapy). If these activities are no longer possible because of various constraints, counselors can invite clients to explore creatively other similar or related practices that might give them joy. For example, if a person loved to dance in his or her youth but is now not able to walk, the counselor and client can brainstorm to find other ways to express this love of dance. Counselors can ask questions such as, "What is it about dance that you loved?" "How can you find ways to experience this today?" "What is stopping you?" "What resources do you have for this?" As a result of this brainstorming, clients may find other ways that they can dance or enjoy dance (e.g., doing creative dance while sitting in their chairs or lying in their beds, watching a television program that focuses on dance).

At some point in the quest for fun, counselors can ask clients to develop a do list or bucket list and make plans to engage in one or more of these activities. After clients have tried an activity, counselors can invite them to describe their experiences and the degree to which they were satisfying or disappointing. Using creative problem solving, counselors can encourage clients to identify ways to continue these activities or try something else.

In addition to helping clients identify and engage in new satisfying activities, counselors can invite clients to focus on things that they currently are grateful for, to stop taking positive things for granted, and to recognize the precious nature of life. Counselors can also encourage clients to recognize that in spite of many negative life events, they can find meaning and joy in their lives. This process will mean something different for each individual and may require lengthy discussions (Davidson, 2011; Saisan, Smith, et al., 2012).

In summary, because counselors know the value of having life-enriching experiences, they can invite clients to (a) identify their interests, (b) determine the parameters they wish to maintain, (c) challenge their lifetime habits of putting off the fun things for work, (d) brainstorm options that might meet their interests and abilities, and (e) work out the logistics for achieving some of these options. Once clients have completed an activity, counselors can follow up to learn whether these experiences were valuable and whether the client would like to find other life-enriching experiences.

Bibliotherapy Focusing on Aging Well and Counteracting Ageism

A number of books have focused on aging well. One such strength-based book involves interviews with 30 people who were age 85 or older and were born between approximately 1901 and 1924 (Loe, 2011). On the basis of these interviews, Loe (2011) presented the following list of suggestions: Continue doing what you always did, resort to tomfoolery (laughter, humor), ask for help and mobilize resources, balance independence and connectivity, foster relationships but value alone time, care for others, reach out to family, connect with peers, get intergenerational and redefine family, insist on hugs, be adaptable, take time for self-growth and reflection, and accept and prepare for death. Counselors could either suggest this book to their clients or perhaps provide the above list as talking points during counseling sessions.

Other books or memoirs that focus on aging well include *Having Our Say: The Delany Sisters' First 100 Years* (Delany & Delany, with Hearth, 1993); *Never too Late: A 90-Year-Old's Pursuit of a Whirlwind Life* (Rowan, 2011); *I Still Have It, I Just Can't Remember Where I Put It* (Rudner, 2008); *Prime Time* (Fonda, 2011); and *Two Old Women: An Alaskan Legend of Betrayal, Courage, and Survival* (Wallis, 1993). These books are easy reads and provide examples of living well that might be useful to older clients. Counselors can invite clients to read these (or watch movies that parallel them) and to consider how they apply to themselves. Counselors can ask questions such as, "What did you learn from this book?" and "How can you apply this book to yourself?"

Resources for Healthy Aging

ACA's Wellness Interest Network
The Center for Healthy Aging of the National Council on Aging, http://www.ncoa.org/improve-health/center-for-healthy-aging
HELPGUIDE.ORG, http://www.helpguide.org
International Longevity Center on an Aging Society
MacArthur Foundation's Research Network on an Aging Society, http://www.macfound.org/networks/research-network-on-an-aging-society
Stanford Center on Longevity, longevity3.stanford.edu
World Economic Forum, http://www.weforum.org/

Summary

Many factors are associated with aging well. Counselors can use the information in this chapter to provide a therapeutic/counseling approach that includes attention to thoughts and behaviors that have been found to have a positive impact on the aging process. For example, counselors might want to include discussions of clients' thoughts about, feelings about, and willingness to engage in appropriate exercise, diet, social interaction, and cognitive training. If clients are interested in and willing to consider these options, counselors can use creative problem solving to encourage clients to find ways to do so. Counselors will also want to focus on clients' typical ways of approaching and appraising issues in their lives and help them develop or strengthen their abilities to gain control over situations, try new ways of dealing with issues, reframe an event, and use problem-focused coping. Because having fun and finding joy are important to one's quality of life, counselors can use brainstorming to encourage clients to find ways to achieve this.

Chapter 5
Health Issues Associated With Aging

One of the issues faced by the aging population is the advent of various health issues or disabling medical conditions. A discussion of all the medical conditions that older people may have is beyond the scope of this chapter. The purpose of this chapter is to discuss general health issues as well as a few of the more disconcerting conditions that older people may experience.

Older people are likely to have more than one medical condition or health issue because of limited resistance to disease, reduced vigor, limited income, and limited access to social programs (Cavanaugh & Blanchard-Fields, 2006; Hoyer & Roodin, 2003; Kampfe et al., 2008). Numerical estimates of the incidence of chronic and/or disabling conditions among older people vary widely. Reports of incidence of disability range from 19% (cited in Research Notebook, 2007) to as high as 75% (Calkins, Bult, Wagner, & Pacala, 1999). This variation is likely attributable to dissimilar definitions, data collection methods, type of analyses, and focus of various researchers (Freedman, Martin, & Schoeni, 2002; Kampfe et al., 2008).

The good news, however, is that life expectancy has increased and functional limitations have decreased in the last century (CDC, 2007). According to the National Center for Health Statistics (1990), the ability to maintain function may be attributable to later onset or reduced onset of disability, increased probability of recovery from injuries or illness, and shorter episodes of disability. Furthermore, as the Baby Boomers reach age 65 or older, it appears that this group will be healthier, will be more attuned to health-promoting behaviors, and will have longer life expectancies than their older counterparts (Schonbrun & Kampfe, 2009).

The percentage of older people who have chronic disability has been dropping, with a projected 40% decrease by 2027 (Devino et al., 2004). Furthermore, coping abilities, accommodations to the physical and social environment, external support, therapeutic regimens, lifestyle, medical care, and rehabilitation are all expected to mediate the progression and effects of the disabling conditions that older people have (Verbrugge & Jette, 1994). Likewise, premorbid personality (i.e., personality prior to the disability) can be an important aspect of adapting to a disability (S. M. Smith & Kampfe, 2000).

When considering the "typical" medical conditions that older people may experience, it is important to remember that not all people will have these. Believing that most older people have these conditions may cause counselors, medical providers, service providers, and so forth to draw false impressions of an individual who is older. I am reminded of a story once told by Dr. Mae Smith that illustrates this point.

> An 85-year-old woman asked her doctor about her sore right knee. After the doctor examined her, he said "Well, you're just getting old, and this is something that happens. You have to expect it." The woman responded, "But doctor, my left knee is as old as my right knee, and it feels just fine."

One aspect of the counselor's job, then, is to avoid making assumptions that because people are older, they will naturally have certain disabling conditions. When older people do have symptoms of a medical conditions, counselors may help them determine the degree to which they wish to (a) identify the causes of the symptoms using medical specialists; (b) identify prevention, treatment, and lifestyle changes that might help; (c) follow through with suggested prevention, treatment, and lifestyle changes; and (d) accept and adjust to the limitations for which there are no alternatives. In the counseling process, counselors will need to recognize that variance is to be expected; that levels of resilience, energy, endurance, and stress are all important factors to consider (Marinelli & Del Orto, 1999); and that the client's perspective is very important in the process. Furthermore, Choate (2008) recommended that counselors focus on wellness, development, positive aspects of aging, and continued growth rather than on pathology.

Potential Disempowerment in the Medical Community

Many organizations and professionals consider the medical model to be disempowering and paternalistic (Chernof, 2011; Sales, 2007; Watson, Roulstone, & Thomas, 2012). In this model, doctors, nurses, and specialists know best, and the client has little opportunity for choice or independence. Although today's medical practice may be less disempowering, older people may have grown up with the concept that doctors should be in charge and may therefore feel powerless in medical situations (Sales, 2007). Thus, it is important for counselors to do all they can to help clients maintain control over medical decisions made about them (i.e., promote person-centered care).

Several novels and movies demonstrate the impact and dehumanizing quality of disempowerment associated with the medical model as well as the empowering qualities of service providers who include clients in choices about their care. These include the novels *Left Neglected* (Genova, 2011) and *A Month of Summer* (Wingate, 2008) and the movie *Whose Life Is It Anyway?* (Bachmann & Badham, 1981). Counselors can read or view these stories with other counselors, clients, caregivers, service providers, and family members and discuss the implications for appropriate and humanistic service.

Health Issues That May Be Experienced by Older People

Metabolic and Other Changes

People's metabolism decreases about 5% per decade (Howard, 2012b). Implications of this slower metabolism are that older people will need to continue to exercise in order to burn off calories and that they are in danger of overmedication or medication side effects because their bodies are not able to process medicine in the same manner as younger bodies (American Geriatrics Society, 2005; Terrell, Heard, & Miller, 2006).

Older people's stomachs may secrete low levels of hydrochloric acid, resulting in lower levels of vitamin B12. Because this vitamin supports many body functions, it is important for clients to take B12 supplements or eat foods rich in B12 (Howard, 2012b; M. Smith et al., 2012). Older people's stomachs may also empty more slowly than younger people's stomachs, which can lead to the risk of acid reflux. Furthermore, when food is moving more slowly through the large intestine, constipation and possibly polyps are likely to occur. Ways to counteract these issues are to drink plenty of water, include fiber in the diet, and get plenty of exercise (Howard, 2012b).

Older people also tend to become dehydrated more readily than younger people. Dehydration can affect the electrolyte balances in the blood and serotonin levels in the brain, resulting in fatigue, problems with memory and concentration, headaches, anxiety, and other altered moods. Because dehydration can have many negative outcomes, clients need to be aware that they should drink water even when they do not feel thirsty (Howard, 2012b). Counselors can model the intake of water by having it available in the office, drinking it themselves, or offering it prior to and during counseling sessions.

Older people tend to have decreased immune response. Furthermore, their response to vaccines may decrease, leaving them vulnerable to illnesses such as flu, pneumonia, and other medical conditions. Because older people are more vulnerable to illness, they are sometimes given higher doses of flu vaccine and can benefit from pneumococcal and shingles vaccinations (Howard, 2012b). Counselors might wish to provide information about these issues in their offices.

A normal part of aging seems to be some degree of incontinence, or at least having to go to the bathroom more often than younger people. There are basically two kinds of incontinence: stress incontinence (urination when one sneezes or coughs) and urine incontinence (urgent, uncontrollable, unexpected need to urinate). Both of these are particularly prevalent among older women, but they also occur in men. Given that one problem with aging is potential dehydration, this seems to be a double-edged problem because older people may decrease liquid intake to avoid having to urinate at inconvenient times, thereby leading to dehydration. Simple practices can help in some situations. For example, women (and men) can practice Kegels (pelvic exercises), which strengthen the muscles that support the bladder, rectum, uterus, and small intestine. Men with incontinence problems should probably see a urologist because more than 50% of men in their 70s tend to have prostate issues, and frequent urination may be associated with this problem (Howard, 2012b). Counselors can invite clients to seek advice from specialists when necessary. Counselors should also assure clients that it is perfectly appropriate to take a bathroom break during a session. It might also be a good practice to preschedule a bathroom break mid-session and to include paper products in the bathroom that can be used in case of an accident.

Decrease in muscle mass (sarcopenia) has been thought to occur over a lifetime. This change seems to accelerate after age 65. Recently, however, studies have shown that those who continue to exercise (e.g., master athletes) do not appear to lose muscle mass. Studies of leg muscles have shown that the muscles of older people (in their 60s and 70s) who remained physically active contained as many healthy mitrochondria (converters of food into fuel for the muscles) as people who are in their 20s and that muscles of older people who had been sedentary had considerably fewer functioning mitrochondria than younger people. Likewise, aerobic capacity has been thought to automatically decrease with age; however, recent studies of older individuals who practice vigorous and regular endurance exercise have found that the decline in aerobic capacity is only about 5% per decade. These new findings imply that being sedentary puts people at risk for decreases in strength, muscle mass, and endurance and that exercise slows the aerobic capacity decline (Reynolds, 2011). Counselors might wish to share this information with consumers who are sedentary or who are considering exercise programs.

Pain

A common myth is that as people grow older, they naturally feel pain. Pain, however, can be an indicator of a medical condition and a signal that medical assistance should be sought. If older individuals believe that pain is a part of being older, they may decide to just live with it rather than seeking medical consultation about the reason for the pain. Another reason for avoiding medical consultation may be fear of what they might learn about the cause of the pain. None of these strategies are health promoting. Having pain can affect one's comfort, hope, enjoyment, and peace of mind. Furthermore, ignoring pain can result in failure to receive treatment for a condition that may be ameliorated (National Hospice and Palliative Care Organization, 2012c).

When clients feel pain, it is important for them to talk with family members, medical professionals, nursing home staff, and counselors. If family members or service providers have the mistaken notion that pain comes with aging, they may ignore the older person's complaints. It is, however, vital that counselors, health care providers, and significant others listen, empathetically and seriously, to older people's statements about pain and help them get a medical evaluation and treatment for the condition causing the pain (National Hospice and Palliative Care Organization, 2012c).

In addition to suggesting that clients seek medical consultation, counselors might encourage clients to discuss their pain with a dietitian or nutritionist. Certain foods can have a significant impact on the reduction of pain. Examples of these kinds of food include red grapes, ginger, soy, cherries, turmeric, and fish. Furthermore, an anti-inflammatory diet that limits processed foods, animal protein, saturated fats, partially hydrogenated oils, and trans fats and increases intake of fish, seeds, nuts, beans, fruits, and vegetables can be helpful (Howard, 2011).

Counselors may find that their clients are interested in using nontraditional forms of pain treatment, such as infrared heat therapy (relieves tension, loosens muscles, and increases flexibility), hydrotherapy bathing (relaxes muscles and improves circulation), and massage (relieves joint and muscle pain). Although most of these techniques provide short-term relief from pain, they may not have long-term effects (Mehul Desai, as cited in Ianzito, 2011). Counselors can listen to clients' discussions of these options, ask questions regarding the efficacy of the options, and then respect clients' decisions regarding their use. Counselors, however, should suggest that their clients seek medical consultation to ensure that these nontraditional treatments are appropriate and that they contact their insurance provider to determine whether these treatments are covered.

Case Example Regarding Pain

Mrs. Lee had quite a high tolerance for pain because of a lifelong pain-inducing condition. Because she was accustomed to pain, she rarely complained about it. Consequently, when she did express feelings of pain, her counselor suggested that she have a medical evaluation. During the evaluation, it was found that she had a potentially dangerous blood clot in her leg. If the counselor had assumed that pain was a natural part of aging or normal for Mrs. Lee, he might have ignored an important sign of a serious medical condition that needed treating.

Falls

Approximately one in three older individuals experience falls each year. Falls can have serious consequences and are considered to be the leading reason for emergency visits and hospitalizations, the primary cause of injury-related deaths and hip fractures, and major contributors to decreased mobility among older people. Furthermore, older people are more susceptible to injury and have greater difficulty recovering from falls than younger people. For example, after a fall, people who are age 75 or older are 4 to 5 times more likely to be placed in long-term care facilities than those who are ages 65 to 74 years (Haslanger, 2012).

Falls can be caused by many conditions or situations, including low vision, insubstantial or no footwear (Haslanger, 2012), loss of peripheral sensation in the feet, vertigo, cerebrovascular disease, arthritic knee joints (Casciani, 2012a; Wickremaratchi & Llewelyn, 2006), brain damage from strokes (National Stroke Association, 2012b), frailty/muscle weakness (Pennar, 2012a), alcoholism (Ivers & Veach, 2012), arthritis, diabetes, and fear of falls (Agility, n.d.). Furthermore, multiple medications can place people at risk of falls, especially if the medications cause drowsiness or dizziness (Agility, n.d.). Because of these multiple medical reasons for falls, counselors can recommend that clients discuss with their physicians ways to minimize the risks. Such strategies might include taking medications at bedtime or with meals, reducing medication dosages (Haslanger, 2012), reviewing interactions among medications, and finding medications that are less likely to cause falls.

Instruments have been designed to measure the risks of falls. One of these, the "Timed Up and Go" (TUG) test, measures the number of seconds it takes for a person to stand up from an armchair, walk about 10 feet, turn, return back to their chair, and sit down. Community-dwelling adults who take longer than 13.5 seconds to complete this task are expected to be "a faller" 80% of the time (Shumway-Cook, Brauer, & Woollacott, 2000). Obviously, this instrument predicts only one aspect of falling; therefore, it may not be appropriate for all clients. Another tool designed to assess the risk of falls in older people is the STEADI, which was developed by the CDC. This instrument is available at http://www.cdc.gov/injury/STEADI.

Falls are often caused by environmental conditions. Examples of common-sense safety rules include keeping floors dry and clear of clutter, installing handrails or grab-bars in stairwells and bathrooms, ensuring that stairs are level and solid, taking care that wires are not lying across floors, removing door sills, marking steps or bumps with easy-to-see colors (e.g., yellow or red), removing loose rugs or using nonslip rugs and mats, arranging furniture to make sure that it is not in central locations, installing a shower chair and a hand-held shower head, and ensuring that all walking surfaces have appropriate lighting (Haslanger, 2012; Hope Heart Institute, n.d.). Counselors can evaluate their own offices as well as other facilities to ensure that they are free of hazards that might create falls. If they are unsure of their abilities to do a proper evaluation, they can contact the nearest independent living center, a rehabilitation technologist, or an occupational therapist for advice.

Muscle strength and balance are vital in avoiding falls. Fortunately, individuals can partake in programs that help them maintain both of these to the best of their abilities. As with many other situations, regular moderate exercise is very important for individuals who may be susceptible to falls. Examples of appropriate exercise include tai chi, walking, yoga, exercise classes, and strength training designed for older people. Individuals may also wish to enroll in balance-retaining programs or hire a balance instructor for private lessons (Haslanger, 2012; National Council on Aging, 2012). Physical therapy is also helpful in reducing vulnerability to falls. Physical therapists will likely provide treatment that focuses on coordination, balance, transfer issues, walking, flexibility, and strength (Agility, n.d.). Counselors can use creative problem solving to help clients identify their options and to decide whether they wish to follow through with any of the choices. At a later date, counselors can follow up with clients to discuss whether the options they chose are working for them.

Assistive devices, such as canes, crutches, or walkers, may be of help in avoiding falls. If such devices are used, however, it is important that they are properly fit to the individual (e.g., correct handle grip size and height), that the person knows how to use them properly, and that the devices are kept in good condition. For example, canes should be regularly inspected to make sure that the rubber tip on the bottom is working effectively. If not, the tips can become hard and contribute to falls (Haslanger, 2012). Occupational therapists, independent living specialists, and rehabilitation technologists are good resources for finding appropriate assistive devices and helping people learn how to use them. Additional information regarding AT can be found in Chapter 2.

Individuals who are susceptible to falls or who live alone may want to consider obtaining a Personal Emergency Response System (PERS). These are devices that can be worn at all times and can be used to request emergency help in situations such as falls. There are many types of PERS, and they are sold by a variety of companies and programs, so clients may wish to discuss the differences between these before purchasing one. Clients may have mixed feelings about these devices. Some may think that PERS will give them less autonomy, whereas others may think that PERS will give them independence and allow them to stay in their own homes. Counselors can use creative problem solving to help clients consider these issues as they make decisions regarding PERS use.

Because falls are common among older individuals and can have devastating effects, the Center for Healthy Aging of the National Council on Aging, a nonprofit advocacy and service organization, helps community-based programs develop evidence-based programs to help prevent falls (National Council on Aging, 2012). Counselors can help clients determine whether these or other such programs exist in their communities. The names and locations of these programs are likely to be available from the Area or County Agency on Aging or the National Council on Aging. Other resources can be found at http://www.ncoa.org/improve-health/center-for-healthy-aging/falls-prevention-awareness.html, at http://www.fallsfree@ncoa.org, and at http://www.cdc.gov/homeandrecreationalsafety/Falls/adultfals.html.

Frailty or Frailty Syndrome

For many years, the term *frail* was used as a catchall term to describe the condition of being old. Currently, however, there are objective markers or instruments for measuring frailty. According to Linda Fried (as cited by Pennar, 2012a), frailty is a syndrome experienced by people age 65 years or older in which three or more of the following five criteria are met: self-reported exhaustion, unintentional weight loss of 10 pounds or more in the past 12 months, grip strength weakness, low physical activity, and slow walking speed. Although the above definition of frailty syndrome seems relatively simple, it involves a complex interaction among many variables. For example, inadequate nutrition can lead to decreased muscle mass, which can decrease strength and result in a slower walking pace, less overall activity, and lower levels of energy. These factors can interact to negatively affect various bodily systems, such as the endocrine and immunological systems (Pennar, 2012a, 2012b).

Pennar (2012a) indicated that among community dwellers, about 7% of those who are age 65 or older and about 18% of those who are age 80 or older are frail. When people have been labeled as "frail," the medical community perceives them as having greater risks for falls and poor postsurgery recovery and may suggest changes in their living arrangements and more care before and after surgeries. Many frail individuals, therefore, live in long-term care settings, with frail men being more likely than frail women to live in nursing homes or hospitals.

Counselors can be aware of the potential cascading effects of frailness and can discuss these with clients. They can use one of the instruments designed to measure frailness to gain some information about their client's vulnerability to frailness. If the client seems to be frail, counselors can ask them whether they want to change the situation and whether they think they can. If clients are interested in improving their strength, counselors can use creative problem solving to help them determine their course of action. Of course, medical consultation would be very important in any plans to improve strength.

Dementia (Cognitive Impairment)

Perhaps one of the most confusing and unsettling topics associated with aging involves dementia and the multiple symptoms, definitions, causes, misconceptions, misdiagnoses, stigmas, treatments, and management strategies associated with this condition. People are sometimes mislabeled with this condition (and its variety of causes)—and the label sticks—without proper evaluation, diagnosis, or treatment. It is, therefore, important for counselors to be aware of the definitions, symptoms, and implications of each of the conditions associated with dementia and to ensure that their clients receive accurate diagnoses.

Dementia has been a described as a loss of cognitive functioning, thinking, reasoning, memory, and behavioral abilities to the degree that it interferes with daily lives and activities (Alzheimer's Disease Education and Referral Center, 2012a, 2012b). Symptoms of dementia may include inability to describe or recall specific instances; difficulty performing simple and familiar tasks, such as dressing appropriately, paying bills, and washing up; being unable to follow directions; frequently forgetting, misusing, or garbling words; repeating stories or phrases several times in the same conversation; getting lost or disoriented in familiar surroundings; showing poor judgment; behaving in socially inappropriate ways; or having a great deal of trouble making choices (M. Smith et al., 2012). Depending upon the cause of dementia, it may involve a progressive deterioration of intellectual functioning that ranges from very mild in the beginning to very severe in the later stages (American Health Assistance Foundation, 2012a).

Dementia can be caused by a wide variety of conditions. The most common cause is Alzheimer's disease, followed by various vascular disorders, which are the second leading cause. Other causes of dementia are Lewy Body disease, Huntington's disease, Parkinson's disease, normal pressure hydrocephalus, hippocampal sclerosis, generalized brain atrophy, Wernicke-Korsakoff syndrome, Creutzfeldt-Jakob disease, and other frontotemporal disorders (Alzheimer's Disease Education and Referral Center, 2012a, 2012b; American Health Assistance Foundation, 2012a, 2012c; Hendrick, 2011). Recent research has shown that there may be some relationship between dementia and other conditions as well. For example, one study found that women who started taking estrogen at a later age were 48% more likely to be at risk of dementia than those who never took estrogen treatment (e.g., Tokar, 2011). It may also be that older people with type 2 diabetes and a history of hypoglycemic episodes are at higher risks of dementia than those who do not have these episodes (Whitmer, Karter, Yaffe, Quesenberry, & Selby, 2009). Additional information regarding all of the above causes of dementia is beyond the scope of this chapter; however, counselors are encouraged to become familiar with each of these causes. Because Alzheimer's disease is the leading cause of dementia and because it is often misunderstood, I am including information about this condition.

Alzheimer's Disease

Alzheimer's disease is a progressive, irreversible brain condition that involves slow deterioration of memory, thinking skills, reasoning, judgment, and the ability to perform ADLs; it also involves behavioral disturbances and, eventually, death. The condition is primarily caused by neurofibrillary tangles (tangled bundles of fibers), amyloid plaques (abnormal clumps), and loss of connections between the neurons (nerve cells) throughout the brain. Eventually, neurons lose the ability to function, and finally they die. Unfortunately, at this time, these conditions cannot be identified until after death (i.e., during an autopsy); therefore, the diagnosis of Alzheimer's disease can often be inaccurate (Alzheimer's Disease Education and Referral Center, 2012a; Hendrick, 2011). Furthermore, Alzheimer's is often used as a catchall phrase, resulting in potentially inaccurate labeling and treatment.

Although older people are more likely than younger people to have Alzheimer's disease, and although people over age 85 are the most likely to experience it, it is not a common occurrence for older people (Aging America, 1991). The Alzheimer's Disease Health Center (2011) has indicated that Alzheimer's disease may often be misdiagnosed because one of its typical symptoms is dementia. To illustrate this point, Hendrick (2011) cited a study in which half of the men who had been diagnosed with Alzheimer's disease when they were alive were found not to have had this disease during autopsies. In other words, these men had other reasons for their dementia than the amyloid plaques and neurofibrillary tangles associated with Alzheimer's disease. At issue is the concern that inaccurate diagnosis will lead to inappropriate treatment (Kampfe et al., 2005).

Because of the danger of misdiagnosis, it is important to ensure that individuals with cognitive dysfunction have not been mislabeled as having Alzheimer's disease (Kampfe et al., 2005). Counselors may, therefore, wish to advise individuals and their family members to obtain a second opinion when they have been diagnosed with Alzheimer's disease. The decision to get a second opinion is sometimes a concern for clients; therefore, counselors can help them understand the importance of such an opinion and help them realize that physicians are typically willing to refer patients to specialists. The types of specialists that might be of assistance are geriatricians, geriatric psychiatrists, neurologists, and neuropsychologists, especially those who specialize in dementia (Alzheimer's Disease Education and Referral Center, 2012b).

Perhaps one of the most disconcerting aspects of Alzheimer's disease is the stigma associated with it. Stigma can be counteracted by improving an understanding of the condition among family members, colleagues, friends, the public, service providers, and legislators. A series of five short films (i.e., *A Quick Look at Alzheimer's*) has been developed by the Alliance for Aging Research to provide basic information about the condition. These are free of charge; can be viewed on cell phones, personal digital assistants, DVDs, laptops, or iPads; come in several languages; and can be accessed on http://www.aboutalz.org or http://www.agingresearch.org. A documentary titled *There Is a Bridge* (Verde & Kay, 2011) describes the importance and possibility of meaningful communication with someone with dementia (which may involve nonverbal communication). This documentary indicates that although many things change about people with dementia, their essence still remains. Another user-friendly and free documentary regarding prevention and treatment of dementia can be found at http://w3.newsmax.com/blaylock/video_briar.

From a psychological perspective, Alzheimer's disease has been described as a dehumanizing condition in which people lose themselves and in which family members and friends gradually lose their loved ones. Counselors, families, and friends can learn a great deal about the psychological and physiological aspects of dementia or Alzheimer's disease by reading personal accounts or novels that describe various aspects of the condition (e.g., *Still Alice* [Genova, 2009]; *Where the River Turns to Sky* [Kleiner, 1996]); by listening to or watching interviews or performances by those who have the condition (e.g., Glenn Campbell's interviews and last singing tour); or by watching movies that deal with this topic, such as the following: *Away From Her* (Egoyan, Mankoff, & Polley, 2007), *Friends With Benefits* (Shafer, Glotzer, Zuker, Gluck, & Gluck, 2011), *Robot and Frank* (Niederhoffer, Bisbee, Bisbee, Accord, & Schreier, 2012), *The Savages* (Hope, Carey, Westheimer, & Jenkins, 2007), *Aurora Borealis* (Disharoon & Burke, 2004), *Firefly Dreams* (Kaneda, Rycroft, Williams, & Williams, 2001), *The Iron Lady* (Jones & Lloyd, 2011), *The Notebook* (Harris, Johnson, & Cassavetes, 2004), *Walking and Talking* (Hope, Schamus, & Holofcener, 1996), *Age Old Friends* (Whitley & Kroeker, 1989), and *Iris* (Fox, Rudin, & Eyre, 2001).

These materials describe the riveting fear and worry associated with losing contact with reality, losing the sense of time, having difficulty finding words, being confused about what one is doing and where one is, and the feeling of losing oneself. They also show the humanity, wisdom, and ability to adjust that can remain even as dementia progresses. Furthermore, they depict family and significant others' reactions to dementia and various methods to adjust to the condition and to interact with the person with this condition. Most of these materials are emotionally difficult to read or watch; therefore, it is very important that counselors read or view them prior to introducing them to family members or clients.

Dementia-Like Symptoms

Because of the many causes of cognitive impairment in older people, dementia can easily be misdiagnosed. A misdiagnosis can result in lack of appropriate treatment and in the advancement of conditions that can be treated (Kampfe et al., 2005). It is therefore vital that counselors understand the difference between dementia (a specific medical condition that includes a variety of symptoms) and dementia-like symptoms (symptoms that are similar to dementia but are usually reversible if treatment is given for the actual cause of the symptoms). This is a very important distinction. I repeat, dementia-like symptoms are usually reversible because they are caused by some condition that is treatable or reversible.

Potential causes of dementia-like symptoms include drug toxicity, short- or long-term side effects of medication, overmedication, infections or tumors in the brain, chronic alcoholism, sleep disturbances, vitamin B12 deficiency, some liver disorders, some thyroid or kidney disorders, urinary tract infections (UTIs), dehydration, malnutrition, stress, or depression (Alzheimer's Disease Education and Referral Center, 2012a, 2012b; American Health Assistance Foundation, 2012a, 2012c; Hendrick, 2011; L. Robinson et al., 2013; M. Smith et al., 2012). Furthermore, people with hearing impairments may be inaccurately thought to have a cognitive impairment because they misinterpret what is said to them and respond inappropriately (Kampfe, 2009).

Other causes of dementia-like symptoms can include multiple losses within a compressed amount of time (e.g., loss of friends; family members; physical abilities, functions, or strengths; life-time employment and identity; income; interaction with children and grandchildren; and personal car or transportation) and many other concerns (e.g., personal or family member illness, residential relocation, mobility problems, reduced family responsibilities, and reduced opportunities for personal choice or decision making). These experiences can lead to feelings of sadness, loneliness, boredom, worry, exhaustion, and meaninglessness and can result in confusion and forgetfulness (Alzheimer's Disease Education and Referral Center, 2012a, 2012b; American Health Assistance Foundation, 2012a, 2012c; Hendrick, 2011).

Because many of these conditions and situations can be treated or have their own implications, and because some health care providers may assume older people are "prone to" dementia, it is vital that the correct cause of dementia-like symptoms be identified. This is important because inaccurate diagnoses will likely lead to inappropriate treatments

(Alzheimer's Disease Education and Referral Center, 2012a, 2012b; *ACA Code of Ethics* [ACA, 2014], Standards E.5. and E.5.c.; American Health Assistance Foundation, 2012a, 2012c; Hendrick, 2011). Counselors must therefore be mindful that various conditions mentioned above may be causing dementia-like symptoms and must advocate for appropriate medical diagnoses and palliative medical treatments.

Case Example of Dementia-Like Symptoms

Mrs. Jones began showing signs of confusion and hallucinations, and her daughter was concerned that she was developing dementia. Knowing that many medical conditions can result in such symptoms, her counselor recommended that Mrs. Jones meet with her doctor and be tested for a UTI and other medical conditions. The family followed through with this suggestion, and it was found that she, indeed, had a UTI. With appropriate medication, she quickly improved, and her hallucinations and confusion stopped. In offering this case example, I am not suggesting that counselors make medical diagnoses, but that they know enough about potential causes of dementia-like symptoms to objectively question the situations that some clients may experience and to advocate for appropriate diagnoses and treatments.

Interpersonal Consequences of the Diagnosis of Dementia

Unfortunately, when people are diagnosed with some form of dementia, they are often stigmatized, spoken about behind their backs, discussed in front of them as if they were not there, not included in decisions, assumed to be unable to make important decisions, and generally excluded from activities that they previously enjoyed. For example, Cotter, Meyer, and Roberts (1998) found that interviewees with dementia indicated that they were not involved in decisions about their discharge destinations (i.e., where they would live after a hospital stay). Some of these individuals preferred that the decision be delegated, but others indicated that they would like to have been included in the decision. Interviewees stated that staff and other people did not listen to them. The counselor's role, in these cases, can be to focus on the client's perspectives, fears, strengths, and personal control when possible; to respect the individual; to model respectful behavior; and to encourage family members, care providers, and community members to do the same.

In some cases, caregivers may follow prescriptive formulas and enforce set schedules and medications without regard for clients' quality of life. On the other hand, some enlightened programs treat the whole person and not just the dementia. They identify people's interests and passions, provide ways for them to experience these, and give them opportunities to decide what they wish to do. These programs are cautious about the types and amount of drugs given. They work to understand what soothes and upsets the client, and they develop individual plans to match these. For example, individuals who have loved to dance, to be with animals, to read books, or to sing are given the opportunity to continue to engage in some aspect of these activities (Abrahms, 2012a).

Personal Strategies for People With Dementia or Dementia-Like Symptoms

People who have dementia or memory loss can use a number of strategies to help themselves function more independently. To remember where they put things, they can make a list of one location where each important item should be placed after using it, or they can stop and look at it the item while verbally saying where they put it. To keep track of schedules and dates, they can make checklists, leave themselves notes (e.g., sticky notes), and put important dates or appointments on calendars (which they leave in one place). To ensure that they can find important contact information, they can make a list of phone numbers and so forth and keep them next to the telephone. To avoid missing appointments, they can set an alarm clock or ask friends or relatives to remind them of these. To shut off electrical equipment, gas stoves, and water faucets in a timely manner, they can use timers or purchase appliances that have an automatic shut-off. To learn new tasks or remember old tasks, clients can do the following: in a quiet place without distractions, ask for explanations of how to complete the task; focus totally on the person explaining the task; ask for multiple demonstrations; write down the steps; repeat the information back verbally; and practice the task several times while the instructor is available (M. Smith et al., 2012).

Counselors can discuss these strategies with clients, their families, and their caregivers to determine whether they are interested in using them. If they elect to try these strategies, counselors and family members will need to be patient in the process. It may be that only one strategy can be considered at a time, and it may take multiple tries to review and learn a task.

One aspect of dementia can involve sleeplessness, fears, wandering, or agitation at night. These behaviors and feelings can be wearing on both the client and the family member or caregiver. One option for these people can be night services such as the Hebrew Home's ElderServe At Night. Essentially, these are day-program services that are offered at night where clients can be in a safe environment and join in various activities (e.g., participating in social activities, painting, receiving a minimassage, listening to live music, practicing yoga, cooking, receiving prescription medications, doing physical therapy, taking part in group reminiscence, and walking the halls; Abrahms, 2012a). Counselors can help identify local programs that offer such services and if they do not exist, they can advocate for their development.

Counseling Clients With Dementia and Their Families

Individuals who are in the early stages of dementia or Alzheimer's disease can benefit greatly from counseling. Because they are facing tremendous personal changes that influence every aspect of their lives, they will need to have someone with whom they can openly express their feelings and experiences (e.g., fear, loss of self, loss of autonomy, anger, confusion, other people's reactions to them). Clients will also need to discuss practical issues associated with their future, such as their family's needs, their own living arrangements, caregiving preferences, medical treatment and specialist options, financial and legal matters, disposition or care of personal property, social support for themselves and their families, and decisions about death (e.g., living will, hospice, place of death, rituals, disposition of the body). They may also want to decide, early on, who they want to make medical decisions for them when they are no longer able to do so, how they want to interact with their family and friends, who should be named as power of attorney, and what type of assistance they need from an attorney.

Counselors are well equipped to focus on any of the client's feelings and to help the client use creative problem solving to make decisions about the remainder of his or her life. An important point when counseling individuals with dementia is that counselors must recognize the need for balance between the ethical rights of clients to make their own choices, their abilities to do so, and the family's legal rights to make decisions on the client's behalf. It is also important that clients be included in decisions, when possible and appropriate (ACA, 2014, Standard A.2.d.).

Clients who have severe dementia can benefit from counseling because they may not have other opportunities to express themselves in a respectful listening environment. In these situations, counselors need to realize that the person may tell the same story several times within a session. Because of this, counselors must learn to be totally "in the present" (which is an important counseling strategy). Instead of reminding the person that he or she has "just said that," counselors need to relax and realize that the person is experiencing the story in the moment, and thus the counselor needs to be in the same moment. In this situation, counselors can listen for patterns across the story and reflect these back to the client. They can listen for the underlying feelings, thoughts, views of self, regrets, or pride that cause the person to replay the event they are speaking of. Counselors can use this time to challenge their own abilities to be in the here and now.

Activity to Enhance Counselor's Ability to "Stay in the Present" (Kampfe, 2003)

1. Find a comfortable place to stand or sit.
2. Close your eyes.

3. Say "Now!" With each "now" statement, make a physical gesture, such as raising your hand, punching the air, clapping your hands, or blinking your eyes.
4. Say "Now!" and move.
5. Say "Now!" and move again.
6. Continue this activity for about 5 minutes, staying totally in the present.
7. Bring this activity to a close by resting quietly for about 1 minute.
8. Either alone or in a group, consider the concept of "now" as it relates to your counseling and how you can use this activity to enhance your ability to stay in the present with your clients.

Counselors typically pay close attention to facial expressions (nonverbal communication) in the counseling process in order to learn about a person's affect, interest level, understanding of the topic, and focus. Clients who have Alzheimer's disease or Parkinson's, however, may have decreased facial or bodily expressions (e.g., a smile, a frown, a shrug, a grimace) to accompany their feelings. In these cases, lack of facial expression may not imply lack of interest, feelings, or understanding. Because it may be more difficult to discern a client's reactions to counseling topics, the counselor may have to ask more direct questions about the client's feelings. Counselors can also help families and significant others understand and adjust to the potential lack of facial or bodily expressions (Casciani, 2012a).

Counseling Family Members of Clients With Dementia
Counselors can help family members and caregivers consider different ways of communicating with their loved one and can help them deal with their feelings in new ways. Following is an example of a statement that might be made to a daughter by a mother who has severe memory loss: "Now you're my daughter?" This statement can generate many feelings within the daughter (e.g., sadness, anger, impatience, fear, etc.). Counselors can use this statement as a role-playing opportunity. The counselor can repeat this statement to the daughter, "Now you're my daughter?" and ask the daughter to consider alternative ways of responding to her parent (e.g., "I've told you that several times." "UmHum, and I love you." "Yes, you are a wonderful mother." "Why can't you remember who I am?" or "I have to leave pretty soon.") Counselors can ask about the value of or the potential harm associated with each response and support the daughter or son in finding a way to respond in a positive and caring way when communicating with a parent who does not remember them. Of course, this strategy can be used to work through other communication issues between adult children and their older parents.

Counselors can invite family members, both caregivers and those who are not caregivers, to read or view the books or movies mentioned earlier in this chapter and to discuss their responses with the counselor and each other. Counselors can ask questions such as, "Did any of this seem familiar to you?" "How did this book/movie affect you emotionally?" "What did you learn from this story?" and "How can you use this story to help you with your own situation?" Counselors can also provide group counseling to family members and significant others. During these sessions, counselors can invite participants to describe their concerns, express their feelings, and identify ways that all members can be supportive of the primary caregiver and the individual with dementia. Resources for issues associated with family counseling include the Association for Specialists in Group Work (http://www.asgw.org) and the International Association of Marriage and Family Counselors (http://www.iamfconline.org).

Family members might also benefit from a support group of individuals who are facing similar issues (Alzheimer's Disease Education and Referral Center, 2012a; American Health Assistance Foundation, 2012b). Such support groups can allow them to express concerns; find respite; discuss coping strategies; give and receive emotional support; and share information about the condition, resources, specialists, and treatments. Support groups are available both online and in person. Counselors, themselves, can lead such groups or, they can help people find a group.

Dementia Resources

Accelerate Cure/Treatments-Alzheimer's Disease (ACT-AD), http://www.act-ad.org
Adult Development and Aging (APA Division 20), http://apadiv20.phhp.ufl.edu/
Alzheimer's Association, http://www.alz.org or 800-272-3900
Alzheimer's Disease Education and Referral (ADEAR) Center, http://www.nia.nih.gov/alzheimers or 800-438-4380
Alzheimer's Foundation of American, http://www.alzfdn.org or 866-232-8484
Alzheimers.gov, http://www.alzheimers.gov or 877-696-6775
American Health Assistance Foundation, http://www.ahaf.org or 800-437-2423
APA Division 20: Division of Adult Development and Family Caregiver Alliance, http://www.caregiver.org or 800-445-8106
HELPGUIDE.ORG, http://www.helpguide.org
Latino Alzheimer's & Memory Disorders Alliance, http://www.latinoalzheimersalliance.org or 708-714-4268
Lotsa Helping Hands. http://www.lotsahelpinghands
NIH SeniorHealth, http://www.nihseniorhealth.gov/alzheimers-disease/toc.html
Palliative Dementia Care Resources, http://www.pdcronline.org

Normal Memory or Cognitive Losses

Extreme memory loss is not an inevitable part of aging (Aging America, 1991; Kampfe et al., 2005; M. Smith et al., 2012). Older people may, however, experience normal cognitive changes that involve some memory loss (i.e., age-associated memory loss). For example, the Pew Research Center (2009) found that 25% of older participants indicated that they had memory loss, and Wilson, Beck, Bieneas, and Bennett (2007) found that 83% developed mild cognitive impairment over a 12-year period. Causes for age-related memory loss and other cognitive changes include a decline in growth hormones that stimulate the growth of, repair of, and protection of brains cells; decrease in blood flow to the brain; deterioration of the hippocampus, a region of the brain that involves the formation and retrieval of memories; and less efficient absorption of brain-enhancing nutrients (APA, 1998; Hoyer & Roodin, 2009; M. Smith et al., 2012).

Examples of age-related forgetfulness involve forgetting why you went into a room and word-finding problems, such as "blanking" on a familiar name, word, street address, book title, or movie title. Other cognitive changes experienced by older people include slower rates of encoding, storing, and retrieving information; longer required periods or repetition to learn new information (APA, 1998); and problems remembering recently acquired information (i.e., short-term memory issues; Hoyer & Roodin, 2009). Implications of these issues are that the counselor may need to allow more time for some older individuals to communicate an idea or to respond to the counselor's questions. Counselors should, therefore, wait for responses when they do not come immediately. Furthermore, counselors should not assume that because it takes longer to process thoughts or to retrieve information that older people are functioning at a lower cognitive level or that they will be unable to process complex thoughts. Counselors might also be sensitive to the need for longer periods of time for older individuals to develop new skills and discuss some of the personal strategies mentioned above to assist them in their daily lives.

Although some memory loss may occur with aging, it is important to remember that older people typically maintain creativity, daily social and occupational functioning, and long-term or institutional memories that can be very assistive to themselves and others (APA, 1998; Hoyer & Roodin, 2009). As discussed in Chapter 11, older people's lifelong skills and experience can be invaluable to trainees, younger workers, and administrative staff.

Stroke

A stroke is an incident in which blood flow is interrupted to a specific area of the brain, causing brain cells to be damaged or die. Because specific brain cells control various functions (e.g., speech, memory, movement, etc.), these functions may be negatively affected, depending on the area of the brain that is damaged. Furthermore, there are many degrees of severity associated with stroke (i.e., some strokes are small, resulting in minor functional problems, whereas other strokes may be larger, paralyzing an entire half of the body). In addition, individuals can experience a series of multiple small strokes (i.e., multi-infarcts). Recovery from stroke varies from complete recovery to severe long-term loss of function, with more than two thirds of survivors having some type of disability (Alzheimer's Disease Education and Referral Center, 2012b; National Stroke Association, 2012c). Risk factors for stroke include high blood pressure, diabetes, sickle cell anemia, smoking, obesity, and having an African American background. For example, African Americans are twice as likely to have a stroke, to die from stroke, and to have more severely disabling conditions from strokes than Caucasians (National Stroke Association, 2012a).

As mentioned above, there are many types of strokes. *Ischemic strokes* are caused by blood clots that slow or stop blood flow. There are two types of ischemic stroke (embolic and thrombotic). *Embolic strokes* are caused by a blood clot (embolus) that forms somewhere in the body and then travels to the brain, where it lodges at any blood vessel that is too small for it to pass. *Thrombotic strokes* are caused when a blood clot blocks one or more arteries that supply blood to the brain or when blood vessels become clogged with cholesterol or fatty deposits. The most common form of thrombotic stroke is *large vessel thrombosis* (i.e., occurring in the large arteries), which involves long-term atherosclerosis followed by rapidly forming blood clots. This condition is often associated with coronary artery disease, and those who have had this type of stroke often die of a heart attack. *Small vessel disease/lacunar infarction* occurs when the flow of blood is blocked to very small arterial vessels. Although little is known about this type of stroke, it is believed to be related to hypertension (high blood pressure; National Stroke Association, 2012c).

Another type of stroke, *hemorrhagic stroke*, is associated with a blowout, breakage, or hemorrhage of a blood vessel in the brain. These can be caused by a number of conditions, such as high blood pressure and cerebral aneurysms (a weak or thin spot in the wall of the blood vessel). There are two types of hemorrhagic strokes (intracerebral and subarachnoid). *Intracerebral* strokes involve hemorrhaging/bleeding that occurs within the brain. *Subarachnoid* strokes involve the burst of a large artery near or on the membrane that surrounds the brain, causing the brain to be surrounded by blood-infused fluid (National Stroke Association, 2012c).

As indicated above, strokes can occur in different areas of the brain. Because each area of the brain governs a specific function of the body, it cannot be assumed that the effects of a stroke will be the same for each person. From a rudimentary perspective, the left hemisphere of the brain typically controls movement in the right side of the body, whereas the right hemisphere controls movement in the left side of the body. Because the left hemisphere controls movement in the right side of the body, a stroke in this area may cause various levels of paralysis of the right side of the body (*right hemiplegia*). The left hemisphere also controls speech and language abilities; therefore, a person with a left hemisphere stroke may develop *aphasia* (a catchall term for a variety of speech and language problems). Problems associated with aphasia vary widely and can include from one to several communication issues. For example, a left-brain stroke can affect people's ability to use the muscles associated with speech but typically does not affect their ability to understand speech and to think clearly. A left-brain stroke, however, can create memory problems that result in difficulty in learning new information, cause shortened attention spans, create problems with generalization and conceptualization, result in a cautious and slow behavioral style, and create a need for frequent assistance and instruction with everyday tasks (National Stroke Association, 2012b, 2012c). Two movies that demonstrate problems associated with a left hemisphere stroke are *Diamonds* (Green & Asher, 1999) and *It Runs in the Family* (Douglas & Schepisi, 2003).

Because the right hemisphere controls movement in the left side of the body, a stroke in this area may cause paralysis in the left side of the body (*left hemiplegia*). A stroke in the right hemisphere can also impair people's perceptions of the environment, spatial relationships, and their abilities to perform certain tasks, such as walking or driving a car. In some cases, individuals with right-brain damage may be unaware of their inabilities to perform these tasks. This lack of awareness can result in their attempts to engage in activities that they cannot do (e.g., walking without aid or driving a car). They may also be unaware or less aware of their left side (*left-sided neglect*). Because of this visual field impairment, they may "ignore" or "forget" people and objects on their left side. Another potential problem associated with right-hemisphere damage includes lack of short-term memory. For example, people with this damage may not be able to remember what they did a few hours or minutes ago but be able to remember specifics about their lives many years ago (National Stroke Association, 2012b). Counselors and family members can sensitize themselves to this issue by reading the novel *Left Neglected* (Genova, 2011).

Two other sites in which a stroke can occur are the cerebellum and the brain stem. The cerebellum is primarily responsible for controlling balance, coordination, and reflexes. A *cerebellar stroke* can therefore cause problems with coordination, balance, reflexes of the torso and head, dizziness, nausea, and vomiting. The brainstem controls all involuntary life-supporting functions, such as blood pressure, the heart, breathing rate, hearing, eye movement, swallowing, and speech. It is also the area through which messages are carried from all parts of the brain to the body. Clearly, a stroke in this area of the brain (*brainstem stroke*) can have devastating consequences (National Stroke Association, 2012b).

Not only are there wide varieties, severity, and locations of strokes, there is also a broad range of recovery. Some brain cells may be permanently damaged, whereas other cells may be temporarily damaged and may resume functioning after time. The brain may even reorganize itself. For example, occasionally one section of the brain may take over the region that has been damaged by a stroke, or the brain can make an unexpected and remarkable recovery. Generally, of those who have strokes, 15% die soon, 10% need long-term care, 40% have moderate to severe impairments, 25% have minor impairments, and 10% nearly completely recover (National Stroke Association, 2012b).

Because of the broad range of types, severity, and location of strokes, it is inappropriate to assume that all strokes result in the same type of problems and symptoms or have the same severity of consequences. I have found that family members, service providers, and friends often assume that a person who can no longer speak can no longer understand speech or think clearly. The result of this assumption can be devastating because these significant others may begin to treat the person in patronizing ways, make decisions for him or her, and talk around or for the person as if he or she does not understand or want to give input. One novel that describes both appropriate and inappropriate behaviors on the part of service providers is *A Month of Summer* (Wingate, 2008).

Counselors can counteract negative community attitudes and behaviors by using respect and directness when interacting with an individual who has had a stroke. The counselor's challenges are to (a) let the client know that the counselor is aware of his or her ability to think without the need for the counselor to be condescending, (b) encourage others (friends, family members, service providers) to recognize that just because the person is unable to speak does not mean that he or she is unable to think clearly, (c) advocate for the rights of the client to make decisions for himself or herself when possible, and (d) find ways for the client to communicate with the counselor and others. For example, I have noted the pleasure and extreme relief in people's faces when I indicated to them that I knew that even though they could not speak, that they were thinking clearly.

It is also important for counselors to work with clients and their family members to help them understand the actual limitations of the stroke. For example, in the case of a right hemisphere stroke in which an individual is unaware that it is no longer safe to drive or to walk without assistance, counselors will need to spend time with them to help them adjust to these new limitations, find ways to become empowered and maintain dignity in spite of these limitations, and continue to have a fulfilling life. Counselors can use creative problem solving to indentify things they can do and find resources that can help. Counselors will also need to invite clients to discuss their fears and apprehensions about living arrangements and to identify post-stroke housing options. Counselors have the skills to assist individuals with their feelings about a disabling condition and can use these skills throughout the counseling process.

Counselors can also use creative problem solving to identify strategies for dealing with new limitations associated with the stroke; however, it is important for clients and their families to work with specialists who have the skills to help post-stroke individuals safely achieve at their highest levels of independence. Speech therapists, occupational therapists, physical therapists, orthotists, independent living specialists, and rehabilitation technologists can provide this function. These professionals typically focus on what clients can do rather than what they cannot do. They also work with clients to identify techniques, community resources, and aids to assist them in optimal functioning and independence. Several of these specialists are funded through the state and federal government at no charge to clients.

Family members of persons who have had a stroke may experience high levels of physical, mental, and emotional stress, especially when they are the primary caregivers. Initially, they are faced with a sudden, often catastrophic event in the life of their family member and consequently in their own lives. Supporting a person with a stroke can require a great deal of time and energy and, depending upon the severity of the stroke, can involve transporting the client to various appointments and activities; assisting with financial management; providing mental, emotional, and physical support; helping with ADLs (e.g., grooming, preparing meals, taking medications); communicating with health care providers and other professionals; managing a health care team; assisting with and encouraging exercise; and advocating for the client. Furthermore, family members may be dealing with Social Security, Disability Determination, Medicare, and Medicaid decisions and follow-up. These activities can take a great deal of time, energy, knowledge, and understanding and can often become very frustrating. The result of all of these responsibilities and frustrations may be disruption of family and work life, discontinuation of leisure activities, failure to take care of oneself, and physical and mental exhaustion (National Stroke Association, 2012a). Additional information about caregiving issues can be found in Chapter 9.

Implications for counselors are that family members may need individual or group counseling, or they may need to join a support group. Another implication is that many of the above caregiving/ family responsibilities are essentially case-management functions that counselors can incorporate into their practices. Counselors who regularly work with these kinds of situations and who obtain additional training in these areas can facilitate and actually carry out many of these functions with greater ease and with less anxiety than a family member might be able to.

Stroke Resources
Lotsa Helping Hands, http://www.lotsahelpinghands
National Institute of Neurological Disorders and Stroke, National
   Institutes of Health, http://www.ninds.nih.gov or 800-325-9424
National Stroke Association, http://www.stroke.org or 800-STROKES

Issues Associated With Medications

It has been estimated that approximately one third of older adults who live in the community take five or more prescription medications (Qato et al., 2008), that approximately half of this population use over-the-counter (OTC) medications or dietary supplements along with prescription drugs (Johnson, 2010), and that many older adults misuse both prescription and OTC medications (Gurwitz & Avorn, 1991). Throughout this and other chapters, I have discussed some of the possible problems associated with medications. These problems include inaccurate diagnoses, inaccurate prescriptions, multiple prescriptions for the same or different conditions, interaction among medications, errors in dispensing medications, and side effects of medications.

According to Howard (2012a), the Institute of Medicine has indicated that medication errors are a severe health risk, resulting in approximately 2.5 million preventable injuries each year. Furthermore, older people seem more likely than younger people to be hospitalized for injuries associated with medication. For example, more than half of the medication errors that result in death occur among people who are over age 60. Furthermore, adverse effects of drugs increase exponentially once individuals take four or more drugs. Given that older people take an average of four to six medications, they are more vulnerable to this effect (Howard, 2012a).

Older people may be seeing more than one health care provider who can prescribe medications. For example, they may be receiving treatment from a general practitioner, a geriatrist, a urologist, a naturopath, a cardiologist, and so forth. The danger here is the potential lack of communication among these physicians regarding the medications and treatments they are prescribing. Without this communication, clients may be taking two different medications for the same condition, multiple doses of the same medication, or medications that negatively interact with each other. A related issue is the use of traditional or alternative medicine healers. Depending upon their cultural beliefs and backgrounds, clients may be receiving treatment from a faith or spiritual healer, a family member, a witch, a medicine woman or medicine man, a curandera/o, and so forth, all of whom might provide alternative treatments. Furthermore, older people may be taking herbs that have been culturally handed down from grandparents but that may interact with prescribed medications.

Another problem can occur when clients are discharged from hospitals with a new set of prescriptions. Discharge instructions may involve continuation of medications, cessation of medications, changes in the dosage of medications, change in the type of medications, or the start of new medications. When clients return home, they may be confused about which medications to take and which not to take, especially if all the previous medications are still in the medicine cabinet, on their bedside table, and so forth (Howard, 2012a, 2012b). If clients return to a residential facility, the staff may misinterpret the instructions, neglect to change to the new drug protocol, or add a drug without deleting its counterpart, resulting in inappropriate and sometimes dangerous care. If primary care physicians do not receive—or if they neglect to review—a list of the new medications prescribed by the hospital physician, they may not know that the person should no longer be taking a prescription that they, themselves, had previously prescribed.

Johnson (2010) indicated that all mental health professionals have a responsibility to monitor for adverse effects of medications. Rather than assuming that a client has a particular condition (e.g., depression, dementia), counselors need to be aware that some of the client's behaviors may be the result of medications and not the result of a disease process. If this situation is suspected, counselors may wish to ask for a review of medications by both the client's regular pharmacist or nursing staff and an outside pharmacist (Shallcross, 2012a). Furthermore, because older people react differently to medications than younger people, have slower metabolisms, and may be taking multiple medications for several conditions; it is important for clients to receive appropriate consultation from a geriatrician who is familiar with aging issues as well as the complex nature of the drugs they may be taking.

In this process, counselors can advocate for cessation or reduced dosage of certain medications, more appropriate or less harmful medications, or alternative treatment modalities that have fewer side effects than medications (Johnson, 2010, 2011; Reid & Kampfe, 2000; Shallcross, 2012a). For example, behavioral intervention techniques and behavioral counseling can be used with some conditions that may currently be treated with drugs (e.g., depression, anxiety). These behavioral interventions, when used appropriately (e.g., the right technique for the right condition), have fewer side effects than medications and will involve personal interaction with a therapist (e.g., social interaction). Functional assessment can also be used to help determine a course of action that focuses on specific rather than broad issues (Johnson, 2010).

Older people who are living independently may be using more than one pharmacy or drug provider. For example, they may have a local, easy-access drug store where they get most of their medications, but they may also order drugs through mail-in drug programs, get drugs as they drop by some other pharmacy, bring drugs home from a pharmacy located in a hospital, or bring free sample drugs home from the doctor's office. Unless one pharmacy is involved in all drug purchases, there may be no single location that maintains a list of medications that can be monitored for dosage, duplication, interaction, side effects, and so forth. It is therefore important for clients to use only one pharmacy or to inform each pharmacy and the primary care physician of the other medications they are taking. Most pharmacies have a computer program that can automatically catch potentially serious drug interactions; however, if they are unaware of all the medications a person is taking, their monitoring system cannot be effective (Howard, 2012a).

There is also the possibility of pharmacy error. Howard (2012a) indicated that a study conducted at Auburn University in Alabama found that one of every five prescriptions contained community pharmacy errors. One type of error involved misreading one drug for another (either looks or sounds alike). For example, hydralazine (a blood pressure medication) may be misread as hydroxyzine (an antihistamine that can result in oversedation or confusion among older people). The result of such an error would be twofold: (a) the person would not receive important blood pressure medicine, and (b) the person may show signs of confusion and sedation. The long-term result could be deteriorated health and misdiagnosis of dementia. Other examples of pharmacy error include giving pills that look alike but have different functions, failing to review the possible interactions among multiple drugs being taken, giving the wrong dosage, giving inappropriate instructions for taking the medication, incorrectly transferring the doctor's instruction onto the drug label (e.g., "take with food"), and dispensing a prescription intended for another person (Howard, 2012a).

Personal misuse of both prescription and OTC medications is also a major concern. Client misuse of drugs and medications can include underuse, excessive use, or inconsistent use of a prescription drug (Gurwitz & Avron, 1991); taking multiple drugs without proper oversight or direction by a physician; sharing medications with friends or family members (Stevens & Smith, 2000); and continuing to use medications that have either expired or are no longer needed. Individually, and in combination, these types of medication misuse can lead to serious adverse consequences (Reid & Kampfe, 2000).

Two Case Examples of Medication Issues

Mrs. Smith's physician changed the diuretic she was taking. The information was sent to her nursing home; however, the medical protocol was changed inappropriately by the nursing staff (i.e., they added the new diuretic but did not cease the old one), resulting in her taking two different diuretics. This overdose lead to progressive dehydration, low potassium levels, and subsequent deterioration of her cognitive functioning. Because Mrs. Smith was becoming more and more confused, her community-based counselor advocated for a review of her medications. The error was discovered, and the medication protocol was corrected.

Mr. Bell moved to a nursing home because he was having difficulty living on his own because of a physical disability. Within 3 months after placement, he began to display extreme memory loss, balance problems, and confusion. This change did not seem to be of concern to the staff members because they assumed he had some form of rapidly progressing dementia, "probably Alzheimer's." Knowing that older people's metabolisms are slower than younger people's and that certain drugs can cause dementia-like symptoms, Mr. Bell's community-based counselor advocated for an immediate reevaluation of his medications. It was found that Mr. Bell had been receiving several drugs that would cause his symptoms. Consequently, his medication regimen was changed, and Mr. Bell's "symptoms of dementia" desisted.

Problems Associated With Psychotropic Drugs

Another concern is that many older people in residential care facilities are taking one or more psychotropic medications (U.S. Department of Health and Human Services, 2001). Basically, there are three types of psychotropic drugs (i.e., antidepressant, anxiolytic, and antipsychotic); however, there are many drugs that fall within these categories. These medications affect brain activities that are associated with behavior and mental processes and are prescribed for behavioral problems, cognitive disorders (e.g., dementia), depression, psychosis, agitation, insomnia, and anxiety (Johnson, 2010). One study showed that 71% of residents in a nursing home were taking antipsychotic drugs for dementia with associated agitated or psychotic behaviors, and 14% were taking these drugs for schizophrenia. In addition, 43% were taking antianxiety medications for Alzheimer's-related dementia and behavioral disturbance. Furthermore, some residents who had not been diagnosed with a mental health condition were given antianxiety and antipsychotic drugs for acute problematic behavior (U.S. Department of Health and Human Services, 2001). Another study of older adults with dementia who were living in nursing homes or acute care facilities showed that 87% were taking at least one, 66% were taking at least two, 36% were taking at least three, and 11% were taking at least four psychotropic drugs (Pitkala, Laurila, Strandberg, & Tilvis, 2004). These estimates are cause for great concern because of the adverse side effects and interactions associated with psychotropic and other medications.

Older people are extremely vulnerable to the side effects of psychotropic drugs and are 3.5 times more apt to be hospitalized as a result of their adverse effects than are their younger counterparts. Adverse effects of psychotropic drugs can include reduced neuromuscular coordination, balance problems, clumsiness, tremor, falls, dizziness, and ataxia; vision changes or blurred vision; sedation, lethargy, drowsiness, or fatigue; headaches; cardiac rhythm changes; weight gain or loss; tardive dysconesia, neuroleptic malignant syndrome, or ataxia; impaired concentration, memory loss, slurred speech, confusion, impaired judgment, slowed thinking, apathy; mood swings, irritability, agitation, nervousness, restlessness, and insomnia; depression or suicidal ideation; delusions, psychosis, or hallucinations; anxiety or tension; euphoria, jittery feelings, or mania; sexual dysfunction; and low white blood cell count, hypertension, nausea, vomiting, constipation, diarrhea, or dry mouth. These adverse affects may increase as the number of medications increases, especially when taken over a long period of time (Johnson, 2010, 2011). These effects may also be misdiagnosed as other conditions.

Because of these concerns, Johnson (2011) has recommended that psychotropic drugs should be used only for specific behavior problems or psychiatric conditions rather than given more broadly, that dosage for medications should be kept at the lowest therapeutic level, that regular monitoring of the effectiveness or side effects of a medication be conducted, and that pharmacological treatment be discontinued when appropriate. He indicated that staff convenience should never justify the use of psychotropic medications, and that treatment should involve the least intrusive methods with the fewest side effects.

Counselor, Case Manager, and Family Strategies Regarding Medication

Counselors, as case managers, can encourage older people or their family members to maintain a list of all medications and dosages that clients are taking (including inhalers, patches, OTC drugs, homeopathies) and make this list available to the client, caregivers, family members, regular physicians, specialists, emergency medical services, nursing homes, and hospitals where they are being served (with client permission). There are several ways to prepare such a list. Clients can provide the counselor or family member with a list of all the medications they are taking. One prompt that can be used to help clients remember all of their medications is to ask them to describe their various conditions and the medications they take for each of these. Counselors, visiting nurses, or family members can also ask clients to show them the medications they are taking, either by asking them to bring them into the office or by visiting their homes to actually see the medications. To ensure that all medications are identified, clients can be asked to show all the places that they keep their medications (e.g., in a medicine cabinet, in a dresser, on a bookcase, on a windowsill, in cupboards, in a purse or wallet, beside a favorite chair, or on a bedside table; Reid & Kampfe, 2000).

Other methods to collect a list of medications are to contact the client's Part D Prescription Drug Insurance program to obtain a list of the prescription drugs that clients have been paying for or to contact the pharmacy or pharmacies that the client uses. AARP offers a service entitled AARP Health Record (available at http://www.aarp.org/healthrecord) that can be used to maintain health records, and some communities have a free service in which individuals can list this information on Smart911.com, which is automatically sent to medics and the police when they receive a 911 call from a client's telephone (Howard, 2012a; Shallcross, 2012c). Case managers, counselors, and family members will likely need authorization from the client to work with these services.

Counselors might also take steps to make certain that health care institutions, agencies, family members, or older people, themselves, maintain and monitor information regarding the possible side effects of medications being taken (Johnson, 2010). To do this, counselors can recommend or develop a grid of the medications being taken and the side effects associated with these. Such a grid would list all medications taken on the left-hand column and all the possible side effects of all these medications across the top of the grid. Simple check marks could then be made for each side effect of each medication. This exercise effectively demonstrates how many medications the client is taking that might result in certain side effects. The result is quite illuminating and often causes a rethink of the medications or of the possible resultant client behaviors.

Counselors might also encourage older people and their family members and caregivers to regularly ask for a consultation from a pharmacist. Such a consultation is free and is typically offered when people pick up a medication. These consultations are important because an estimated 89% of reported medication errors have been discovered at the time of the consultation. During this consultation, clients can discuss the dosage and confirm that it matches what the physician has indicated. They can also ask the pharmacist if the medication seems appropriate for their condition, their weight, and their age. Even if the medication is a refill, clients may wish to open the container to ensure that it is the same pill and same dosage that they usually take. It might also be helpful to schedule a consultation appointment during which the client or family member brings every prescription and OTC medication that the person takes. This will allow the pharmacist to determine whether there are any side effects of, interactions between, or duplications of medications. Furthermore, because pharmacy errors tend to increase during their busiest times, clients or their caregivers might want to consider refilling their prescriptions during a less busy time of the day, get refills during the last 3 weeks of the month (errors increase in the first week of the month), or use the automated refill system, which gives the staff plenty of time to fill a prescription (Howard, 2012a).

Summary

Counselors need to be aware of and sensitive to the possibility of misdiagnosis of their clients by the medical community. In addition to the situations mentioned above, some illnesses are commonly misdiagnosed because there are no definitive tests for these illnesses; because even when a person has a disease, they may not "test positive" for it; and because their symptoms are similar to symptoms of other conditions. For example, Parkinson's disease may mimic Alzheimer's disease, stress, stroke, traumatic brain injury, or an essential tremor. Chronic fatigue syndrome may mimic hepatitis, sinus problems, rheumatoid arthritis, lupus, or fibromyalgia. Multiple sclerosis may mimic lupus, bipolar disorder, viral infection, or Alzheimer's disease. Because of these similar symptoms across several conditions, it is difficult for physicians to make an absolute diagnosis. Furthermore, misdiagnosis can occur because a client is referred to a specialist because specialists typically have a narrow range of focus and expertise. Thus, they may make a diagnosis on the basis of the conditions they have experience with, rather than recognizing that symptoms might be the result of a condition they are less familiar with (M. A. Fisher, 2011).

Counselors can encourage clients and their families to keep records of their medical history (e.g., lab tests, medications, hospital admission records, X-rays, etc.) that can be shared with specialists and their primary care physicians. Counselors can also help individuals prepare for visits to their doctors by brainstorming and practicing questions that they need to ask, suggesting that they take a second person to be with them during the doctor's visit, encouraging them to be honest with their doctors about their symptoms and any treatments they may have tried, and encouraging them to ask for a second opinion. If there is some concern about a diagnosis, counselors can give clients the name of patient advocacy organizations, such as In Need of Diagnosis (M. A. Fisher, 2011).

Chapter 6
Mental Health Issues Among Older People

The purpose of this chapter is to discuss mental health issues among the older population and to provide counseling strategies that can be used in various situations. A general discussion regarding mental health of older people is provided, followed by foci on anxiety and stress, depression, suicide, sleep issues, PTSD, substance abuse and addictions, and psychiatric issues.

In general, the prevalence rates of mental health disorders among older people appear to be lower than in any other age group. Life satisfaction has been found to be as good as, and perhaps better than, other age groups. Furthermore, many older people have indicated that they are generally happy and satisfied with their lives (APA, 1998; M. A. Fisher, 2011; Gomez et al., 2009; Howard, 2012b; J. E. Myers, 1999; Pew Research Center, 2009; Werngren-Elgstrolm et al., 2009). Furthermore, Pleis, Benson, and Schiller (2003) found that older women experience lower rates of emotional distress (e.g., feelings of hopelessness, sadness, and worthlessness) than younger women.

In spite of the statistics that show that many older people view their lives positively, it has been estimated that approximately 20% of the older population have mental health conditions ranging from emotional distress or anxiety to depression and suicidal tendencies (Morrissey & Krahn, 1995; Stanley & Averill, 1999). They also experience sleep issues (L. Robinson et al., 2013), PTSD (Wilke & Vinton, 2005), and substance abuse (Colliver, Compton, Gfroerer, & Condon, 2006). All of these mental health conditions are discussed in this chapter.

The good news is that older people are thought to respond to counseling as well as or better than younger people (J. E. Myers & Harper, 2004; J. E. Myers & Schwiebert, 1996); therefore, counselors can use the techniques that they are familiar with and that have been effective for them in the past (Hazler, as cited in Shallcross, 2012a). As indicated throughout this book, however, counselors may need to adjust their techniques because of medical or sensory conditions that might influence older clients' abilities to communicate, process the content of the session, maintain focus without tiring, sit through a 1-hour session, and retain newly learned information. Adjustment of techniques might include having more sessions, shortening sessions, giving breaks during sessions, using communication aids, repeating content, and adjusting the physical office.

Anxiety and Stress

As indicated above, older people may experience anxiety or stress (Stanley & Averill, 1999). The concern is that because older people are faced with a multitude of negative life transitions, their anxiety or stress levels may be high (Glicken, 2005; Kampfe, 1999; Kerson, 2001). There are mixed findings, however, regarding this topic, with studies reporting broad ranges of stress or anxiety among older people (e.g., L. L. Fisher, 2010). One reason for the diversity in findings regarding anxiety may by that many of its symptoms are the same as symptoms for other medical conditions (Choate, 2008; Kerson, 2001). Another reason for the diversity in findings is that older people are a diverse group with multiple and varied coping strategies.

An AARP survey found that among men age 60 through 69, 21% experienced high levels of stress, and 32% experienced moderate levels of stress. Among women age 60 through 69, 20% experienced high levels of stress, and 44% experienced moderate levels of stress. The stress ratings for people age 70 years or older were lower than for their younger counterparts. Among men age 70 or older, 6% experienced high levels of stress, and 33% experienced moderate levels of stress. Among women of this age, 9% experienced high levels of stress, and 39% experienced moderate levels of stress (L. L. Fisher, 2010). These findings seem to be an indication that as people reach age 70 or older, they experience less stress even though they have many potential stressors.

Professionals are concerned about the multiple stressors in older people's lives. These stressors include (but are not limited to) isolation, lack of autonomy, health problems, family or marital conflict, loss of significant others, financial issues, lack of social support, residential relocation, and societal ageist attitudes toward older people (Glicken, 2005; Kampfe, 1999; Kerson, 2001; J. E. Myers & Schwiebert, 1996). Individually, and in combination, these stressors can create anxiety.

Anxiety can manifest itself as night sweats, essential hypertension, shortness of breath, heart palpitations, and chest or generalized pain (Glicken, 2005; Richardson, 2001). Because these symptoms of emotional distress are similar to signs of other physical conditions, they can sometimes be misdiagnosed and treated as a physical condition rather than as emotional disorder (Choate, 2008). Conversely, these symptoms also coexist with physical conditions such as seizure disorders, cardiac conditions, respiratory illness, and metabolic disorders. A misdiagnosis of anxiety rather than a physical condition can lead to failure to provide appropriate medical treatment (Kerson, 2001). Counselors must, therefore, be cautious about a misdiagnosis. Furthermore, the *ACA Code of Ethics* indicates that counselors need to "take special care to provide proper diagnosis of mental disorders. Assessment techniques (including personal interviews) used to determine client care (e.g., locus of treatment, type of treatment, recommended follow-up) are carefully selected and appropriately used" (ACA, 2014, Standard E.5.a.).

Anxiety is linked with physiology. People of all ages are subject to the fight-or-flight response. This response is based on our natural, ancient, animal instinct to protect ourselves. Animals, when frightened, can run, fly away, or fight. Their bodies prepare to do these protective things in many ways. For example, chemicals are produced, the heart rate increases, and blood leaves extremities (e.g., hands). Once the animal has run, flown, or fought to protect itself, the body returns to homeostasis (B. Martin, 2006).

Through socialization, or perhaps because of physical limitations, human beings have learned that running, flying, or fighting are inappropriate, impossible, or ineffective behaviors. However, our bodies continue to respond to stressful or frightening situations by preparing to take action. If people have stress and do not have a way to release the fight-or-flight response, their body chemicals, heart rate, and circulation can remain in the "protective mode." This state may negatively affect their medical and neurological well-being (Jansen, Nguyen, Karpitskiy, Mettenleiter, & Loewy, 1995; B. Martin, 2006). It is, therefore, important for people to identify other methods to proactively control stress and reactively respond to stressful situations in ways that can help them maintain a sense of well-being or to release physiological reactions to stressful events. Running, walking briskly, and swimming can help maintain bodily homeostasis. Because older people are likely to experience many stressors, it is important for them to engage in one or more of these activities or to find other activities that have similar results. The chapter on aging well (Chapter 4) provides information on these kinds of wellness behaviors.

One theory that focuses specifically on adjustment to life events is the cognitive–phenomenological theory of psychological stress (Folkman & Lazarus, 1980), also referred to as the cognitive–phenomenological theory of stress and coping (Folkman, Lazarus, Dunkel-Schetter, DeLongis, & Gruen, 1986). This theory and related research indicate that how people perceive a potentially stressful event will influence how they cope with that event; these two variables (perceptions and coping), along with other intervening variables, will influence the outcome of that event. For example, when people perceive an event to be controllable, they typically engage in health-promoting coping strategies such as using problem-focused coping (e.g., facing and dealing with the problem) and seeking social support; on the other hand, when people perceive a situation as uncontrollable, they may use ineffective strategies such as wishful thinking and avoidance. Taken together, perceptions of an event and coping strategies are thought to influence people's stress levels and overall psychological well-being (Kampfe, 1995, 1999; Kampfe & Kampfe, 1992). Counselors can help clients rethink their perceptions of each event to gain some sense of control over it, and they can help clients identify health-promoting strategies to deal with these stressors.

Counselors can use a variety of techniques to assist older individuals with anxiety. Some of these techniques can be practiced both individually and in small groups. First and foremost, counselors need to provide a nonjudgmental atmosphere and advanced empathy so that people can discuss their stressors and/or their anxiety. Cognitive behavior therapy can be used to encourage clients to examine their thoughts about certain stressors, to modify their thoughts (e.g., decatastrophizing, thought stopping), to consider using new coping strategies and actions, and perhaps to gain some control over their situation. Another behavioral strategy is desensitization, that is, inviting the client to face and practice responses to anxiety-producing events that move from the least anxiety-producing event to more anxiety-producing events. In addition to therapeutic counseling, counselors can provide information about anxiety and encourage clients to use self-monitoring. Other strategies that are effective in reducing stress or reducing the bodily reactions to stress are meditation, progressive relaxation, and biofeedback (Bernstein et al., 2000; Choate, 2008; Johnson, 2011; J. E. Myers & Harper, 2004; Stanley & Averill, 1999).

Depression

The CDC has indicated that the rates of depression are lower for people age 60 or older than for their younger counterparts (cited by Chatters & Zalaquett, 2013). Although the rate of depression is thought to be lower for older people, the National Alliance on Mental Illness has indicated that more than 6.5 million (approximately 18%) of individuals who are age 65 or older experience depression (Shallcross, 2012a). Etaugh and Bridges (2004) reported similar rates, indicating that approximately 15% of older people experience depression, with men's rates increasing after age 60 and women's rates remaining the same or decreasing as they grow older. Likewise, the Pew Research Center (2009) found that among 3,000 older interviewees who were ages 65 or older, 20% felt sad or depressed, and 17% felt lonely. Of those age 75 years or older, 19% rated themselves as not too happy. Furthermore, in 2011, those age 85 and older had the second highest suicide rate of any age group in the United States (16.9 per 100,000); the rate for those age 65–84 was 15.1 per 100,000 (American Foundation for Suicide Prevention, 2011). For this reason, a major concern is depression and suicide among the older population, especially among men (U.S. Department of Health and Human Services, 2007).

The percentage of older people who have depression may be underestimated. It is speculated that depression often goes undiagnosed among this age group; therefore, statistics may underrepresent the number of older people who have this condition. For example, in some cases, symptoms of depression may be mistaken for "normal" aspects of aging. Thus, depression may not be recognized or diagnosed. If family members, counselors, physicians, psychiatrists, and other health care providers believe that older people typically feel sad or depressed, they may not identify these as symptoms of clinical depression (Chatters & Zalaquett, 2013; J. E. Myers & Schwiebert, 1996; Shallcross, 2012a). Furthermore, depression may present itself differently in older people than in younger people. For example, older people with depression may show a lack of interest in doing certain activities rather than experience a significant depressed mood (Shallcross, 2012a).

In trying to determine whether an older person has depression, it is important to separate symptoms of depression from symptoms of other physical conditions. The concern is that a medical condition may present as depression; conversely, depression may present as a medical condition. Unless counselors and physicians are alert to this possibility, there is a danger of misdiagnosis of either depression or another physical problem (Shallcross, 2012a). It is therefore important for counselors to invite clients to consult with a physician and perhaps a psychiatrist to determine whether there is some medical condition causing the depressive symptoms.

There is also concern that older people who display mild to moderate depressive symptoms may actually be severely depressed (Duberstein & Conwell, 2000; Whitbourne & Whitbourne, 2011). A large cohort of older people lived during a time in which psychological symptoms were hidden or minimized—a fact that may be especially true for men. Thus, older people may be unlikely or unwilling to bring up or discuss their symptoms (Shallcross, 2012a). Furthermore, depression is often misdiagnosed as dementia because both conditions involve similar symptoms with regard to memory loss (M. Smith et al., 2012). For example, some specialists have estimated that 20% to 30% of older people who have been diagnosed with dementia actually have depression (Hope Heart Institute, n.d.).

These issues are cause for concern because undiagnosed and untreated depression can have serious medical and psychological consequences (Shallcross, 2012a). For example, there is a strong relationship between severe depression and suicide (Duberstein & Conwell, 2000; Whitbourne & Whitbourne, 2011). For this reason, counselors need to be cognizant of and alert to the signs of depression among their older clients.

Older individuals may experience reactive depression (a reaction to a situation). They can become depressed because they have experienced one or more significant physical, sensory, mental, vocational, personal, or interpersonal losses in a compressed amount of time (Kampfe et al., 2005; Shallcross, 2012a). For example, the danger of depression increases for women after multiple losses or after a single loss (e.g., loss of a partner) that results in a series of subsequent losses (Kerson, 2001). Another cause for reactive depression may be the ageist society in which they live, which often devalues older people (Shallcross, 2012a).

Older people may also experience clinical depression (a medical condition). Genetics can increase the likelihood of clinical depression. It has been suggested that if close blood-relatives have had depression, clients will be more likely than others to experience this condition at some point in their lives (Shallcross, 2012a). For older people, it may be difficult to determine whether their parents or grandparents experienced depression because their ancestors may not have been diagnosed or treated for such a condition, or they may not have had records of their medical histories.

Symptoms of depression can include the following: experiencing depressed mood, despair, malaise, or "the blues"; suffering from bouts of crying; displaying suicidal ideation or gestures; feeling anxious; experiencing low energy, fatigue, or achiness; having no desire to do anything; experiencing either a loss of appetite, digestive problems or eating to feel better; displaying decreased socialization; losing pleasure or interest in usual activities; experiencing insomnia or sleeping more than usual; having problems with decision making, concentration, memory, or confusion; feeling as though there is a lack of meaning, motivation, or direction; withdrawing from responsibilities; experiencing psychomotor retardation or agitation; being overwhelmed or underwhelmed; feeling worthless, guilty, empty, helpless, hopeless, or like one is a victim; finding fault in others or self; complaining of physical problems; exhibiting sudden irritability; having a decreased sex drive; and participating in compulsive gambling. Behavioral signs, while in the counselor's office, may include strained muscles around the mouth and eyes, poor eye contact, slowed movements, slowed speech, excessive crying, and slumped posture (Choate, 2008; J. E. Myers & Schwiebert, 1996; Saisan, Segal, Smith, & Robinson, 2012; Shallcross, 2012a).

As indicated earlier, the *ACA Code of Ethics* stresses the importance of obtaining an accurate diagnosis for various conditions (ACA, 2014, Standard E.5.a.). One recommendation is to ask direct questions associated with some of the above signs and symptoms of depression as well as the signs and symptoms described in the *DSM* (as advocated by Shallcross, 2012a). Other diagnostic tools include the International Classification of Diseases (also encouraged by Shallcross, 2012a) and the Geriatric Depression Index (a quick, transparent, 20-question list to gauge the extent of a client's depression; Kimmel, 2012).

Psychotherapy has been found to be effective in treating depression among older individuals. Cognitive behavior therapy (CBT) and interpersonal therapy/psychotherapy, for example, are thought to be as effective as medication in treating depression and are also effective in prevention of or recidivism of depression (Chatters & Zalaquett, 2013; Shallcross, 2012a).

Cognitive therapy, or CBT, is helpful when depression is associated with negative thoughts and beliefs. Using cognitive therapy, counselors identify and challenge clients' negative core beliefs about themselves, others, and the future. They also ask clients to determine whether there are other ways of thinking about situations. In addition to challenging negative thoughts, CBT focuses on problem solving and on coping skills (Chatters & Zalaquett, 2013; J. E. Myers & Harper, 2004; Shallcross, 2012a).

Interpersonal psychotherapy has been found to be effective with older clients with depression (both those with and those without cognitive dysfunction). Interpersonal psychotherapy can be especially helpful when a client's depression is associated with relationships with other people. Treatment methods can focus on current interpersonal issues, including role transitions, role disputes, abnormal grief, and interpersonal deficits. Therapy typically involves face-to-face sessions during which therapists use clarification, exploration, communication analysis, encouragement of affect, and identification of alternative coping strategies. Working through relationship issues can help clients gain perspective about how these issues affect their mood and what they can do to change their situations (Chatters & Zalaquett, 2013; Miller et al., 2001; Shallcross, 2012a).

Hinrichsen (1999) indicated that interpersonal counseling is important because of the many interpersonal losses that older people experience. Counselors can focus on both current and past relationships that may be linked to depressive symptoms. Clients can be invited to examine these relationships and to determine the kinds of changes they wish to make, with special focus on problem areas. Interpersonal issues can include mourning a loss of one or more people, reconnecting with other people, establishing a plan to resolve interpersonal disputes, and developing social skills to achieve and maintain positive interpersonal relationships. Interpersonal issues can also include mourning and accepting role losses, identifying new roles, and developing mastery of these new roles.

Other counseling strategies that have been useful for older people with depression are group therapy, bibliotherapy, and reminiscence therapy (J. E. Myers & Harper, 2004). Information about these therapeutic approaches is provided in Chapter 2.

With regard to choice of counseling strategy, Richard Hazler (as cited in Shallcross, 2012a) indicated that counselors may wish to focus on the strategies that they, themselves, have found to be most effective for clients with depression; a combination of strategies may be needed, depending upon the underlying issues associated with the condition. He emphasized that the core relationship and basic counseling skills are vital to the counseling process, and these can be used no matter which counseling theory or strategy a counselor chooses to use.

Medications (e.g., antidepressants) are often prescribed for older people with depression, though medications are more frequently used with those who have moderate to severe, rather than mild, depression. Medications are primarily used to ease depressive feelings and thoughts so that clients can consider and perhaps change thoughts and actions associated with the condition. In other words, antidepressants may act as an adjunct to counseling, not as the primary or single treatment. Using medications as an adjunct to counseling may be especially appropriate when the client has a history of suicide attempts or ideation, has family members with depression, has chronic pain, or has an underlying medical condition causing the depression (Shallcross, 2012a). There are many problems associated with medication, however, and these are discussed in Chapter 5.

Depression is multidimensional. For this reason, wellness activities—such as regular age-appropriate exercise, healthy diet, consistent sleep, spirituality, socialization, daily responsibilities, and leisure activities—may help. Conversely, it appears that people who are depressed tend either not to engage in these activities or to decrease these activities. Because of the positive benefits of these types of activities, counselors can encourage and challenge clients to make decisions about and take actions regarding these practices (Shallcross, 2012a).

Suicide

Although variation in reports exist, the suicide rate for older adults is quite high (National Institute of Mental Health, as cited by Shallcross, 2012a). Older people who are particularly at risk are Caucasian males who are age 85 and older, are socially isolated (i.e., live alone), have become widowers within the past 2 years, have lost a physical function, and/or have been diagnosed with cancer or cardiovascular disease (APA, 1998; CDC, 2010; Conwell, Duberstein, & Caine, 2002; U.S. Department of Health and Human Services, 2007). The concern about suicide among older people is so great that Medicare and Medicaid now pay physicians to screen depressed clients for risk of suicide (Shallcross, 2012a).

Because the lethality of attempted suicide is quite high among older people (Osgood, 1985), family members and counselors should not take the symptoms lightly or assume these symptoms are necessary components of aging. Symptoms might include statements such as, "I'm just not worth anything anymore," "I just don't feel like going on," and "My family would be better off without me." Certain behaviors might also be signs that a person is thinking of suicide. These behaviors include giving things away, doing paperwork and making plans associated with death and inheritance, and having a sudden behavioral change (J. E. Myers & Schwiebert, 1996). It must also be noted, however, that many of these behaviors (e.g., giving things away, doing paperwork, and preparing for death) are normal and productive in many cases (see Chapter 13). Other risk factors for suicide, for both men and women, include depressive symptoms or a major depressive disorder; personality disorder; use of antidepressant medications; family history of attempted or completed suicides; personal history of mental or physical illness; newly diagnosed physical condition; substance abuse (drug or alcohol); impulsivity; risk-taking behavior; poor decision making; loss of a close friend or a significant other because of suicide; lack of, loss of, or withdrawal from significant relationships or responsibilities; perceived lack of tangible emotional resources; increased agitation, anxiety, emotional outbursts, hostility, or rage; unwavering and pervasive feelings of helplessness, worthlessness, hopelessness, guilt, or despair; and presence of sleep difficulties (Barnow, Linden, & Freyberger, 2004; Conwell et al., 2002; Liu & Chiu, 2009; Shallcross, 2012a).

Counselors may also need to consider a client's cultural background and its relationship to suicide. As mentioned above, older Caucasian males, under certain circumstances, are at high risk of suicide. Native Americans may also be at risk. For example, Nikki Kirkendoll (a licensed professional counselor and director of behavioral health at the Oklahoma City Indian Clinic) has indicated that (a) among Native American tribes, historical trauma, substance abuse, and problems with access to care may contribute to the risk of suicide; and (b) suicide is a leading cause of death among Native American and Alaskan Native populations (Daniel-Burke, 2012). On the other hand, women of color have been found to have the lowest suicide rate for all age groups (National Center for Health Statistics, 1990) and to be more satisfied with their lives than Caucasian women (Armstrong, 2001).

If clients show high risk of suicide and/or indicate that they are considering this action, counselors should determine their intentions and whether they have a plan and a means to follow through with it. In other words, counselors will want to determine how lethal, specific, proximate, and available the suicide plan is. To do this, counselors will want to ask closed-ended questions that require "yes" or "no" answers, such as, "Have your problems been getting you down so much lately that you've been thinking a about harming yourself?" or "Have you been feeling so hopeless that you've been thinking about killing yourself?" (Shallcross, 2012a, p. 38). If clients answer yes, counselors must act quickly to determine the degree of risk for suicide. Questions such as, "How would you do this?" "Do you have a plan?" "Do you have the gun, the drugs, etc.?" should be asked. One very important strategy is to develop a verbal and written contract between the client and counselor that indicates that the client will contact a crisis hotline before deciding to commit suicide and that he or she will dispose of the means by which to follow through with the suicide. Talking about the issue of suicide at this stage may help reduce clients' agitation and decrease the lethality of the situation (Shallcross, 2012a); however, if they report that they have the means to carry out their plan, the counselor must take action. The *ACA Code of Ethics* (ACA, 2014, Standard B.2.a.) indicates that confidentiality "does not apply when disclosure is required to protect clients . . . from serious and foreseeable harm or when legal requirements demand that confidential information must be revealed." Counselors can gain further insight about clinical skills needed in assessment, prevention, and treatment issues associated with issues of suicide from McGlothlin's (2008) text on this topic.

An overriding aspect of counseling people who are depressed and who might be considering suicide is for counselors to demonstrate that they understand that the client is having intense psychological pain and that he or she wants to be relieved of this pain. It is important for counselors to listen calmly and openly and to show that they care. In this process, counselors should not ignore or avoid discussions of suicide and should not be afraid to discuss the situation or the problems that have led to the desire to commit suicide. In other words, it is important for counselors to convey to clients that it is OK to talk about their deep feelings and thoughts of suicide, and that the counselor is trying to understand the pain and circumstances associated with their feelings (Shallcross, 2012a).

Additional counseling strategies can include helping clients identify alternatives to suicide or find ways to improve their lives. Creative problem solving might be used here. Counselors can ask clients to identify and verbalize other options to suicide. If clients are unable to think of other options, counselors can help them identify these. If suicide remains one of their options, counselors can invite them to give it lower priority than other options. In this process, counselors can use the information that clients have provided about their lives to examine ways to make changes in situations that are difficult and add new activities that might enhance their lives. For example, counselors might help them find ways to develop a support network; reconnect with important others; identify the positive aspects of themselves and their lives; recognize their skills and positive attributes; work through feelings of guilt; identify doable and desirable activities that might give them a new sense of purpose and joy; engage in wellness behaviors, such as exercising and eating healthy food; and take on responsibilities that they may have been avoiding or that someone else has taken over. One note of caution is that as the client's mood or depression improves, it is important not to lose sight of the suicidal threat. Indeed, medication or therapy may result in higher energy levels that can be used to carry out a suicide plan (J. E. Myers & Schwiebert, 1996; Shallcross, 2012a).

Sleep Issues for Older Adults

As a preface to this section, counselors should be aware that although older people can experience sleep issues, it also appears that older people may need less sleep than younger people, with older people's average need for sleep being approximately 7.5 hours per night. It is also important to recognize that sleep requirements vary from person to person, and that shorter number of hours of sleep may not necessarily be an indication of a sleep disturbance (L. Robinson et al., 2013).

Sleep is essential to both emotional and physical health. It can contribute to memory function, concentration, body repair, and the maintenance of the immune system (L. Robinson et al., 2013). It is of some concern, then, that older adults typically have some sleep issues. For example, about half of individuals over age 80 report having sleeping problems (APA, 1998). Typical sleep issues for older people include having less deep sleep, waking up earlier, getting sleepy earlier, and having reduced ability to fall asleep and to stay asleep. Abnormal sleep issues include waking up tired every day, not feeling rested, having major problems falling to sleep even when tired or getting back to sleep during the night, relying on alcohol or sleeping pills to fall asleep, feeling sleepy or irritable during the day, being unable to stay awake when driving or sitting, being unable to control emotions, and having difficulty concentrating when awake (L. Robinson et al., 2013).

Counselors should be aware that it is not always clear whether sleep problems cause or are caused by certain conditions; however, there are relationships between sleep disturbance and depression, anxiety, memory problems, daytime sleepiness, attention problems, sensitivity to pain, night-time falls, cardiovascular disease, weight problems, diabetes, and breast cancer. There may also be a cycle in which anxiety or depression causes sleeplessness that, in turn, contributes to anxiety or depression (L. Robinson et al., 2013; Whitbourne & Whitbourne, 2011).

Regardless of the causes or effects of sleep disturbance among older people, a secondary problem is that individuals who are unable to sleep may take OTC or prescription sleep or anxiety aids that may not be health-promoting (Nordqvist, 2012; L. Robinson et al., 2013). These aids may have side effects or may not be meant for long-term use. They may even contribute to insomnia because they are used to alleviate symptoms, not the causes of sleeplessness. It is therefore best to limit sleeping pills to situations where a person's health or safety is threatened. Examples of drugs that are widely prescribed for older people are Valium, Ativan, Klonopin (clonazepam), and Xanax, all of which contain benzodiazepine, which may potentially contribute to dementia (Nordqvist, 2012).

Sleep/wake cycles are controlled, to some degree, by melatonin, which is a hormone that is produced deep within the brainstem. Because the production of melatonin declines with age, some researchers believe that this decline may affect the circadian rhythm (daily variations in body functions) of older people and thus their sleep/wake cycles. Researchers have found that for women, melatonin supplements can reduce sleep disturbance; however, the side effects of taking prescription or OTC melatonin can involve drowsiness, confusion, headaches, and constriction of blood vessels. Furthermore, OTC melatonin supplements may contain a great deal more melatonin than found in the normal body (Whitbourne & Whitbourne, 2011).

Because many of the causes of insomnia and sleep disturbance are treatable, it is important to identify the underlying causes of these conditions. These causes can include various forms of dementia, general stress, specific stressors (e.g., caregiving, loss of a loved one, recent move), depression, anxiety or worry, sadness, traumatic experiences, diabetes, asthma, heartburn, need for frequent urination, pain, asthma, arthritis, osteoporosis, restless legs syndrome, sleep apnea, side effects of medications, or interaction between medications. Other common causes for insomnia among older people include poor daytime and nighttime sleep habits, irregular sleep hours, alcoholic beverage intake before bedtime, and falling asleep while watching television. Difficulty sleeping may also be a learned behavior that occurs when people initially are not able to sleep because of a specific and short-term stressor but eventually teach their bodies not to sleep even after the reason for not sleeping has been resolved (L. Robinson et al., 2013; Whitbourne & Whitbourne, 2011).

Counselors can use this information to help clients identify their reasons for not sleeping and then identify various methods and specialists that can help them with their sleeping problems. It might also be appropriate to make a referral to a physician to be sure that the sleep disturbance is not caused by side effects of medication, interaction among medications, or some medical problem that can be treated.

Because stress or worry about specific events seems to be a major cause of sleep disturbance, counselors can use their listening skills to help people discuss and resolve their worries about specific stressors in a nonjudgmental, supportive atmosphere. In addition, counselors can use behavioral counseling to help clients determine how their thoughts are influencing their sleep habits and how they might change these. Counselors can also incorporate progressive or autogenic relaxation and other relaxation strategies into their practices.

In addition to helping clients work through their concerns and develop relaxation skills, counselors can invite them to explore various strategies that might improve their ability to get an appropriate amount of sleep each day and night. L. Robinson and colleagues (2013) suggested many strategies to improve sleep or to ensure that people get sufficient sleep. These strategies can be divided into the following categories: keeping a regular bedtime routine, enacting certain bedroom and sleeping practices, establishing middle-of-the-night practices, changing daytime habits, and taking naps appropriately. Counselors can use this list as a point of discussion during creative problem solving with clients, or they can use L. Robinson and colleagues' (2013) easy-to-read book *Insomnia in Older Adults* as bibliotherapy.

PTSD

Until recently, PTSD had been thought to be a severe reaction to combat; however, it is now acknowledged that PTSD can result from any traumatic event. Traumatic events can include serious accidents or events, sexual or physical abuse or assault, terrorist attacks, and natural disasters. Because older people may have experienced extreme noncombat trauma in their lifetimes, PTSD may be an issue for them (Wilke & Vinton, 2005).

In PTSD, the reaction to an event is so severe that it disrupts a person's life and is persistent over time. Symptoms can include vividly reliving a traumatic event, avoiding certain situations that are reminders of a traumatic event, being hyperaroused, feeling numb, and/or feeling guilty. Reliving traumatic events or reexperiencing memories of events can happen at any time and can involve flashbacks and nightmares during which people feel like they are actually going through the event again. Avoiding situations involves staying away from people or events that bring back memories of the event. Hyperarousal can involve feeling jittery and being constantly watchful and fearful for dangerous situations, being irritable, and having sudden feelings or outbursts of anger. Numbness involves the inability to remember or talk about certain aspects of the trauma or difficulty expressing one's feelings about it. Guilt involves blaming oneself for some aspect of the traumatic event. Any of these reactions can interfere with enjoyment of life, interpersonal relationships, productivity, and focus (National Center for PTSD, 2011b).

Although there are relatively few studies that have examined PTSD among older people, existing studies reveal the prevalence of PTSD among people who are over age 60 to be from 1.5% to 4% (van Zelst, de Beurs, Beekman, Deeg, & van Dyck, 2003). The number of older people with PTSD may be underestimated, however, because diagnosticians may incorrectly connect PTSD symptoms with some other condition common among the older population (e.g., sleep disturbance, cognitive impairment), or they may believe that the symptoms are simply typical of older people. Furthermore, research suggests that older people may differ from younger people with regard to both the types of traumatic events they have experienced and the subsequent reactions to these traumatic events (i.e., their symptomatology; Kaiser, Wachen, Potter, Moye, & Davison, 2013). Older adults who have experienced a traumatic event later in life have been found to have hyperarousal, avoidance, memory problems, sleep issues, and reduced appetite; whereas younger adults have been found to have hostility, depression, and guilt (Owens, Baker, Kasckow, Ciesla, & Mohamed, 2005; Thorp, Sones, & Cook, 2011). The implication is that PTSD may go undetected in older people. Furthermore, when it is detected, treatment methods may need to be customized for this population.

PTSD symptoms may emerge for the first time or may reemerge as people become older (Kaiser et al., 2013). This phenomenon has been labeled Late-Onset Stress Symptomatology (LOSS). LOSS can happen because older people may have more time to dwell on the past, have fewer opportunities to engage in activities that divert their thoughts from past upsetting events, have medical conditions that result in a sense of vulnerability, and engage in life review and in efforts to make sense of their lives (National Center for PTSD, 2012). They may have functional losses or cognitive impairment, and they may be dealing with role changes, retirement, reduced income, decreased sensory capacities, decreased social support, and loss of one or more loved ones—all of which might interfere with their ability to cope with old memories (Cook, 2001; Kaiser et al., 2013). It may also be that the strategies for dealing with troubling memories that were available to them in the past (e.g., overcommitting to work or other projects, drinking) are no longer available to them. On the positive side, older people may have developed resilience and adaptation strategies over a lifetime that can be used as coping resources when dealing with traumatic events (Kaiser et al., 2013).

Much of the research on PTSD among older people has focused on men who were in the military; therefore, we know less about this condition for women and nonmilitary individuals. Older women can have many types of trauma in their lives, including domestic violence and rape, which can lead to long-term interpersonal consequences as well as PTSD (Kaiser et al., 2013). A study of community-based older women whose average age was 70 found that 72% had experienced at least one type of interpersonal trauma during their lives (i.e., childhood sexual or physical abuse, rape; Wilke & Vinton, 2005). One event that seems especially common among older women (ages 45–70 in the 1990s) is violence on the part of an intimate partner that has extended over a long time-span (Goenjian et al., 1994). These types of traumatic experiences seem to be more common among older than younger women (Frueh et al., 2004; Wilke & Vinton, 2005). An implication is that more older people (i.e., women) may have PTSD than have been diagnosed or reported in the literature. It has been speculated that as women's roles change, over time, we will see different statistics regarding trauma that are based on the experiences of their age cohorts (Kaiser et al., 2013).

PTSD is often found to co-occur with various other conditions. These conditions include multiple medical problems (e.g., gastrointestinal issues, musculoskeletal disorders, arterial disorders, dermatological issues, chronic pain), cognitive issues (e.g., dementia), and psychiatric/mental health issues (e.g., lower psychosocial functioning, substance abuse, anxiety disorders, mood disorders such as major depression; Kaiser et al., 2013). Counselors working with clients who have PTSD should be alert to these other possible conditions. Likewise, counselors might want to be watchful for possible undiagnosed PTSD among clients who have these other symptoms.

Various treatments have been found to be effective for people with PTSD (National Center for PTSD, 2007b, 2011b). These include medical treatment (medications) and various forms of psychotherapy.

Treatment for PTSD

Medical treatment for PTSD typically involves prescription medications. Selective serotonin reuptake inhibitors (SSRIs) increase the serotonin levels in the brain, resulting in a sense of "feeling better." In other words, they are antidepressants. The two SSRIs that have been approved by the FDA for use with PTSD are paroxetine (Paxil) and sertraline (Zoloft). Other SSRIs include citalopram (Celexa) and fluoxetine (e.g., Prozac). SSRIs may have side effects that include nausea, drowsiness/tiredness, and decreased sexual interest, and they can interact negatively with other medications. Patients typically take these medications indefinitely; however, some physicians may gradually reduce the medications once clients have been symptom free for a year. There is some concern that physicians may prescribe benzodiazepines for PTSD. These drugs are not recommended because they can be addictive to people who have had drug and alcohol problems and because they do not treat the core symptoms of PTSD (National Center for PTSD, 2007b, 2011b).

Counseling/psychotherapy can be a very effective modality when working with people who have PTSD because many times those with this condition keep their feelings to themselves, and because counseling can encourage clients to face their memories and feelings and find new ways to deal with them. Furthermore, therapeutic work can be completed within several months (e.g., 4 to 6 months) unless other coexisting mental health problems exist. Techniques found to be especially successful in treating PTSD are eye movement desensitization and reprocessing (EMDR) and various forms of CBT. These techniques are based on the notion that talking about the traumatic event with a therapist can help, and they have been found to be effective even for those who have experienced PTSD for a long time (National Center for PTSD, 2007b, 2011b). Other therapeutic approaches involve brief psychodynamic psychotherapy, family therapy, group therapy, and support groups. Regardless of which therapeutic techniques counselors use, it is vital that they receive sufficient training, supervision, and experience in each before using them with clients.

EMDR involves inviting the client to learn specific eye movements or simply asking them to watch the counselor's finger move back and forth in front of the client's eyes (eye movements help clients relax); asking them to identify a target image, memory, or belief about the traumatic event; using desensitization and reprocessing, which involves focusing on mental images while doing learned eye movements; and, once the original negative images are no longer stressful, helping the client install positive images and thoughts. Once clients have worked successfully through this process, therapists can invite them to do a body scan that involves focusing on other unusual sensations or tensions in the body that may need to be addressed in later sessions (National Center for PTSD, 2011b).

CBT has been found to be very effective in treating PTSD. The two forms of CBT that have been most researched are cognitive processing therapy (CPT) and prolonged exposure therapy (PE or PET). Furthermore, these therapeutic approaches can be completed in up to 4 months.

CPT involves helping clients become more aware of their thoughts and feelings, helping them understand the typical belief changes that happen after a trauma, and encouraging them to challenge their negative thoughts and feelings about the event (cognitive restructuring). Counselors ask clients to examine what they are thinking or telling themselves about the trauma and to decide whether those are accurate or inaccurate. Counselors can challenge thoughts that cause distress and invite clients to consider other more accurate, balanced thoughts. In other words, counselors invite clients to change the things they are telling themselves about the traumatic event (National Center for PTSD, 2007b, 2011b).

PET is based on the premise that repeated exposure to thoughts, feelings, and events that people have been avoiding can help them learn that memories or fears about a traumatic event cannot be avoided. In other words, facing a trauma in a safe environment can help people work through their thoughts and feelings about it. This is especially true of the fears that people associate with a traumatic event. PET involves learning about PTSD symptoms and how treatment can help, learning to use breathing to help relax and manage stress, repeatedly talking about and facing the traumatic event to gain control over troublesome thoughts and feelings associated with that event, and practicing new learned behaviors in real situations. Therapists may use flooding and desensitization techniques in this process (National Center for PTSD, 2007b, 2011b).

Brief psychodynamic psychotherapy involves learning how the past affects the present and finding ways of dealing with emotional issues caused by past trauma. Therapists help clients become aware of their thoughts and feelings, identify the triggers that set off stressful memories and symptoms, discover ways to cope with intense feelings associated with these memories or symptoms, and find healthy ways to feel better about themselves (National Center for PTSD, 2007b).

Family therapy can be very important because PTSD can affect the entire family. Parents, children, grandchildren, partners, and so forth may feel frightened, angry, or guilty about the person's thoughts and behaviors, and they may not understand why those with PTSD behave or feel as they do (e.g., express anger, feel so much guilt). In family therapy, members can learn about PTSD and how it is treated, express their feelings and concerns about the condition and its symptoms, be honest with and listen respectfully to each other, learn what triggers PTSD symptoms, and find new ways to interact that may be helpful (National Center for PTSD, 2007b).

Group therapy gives clients opportunities to discuss their stories and symptoms with others who have experienced trauma. In other words, it helps build relationships among people who understand, to some degree, what the client has been through. Group therapy can include discussions of the events themselves, the group members' cognitive and emotional responses to these events, and a focus on the present rather than on the past (National Center for PTSD, 2007b).

Support groups are available for individuals with PTSD. There are many types of foci in such support groups. For example, some focus on relaxation, some focus on war memories, and some focus on the here and now (National Center for PTSD, 2012).

As indicated above, it is common for those who have PTSD to have a coexisting mental health issue, such as alcohol and drug abuse, depression, panic disorder, or other anxiety disorders. In many cases, the treatments described above can also apply to some of these other conditions. It has been recommended that PTSD and the other issues be treated at the same time rather than separately (National Center for PTSD, 2007b).

Addictions, Alcoholism, and Substance Abuse

It has been projected that among individuals age 50 years or older, substance abuse will increase from 719,000 individuals in 2002 to

3.3 million individuals in 2020, a 355% increase (Colliver et al., 2006). Estimates of alcohol abuse among the older population range from 2% to 20%. Estimates of drug dependence and abuse are difficult to determine; however, the older population is thought to take from 2 to 3 times more prescribed psychoactive drugs and more OTC drugs than the younger population (Benshoff, Koch, & Harrawood, 2003).

The general signs or symptoms of the misuse of alcohol, nonmedical drugs, OTC drugs, or medications include unsteadiness, falls, depression, tremors, constipation, fatigue, malnutrition, memory loss or other dementia-like symptoms, sleep disturbance, and anxiety. Substance abuse is difficult to recognize because the behaviors associated with this condition can be similar to the behaviors associated with depression, chronic pain, fatigue, cognitive processing difficulties, anxiety, dementia, side effects of medications, interaction among medications, infections, frailness, tumors, vitamin B12 deficiency, and disorders of the liver, thyroid, or kidneys. Because of these shared behaviors and symptoms, there is a possibility for misdiagnoses and/or lack of treatment of any of these conditions (Benshoff et al., 2003; Gomberg, 1995; Kampfe et al., 2008; Reid & Kampfe, 2000; Stevens & Smith, 2000; Williams, Ballard, & Alessi, 2005).

Numerous assessment instruments for substance abuse have been used with the general population. These instruments include the Addiction Severity Index, the Substance Abuse Subtle Screening Instrument (SASSI), the Michigan Alcohol Screening Test (MAST), and a screening tool that focuses on cutting down, annoyance, guilt, and eye opening (CAGE). Counselors can also use the most recent National Council on Alcoholism Criteria for Diagnosis of Alcoholism and the American Psychiatric Association's (2013) *DSM* as references. Counselors will need to clearly understand the purpose, administration, scoring procedures, and (where appropriate) the validity and reliability of assessment tools before using them. It is doubtful that any of these has been standardized for older people; therefore, counselors will need to use them with caution. The following activity provides counselors with the opportunity to consider the efficacy of certain assessment tools.

Assessment Activity

1. Personally take each of the following substance abuse assessments: SASSI, MAST, CAGE. After completing all three tests, ask yourself the following questions:
    a. Did any of the tests have an ageist or cultural bias?
    b. Were the results similar or different across the tests?
    c. What did each test focus on?
    d. Were there any problems within the test that might affect an older person's score?

2. Now take the same tests but simulate several physical or mental health conditions that an older person might have (e.g., generalized tremor, depression, memory loss, sensory loss). After taking the tests, ask yourself the following questions:
   a. If I had this particular condition, would there be a possibility that the test results are inaccurate with regard to screening for substance abuse?
   b. Did some tests have error or bias toward people with the conditions I simulated?

Once identified, substance abuse can be treated, and individuals can live substance-free lives (Kampfe et al., 2005; Williams et al., 2005); however, little data-based information is available regarding the unique needs of older individuals who experience alcohol and drug problems (Benshoff et al., 2003). Information regarding treatment is provided in the following sections of this chapter. Furthermore, Yalisove (2010) and Brooks and McHenry (2009) provide detailed information about substance abuse counseling that can be applied to the older population.

Alcoholism

Professionals have suggested that as the older population increases, so will the problems associated with alcoholism. Older people may be at risk because of the multiple losses that they experience (e.g., income, friends, family, residence, occupation, autonomy). These losses may result in grief, reduced mobility, reduced social support, excessive time on their hands, and a sense of disempowerment (Kampfe, 1999; J. E. Myers, 1990; Stevens & Smith, 2000; E. B. Waters & Goodman, 1990).

There is a difference in opinion about the extent of alcohol abuse among older people, with estimates ranging from 2% to 20% (Benshoff et al., 2003). A number of community surveys have shown that people who are over age 65 drink less and have fewer alcohol-related problems than younger people. These surveys have also shown that older people's alcohol intake remains relatively stable over time (National Institute on Alcohol Abuse and Alcoholism, 2013). Surveys of people admitted to health care settings have found that only 6% to 11% of older people admitted to hospitals, 14% of older people in emergency units, and 20% of older people admitted to psychiatric units show signs of alcoholism (as reviewed by National Institute on Alcohol Abuse and Alcoholism, 2013). These findings are in contrast to the finding that 50% of people of all ages who have been admitted to trauma centers have alcohol-related injuries (Ivers & Veach, 2012).

The mixed findings between studies of older people may have to do with the definitions, measuring instruments, and health care workers associated with the studies. For example, the low percentage of people showing alcohol-related problems in some of the surveys may be attributable to inappropriate screening instruments and the inability for hospital staff to recognize alcoholism in older people because they mistake signs of heavy drinking for other conditions that older people might have (e.g., poor nutrition, insomnia, depression, frequent falls, and congestive heart failure; National Institute on Alcohol Abuse and Alcoholism, 2013).

There is speculation that late-onset alcohol-related issues may occur in retirement communities because of the social norm of drinking at parties or at cocktail hour; however, no data regarding this speculation were found. One report did indicate that alcoholism may exist among as high as 49% of people in nursing homes; however, this percentage may reflect the use of nursing homes for short-term stays for alcoholism (National Institute on Alcohol Abuse and Alcoholism, 2013). My experience with nursing homes does not match these data.

Alcoholism among older people is of great concern because heavy drinking can result in higher risks of cirrhosis of the liver, insomnia, depression, vascular strokes, heart attacks, gastric bleeding, falls (Ivers & Veach, 2012), hypoglycemia, increased heart rate (Stevens & Smith, 2000), car crashes, hip fractures, decreased bone density (National Institute on Alcohol Abuse and Alcoholism, 2013), brain deterioration (especially in the frontal lobes and the cerebellum), dementia, and memory loss (National Institute on Alcohol Abuse and Alcoholism, 2013; M. Smith et al., 2012). Heavy drinking may also influence one's ability to manage medical or psychological conditions such as diabetes and anxiety (Ivers & Veach, 2012), to drive safely (AARP, 2010; National Institute on Alcohol Abuse and Alcoholism, 2013), and to use motor skills (Stevens & Smith, 2000). Furthermore, long-term alcohol use can lead to activation of enzymes that may influence the breakdown of prescription medications. Because older people typically take multiple prescription drugs, there is a risk of alcohol–medication interaction. Furthermore, older people with alcoholism are about 3 times more liable to experience a major depressive disorder than those who do not have alcoholism and are 16% more likely to die of suicide than nondrinkers (National Institute on Alcohol Abuse and Alcoholism, 2013).

Older people have a lower tolerance for alcohol than younger people because they have less body water with which to dilute the alcohol, resulting in a higher blood alcohol concentration. In addition, older people are typically unable to metabolize drugs or alcohol as efficiently as younger people. Because of the lower tolerance for alcohol, they can experience effects of alcohol with fewer drinks than when they were young (National Institute on Alcohol Abuse and Alcoholism, 2013; Stevens & Smith, 2000). Furthermore, because older people are likely to be taking one or more medications, there is an increased risk of negative interaction between alcohol and medications (AARP, 2010).

As a caveat, it must be noted that moderate alcohol use can also have a protective effect against heart disease. For older people, moderate alcohol use is defined as one to two drinks a day (National Institute on Alcohol Abuse and Alcoholism, 2013; M. Smith et al., 2012).

Treatment for alcoholism has been shown to be as effective for older people as for younger people; therefore, older people have much to gain from traditional treatment. Treatment for those with late-onset drinking problems tends to be more effective than for those who have had long-term drinking problems. There is also some evidence that group work is more effective for older people when given with a similar-aged cohort (National Institute on Alcohol Abuse and Alcoholism, 2013). Spirituality may be a helpful tool in working with older people who have an addiction, especially if the counselor is well informed about various religious/spiritual practices (Diallo, 2013). It should also be noted, however, that some people do not profess to have spiritual or religious beliefs. Counselors might invite these clients to discuss their worldviews and identify the value systems that may be helpful in dealing with their addictions (Reid & Kampfe, 2000).

Ivers and Veach (2012) have suggested that because a large proportion of all ages who have been admitted to trauma centers have alcohol-related injuries, it is important to provide alcohol screening and brief counseling to patients while they are in such settings. They indicate that even two sessions with a qualified counselor can affect a client's decision to make long-lasting healthier choices regarding his or her alcohol use, because the trauma is a "teachable moment," making clients amenable to change. During screening and counseling sessions, counselors can use their skills in rapport building, active and empathetic listening, and cultural sensitivity to encourage clients to consider the connection between their alcohol use and the trauma they are experiencing. Counselors can also encourage these patients to seek additional counseling or assistance upon release from the hospital and can make referrals to appropriate programs or counselors. Because so many older people are admitted to emergency units for falls, this type of screening and short-term counseling might be of great benefit to the older population, especially if it is done by a qualified counselor.

Because of older people's multiple risk factors for developing alcoholism, counselors will need to identify the specific risk factors for each of their clients. As a preventative measure, counselors can help clients identify ways of coping with their losses and stressors and find new meaningful ways to live their lives. As indicated in other chapters, a variety of counselors' attitudes and skills are involved in helping people deal with their multiple losses. As a basis, counselors need to understand and respect clients' unique views of and feelings about their situations. There is great power in paraphrasing content, reflecting feelings, using advanced empathy, asking open-ended questions, and summarizing content and feelings (Kampfe, 1994, 1995; J. E. Myers & Schwiebert, 1996; E. B. Waters & Goodman, 1990). Furthermore, counselors can ask clients to focus on the positive and meaningful aspects of their lives, develop a sense of control over their circumstances, identify social support resources, and develop their sense of resilience (Kampfe, 1999; Reid & Kampfe, 2000; E. B. Waters & Goodman, 1990).

Counselors can also work with older clients' environments to encourage opportunities for social interaction that do not focus on drinking (Stevens & Smith, 2000). In this process, counselors can give health care providers and family members information about the importance of social interaction and social support. Counselors can also identify and refer clients to social support agencies, support groups, and other organizations or programs that encourage social interaction (Reid & Kampfe, 2000).

Other Issues Associated With Addictions

As our population ages, more and more people who were exposed to illicit drugs and the accompanying subculture during their youth will be classified as older people. For example, the 1960s and 1970s youth will soon reach or have already reached age 65. When considering addictions, especially to illicit drugs, counselors may want to consider the possibility that an older person who has had a lifetime addiction may be involved in a subculture that has its own rituals, lifestyle, beliefs, worldview, values, language, and experiences. For this reason, multicultural counseling theory and practice may be relevant with this population. This particular culture may be at odds with, or transcend, other cultures (e.g., race, religion, gender, family, socioeconomic status) that the older person identifies with (Reid & Kampfe, 2000). Counselors will therefore need to be aware of strategies that work best with a subculture of drug users as well as strategies for working with people who have multiple cultures.

Issues Associated With Older Psychiatric Patients

It has been reported that approximately 15% to 20% of people over age 65 display symptoms of psychiatric disorders (Aging America, 1991). These conditions may be associated with a true psychiatric disorder or may be attributable to recent circumstances or long-standing troublesome situations (Kelley, 2003; Swett & Bishop, 2003).

Care for clients who have psychiatric conditions such as schizophrenia or bipolar disorder can be extremely complex and will likely require the services of psychiatrists, counselors, and other mental health professionals. Counselors will therefore need to establish appropriate communication with these specialists. Counselors may also need to provide counseling to family members who need assistance with the issues they are facing.

Prior to deinstitutionalization in the 1970s, many people with psychiatric disorders, mental retardation, behavior disorders, and even stroke were "placed" into "state mental institutions." These people are now or will soon be among our older population. I worked part-time at one of these mental institutions from approximately 1966 through 1968; therefore, the following information is anecdotal. Client ages ranged from late teens through older adulthood, and severity of their conditions ranged from mild to severe. Living in an institution was not ideal. The campuses had many old buildings that were often surrounded by high fences. Many people lived in dismal wards, bed-beside-bed, with bars on the windows. People were heavily medicated with the drugs that existed in those days and received treatments that may or may not have been necessary or helpful (and may even have been harmful). Often, "patients" were expected to behave in specific ways and given very little opportunity to think and do for themselves. A movie that provides some insight into this experience is *One Flew Over the Cuckoo's Nest* (Zaentz, Douglas, & Forman, 1975).

Whitbourne and Sherry (1991) found that older psychiatric patients who had this experience earlier in their lives tended to develop their own view of their history in order to emphasize the positive aspects of their life stories and to minimize or deny the potentially upsetting experience of spending a major part of their lives in a state mental hospital. Doing so allowed them to feel less distressed as they thought back on their life stories. As indicated in the chapter on psychological well-being, this process is called *identity assimilation* and involves reinterpretation of a past negative event in order to maintain a positive identity (Whitbourne & Whitbourne, 2011). If such consumers want to talk about their earlier experiences, counselors will want to listen respectfully to these histories and perhaps expect that identity assimilation is a positive way of reflecting back on their experiences.

There is current concern about the use of PRN medications in in-patient psychiatric hospitals, regardless of the age of the patient. (PRN stands for *pro re nata*, a Latin phrase that means "in the circumstances" or "as the circumstance arises.") In this situation, PRN refers to a practice in which physicians prescribe a psychotropic medication that can be given at the discretion of the nursing staff to contain violent or agitated patients. When nursing staff have this option, there is the danger of higher than necessary doses, adverse drug reactions, a mixture of multiple medications, and possible high death rate (Mugoya & Kampfe, 2010). This danger may be greater for older people than for younger people because of their metabolic rates and multiple drugs they may be taking. Counselors will need to be aware of these practices and advocate for their older clients who are in these situations, both individually and systemically (i.e., advocate for changes in policies and procedures).

Resources for Mental Health Issues

About.com, *Alcohol Alert: Alcohol and Aging*, http://www.alcoholism.about.com/library/naa40.htm

ACA Trauma Interest Network (TIN), http://www.counseling.org/knowledge-center/trauma-disaster

Aging and PTSD, http://www.ptsd.va.gov/professional/continuing_ed/aging-ptsd.asp

Alcoholics Anonymous, http://www.aa.org

American Mental Health Counselors Association (AMHCA), http://www.amhca.org/

Division 20, American Psychological Association (Division of Adult Development and Aging), http://apadiv20.phhp.ufl.edu/

HELPGUIDE.ORG, http://www.helpguide.org

International Association of Addictions and Offender Counselors (IAAOC), http://www.iaaoc.org/

National Center for PTSD, U.S. Department of Veterans Affairs, http://www.ptsd.va.gov/

National Coalition on Mental Health and Aging, http://www.nc-mha.org

National Institute on Aging/National Institute on Health Organizations Directory, http://www.nia.nih.gov

National Suicide Prevention Lifeline, 800-273-8255

U.S. Department of Veterans Affairs, http://www.mentalhealth.va.gov/substance abuse and http://www.ptsd.va.gov/public/where-to-get-help.asp

Summary

Although older people are typically aging well and are mentally healthy, a portion of this population has mental health issues. These issues include anxiety or stress, depression, suicide, PTSD, substance abuse and addictions, and psychiatric issues. A major concern associated with these conditions is diagnostic error, so counselors will need to be vigilant about this issue. Many of the techniques designed for the general population with these conditions are appropriate for older people; therefore, counselors can use these to improve the lives of this population.

Chapter 7
Special Issues Associated With Aging

The purpose of this chapter is to discuss special issues that are not otherwise discussed in the book but that are relevant to counseling older people. Topics include multiple losses and transitions, financial issues, elder abuse, driving and transportation, veterans' issues, and forensic vocational analysis.

Multiple Losses and Transitions

Older people are faced with multiple transitions that are often associated with loss (Deggs-White & Myers, 2006). They can experience loss of health, energy, physical flexibility and strength, vocational identity, specific jobs, social support, important family and community roles, hearing, vision, physical appearance, independent living, physical independence, autonomy, sexuality, income, identity, memory, sense of worth, close relationships, and their own lives. They can also experience deaths of partners, parents, children, grandchildren, and long-standing friends. All of these losses or transitions may be experienced in a relatively compressed amount of time (Kampfe et al., 2005).

Any one of these transitions can be stressful and requires strength and support to deal with, but in combination, these potential stressors can be overwhelming. Reports have indicated, however, that older people typically adjust positively to transitions (J. E. Myers & Harper, 2004). Counselors can promote this positive adjustment by fostering and focusing on clients' strengths, social support, spirituality, adaptability, optimism, resilience, continued growth and development, and wellness behaviors (Borman & Henderson, 2001; Choate, 2008). Counselors can help clients identify their perceptions of these events, opportunities to maintain independence within these events, and effective coping strategies to deal with them (Kampfe, 1995, 1999, 2002). Counselors can also help clients examine the degree to which they can redefine the transition or themselves and can ask clients to consider the possibility that when one door closes, another one may open. Because of the multiple and varied transitions that can occur in older age, several chapters in this book include the concept of transition.

Financial Issues

One of the biggest issues facing the older population is inadequate income from private and public sources. The Administration on Aging (2007) reported that in 2006, 23.3% of people age 65 or older had incomes of less than $10,000 per year, and only 32.5% of this population had annual incomes of $25,000 or more. The median income was $15,000 for women and $23,000 for men. Household incomes of persons age 65 years or older were low for many older people, with approximately 7% having incomes of less than $15,000 per year, and 46.8% having incomes of less than $35,000 per year. Furthermore, many of the older population have little or no retirement savings (Dixon et al., 2003; Helman, Copeland, & VanDerhei, 2006).

The Administration on Aging (2007) reported that in 2005, major sources of income for persons age 65 years or older were Social Security (89% of the population), asset income (55% of the population), private pensions (29% of the population), earnings from current work (29% of the population), and government employee pensions (14% of the population). A major concern is that pensions are shrinking because of the economy; thus, although older individuals may have pensions, these may be decreasing in value (Kwan, 2003).

There seem to be several reasons for lack of savings. One is that many people have been unemployed or have worked for such low salaries that they have been unable to set aside money for the future (Devino et al., 2004). For example, Devino et al. (2004) cited a 2002 American Express survey of individuals who had recently left or lost their jobs and found that more than half of them had previous annual incomes of less than $25,000, and one third had incomes from $25,000 to $50,000 but had no retirement savings. Another reason for lack of savings is that many people have not had health insurance coverage. Devino et al. reported that 41% of American citizens were experiencing medical debts and were therefore unable to set aside savings for their retirement. This situation was of major concern because they estimated that in 2003, the savings required to cover prescriptions, insurance premiums, and other expenses from age 65 to age 85 would range from $100,000 to $121,000.

Because of inadequate pension plans and retirement saving, Social Security has been the primary source of income for many people. Social Security benefits, however, were never intended to fully support individuals after retirement. Furthermore, Social Security payments are based on the highest 35 years of earnings while one is in the Social Security system (Social Security Administration, 2011f); therefore, people with low lifetime incomes will have small Social Security checks and be likely to have little or no income from savings or pensions.

Baby Boomers may also have financial problems at retirement. It has been speculated that although the income levels are higher for this group, they may experience postretirement financial difficulties because their financial resources may not be sufficient for the economy at that time (Munnell, Golub-Sass, & Webb, 2007) and because their savings may be insufficient for how long they are expected to live (Institute on Rehabilitation Issues, 2009).

A recent survey of working Baby Boomers (AARP, 2011) found that 55% were at least somewhat satisfied with their proposed retirement savings, 35% thought they may not be able to afford retirement, and 44% thought they would not be able to do the things they want to do in retirement. These Baby Boomers expected that their retirement income would come from several sources: 61% had 401Ks, 55% had other savings or investments, 49% had pensions, and 59% expected to need Social Security income. These Baby Boomers fell into the following five categories. The self-reliant category was composed of 22% of Baby Boomers; people in this category were affluent and optimistic, planned on continuing to work especially for enjoyment, and planned to rely on their own investments. The enthusiasts accounted for 10%; they were affluent, optimistic, enthusiastic about retirement, and satisfied with their retirement savings. The traditionalists accounted for 26%; they were cautious but optimistic and intended to rely on continued work and Social Security for income. The anxious category was composed of 22% of Baby Boomers; they had lower levels of education and income, were less positive about their retirement income, and were particularly concerned about health issues. The strugglers accounted for 20%, had the lowest income and educational levels, were pessimistic about retirement, and had already experienced negative life events such as death of a spouse, loss of a job, and serious illness. The implication is that Baby Boomers may need assistance with a variety of financial issues as they reach retirement age.

On the basis of the above information, counselors are likely to discover that many of the older people with whom they work will be experiencing financial difficulties. It will therefore be important for counselors to be aware of the various programs designed to assist individuals in these situations. Because these programs can have significant impact on people who need and wish to use them, counselors will need to help clients explore the positive and negative aspects of each (Kampfe et al., 2008; Mamboleo & Kampfe, 2009) and have lists of programs and impartial consultants who can provide clients with assistance in this matter. Counselors also need to be aware that older people may need to continue to work even after they reach retirement age. Thus, it is important for counselors to have knowledge of and skills in vocational counseling, issues associated with older workers, and programs designed to assist clients who are seeking employment. Chapter 11 includes a detailed discussion of this topic.

Elder Abuse

According to the National Center on Elder Abuse (2005), there were no official annual statistics regarding the number of older people who were abused. One reason for this lack of definitive statistics is that there is no standard definition for abuse. Each state is responsible for its own laws and regulations regarding elder abuse, resulting in various definitions and methods for reporting such abuse. Other reasons for lack of definitive statistics are that elder abuse is not always reported by elders, family members, or service providers (Bulman, 2010; Lawson, 2013; O'Neill & Vermeal, 2013), and research is often based on random samples of specific populations rather than on all-inclusive national figures (Lawson, 2013). Furthermore, behaviors on the part of the abuser may be a factor in failure to recognize abuse. For example, some abusive caregivers may accompany the elder individual to all appointments, making it impossible for clients to express their concerns regarding abuse (Ahmad & Lachs, 2002; O'Neill & Vermeal, 2013). In spite of the lack of a national understanding of the degree to which elder abuse exists, a number of statistics are available. Lawson (2013) provides a review of these data in his book on family violence.

Types of Abuse

There are many types of elder abuse. According to an APS survey (Teaster et al., 2006), these types include self-neglect (37.2%); caregiver neglect (20.4%); financial exploitation (14.7%); emotional, psychological, or verbal abuse (14.8%); physical abuse (10.7%); sexual abuse (10%); and other (1.2%).

Neglect can involve a wide variety of issues, including failure or refusal to provide shelter, safety, food, water, health care, clothing, personal hygiene, comfort, and medicine by a caregiver or person with fiduciary responsibility. Neglect also involves self-neglect in which older people are no longer able to take care of themselves, which threatens their safety and health. This type of neglect is thought to account for the largest percentage of neglect (Lawson, 2013; National Center on

Elder Abuse, 2012), and it typically involves people who have some degree of confusion, disorientation, cognitive impairment, or depression (Abrams, Lachs, McAvay, Koehane, & Bruce, 2002). Signs of neglect can include soiled or urine-soaked bedding or clothes, feces on the body, body odor, dirty clothes or body, bedsores, inappropriate or insufficient clothing for the weather, lice or fleas on the individual, dehydration, malnutrition, isolation, depression, and inappropriate or lack of medication (Arizona Department of Economic Security, n.d.; Dyer, Connolly, & McFeeley, 2003).

Financial abuse or exploitation can take the form of misusing debit or credit cards or joint bank accounts; making unauthorized transfers across accounts; cashing checks without authorization; misusing or stealing people's possessions or money; engaging in identity theft; forging people's signature or coercing them to sign documents; setting up scams designed to talk people into giving money for an immediate and urgent need; and misusing one's guardianship, conservatorship, or power of attorney (Arizona Department of Economic Security, n.d.; National Center on Elder Abuse, 2012; O'Neill, n.d.).

Warning signs of financial abuse include client concerns or confusion about missing funds in bank accounts, being asked to sign documents that give another person power of attorney, being accompanied by a stranger or family member to the bank in order to withdraw large amounts of cash or to make transactions, becoming dependent upon one particular person (i.e., isolated from other people), appearing to be anxious or nervous around a particular person, having a new friend who seems particularly interested in the person's finances, having new concerns about missing funds or possessions, indicating the need for more money, and taking out loans that do not seem necessary (Arizona Department of Economic Security, n.d.; O'Neill, n.d.). Although many of these situations may be signs of financial exploitation, some may also be perfectly innocent, supportive, and natural practices among parents and their children or other family members (e.g., children being given power of attorney, paying the bills, working with financial institutions when the parent can no longer do so or does not wish to do so). Thus, it is important to understand the cultural views and typical family practices regarding money matters before assuming that financial abuse is occurring.

Emotional, psychological, or verbal abuse involves engaging in nonverbal or verbal acts that cause older people to experience distress, anguish, or mental pain. Examples of this kind of abuse include insults, intimidation, verbal assaults, threats, harassment, and humiliation. Emotional abuse can also include treating people as if they were children, ignoring them, and isolating them from other people or activities (Lawson, 2013; National Center on Elder Abuse, 2012). These types of abuse can apply to many situations and are therefore discussed throughout this book.

Physical abuse involves threatening or inflicting physical injury or pain. Behaviors that constitute physical abuse include shaking, shoving, pushing, hitting, slapping, pinching, kicking, burning, giving inappropriate drugs or dosages, force feeding, and using physical restraints (Lawson, 2013; National Center on Elder Abuse, 2012). Warning signs for physical abuse can include injuries that are not properly cared for, delay in seeking treatment for injuries, multiple injuries that are in various stages of healing, explanations of injuries that are not consistent with the location or type of injury (Arizona Department of Economic Security, n.d.), burns, bruises, and fractures (Dyer et al., 2003). Sexual abuse has been described as sexual contact when a person is unable to give consent or does not wish to give consent. Such contact can range from unwanted touching to sexual assault, such as forced nudity, sexual photography, sodomy, and rape (Lawson, 2013; National Center on Elder Abuse, 2012).

Abuse in Institutions

Elder abuse also occurs within institutions. Although government regulations and statutory reporting requirements exist to protect people in institutions (Summers & Hoffman, 2006), elders who live in long-term care settings are at high risk for abuse or neglect because they are likely to be extremely dependent on the staff because of disabling physical and cognitive conditions (Atlanta Long-Term Care Ombudsman Program, 2000; Burgess, Dowdell, & Prentky, 2000; Hawes, 2003; Hawes, Blevins, & Shanley, 2001; Lawson, 2013; Schiamberg et al., 2012). Institutional abuse includes not turning the older person regularly (which can result in bedsores), failing to give adequate assistance at mealtimes, leaving the older person wet and soiled, turning call lights off without responding (Atlanta Long-Term Care Ombudsman Program, 2000), shoving, pinching, pushing, grabbing, slapping, hitting, and using excessive restraints (Hawes, 2003).

Identifying Elder Abuse

One method of identifying elder abuse is to watch for the risk factors. Client-related risk factors are client dependency (Burgess et al., 2000; Hawes et al., 2001; Schiamberg et al., 2012), cognitive disability (Wiglesworth et al., 2010), earlier traumatic experiences (Acierno, Hernandez-Tejada, Mussy, & Steve, 2009), social seclusion (Lachs, Williams, O'Brien, Hurst, & Horwitz, 1997), and gender (because women are more likely to be abused than men; Teaster et al., 2006). It is not clear whether depression is a risk factor or a result of abuse; however, it certainly can be one indicator that elder abuse is occurring (Brandl & Cook-Daniels, 2002). Client risk factors for self-neglect may include advanced age (ages 75 or older), frailness, being Caucasian, and being disoriented or confused (Abrams et al., 2002).

Other risk factors associated with elder abuse are the characteristics of caregivers. These characteristics include being middle-aged (Teaster, Nerenberg, & Stansbury, 2003), having a mental illness (Williamson & Shaffer, 2001), and being a substance abuser (Anetzberger, Korbin, & Austin, 1994). It has been suggested that the perpetrator of elder abuse or neglect is often a family member (e.g., adult child, partner; Ahmad & Lachs, 2002; Laumann, Leitsch, & Waite, 2008; Teaster et al., 2006). For example, Teaster and colleagues (2006) reported that 65.5% of elderly abuse cases involved family members, with adult children being responsible for 32.6% of the cases. One other risk factor is sharing a living situation, usually with family (Lachs et al., 1997).

Risk factors of physical abuse within institutions include persistent staff problems, lack of supervision, poor hiring or screening practices, poor training in problem behavior management, staff burnout, stressful working conditions, resident aggression, and resident–staff conflict. Risk factors and predictors of psychological abuse include staff burnout, negative attitudes about residents, physically aggressive residents, and age of staff (i.e., younger staff are more likely to be abusive; Hawes, 2003; Pillemer & Bachman-Prehn, 1991).

Counselors can also be watchful for psychological consequences of abuse that might be signals that a client is being abused. These reactions might include depression, PTSD, learned helplessness, shame, guilt, anxiety, and denial (O. Barnett, Miller-Perrin, & Perrin, 2011; Lawson, 2013). Noting these signals is important both for detecting abuse and for intervening and treating the abuse. A tip for ferreting out elder abuse is to spend some time alone with clients to give them the opportunity to express their fears or concerns about safety, living arrangements, or financial issues. In addition, there are many instruments that have been used to screen for elder abuse, including the following: the Suspected Abuse Tool, the Screen for Various Types of Abuse or Neglect, the Questions to Elicit Elder Abuse, the Hwalek–Sengstock Elder Abuse Screening Test, the Elder Abuse Suspicion Index, the Brief Abuse Screening for the Elderly, the Partner Violence Screen, and several others. Counselors can use one or more of these instruments during interviews with clients when they suspect some type of abuse; however, the instruments' reliability and validity have not been tested in many settings (O'Neill & Vermeal, 2013).

Intervention

Intervention can involve legal, educational, advocacy, and therapeutic components (Reis & Nahmiash, 1995). One imperative intervention is reporting the abuse. It is important to note that after a case has been reported, assessment and legal and physical interventions are primarily done by each state's APS, and counselors are not informed of or included in these activities (see Chapter 3). A recent literature review of studies of certain interventions (i.e., home visits, advocacy, social services, psychoeducational support groups, legal interventions), however, showed that these interventions had little effect on abuse (Ploeg, Fear, Hutchinson, MacMillan, & Bolan, 2009). The implications of this finding are that counselors may become disappointed or upset if their reporting makes no difference in their clients' lives and may refrain from making future reports. In the past, one of the most effective interventions involved helping clients change their place of residence; however, this intervention is effective only if the client is willing to make a residential relocation (Wolf & Pillemer, 1989).

Because of the possible psychological consequences of abuse, counselors may wish to focus on the sequelae of abuse. Counselors have the skills to work with depression, PTSD, learned helplessness, shame, guilt, anxiety, and denial and can use these skills when working with clients who have been or are being abused. Unfortunately, three studies of psychosocial interventions found no difference in well-being, family relations, self-esteem, guilt, or depression between those who did and did not receive psychosocial intervention (as reviewed by Ploeg et al., 2009). Nahmiash and Reis (2000), however, found that among 473 strategies used with 83 older individuals who had been abused, the most effective psychological interventions included education and individual counseling that focused on reduction of depression, stress, and anxiety. With regard to specific strategies, Fraser (2006) indicated that on the basis of anecdotal reports, a combination of person-centered therapy and CBT is effective. Additional information regarding strategies for counseling elders who have experienced abuse can be found in the discussions of PTSD in Chapter 6.

Resources for Elder Abuse

National Center on Elder Abuse, http://www.ncea.aoa.gov/
National Committee for the Prevention of Elder Abuse, http://www.preventelderabuse.org/index.html
U.S. Department of Health and Human Services Administration on Aging, http://www.aoa.gov/about.asp

Driving and Transportation Issues

According to the National Household Travel Survey (cited by Abrahms, 2013), more than 20% of older Americans (ages 65 years or older) do not drive. It appears that older men outlive their driving days by 7 years, whereas older women outlive their driving days by 10 years. Reports vary regarding older people's driving records. Some have a negative perspective, and others have a positive perspective; therefore, older people, their significant others, and counselors will need to be both open-minded and skeptical when reviewing these reports.

Reports with a negative perspective indicate that drivers typically tend to have higher crash rates and driver death rates once they reach 70 to 75 years of age. According to Saisan, White, and Robinson (2012), older people are more likely to have accidents and receive driving citations than younger people, and the rate of fatal car accidents increases when people reach age 70. According to Waller (1998), the crash risk per mile increases at age 55, and at age 80, it exceeds the crash risk of young beginning drivers. According to the Fatal Analysis Reporting System of the Insurance Institute for Highway Safety, driver deaths caused by crashes increase somewhat at age 70 and more markedly at ages 75 and 80 (especially for men). In addition to having more fatal accidents, older people tend to be more seriously injured than younger people in similar kinds of crashes—perhaps because they are less able to recover from injuries (cited in AARP, 2010).

Reports with a more positive perspective indicate that the driving problems associated with older people may have been exaggerated, and that older people have other resources and abilities to compensate for some of the deficits associated with driving. For example, reports have indicated that drivers who are 65 years or older are 4 times less likely to be in a crash than drivers who are age 16 to 19, fatality rates are lower for people age 65 or older (i.e., 18 per 100,000) than for people age 16 to 25 (27 per 100,000), older drivers are far less likely to drink and drive than drivers who are under age 25, and older individuals are far less likely to have alcohol-related fatal car accidents than younger individuals (Whitbourne & Whitbourne, 2011).

The majority of driver violations and crashes for older people occur at intersections and involve right-of-way issues, improper left turns, and driving through stop signs or traffic lights (Waller, 1998; Whitbourne & Whitbourne, 2011). Signs that a person may not be driving safely include the following: leaving the blinker on; failing to use the blinker when turning; missing exits that are familiar; drifting from one lane to another; accelerating or braking suddenly without need; having multiple close calls; receiving multiple warning tickets from traffic officers; and having an unusual number of dents and scratches on the car, curb, mailbox, and garage door (Saisan, White, & Robinson, 2012).

The potential for car accidents among older people is thought to be attributable to stiffness or pain in the neck that impairs the ability to look left and right over one's shoulder; pain and stiffness in legs, hands, arms, or shoulders that reduce the ability to use the gas pedal, brakes, and steering wheel; visual problems that reduce the ability to see cars and pedestrians, road signs, and signs of danger; increased sensitivity to glare and difficulty seeing at night; difficulty with dividing one's attention between more than one situation while driving; hearing problems that cause people to miss their own car noises and warning signs from other vehicles and the environment; reduced reflexes that cause slow reaction times; medications that interfere with reaction times, memory, or judgment; decreased tolerance for alcohol that may influence alertness and reaction time; mental or physical slowness of reaction time to unexpected situations or to emerging traffic; memory loss or judgment problems that may cause the driver to become lost or forget where to turn; and concerns, fears, or uncertainties about their own driving abilities, which may cause them to hesitate, be preoccupied, or use their brakes much more than necessary (AARP, 2010; Saisan, White, & Robinson, 2012; Whitbourne & Whitbourne, 2011).

If older people or their family members are uncertain about the safety of their driving, they can enlist the help of a certified driver rehabilitation specialist, rehabilitation technologist, or occupational therapist to evaluate the individual's ability to drive. Clients may also wish to talk with their doctors about this issue. Using this third party will help assuage or confirm the worries of family members, friends, or the older person. Furthermore, these specialists can often recommend accommodations or modifications that will allow the person to continue to drive safely. Depending on the community, driver assessments may be obtained from occupational therapy driving specialists (see http://www.aota.org/olderdriver), the city or county Office on Aging, the Area Agency on Aging, the U.S. Department of Veterans Affairs (VA), private evaluation and training agencies, or the state bureau/department of motor vehicles (AARP, 2010; Saisan, White, & Robinson, 2012).

Older people may also wish to do a self-evaluation of their skills. Examples of computer or online evaluation programs are the AAA Roadwise Review (a computer CD program), AARP Driver Safety Program website quizzes, and the AARP Driver Safety Program on-line course. Other self-evaluation resources are listed at http://www.helpguide.org. Discussions of each of these programs is beyond the scope of this chapter; however, one example might help counselors understand how these programs work. The AAA Roadwise Review is a screening tool that gives older people the opportunity to test their skills at home. This evaluation tool is free online or can be purchased on CD-ROM. It is designed to evaluate eight functions that have been linked to automobile accidents. One word of caution regarding any computer-based program is that many older people may not be familiar with computers and/or may be intimidated or frightened by them. Because of this, they may be so stressed or confused about how to use the computer that they cannot concentrate or focus on the tasks of the program. If this is the case, there is a strong probability of inaccurate negative driving skills ratings. Counselors will, therefore, need to be cautious about the results of these technologically administered assessments and help clients understand the results (ACA, 2014, Standard E.7.c.).

In addition to offering this free evaluation of older people's fitness to drive, AAA also offers them a free "CarFit" evaluation, which is a personalized assessment of the fit between drivers and cars. An evaluation can include the ease with which drivers can reach peddles, twist their bodies, see over the dashboard, and see overhead and side mirrors. The evaluation also includes a check for blind spots and distance between the steering wheel and the driver's chest. If there is a need for modifications, evaluators can give advice and refer drivers to programs or services that can modify their vehicles to better match them (Highroads, 2012).

Older people may wish to improve or maintain their driving by taking various classes or workshops that focus on safe driving or defensive driving. These classes can be found by contacting senior centers, an Area Agency on Aging, the AARP, or AAA. Some options involve sitting through a half-day lecture that includes workbooks and audiovisual aids. Other options include computer programs that are designed to enhance mental quickness in driving or online courses that provide information about laws and driver safety (Highroads, 2012; Saisan, White & Robinson, 2012). Edwards, Delahunt, and Mahncke (2009) found that individuals who completed a computer course (i.e., Drive Sharp) were 50% less likely to cause an accident within the next 6 years and were 40% less likely have to give up driving within 3 years than those who had not taken the course. Furthermore, insurance companies generally reduce annual premiums for those who have taken driver safety courses because there is actuarial evidence that such courses can improve one's driving (Highroads, 2012; Saisan, White & Robinson, 2012).

In addition to driver training, older people can use a number of strategies to minimize the negative issues associated with aging and maximize their ability to drive. They can obtain regular eye appointments and use appropriate eyewear to improve their vision; increase or decrease the brightness of the lights on their dashboard; keep all lights, windows, and mirrors clean; have the car serviced on a regular basis; keep the car filled with gas; obtain a hearing evaluation and hearing aids if necessary; wear tinted glasses or get tinted glass on the car windows to reduce glare; speak with a physician to understand and control the effects of medications; obtain suggestions from a physical therapist regarding exercises that can help maintain or improve physical flexibility and strength; get enough sleep and rest to maintain clarity of thinking and memory; and purchase a car with windows that are large and unimpeded by metal or tags. If a physical disability other than hearing or vision is the problem, they can select a car with power brakes and steering and automatic transmission, or they can ask a rehabilitation technologist or occupational therapist to suggest automobile modifications. If they have had driving problems associated with alcohol consumption, they can avoid alcohol before driving, identify a designated driver before drinking, or have a certified emission interlock inserted into their cars that requires that they pass a breathalyzer test prior to starting the car (AARP, 2010; Saisan, White & Robinson, 2012).

Other strategies for safe driving include focusing only on driving, paying extra attention when approaching or driving through intersections, avoiding distractions such as using the phone or talking to a passenger, avoiding looking down at a global positioning system (GPS) or map, leaving plenty of space between cars to allow for braking, and remembering to leave much more space in fast traffic. If drivers are unfamiliar with the road, they will want to plan and study that route prior to driving. Drivers with certain vision problems will want to avoid driving at night or into the sun. Drivers may also wish to avoid driving in stormy weather. It is also important for drivers to realize where they feel most uncomfortable driving and avoid those situations (Saison, White, & Robinson, 2012).

Counselors can use all of this information in discussions regarding driving issues. After empathetic listening to a client's concerns, counselors can use creative problem solving to determine what actions the client wishes to take (e.g., other- or self-evaluation of their driving, evaluation of the person–car fit, alterations of the automobile, training programs, use of specialists to improve flexibility and strength, etc.). Counselors may need to describe the options that are available, because having the knowledge of the various resources and options will give clients more opportunities for choice.

Occasionally, the family, physician, or court may believe that an older person is no longer able to drive safely. If this is the case, counselors can brainstorm and practice the strategy that family members will use to discuss this concern with their older relative or friend. Counselors can help families recognize the importance of approaching the older person in a respectful manner, empathizing with their potential loss, and providing specific examples of potential problem-driving issues and events.

These discussions can be difficult because driving can be a source of pride and identity, a primary method by which to maintain independence, and a symbol of freedom and responsibility. Losing the ability or opportunity to drive can therefore be a profound loss, and this sense of loss should be honored and respected. It is also important that other methods of transportation be identified so that the loss is not complete. It might be helpful to develop a plan to make the transition out of driving in stages, such as giving up driving at night or on freeways and occasionally using public transportation. This transition period might give the person time to adjust to and learn new strategies for maintaining independent travel while not driving his or her own car (Saison, White, & Robinson, 2012).

Because transportation seems to be a key to staying in one's own home, being independent, being able to socialize, and continuing to work, it is important to discuss alternative forms of transportation that will give the individual as much flexibility and freedom as possible. With the increasing older population, transportation may become a serious issue for this group and for the community. For example, Transportation for America, an advocacy group (as cited by Abrahms, 2013), has indicated that in 2015, 15.5 million older Americans will have poor or no access to public transportation, especially those who live in rural areas.

On the other hand, the growing older population can be an impetus to communities to develop their public transportation systems. For example, the use of public transportation increased by 40% from 2001 to 2009 (Abrahms, 2013), which may result in more and better systems. Counselors, as case managers, can make themselves aware of their local transportation systems; if such systems do not exist or are ineffective, counselors can advocate for a workable public system. Examples of for-profit and nonprofit transportation systems that can be used as models include the California SilverRide, the South Carolina Lower Savannah Council on Governments, the Maryland Ride Partners, and the South Dakota River Cities Public Transportation (Abrahms, 2013). Some of these transportation programs (e.g., SilverRide) provide more than transportation in that they offer one-on-one help and companionship during a ride.

Resources for Transportation

Independent living centers, Councils or Area Agencies on Aging, church-related groups, and city transportation systems are likely to have information about available transportation systems. National resources associated with transportation include the following:

Beverly Foundation, http://www.beverlyfoundation.org
Community Transportation Association of America, http://www.ctaa.org
Independent Transportation Network, http://www.itamerica.org/
National Association of Area Agencies on Aging, http://www.n4a.org
Older Road Users—Federal Highway Administration (FHWA) Safety
    Program, http://www. safety.fhwa.dot.gov/older_users/
Transportation America, http://www.transportationamerica.com

Veterans' Issues

The growth of the aging population will be paralleled by the growth in the veteran population. Older veterans represent a broad range of unique individuals, rather than a homogeneous group. Assuming they may have joined the military at age 18, this group is composed of people who may have joined the military from approximately 47 years ago (for those who are age 65) to 87 years ago (for those who are age 105). They may have served for a short time or they may have made the military their career, and they will have served in a variety of ranks. They may have fought in one or more conflicts, or they may not have served in combat at all. If they served in war, their experiences will have been unique. For example, those who served in World War II (WWII) had very different experiences than those who served in Vietnam or Korea. Furthermore, some veterans may have been injured, whereas others were not. While in the military, they may have served in a wide variety of capacities (e.g., clerical, educational, medical, combat, mechanical). They will have served in different military branches (e.g., Army, Navy, Air Force, Marines, etc.), had varied reasons for joining the military, and had varied feelings and thoughts about their connections with the military. It is not, therefore, appropriate to categorize all veterans into one group or to make assumptions about their experiences (Monroe, 2012).

On the other hand, veterans may have many things in common that are associated with military culture. As the *ACA Code of Ethics* (ACA, 2014) indicates, "Counselors actively attempt to understand the diverse cultural backgrounds of the clients they serve" (Section A, Introduction). The military culture is, therefore, an important consideration when counseling veterans. If counselors are not familiar with the culture, this may damage client–counselor rapport, lead to misdiagnosis, and limit quality of care. Furthermore, counselors should not put too much faith in tools that are standardized on nonmilitary populations when working with someone from the military (Monroe, 2012; K. Myers, 2013).

When considering veterans from a cultural perspective, counselors will need to be aware that clients will likely have experienced a military governing system that honors the commanding officer and relies on the military court system. Veterans may be familiar with and use many unique terms and phrases (e.g., hooah, roger, SNAFU), respond emotionally to certain songs associated with the military (e.g., "Over There" or "The Army Goes Rolling Along"), and have experienced unique cuisine (e.g., meals ready to eat, or MREs). Furthermore, counselors who are working with military clients should learn general information about rank, terminology, military structure, and so forth so that they understand, to some degree, the world of the veteran and so that they do not have to ask the client for clarification on these topics (Monroe, 2012).

Another important aspect of the military culture is the concept of inner strength, or "grit." Grit is a part of military training that is thought to keep military personnel alive and safe. It is what gives them the motivation to continue in the face of difficulty or danger (K. Myers, 2013). Military personnel have been taught that displays of emotion or a lack of control are considered signs of weakness and that composure is a sign of strength. Thus, they may view the need for mental health care as a weakness and may either avoid counseling or display behaviors that seem inappropriate for the topic. For example, a client's tone, rate of speech, or affect may not match a potentially emotionally charged topic (e.g., seeing a buddy die, losing a family member). Rather than being an indication of inappropriate affect or expression, a flat affect may actually be an attempt to appear composed, as expected in the military culture. Being aware of this cultural requirement will help counselors avoid client misdiagnosis (Monroe, 2012). Furthermore, counselors can invite clients to use this grit to face issues and achieve therapeutic outcomes (K. Myers, 2013).

Counselors should also be aware of other military cultural values such as loyalty, duty, respect, selfless service, honor, and integrity. These values can either cause difficulties for clients or can be used to work through personal issues. The counselor's recognition of these and other values can lead to a strong and trustful client–counselor relationship. Although counselors should be aware of military culture and expected behaviors, "there is a fine line between informed multicultural consideration and stereotyping" (Monroe, 2012, p. 53). It is, therefore, important for counselors to keep a clear demarcation between the two.

Counselors can enhance the client–counselor relationship by showing respect for the client's service in the military. This respect can be shown by recognizing military holidays, acknowledging the disrespect that was shown to Vietnam veterans when they returned from the war, and attending specific ceremonies that recognize veterans. Counselors can also inform veterans that it is an honor to work with them, provide them with information about their previous work in clinical settings, and tell them about their own or family members' military service, if this is relevant (K. Myers, 2013).

Counselors should also be aware that spirituality may be very important to veterans. K. Myers (2013) indicated that it is common for veterans (especially those who have been involved in combat) to have a need to explore their spiritually/faith during counseling. Counselors might wish to read *War and the Soul* in which Tick (2005) asserted that PTSD is a soul wound, and that veterans may, therefore, need to come to a reconciliation of their war experiences and their beliefs. He indicated that rituals or rites for returning warriors are important, and that these rituals can be carried out in reconciliation retreats that include storytelling and spiritual and aesthetic healing. Counselors involved in this process must be knowledgeable about faith and spirituality as well as about the possible effects of war on one's spirituality.

Monroe (2012) indicated that although it has become standard practice to assess military personal for PTSD, it is not appropriate to assume that the majority of military personal have this disorder. On the other hand, a large proportion of older veterans are likely to have experienced traumatic events because of war-related incidents (Kaiser et al., 2013). For example, scholars have reported that 85% of older male American veterans had been exposed to traumatic events over a lifetime (Higgins & Follette, 2002) and that older males (median age 71) who had seen combat or were ex-prisoners of war (POWS) of WWII or the Korean War had a PTSD lifetime prevalence rate of 53% and a PTSD current rate of 29% (Iverson et al., 2013). The PTSD rate for veterans who have sought psychiatric treatment is much higher than for other veterans, with estimates ranging from 37% to 80% (Tjaden & Thoennes, 2000). Although older veterans may not exhibit all the criteria for PTSD, between 7% and 15% of this population have demonstrated subclinical levels of PTSD symptoms (Kaiser et al., 2013).

Combat events can continue to be upsetting long after they have been experienced; therefore, older veterans may still be affected by such events. Furthermore, symptoms of PTSD may increase as people grow older. Veterans may also begin to experience PTSD symptoms later in life, even though they had not experienced them as younger people. This delayed response to wartime experiences has been labeled late-onset stress symptomatology (LOSS). As indicated in Chapter 6, LOSS may be similar to PTSD but involves fewer and less intense symptoms. As with PTSD, LOSS can be triggered by a variety of age-related stressors, such as deteriorating health, retirement, and loss of one or more loved ones (Kaiser et al., 2013; National Center for PTSD, 2012).

Because of the potential for PTSD or LOSS, it is important for counselors to recognize and treat the symptoms when they exist. Symptoms can include mentally and vividly reliving the event, avoiding situations that are similar to the event, feeling fear or guilt, losing interest in activities, startling easily, feeling a high degree of stress, being hypervigilant, having nightmares or trouble sleeping, and feeling anger at inappropriate times (Kaiser et al., 2013; National Center for PTSD, 2011a). More detailed criteria for this disorder can be found in the *DSM*.

It is also important not to mistake certain behaviors as symptoms of PTSD. For example, counselors should avoid automatically assuming that sleep disorders have to do with postcombat nightmares. Sleep disorders may be the result of a lifetime of factors that have contributed to difficulty with sleep. These factors might include living on a base where they had to share rooms with roommates who came and went at all hours, having a work schedule that was often switched from night to day, and living near an airfield where various noises could have kept them awake (Monroe, 2012).

Various treatments have been shown to be effective for PTSD (see Chapter 6); however, it is very important that counselors get the appropriate training and supervision in effective treatment before working with this issue. Counselors should be aware of the effectiveness of certain counseling strategies and know how to use them. Further information about treatment of veterans with PTSD can be found at VAPTSD Treatment Programs at http://www.ptsd.va.gov. One free online course provides an in depth discussion of PTSD (see http://www.ptsd. va.gov/PTSD/professional/ptsd101/ptsd101-pdf/brch-aging.pdf). A book titled *Healing War Trauma: A Handbook for Creative Approaches* (Scurfield & Platoni, 2013) might also offer insight into working with people who have had war trauma.

Counselors can support those with LOSS or PTSD by letting them know that asking for help is a sign of strength and wisdom. In the treatment process, counselors might invite veterans to talk to others who have been through the same kind of experience, to discuss their LOSS or PTSD with their family and friends, and to let them know that the old memories of war may be the source of current memory problems, sleep issues, anger, or nervousness. Counselors can also help clients indentify activities that contribute to their sense of personal strength and safety (e.g., eating well, exercising, socializing, being productive; National Center for PTSD, 2012).

One important point associated with wartime experiences is that for some individuals, old wartime memories might be uplifting and help them find meaning in their lives (National Center for PTSD, 2012). For that reason, it is important for counselors not to make assumptions about the meanings and responses to war experiences; instead, they should respectfully listen to their clients without jumping to conclusions about possible PTSD.

Counselors should be aware of the many programs designed to provide both medical and mental health services to veterans. These programs are available through the VA for all veterans who (a) have completed active service in the Navy, Army, Air Force, Marines, or Coast Guard; (b) served in the Merchant Marines during WWII; (c) were National Guard members or reservists who completed a federal deployment to a combat zone; and (d) were discharged from the military for any reason except dishonorable discharge (National Center for PTSD, 2007a).

The VA is intended to be a resource for older veterans, providing a vast number of medical services as well as long-term care, nursing home care, and assisted living. Other services available to veterans include drug and alcohol programs, mental health programs, PTSD services, homeless programs, vision and hearing loss programs, physical therapy, occupational therapy, rehabilitation counseling, job placement for older veterans, and so forth. These programs are often offered on the grounds of large veterans hospitals but can also be found in the community. Furthermore, the VA has partnered with the National Hospice and Palliative Care Organization (NHPCO) to develop the *We Honor Veterans* campaign designed to provide health care providers with information about the unique needs of dying veterans through the distribution of free tools and support.

Counselors who wish to serve veterans should be aware that veterans are usually served by VA programs; typically, priority for employment in the VA is given to veterans. It is also important to note that private contracts can be negotiated with independent counselors, especially when VA services are not locally available. Qualified counselors who are interested in serving veterans need to be aware of Tricare, an insurance plan associated with the U. S. Department of Defense (DOD). Counselors who are listed as a Tricare in-network provider will be allowed to receive referrals directly from the DOD (K. Myers, 2013). Counselors may also wish to join ACA's Association for Counselors and Educators in Government, which focuses on counseling clients and their families in military-related agencies and in local, state, and federal government agencies.

Resources for Veterans

American Legion Veterans Career Center, http://www.legion.org/careers; and regional call centers for VA services, 800-827-1000.
Farmer Veteran Coalition, http://www.farmvetco.org
National Center for PTSD, U.S. Deptment of Veterans Affairs, http://www.ptsd.va.gov/public/pages/ptsd-older-vets.asp
NHPCO HelpLine, 800-658-8898
We Honor Veterans Organization, http://www.WeHonorVeterans.org/Support
U.S. Department of Veterans Affairs (VA), http://www.va.gov
U.S. Department of Veterans Affairs NHPCO's Caring Connections, http://www.caringinfo.org
Veterans Farm Program, http://www.veteransfarm.com

Forensic Vocational Analysis

Some counselors may engage in forensic vocational analysis, which typically involves a professional review of documents (usually for lawsuits or legal decisions) to provide opinions regarding the loss of earning capacity, the need for vocational training or rehabilitation, and/or case management of people who can no longer work because of a disabling physical condition that has been caused by an outside source. These opinions are used by lawyers or insurance companies to develop their cases. According to the *ACA Code of Ethics*, "When providing forensic evaluations, the primary obligation of counselors is to produce objective findings that can be substantiated based on information and techniques appropriate to the evaluation . . . Counselors define the limits of their reports or testimony, especially when an examination of the individual has not been conducted" (ACA, 2014, Standard E.13.a.).

To conduct a document review, counselors need substantiated information regarding what is typical in the work force. This information is based on the history of work-related issues of people within the age group of the person whose case is being reviewed and a projection of the earnings they might have made if they were able to work after a disabling event. Counselors can get much of this information from standard worklife expectancy tables (e.g., average number of years an average person is expected to work over a lifetime) that are based on the history of work among the population similar to the individual whose case is being considered (Schonbrun & Kampfe, 2009).

As indicated in other chapters, life expectancy has increased over the years, older people are less likely to have disabling conditions or functional limitations than they did in the past, and many older people are likely to work beyond the traditional retirement age. The implications are that counselors who specialize in forensic vocational analysis may find that the heretofore standard information on worklife expectancy may no longer be appropriate. In other words, traditional worklife expectancy tables may not take into account the new group of older people who work past age 65. Therefore, it is important for counselors who are engaged in forensic work to be aware of the population shifts and the changes in what has been thought to be typical among older people with regard to worklife expectancy. This advice applies whether counselors are reviewing a younger person's or an older person's case, because the tables are used to estimate future needs and losses of projected income of that person (Schonbrun & Kampfe, 2009).

Summary

To work with older people, counselors must have knowledge and information regarding a vast number of topics. Elder abuse is a concern because it can have serious physical and psychological consequences and because there is some uncertainty about how to effectively deal with this situation. Issues associated with driving and transportation are vitally linked to independence, autonomy, and a sense of self-worth; therefore, counselors will need to be sensitive to and knowledgeable about this situation. Understanding the issues associated with older veterans is important given the uniqueness and growth of this population. Having some knowledge about how the older population can affect forensic vocational analysis is important to the counselor who functions as an expert witness.

Chapter 8

Sensory Loss Among the Older Population

The purpose of this chapter is to provide information that counselors can use when working with persons who have sensory losses. Sensory loss is typically associated with the aging process (Papalia, Sterns, Feldman, & Camp, 2003). There is some evidence, for example, that certain sensory losses tend to accelerate at the following ages: vision = mid-50s, hearing = mid-40s, touch = mid-50s, smell = mid-70s, and taste = mid-60s (Kemmet & Brotherson, 2008). Because sensory loss can sometimes be misinterpreted as a decline in intellectual function and because it can have a significant effect on many aspects of people's lives (e.g., lower quality of life, social isolation, depression), it is important for clients, counselors, and significant others to be knowledgeable about these losses, the problems they present, and methods for dealing with them (Bromley, 2000; Kemmet & Brotherson, 2008).

Vision Loss and Blindness

Visual impairment (i.e., difficulty seeing even when wearing glasses) affects approximately 15.1% of men and 15.7% of women who are age 70 or older. As people age, the percentage increases, with 11% of those age 70 through 79 years and 24.6% of those age 80 years or older having a visual impairment (Dillon, Gu, Hoffman, & Chia-Wen, 2010). There are several conditions that cause late-onset low vision or blindness. The most common of these include age-related macular degeneration (AMD), glaucoma, and cataracts.

AMD is the primary cause of severe vision loss among Caucasians over ages 60 to 65 as well as among other groups. In AMD, people's central vision is affected, that is, they may have dark areas or distortions in their visual field, blurriness, problems with both near and far vision, and/or distortions in distinguishing sizes and shapes. Having this condition affects the ability to perform functions such as reading and driving. Macular degeneration does not typically affect people's peripheral vision and does not result in total blindness. In some cases, vision is not affected a great deal, and in most cases, people have enough peripheral vision to perform most ADLs (American Academy of Ophthalmology, 2002; American Health Assistance Foundation, 2012e; Casciani, 2012b).

Glaucoma involves increased pressure within the eye that can result in optic nerve damage. There are often no early symptoms of glaucoma; however, regular eye examinations can detect this condition. Risk factors for glaucoma are increased age, family history, African ancestry, health problems such as high blood pressure and diabetes, and previous surgeries or injuries to the eye. There are several types of glaucoma, but the two most common types are open-angle glaucoma and closed-angle glaucoma—both of which result in loss of peripheral vision and, in some cases, complete blindness (American Health Assistance Foundation, 2012d; Koo, 2008b).

Cataracts involve the clouding of the eye lens (front of the eye), which impedes the amount of light that can enter the eye, thus causing blurriness. Cataracts typically advance slowly but can occur quickly. Possible causes of cataracts are aging, previous eye injuries or infection, diabetes, use of certain medications (e.g., steroids), exposure to ultraviolet (UV) light, tobacco use, and family history. Surgery (i.e., the removal of the clouded lens and replacement by a clear artificial lens) can be used to restore normal vision. Typically, surgery is done on one eye at a time, and sometimes people still need to wear glasses for clear vision (Koo, 2008a).

Other visual losses associated with age include decreased pupil size, loss of lens elasticity, loss of lens transparency, susceptibility to glare, diabetic retinopathy, and vision loss caused by stroke. Decreased pupil size reduces the amount of light that reaches the retina; therefore, people with this condition will need additional light to see. Loss of lens elasticity reduces the ability to adjust to sudden light changes; consequently, people with this condition may feel uneasy and be unable to see when moving from a bright room to a dark room or vice versa (e.g., they may have problems finding a seat in a theater until they have time to adjust to the dark, or they may have problems with abrupt lighting changes). Loss of lens transparency (different from cataracts) involves a yellowing of the eye lens. This yellowing reduces color discrimination, with greens and blues being more difficult to see than reds and yellows. Susceptibility to glare involves feeling discomfort when exposed to glaring lights and requiring a longer amount of time to recover from the effects of glare. Diabetic retinopathy involves damage to the retina and can range from some loss of vision to blindness. Visual loss caused by stroke is associated with the brain being unable to interpret the images that the eyes send to it (Casciani, 2012b). Extended information about visual impairment can be found at http://www.eyesmart.org.

Activity: Vision Loss

In order to be sensitive to and understand vision loss, it is sometimes helpful to simulate the experience.

1. To simulate several phases of glaucoma (loss of peripheral vision), cut 3-inch holes from the center of one or two paper plates (the holes should be jaggedly cut). Hold the plate(s) 2 inches from the eyes and try to engage in your daily activities. Next, cut 1-inch holes in the center of one or two more paper plates. Place the paper plate(s) two inches from the eyes and try to engage in the same activities.
2. To simulate one of the major effects of macular degeneration, place your hands about 7 inches in front of each of your eyes with slightly open fingers. Then try to engage in your ADLs. Now move your hands to about 2 inches from your eyes and try the above activities again. At this stage, you should have difficulty seeing what is directly in front of you. You are experiencing what it might be like to have only peripheral vision.
3. To experience the early stages of cataracts, place small dots of petroleum jelly on some parts of a pair of sunglasses or eyeglasses and engage in your daily activities. To experience later stages of cataracts, place a smear of jelly over the glasses and try to engage in the same daily activities.

When engaging in these experiences, one should remember that simulation can offer only one small aspect of the experience of any of these conditions. People who are doing these activities can always remove the plates, put down their hands, or take off the jellied glasses at any time. They have not experienced other aspects of the conditions, and they do not have to experience the emotional overlay associated with true and lasting vision loss.

Issues Associated With Late-Onset Blindness or Low Vision

Acquiring low vision as an older adult can be very difficult and may result in frustration, dependency, anger, fear, isolation, loneliness, depression, and reduced quality of life. These outcomes can occur because individuals may be unable to accomplish routine tasks or perform lifelong leisure activities. In addition, they may be subject to falls, dependent upon other people to perform certain activities, treated as if they are no longer able to do or decide for themselves, avoided by others who are uncomfortable with or hampered by their disability, overprotected by others who love them, and relieved of their regular responsibilities and decision making (Casciani, 2012b; Cotter et al., 1998; Haslanger, 2012; Kemmet & Brotherson, 2008). For example, in interviews with individuals who were placed into a long-term care setting, one blind man indicated, "I haven't been consulted about anything. I am a blind man, and if you are blind it means you are out of it . . . it can play on your nerves" (Cotter et al., 1998, p. 252).

People who have lost their vision are also unable to see many of the sights that once gave them joy or relaxation. For example, they may no longer be able to see a beautiful sunset, a loved one's face, glistening snow, and so forth. These losses can affect people in different ways, depending upon their nature and desires; however, they may result in a lower quality of life and feelings of depression (Kemmet & Brotherson, 2008).

The National Federation of the Blind (NFB; 2011a), an empowerment-based association, has indicated that seniors who are losing their vision do not have to give up most of the things they love to do. With alternative techniques, they can maintain or find new jobs, cook or barbeque, knit or sew, listen to recorded books, do gardening, entertain family and friends, do arts and crafts, take care of their grandchildren, go hiking, and generally live full and independent lives. Many of these activities require training, aids, appliances, encouragement, and positive attitudes. The NFB and other organizations provide detailed information regarding where to obtain aids and appliances and how to use them. Furthermore, each NFB state affiliate or chapter typically offers monthly support group meetings where people discuss their feelings and learn about local resources.

Low-vision or blindness-related aids can help people perform everyday tasks and empower them to live more fulfilling and productive lives. For this reason, counselors as case managers can help clients identify and access these aids. Items that can be of help are labeling aids, adapted games, print and Braille writing aids, talking medical and household devices, talking or Braille clocks and watches, sewing and kitchen aides, book reading and recording devices, handheld magnifiers, and software that converts written materials to audio recordings. A white cane is a symbol that the person using it is blind, which helps with safety issues. Because it is a symbol of blindness, however, clients may not wish to use such a cane. Many materials are provided free of charge from a variety of resources, and others are available for a cost (American Health Assistance Foundation, 2012d, 2012e; NFB, 2011b).

Other strategies that can contribute to a client's independence include developing or focusing on other senses, such as hearing, touch, and smell, to get environmental clues. It has been suggested that as people begin to focus their full attention on what they hear, they begin to use their hearing more effectively and gradually improve the ability to remember what they hear. The use of touch (e.g., to discern an object's size, texture, weight), the feel of the cane or walker on surfaces (e.g., dirt, cement, flooring, rises, steps), and other messages received from hands and feet can all enhance awareness of the environment. Furthermore, skills in using these alternative contacts with the environment can gradually improve with practice. Various environmental smells can also be helpful. For example, the smell of gasoline, mown grass, one's own room, or another person's scent can all provide clues to the environment. Furthermore, people can learn to use their residual vision more effectively. For example, if people have lost central vision, they can use their peripheral vision (side, upper, and lower vision) to help them engage in ADLs. They can start by finding the part of the eye that sees the best and then practice using this for environmental clues. With consistent practice, individuals can gradually develop this skill (American Health Assistance Foundation, 2012e).

In addition to learning new ways to get environmental cues, people with visual loss must also protect the vision that they still have. For example, they must protect their eyes from UV radiation by wearing brimmed hats and sunglasses that block both UV-A and UV-B rays. Other techniques to protect one's eyes can be learned by consulting with a therapist who specializes in low vision; this therapist can make specific recommendations on the basis of the individual's needs (American Health Assistance Foundation, 2012d, 2012e).

Strategies for Counselors Working With Adults With Low Vision or Blindness

Because of the strong emotional overlay associated with late-onset vision loss, counselors can encourage individuals and their families and friends to engage in frank discussions of their concerns and feelings (American Health Assistance Foundation, 2012d, 2012e). Having a safe environment in which to express themselves and work through their losses can be very helpful. This environment can be provided in individual or group counseling sessions.

Bibliotherapy can also help clients and their families. One large-print book, *Old Dogs and New Tricks* (Jernigan, 1996), is quite useful because it focuses on the emotional and practical experience of vision loss in adulthood. As the title suggests, the book is written to encourage newly visually impaired individuals to be open to what they can do versus focusing on what they cannot do. It also gives practical advice about day-to-day issues of living with blindness. Another newer book, *So You Don't See as Well as You Used to* (National Organization of the Senior Blind, 2006), includes inspirational short stories by and about seniors who are blind or have low vision but who have not allowed age or blindness to interfere with leading full lives. The book includes a list of resources and is available in large print.

Counselors can invite clients to read one or both of these books and then discuss them in follow-up sessions. Questions can include, "Were you able to read this book in the format provided?" "What do we need to do for you to read this book?" "What were the most important things that you got from this book?" "How can you apply this information to your own life?" "Let's make a list of the things you might try." and "Which of these things would you like to try first?" If clients are unable or unwilling to read these books on their own, counselors can read appropriate passages aloud to them and ask some of the above questions. Doing so might help clients begin to discover possibilities that they had not previously considered. Asking clients to read these books might also open the door to discussions about ways to make written materials accessible to them.

A wide variety of strategies can be used by counselors to ensure their offices are accessible, safe, and respectful for persons with low vision. Because lighting is important, counselors can arrange their offices so that the light source (electric light or window) is behind the client; use overhead nonglare lights and dimmer switches; control glare with curtains or blinds; avoid turning bright lights on and off; and use bright colors (perhaps reds and yellows) to mark switches, levers, and so forth. Counselors can install grab bars in restrooms, avoid throw-rugs or mats, ensure that thresholds to doors are flush to the floor, paint doors and thresholds in contrasting colors, avoid placing furniture or shelves in walkways, leave open spaces for walking rather than placing furniture in the center of the room, avoid any kind of raised flooring (e.g., single steps, raised tiles), and avoid changing the location of objects in the office. Because stairways can be dangerous, counselors will want to install extra nonglare lighting, handrails on both sides of the stairs, color-contrasting first and last steps, and bright colors on the edges of individual steps of stairways. Because clients may use their hearing for environmental cues, counselors can keep their offices quiet so that the client can hear important cues as well as the counselor's words, location, and tone of voice (American Health Assistance Foundation, 2012d, 2012e; Casciani, 2012b; NFB, n.d.).

Counselors might wish to include low-vision aids in their offices or briefcases for clients who will need to read and sign statements or review other written materials. Such aids can include a signature guide, a 20/20 (felt-tip) pen, a magnifier, an enlarger, large-print forms, and a computer with various low-vision functions, such as large print and software to convert written material to audio material.

The counselor's behavior can also enhance communication. It is important for counselors to avoid assuming what the client can and cannot see. For example, counselors can speak normally and directly to the client rather than to an aide or family member; let the client know who is in the room; inform the client when entering or leaving the room; describe the surroundings to help familiarize the client with the environment; tell the client if furniture has been moved; inform the client when handing him or her an object (e.g., "Here is a pen"); hand objects to the client from the side that they see best; avoid feeding, petting, or talking to the client's guide dog without permission; avoid grabbing the client's cane or arm; allow the client to hold the counselor's arm just above the elbow as the client walks about a half-step behind; and avoid moving the client from a bright to a dark room and vice versa (American Health Assistance Foundation, 2012d, 2012e; Cascinai, 2012b; NFB, n.d.).

Each year, new and exciting technology becomes available to people with low vision; therefore, counselors will need to keep abreast of any new developments in this area. It may also be helpful to maintain an updated copy of catalogs of assistive devices. The counselor and client can use these catalogs in creative problem solving in the following manner: (a) the client describes, in detail, the tasks he or she is having difficulty with; (b) the counselor and client review the catalog to brainstorm for items that might be of assistance; (c) the client decides which items he or she might wish to purchase; (d) the counselor and client identify financial resources for such purchases and order the items; and (e) the counselor and client discuss the importance of obtaining consultation from an AT specialist to learn how to properly use the items. Often, local programs are available to help evaluate the need for aides and to show people how to use them. Follow-up is very important in the use of any type of aides, so counselors will want to ask their clients how these are working for them. It is also important for counselors and clients to know that there are many vendors of assistive devices, a few of whom even provide free items. Many of these resources can be found at http://www.ahaf.org/glaucoma or http://www.ahaf.org/macular.

Some older individuals with vision loss may wish to consider long-term living arrangements that provide assistance with daily living. Counselors, as case managers, can help individuals consider their options by taking into account their projected levels of care needs, their budget constraints, their favored locations, and the options that are available (American Health Assistance Foundation, 2012d, 2012e). The chapter on housing options (Chapter 12) includes information regarding a variety of considerations that must be taken into account when considering a residential change.

Counselors can act as advocates for seniors who have a visual loss. If they suspect that an older visually impaired person is being discriminated against in the areas of employment, housing, public transportation, public facilities, and so forth, they can encourage the client to contact a local or state disability law office or the NFB for assistance. Counselors can also use the techniques described in Chapter 3 to support their clients. One very simple but powerful form of advocacy is to demonstrate appropriate communication with blind clients (e.g., addressing them and asking them questions rather than asking their caregivers or family members; and speaking directly to them, adult-to-adult, rather than using a childlike voice).

Resources for Low-Vision or Blindness

American Academy of Ophthalmology (AAO), http://www.aao.org or 415-561-8500

American Council of the Blind, http://www.acb.org or 800-424-8666

American Foundation for the Blind, http://www.afb.org or 800-232-5463

American Macular Degeneration Foundation, http://www.macular.org or 413-268-7660

American Optometric Association (AOA), http://www.aoa.org or 800-365-2219

Association for Education and Rehabilitation of the Blind and Visually Impaired, http://www.aerbvi.org or 877-492-2708

Braille Institute of America, http://www.brailleinstitute.org or 800-272-4553

EyeCare America's Senior EyeCare Program, www.eyecareamerica.org

Foundation for Fighting Blindness, http://www.blindness.org or 888-394-3937

Glaucoma Foundation, http://www.glaucomafoundation.org

Lighthouse International, http://www.lighthouse.org or 800-829-0500

Lions Sight and Hearing Foundation, http://www.lions-sight-and-hearing-foundation.org

Low Vision Resource Kit for Seniors, NFB, http://www.nfb.org or 410-659-9314 ext. 2216

Macular Degeneration Support, http://www.mdsupport.org or 816-761-7080

National Glaucoma Research and Macular Degeneration Research, American Health Assistance Foundation, http://www.ahaf.org or 800-437-2423

National Library Services for the Blind and Physically Handicapped, http://www.loc.gov/nls/ or 888-657-7323

NFB Senior Division, http://www.nfb.org or 410-659-9314

The Seeing Eye, http://www.seeingeye.org or 973-539-4425

Vision Aware, http://www.visionaware.org or 914-528-5120

Vocational Rehabilitation Vision Specialists (addresses and titles vary by state)

Hearing Loss and Deafness

Late-onset hearing loss is relatively common among the older population, particularly among males (National Institute on Deafness and Other Communication Disorders, 2008). It has been reported that by age 54, approximately 14% of the population has a hearing loss (trouble hearing or deaf in one or both ears; Adams & Benson, 1992); by age 70, 20.7% of women and 33.9% of men have a hearing loss (Dillon et al., 2010). Other reports indicate that 25% of individuals who are ages 70 through 74 years and 50% of those who are age 85 years or older have a hearing loss (Cavanaugh & Blanchard-Fields, 2006). Deafness is less common. Approximately 5% of people ages 70 through 74 years and 17% of those 85 years or older experience deafness (Hoyer & Roodin, 2003).

The term used for late-onset hearing loss is *presbycusis*, and it is most commonly associated with damage to the inner ear. Conditions that can cause inner-ear damage include noise exposure, reactions to medications (e.g., myacins), strokes, heart disease, heredity, tumors or head injuries, poor health, zinc deficiency, Meniere's disease, the aging process itself, or any combination of these (Gant & Kampfe, 1997; Kampfe, 2009; Kampfe et al., 2007; Kampfe & Smith, 1999).

Regardless of the cause, late-onset hearing loss typically involves a slow degeneration of the nerve cells (sensorineural) in the cochlea and the eighth cranial nerve that connects the inner ear to the brain. Hence, hearing loss is sensorineural and results in the distortion of or inability to hear high-frequency sounds, especially those associated with speech (e.g., the letters *m*, *l*, and *p*). Because of this distortion of sound, increased volume does not usually help. Another implication of the distortion is that people cannot accurately hear their own voices or monitor the volume of their speech. Hence, they may progressively speak less distinctly and/or more loudly or softly than necessary (Hoyer & Roodin, 2003; Kampfe, 2009; Kampfe & Smith, 1997, 1998, 1999; S. M. Smith & Kampfe, 1997).

Late-onset hearing loss can be mild to profound and can affect one or both ears. Because of the slow progression of hearing loss and because presbycusis does not typically affect low-frequency sounds, many people are not aware that they have a hearing loss, or they may not realize how profound their loss is. Furthermore, because each ear may have a different level or type of loss, a person with a hearing loss will likely hear at different levels from each side of the head. This situation may result in inconsistent hearing, depending upon which ear is facing the sound source; in addition, it may cause others to question whether the person really does have a hearing loss (e.g., "He can hear when he wants to" and "She sometimes hears and then she doesn't"; Kampfe, 2009; Kampfe & Smith, 1998).

Speech discrimination is more difficult when ambient noise (background sound) is present. Furthermore, loud and persistent ambient noise can contribute to further deterioration of the inner-ear nerves. Examples of ambient noise include machine sounds, people speaking at the same time, radio, television, music, running water, and medical equipment such as a nebulizer or oxygen machine. Because ambient noise can have a negative effect on people's ability to hear, it is important to keep this type of noise at a minimum. Individuals with nerve damage may also experience recruitment, which is when one's perception of sound is exaggerated such that even though there is only a small increase in the noise levels, sound may seem much louder. The implication is that people may be bothered or surprised when this unexpected loudness happens, and they may interpret an increase in volume as a shout or some kind of warning signal (Kampfe, 1999).

In addition to presbycusis, older people may have outer-ear canal or middle-ear damage (conductive loss), which involves blockage of some sort in the outer ear, damage to the tympanic membrane (eardrum), or damage to the ossicles (middle-ear bones). This kind of loss is called *conductive loss* because the outer and middle ears conduct the sound waves, mechanically, to the inner ear. Because this type of loss is mechanical and not neurological, hearing aids, increased volume, and sometimes surgery may help.

In addition to hearing loss, older people may experience tinnitus and/or vertigo, which, in combination, can be quite debilitating (Kampfe, 2009). Tinnitus involves a whistling, roaring, hissing, or buzzing in the ears. These sounds can be persistent or intermittent, can range from soft to very loud, and can interfere with the ability to hear speech and other sounds. Furthermore, these head noises can be irritating and cause a great deal of stress. Tinnitus can be caused by a wide variety of conditions, such as middle-ear infection, reaction to medication, tumor, and high blood pressure. In addition, using alcohol, smoking, or being exposed to loud noises can accentuate head noises. Because of the wide range of possible causes for tinnitus, it is appropriate for counselors to suggest that clients with this condition consult a general physician and/or an otologist (Gant & Kampfe, 1997; Kampfe & Smith, 1999; National Institute on Deafness and Other Communication Disorders, 2008; Rothschild & Kampfe, 1997).

Vertigo involves a loss of balance or dizziness, typically because of problems in the inner ear. Vertigo can be mild or very severe, causing extreme dizziness, falls, and even the sense of physical illness and vomiting. Because vertigo involves so many symptoms, it can cause a great deal of difficulty with any activity (Kampfe, 2009; Kampfe & Smith, 1999). Again, medical diagnosis and treatment by an otologist or otorhynolaryngologist are important for this condition.

Activity: Simulated Hearing Loss

Counselors will have a much better understanding of what it is like to have presbycusis if they simulate this loss for themselves. The following activity is designed for this purpose.

1. Turn on a radio with the sound at normal volume.
2. Adjust it to simulate distortion of the speaker's voice and static or fuzzy background noises. No matter how loudly you set the volume, the station will still be out of tune and may be irritating to listen to.
3. Turn the volume down and try to listen to the program.
4. Next, turn on a humming/buzzing furnace, air conditioner, or some other machine (i.e., ambient noise) while listening to the out-of-tune radio.
5. Now imagine that two people enter the room talking with each other, and one of them is wearing a bracelet that rattles and jingles (i.e., more ambient noise).
6. At this point, it is likely that it will be very difficult to understand the program. It may be so difficult that you decide to turn the radio off and miss the whole thing. If this happens to you several times, you may even stop trying to hear at all.
7. Ask yourself about the kinds of psychosocial effects that this situation might have on a day-to-day or hour-to-hour basis, especially if the radio represents other people's one-to-one conversations with you.

Psychosocial Issues Associated With Late-Onset Hearing Loss or Deafness

To appreciate the psychosocial effects of hearing loss, it is helpful to understand the three functions of hearing: the primitive function, the warning or signs function, and the symbolic function (Kampfe, 2009; Kampfe & Smith, 1998).

The primitive function has to do with the unconscious awareness of one's own bodily noises (i.e., breathing, chewing, body movements) and subtle environmental sounds (i.e., creaking of a chair, sound of a cooler system). People with late-onset hearing loss may be unable to hear these sounds, which may result in a feeling of detachment from themselves and their environments and may ultimately lead to a sense of deadness or isolation at an unconscious level (Kampfe, 2009).

The signs or warning function provides a conscious level of awareness of the environment and of everyday signals such as alarms and doorbells. This function helps people prepare for events and respond appropriately. People with presbycusis may either be unable to hear these sounds or misinterpret what they hear because of distortion. For example, they may hear loud thunder and think it is a roaring car, or they may not hear a burglar or fire alarm or may misinterpret what the sound signifies. Inability to hear or misinterpretation of warning signals can lead to vulnerability, apprehension, real danger, disorientation, and faulty or inappropriate responses to sounds. These consequences may ultimately lead to isolation, loss of personal control over the environment, and misdiagnosis because of the seeming disorientation. The signs or warning level of hearing also involves the ability to hear pleasant sounds, such as laughter, music, and the sounds of nature. Not having these experiences may decrease quality of life, especially for those who have loved these sounds throughout their lives (Kampfe, 2009; Kampfe & Smith, 1998, 1999; S. M. Smith & Kampfe, 1997).

The symbolic function has to do with communication (both understanding speech and monitoring one's own speech sounds). It is the vital link between people. From a psychosocial perspective, loss of this function is perhaps the most devastating of all. Reduced ability to hear or understand speech may result in (a) concrete or simplistic communication that is less intellectually stimulating, less complex, and less rich than it was before the hearing loss; (b) reduced interaction and comfort levels with significant others; (c) reduced ability to access medical and other services; (d) lack of access to news programs; (e) being left out of important family discussions and decisions; (f) losing one's role in the family, community, or job environment; (g) having fewer opportunities to understand, disagree with, or sympathize with significant others; (h) having to increasingly rely on family members, friends, and service providers to obtain information and interact with members of the community; (i) being helped too much by significant others; and (j) being treated with impatience when communication is difficult. Furthermore, a hearing impaired person's misinterpretation of, or inappropriate response to, a conversation may be inaccurately perceived by others as a deterioration of intellectual abilities and may even result in a misdiagnosis of cognitive or behavioral issues (Hoyer & Roodin, 2003; Kampfe, 2009; Kampfe & Smith, 1997, 1998, 1999; M. A. Myers, 2012; S. M. Smith & Kampfe, 1997).

The interpersonal and environmental problems associated with a hearing loss can also result in intrapersonal issues. People with late-onset hearing loss may experience anxiety, depression, frustration, loneliness or isolation, loss of confidence, embarrassment, helplessness, disempowerment or lack of autonomy, self-consciousness, resentment, anger, and crankiness. Furthermore, loss of hearing may have strong connotations of being old in a youth-oriented culture, requiring individuals with this perception to accept not only the functional limitations associated with hearing loss, but also the negative connotations that they are becoming old (Kampfe, 2009; Kampfe & Smith, 1997, 1998, 1999; M. A. Myers, 2012; S. M. Smith & Kampfe, 1997).

It takes a great deal of energy and concentration to hear and understand speech and environmental sounds. Furthermore, individuals with late-onset hearing loss are faced with their own emotional reactions to the loss as well as the emotional and behavioral reactions of significant others. This situation may be accompanied by a need for additional energy to cope with other age-related physical conditions and a generally lower level of energy associated with the aging process. The result of these energy-draining situations may be fatigue, exhaustion, and withdrawal from situations in which they must verbally communicate (Kampfe, 2009; Kampfe & Smith, 1998; S. M. Smith & Kampfe, 1997).

It is also important to recognize that each person and family member will respond uniquely to the hearing loss, depending upon a number of variables, such as the type and degree of hearing loss, the person's and their significant others' perceptions of the hearing loss, the amount of support that is needed, the type of support or services available, the person's or significant others' basic coping strategies, and so forth. Because of this variability, counselors cannot assume that a client with a hearing loss or their families will respond in the same way as others respond.

Strategies for Counselors Working With Adults With Late-Onset Hearing Loss

Because of the loss of various functions associated with hearing and because of the potentially strong intrapersonal and intrapersonal issues associated with late-onset hearing loss, counselors can provide a variety of levels of assistance. At the case-management level, they can help clients identify methods, techniques, and mechanisms to deal with losses of their primitive, warning, and symbolic functions. More important, counselors can provide clients with the opportunity to discuss and work through thoughts and feelings associated with their hearing loss and its consequences.

Because many issues have to do with communication, counselors can encourage clients and their significant others to openly and frankly discuss their feelings about the hearing loss and strategies that can improve the situation. It might also be important for people with late-onset hearing loss and/or their families to join groups with similar issues. Typically, however, it is difficult for people with a late-onset hearing loss to meet in groups because of the tendency for group members to all speak at the same time, to move their heads backward and forward at each different person, and to switch speakers without notification. For this reason, ground rules for family and other group meetings need to ensure that the person with a hearing loss has access to what is being said. Such rules can include requiring that one person speaks at a time, the speaker or other members make some type of hand gesture to identify who is speaking, and the speaker waits until the person with a hearing loss can see his or her face. Although these types of rules can be frustrating for group members, they are vital to the person with a hearing loss. Therefore, at the beginning of each group session, it is important to discuss the rules in detail and to offer an explanation of why they are important. Another way to control the problems associated with group counseling or meetings is to keep groups very small and to meet in locations with good lighting and minimal ambient noise.

Counselors can also meet individually with clients or their family members to discuss their feelings and thoughts about the hearing loss and to explore strategies for dealing with decreased ability to hear. Because one-on-one verbal communication is vital in counseling, counselors need to use strategies to enhance this communication. There are many ways to do this, as outlined in the following sections.

Controlling the Environment

Counselors can enhance the hearing-impaired client's ability to hear and communicate by making a variety of changes to their offices, waiting rooms, or any environments where they meet with the client. These changes include containing or decreasing ambient noise, improving lighting, and using techniques that enhance speech recognition.

Because ambient noise can create tremendous problems for a person with a hearing loss, it is vital that counselors meet with clients where background noise is controlled or does not exist. Containing noise not only enhances the ability to communicate, but it also provides an atmosphere that is less stressful and exhausting for the client. Examples of ways to avoid or attenuate extraneous noise include meeting in a private room, meeting as far away from groups of people as possible, meeting in places that do not have noisy equipment, turning off noisy machines, keeping necessary equipment oiled and running smoothly, and asking the client to sit with his or her back to a wall in order to avoid reflection of room sounds. Noise can also be reduced by placing soft materials on all hard surfaces (e.g., soft, textured ceiling tiles or sprays; textured wallpaper; carpeted floors; curtained or draped windows; cloth-covered furniture; and padded chairs; Kampfe, 1990a, 2009; Kampfe & Smith, 1999; S. M. Smith & Kampfe, 1996).

Proper lighting is also important because poor lighting can impede the client's ability to see the counselor's mouth and lips and to pick up any facial or hand gestures that the counselor makes. Examples of poor lighting are glaring light, dim light, light that shines directly into the client's face, and flickering light. The room should be set up such that windows are not behind the counselor but rather are to the side of or behind the client. Counselors can also ask clients if the light is bothering them and can move chairs or adjust the lighting accordingly (Kampfe, 1990a, 2009; Kampfe & Smith, 1999; S. M. Smith & Kampfe, 1996, 1997).

Counselors can advocate for noise control and proper lighting with family members and service providers (e.g., medical rooms, receptionist desks, long-term care facilities, community meeting places). From an empowerment perspective, it will also be important for clients and their families, themselves, to advocate for noise attenuation and proper lighting. They can also make their own homes and places of business less noisy and easier in which to hear or see by following the above practices (Kampfe, 2009).

Counselor Communication Behaviors

Counselors can practice the following behaviors that will enhance communication with their clients: look directly at the client, be sure the client is focusing on the counselor's face before speaking, use appropriate facial expressions, use hand gestures for clarity, keep one's voice at a deeper tone or pitch, sit or stand no more than 4 feet away from and at the same level as the client, speak somewhat slowly (but not too slowly), provide contextual cues (e.g., pointing, introducing a subject matter) to ensure that the client knows the topic of conversation, use short phrases instead of single words, and enunciate clearly without exaggerating the lip movements. It is important for counselors to check in with clients to be sure they understand what the counselor has said and to invite them to ask the counselor to repeat statements when needed (Kampfe, 1990a, 2009; Kampfe & Smith, 1999).

Counselors should also avoid a number of practices when communicating with a person who has late-onset hearing loss. For example, they should avoid quickly changing the topic, speaking at a rapid pace, turning their heads back and forth or up and down while talking, allowing hair to cover the face (e.g., long hair or facial hair), exaggerating facial or mouth movements, placing objects or hands over their faces, and chewing gum or eating food. Counselors should also be aware that people who have late-onset hearing loss may shake their heads as if they are nonverbally saying "yes" when, in fact, the up-and-down head motion is an effort to concentrate and consider what is being said. These seemingly positive head shakes may be misinterpreted by the counselor to mean that the client understands or agrees with the counselor. Counselors should therefore not assume that this particular body language means that the message has been understood (Kampfe, 1990a, 2009; Kampfe & Smith, 1999).

Counselors also need to remain cognizant of the wide variety of conditions that might influence a client's ability to understand speech and to communicate with the counselor. Variables such as level and type of hearing loss, age of onset of the loss, visual acuity, familiarity with the counselor, knowledge of the topic and vocabulary, presence and degree of tinnitus, energy level, other medical conditions, and medications being taken can all influence an individual's ability to understand speech (Kampfe, 2009).

When clients do not understand what has been said, counselors can rephrase the sentence rather than repeat it exactly as said the first time. This rephrasing is helpful because some words are more difficult to hear or lip read, and rephrasing may provide words and sounds that are easier to see and hear than the ones that were not understood. Counselors and clients can also communicate in writing using technology that is comfortable for them (e.g., paper and pencil, computer). This type of communication may be particularly useful if they are discussing lists or a complex number of things. The method of communication methods should be the clients' choice, so counselors can ask clients their preference. Being asked this question can contribute to clients' sense of personal power, which might counteract the disempowering situations they may be encountering elsewhere (Kampfe, 1990a, 2009; Kampfe & Smith, 1999).

Remembering that it takes a great deal of energy just to understand speech, counselors can be watchful for signs of client fatigue and exhaustion during counseling sessions. One sign of fatigue may be reduced ability to understand verbal communication as the session progresses. Counselors can respect this and perhaps shorten the sessions to meet the client's needs or suggest a short break within a counseling session. Counselors may need to schedule more sessions because of the communication barrier and the exhaustion that accompanies it. Counselors might also wish to monitor and ameliorate their own potential feelings of impatience or irritation because of having to repeat themselves and to take longer for communication to occur. In other words, they may need to find ways to remain relaxed, calm, positive, and patient (Kampfe, 1990a, 2009; Kampfe & Smith, 1999).

Counselor–Client Focus on Hearing Loss

Because of the potential interpersonal and intrapersonal problems that can result from late-onset hearing loss, it may be important to focus on clients' feelings about the loss, to allow them to mourn the loss, and to provide an accepting and supportive environment as they do so. Counselors can also invite hearing-impaired clients to identify possible strategies that they can use to improve communication with other people (symbolic level), to gain environmental information (warning level), and to be more aware of unconscious sound (primitive level). For example, clients may wish to consider the positives and negatives of obtaining training in lip reading, of having an ear examination from an otologist or an otorhinolaryngologist, or of getting a hearing evaluation from an audiologist (not a hearing aid dealer).

Counselors can ask clients to consider the efficacy and their comfort levels associated with strategies that have been shown to improve communication. These strategies include informing other people of their hearing loss, letting speakers know that they do not understand what was just said, repeating or paraphrasing a speaker's statement to be sure that they understood the message, and asking the speaker if "X" is what they just said. Clients can also consider asking speakers to look directly at them, clarify the topic of conversation before continuing, enunciate more clearly, speak without raising the volume of their voices, repeat what they just said using different words, move to a quieter room or place in the room where it is easier to hear and see, meet in public places (e.g., dinner at a restaurant) during a non-busy time, and meet in places that have good acoustics (Kampfe, 1999, 2009; M. A. Myers, 2012).

The counselor and client may wish to use brainstorming to identify assistive devices, which are rapidly being developed to ameliorate communication problems. The list of these devices is vast, yet many clients may not be aware of them. Each year, new computer and telecommunication devices and programs are developed that do not require hearing for communication, and these are sometimes offered at no cost to people with a hearing loss. Communication aids include a vast variety of hearing aids (which are now very sophisticated), telephone systems, computer systems, and cochlear implants (for those who are deaf). Closed captioning (i.e., written text that provides the dialogue and descriptions of background sound effects) can be available on television and in movie theaters. Certain public meeting places (e.g., lecture halls, movies theaters) can send sound directly to hearing aids (e.g., induction loops or room loops; Kampfe, 2009).

Clients may also want to explore devices that can help with their awareness of the environment. There are many alternatives to the traditional warning devices, such as smoke detectors, fire alarms, alarm clocks, and doorbells. Often these alternatives involve vibrating alarms, flashing lights, or assistive animals (Kampfe, 2009).

There are several very important points to consider regarding any type of assistive device or practice. It must be remembered that presbycusis involves a broad range of hearing problems. Furthermore, people will have various levels of comfort with, and abilities to use, technology. These broad ranges of hearing loss and comfort levels, combined with the wide array of technological devices, can create either a mismatch or a perfect match between a person's needs and the technology he or she eventually uses. Hence, a great deal of thought and exploration of alternatives should go into choices of technology. Counselors and clients can obtain assistance with these choices from a variety of sources, including audiologists, otologists, local hearing loss associations, the Job Accommodation Network, the National Institute on Deafness and Other Communication Disorders (NIDCD), rehabilitation technologists, speech therapists, specially trained occupational therapists, and local support groups or organizations that focus on late-onset hearing loss (Center for Disability Law, 2012; Kampfe, 2009). It is very helpful to visit local nonprofit organizational offices, which often have examples of technology available for examination. These organizations might also allow individuals to try a device at home and/or provide training in its use. Again, the keys to successful use of technology are appropriate match between the person's needs and the technology, the level of comfort in using the technology, training in its use, and follow-up (Kampfe, 2009). See Chapter 2 for additional information about AT.

In addition to being alert to the possibility of hearing loss among clients, counselors also need to be alert to the potential for tinnitus. Because this condition can interfere with speech comprehension, counselors and clients can brainstorm to identify strategies to reduce these head noises. For example, because smoking and alcohol use can exaggerate tinnitus, clients may decide to obtain assistance in reducing intake of these. Because stress has been known to exacerbate tinnitus, counselors may wish to use counseling strategies that focus on reduction of stress, meditation, or other relaxation techniques. Other suggestions for obtaining relief from tinnitus are the use of music or white noise machines that mask the head noises (Kampfe, 2009; Kampfe & Smith, 1999).

Clients may wish to discuss their vertigo if applicable. In addition to discussing this potentially intense experience and how it affects clients' lives, counselors can help them brainstorm to find appropriate service providers who can evaluate their condition. For example, they may need to identify a local balance disorder clinic, an otologist, or a general medical doctor who is knowledgeable about this condition. They may also need to learn about and use organizations that can provide information and support regarding balance problems and how to control them (e.g., the Vestibular Disorders Association or the Meniere's Network; Kampfe, 1999; Kampfe & Smith, 1999).

Counselors who are working with friends and family members of people with late-onset hearing loss can focus on a variety of content areas and levels of feeling. In addition to offering them the opportunity to discuss their frustrations, worries, and sometimes anger, counselors can provide information to help them understand the implications of a hearing loss as well understand the implications of their own behaviors toward the person with a hearing loss. For example, significant others may have been excluding clients from conversations, talking around them rather than having conversations with them, or failing to use strategies that will improve communication with them.

Resources for Hearing Loss and Deafness

American Tinnitus Association, http://www.ata.org

Lions Sight and Hearing Foundation, http://www.lions-sight-and-hearing-foundation.org

Menieres.org, http://www.menieres.org/

National Institute on Deafness and Other Communication Disorders (NIDCD), http://www.nidcd.gov/

Vestibular Disorders Association, http://www.vestibular.org

Loss of the Sense of Touch

The sense of touch involves the ability to perceive mechanical stimuli (e.g., tactile, vibration), temperature, pressure, pain, body position in space, and localization. More simply stated, touch alerts people to movement, pain, temperature, and so forth. The loss of touch can occur throughout the exterior portions of the body (e.g., hands, feet, upper arms, lips, skin) as well as in the mouth. Although older people may lose the sense of touch, this sense is the one that is considered to be the most likely to remain intact (Casciani, 2012a; Wickremaratchi & Llewelyn, 2006). It is also important to note that loss in one area (e.g., the foot) does not mean loss in some other part of the body (e.g., the forearm).

Practitioners often discuss the loss of touch as a "high tolerance for" or "high threshold to/of" certain sensations, such as sharp or prickly objects, heat, and vibration. For example, clients may be described as having a high tolerance for pain or a high threshold of pain when they have a reduced ability to feel pain. Counselors need to be aware that clients with high tolerance to pain may be at risk because they do not receive warning signals of potential danger or are not aware that they have hurt themselves. Likewise, counselors need to know that people who have been described as having a "high threshold to vibration intensities" will have less ability to feel vibrations. In other words, high tolerance or threshold to a particular sensation means low ability to feel that particular sensation (Wickremaratchi & Llewelyn, 2006).

One of the most common and pronounced losses of touch is in the feet, affecting 24% of people age 70 to 79 years and 34.3% of those age 80 years or older (Dillon et al., 2010). Peripheral sensation in the feet is very important to postural stability; consequently, this type of loss can lead to tripping or falling, especially if the individual has other conditions that affect balance or motor function (e.g., arthritis, cerebrovascular disease, or vertigo; Casciani, 2012a; Wickremaratchi & Llewelyn, 2006). As noted in Chapter 5, falls are the primary reason that older people make medical emergency visits, are hospitalized, or have injury-related deaths. Thus, the loss of touch in the feet can be critical to older people's well-being.

The loss of touch and sensitivity in the hands (especially the fingertips) is also one of the most common losses experienced by older people. The loss of sensitivity in the hands can be attributable to a complex variety of conditions of the nervous system and can be experienced as diminished sensitivity and difficulty with fine manipulations. In addition to losing sensitivity in the hands, older people can experience a number of other conditions, such as reduced finger and hand strength, ability to maintain a pinch, and finger and hand speed. These types of losses can lead to decreased ability to do fine-motor activities, lessened ability to use hands for support or balance, and decreased hand grip, with ultimate results of burning oneself, dropping things, or being unaware that one has hurt oneself in these areas (Casciani, 2012a; Wickremaratchi & Llewelyn, 2006). Earlier in this chapter, I suggested that people can use their sense of touch to assist them when they have lost their vision or have decreased vision. Unfortunately, older people who have lost their sense of touch may not be able to utilize this sense to help them sense their environment.

The loss of touch in the lips and palate or other oral areas can affect older people's ability to articulate speech sounds and therefore can interfere with communication with significant others and service providers (Wickremaratchi & Llewelyn, 2006). This loss—especially in conjunction with a significant hearing loss that affects people's ability to hear their own speech or a left brain stroke that affects people's ability to speak—can create tremendous communication difficulties.

Overall, then, the loss of the sense of touch in various parts of the body can have a variety of negative outcomes. These losses, in conjunction with other conditions associated with aging, can result in a wide range of safety issues for older people. For example, older people may not experience pain until their skin has been damaged, may bruise or tear their skin without being aware of it, may not treat a cut or blister because they do not feel it, may not be aware that they need to wear a coat because they do not feel that the temperature is cold, may have reduced reaction time because of their lack of awareness of the need for action, may have difficulty picking up or working with small objects, may have difficulty differentiating between small objects such as buttons and coins, may have problems writing, may have problems with toileting, and may generally have overall difficulty with tasks that require fine dexterity (Kemmet & Brotherson, 2008; Wickremaratchi & Llewelyn, 2006).

Loss of the Sense of Smell

The ability to smell typically decreases with age. For example, about 5% of the general population experiences the loss of the sense of smell, whereas about 25% of people who are age 50 years or older experience this loss. The loss of the sense of smell is often a progressively slow process; therefore, as people age, they may not be aware of the loss. Women of all ages are more likely to have higher levels of olfactory sensitivity and to be more aware of odors such as body odors and the smell of food than men. Furthermore, men are more likely than women to lose the sense of smell (Hummel, Landis, & Hüttenbrink, 2011; Kemmet & Brotherson, 2008). There are several terms for the loss of the sense of smell (i.e., *anosmia* = lack of ability to smell; *syposmia* = reduced ability to smell; *parosmia* = misperceiving a smell; and *phantosmia* = smelling things that do not exist in the environment), and all of these types can be disconcerting. Another method of classification for loss of smell is based on whether or not the loss is experienced daily, is intense, or results in notable consequences (e.g., weight loss or gain; Hummel et al., 2011).

The sense of smell (olfactory sensitivity) has several functions: interpersonal communication, warning of danger, enjoyment or dislike, effect on mood, and enhanced taste when eating and drinking. The sense of smell is also the source of odor memories (i.e., memories that people experience when they smell certain scents). Associated with the sense of smell is the trigeminal sensation that identifies the sense of cooling, tingling, or sharpness of something that is eaten (Hummel et al., 2011; Kemmet & Brotherson, 2008).

Without the sense of smell, people lose or have a reduced ability to detect pleasant or unpleasant odors (of themselves, others, and the environment) and to detect dangerous smells (e.g., smoke, gas leaks). Furthermore, the sense of smell is closely linked with the sense of taste, influencing people's ability to detect the delicious, distasteful, dangerous, and other qualities of items that they put into their mouths. Because the sense of smell offers many opportunities to enjoy the environment (e.g., scent of flowers, food, children, loved ones, fresh air, mowed grass, rain, perfume, candles, vanilla), the loss of smell can be associated with a lower quality of life (Kemmet & Brotherson, 2008). For example, in some cases, people who experience loss of smell have been found to also have symptoms of depression (Hummel et al., 2011).

The physiology associated with the sense of smell is very complex and has to do with both mechanical and neurological functions. Hence, the loss of smell can be associated with one or more health problems, and people with loss of smell may have a shorter life expectancy, depending upon the cause of the loss. For example, loss of smell can be caused by the following: certain medications; head trauma; vitamin A or B12 deficiency; viral infections of the upper respiratory tract; allergies; exposure to toxic chemicals; congenital insomnia; certain psychiatric conditions (e.g., depression and schizophrenia); endocrine disorders, such as liver failure, kidney failure, diabetes, or hypothyroidism; obstructing polyps; inflammation; neurosurgery; brain tumors; lupus erythematosus; smoking; and neurological conditions, such as Alzheimer's disease, Parkinson's disease, Huntington's disease, and Lewy-Body Dementia. The loss of sense of smell is so closely linked to idiopathic Parkinson's syndrome and Alzheimer's disease that it may be an early symptom of these diseases. The important point is that clients, counselors, and family members need to be aware that the loss of the sense of smell may be a signal for some other medical issue; thus, a thorough medical, neurological evaluation may be needed (Bromley, 2000; Casciani, 2012a; Hummel et al., 2011; Kemmet & Brotherson, 2008).

Because the loss of the sense of smell can have many negative consequences, counselors should be prepared to discuss people's feelings associated with this loss in the same way that they would discuss other losses. Counselors might also wish to use creative problem solving to help clients and their families decide what types of protective measures they wish to take to avoid the dangers associated with the loss of the sense of smell. For example, they may wish to install smoke and gas detectors and to regularly check cupboards and refrigerators for spoiled food (Casciani, 2012a; Kemmet & Brotherson, 2008).

Loss of the Sense of Taste

Loss of the sense of taste is a slow process and has been associated with advanced age (Bromley, 2000). Typically, a person who is age 30 will have approximately 245 taste buds per papilla (i.e., tiny elevations on the tongue), whereas a person who is age 70 will have approximately 88 taste buds per papilla. The tastes of sweet and salty appear to be affected first; therefore, older people may be inclined to add salt to their food to enhance the flavor (Kemmet & Brotherson, 2008).

As with all other senses, the sense of taste is complex, involving the central nervous system and other parts of the body. Furthermore, taste receptors are located in a variety of places in the body, including the tongue, the palate, the oropharynx, the epiglottis, and the small intestine. Sensations from these are transported to the brain via cranial nerves. Other aspects of taste such as texture, spiciness, and temperature are sent to the brain via several pathways (Hummel et al., 2011; Kemmet & Brotherson, 2008). Although loss of the sense of taste is commonly experienced by older people, it has also been associated with conditions such as head trauma, glossodynia (i.e., burning mouth syndrome), epilepsy, schizophrenia, dysgeusia (taste disturbance), lung tumors, Bell's palsy, upper respiratory tract infections, bulimia, Cushing's syndrome, liver disease, diabetes mellitus, and hypothyroidism. The loss of the sense of taste can also be caused by oral appliances (e.g., dentures), dental procedures, oral infections, medications, smoking, poor oral hygiene, and chewing tobacco (Bromley, 2000; Casciani, 2012a; Hummel et al., 2011).

Like the sense of smell, the sense of taste has three functions: interpersonal communication, warning of danger, and eating and drinking (Hummel et al., 2011). Hence, the loss of the sense of taste can have a dramatic negative effect on quality of life and health. People may find that food no longer tastes pleasant, or that it is bland or unappetizing. Thus, they may reduce the amount of food they eat or stop eating, increasing the risk of dehydration and malnutrition. They may also tend to add salt to their diet, increasing their risk of high blood pressure. Furthermore, people who are unable to detect distasteful flavors run the risk of eating foods that are spoiled or bitter (Bromley, 2000; Casciani, 2012a; Hummel et al., 2011).

Counselors may wish to discuss the implications of the loss of the sense of taste with their clients and discuss ways to enhance the eating experience, such as adding herbs; preparing foods with contrasting textures, flavors, colors, and temperatures (Kemmet & Brotherson, 2008); serving food in the most attractive manner to enhance the visual response (Saisan, Smith, et al., 2012); and eating with other people. It is also be important that counselors are aware of the possible causes of taste disorders and suggest that the client get a medical examination. A resource that offers information about the loss of the sense of smell is the Olfactory Research Fund, Ltd. (http://www.olfactory.org).

Multisensory Loss

The literature on multisensory loss typically focuses primarily on the loss of vision and hearing. The prevalence of self-reported dual sensory impairment (DSI) among older individuals is not yet definitively known. Brennan, Horowitz, and Sue (2005) found that 21% of individuals age 70 years or older reported having a loss of both hearing and vision; however, degree of loss was not discussed. A study of veterans, using objective measures of hearing and vision loss, found that the DSI rate was from 1% to 4% of those age 65 through 74 years, from 9% to 13% of those age 75 through 84 years, and from 22% to 26% of those age 85 years or older (S. L. Smith, Bennett, & Wilson, 2008).

With DSI, especially when the losses of each sense are severe, communication and interaction with the environment are extremely difficult because individuals are not able to use the alternate sense (hearing or seeing) to compensate for the other loss. This situation can result in significant functional limitations, extreme isolation, and a combination of psychosocial issues associated with both hearing loss and vision loss (Chia et al., 2006; Kampfe, 2009; Kampfe & Smith, 1997, 1998, 1999; S. L. Smith et al., 2008; S. M. Smith & Kampfe, 1997). Because of their functional limitations, individuals with severe multiple sensory losses may experience confinement to a chair, bed, or room without environmental clues regarding the time of day, activities around them, and changes in their environment. This extreme sensory deprivation may cause people to become severely disoriented and lonely and to resort to behaviors such as rhythmic rocking or pounding, chanting, and calling out in order to gain some control of their environment or to self-stimulate. Unfortunately, these behaviors may be misperceived as symptoms of dementia or psychosis. Family members and staff may also resort to simple assistance rather than some form of comforting and loving interaction or may avoid the person who is displaying these behaviors. These actions only exacerbate the sensory deprivation experience (Casciani, 2012a, 2012b).

Because of these types of circumstances, DSI can have devastating consequences, such as depression, apathy, and low quality of life. People with DSI have been found to have more depressive symptoms (Capella-McDonnall, 2005; Lupsakko, Mantyjarvi, Kautiainen, & Sulkava, 2002), a lower health-related quality of life (Chia et al., 2006), and a higher level of mortality (Lam, Lee, Gomez-Marin, Zheng, & Caban, 2006) than those without DSI.

Programs and specialists for DSI are rare. This is a serious situation because typically, neither specialists in hearing loss/deafness nor specialists in vision loss/blindness have received extensive training in the loss of the other sense. Their techniques often involve teaching people to use the one sense to compensate for the loss of the other sense; therefore, these techniques either no longer work or are less effective (S. L. Smith et al., 2008). Fortunately, DSI was finally listed in the International Classification of Diseases manual in 2007 (9th revision; i.e., the ICD-9-CM), which is an indication that DSI is now a medically recognized issue that will, it is hoped, receive more attention, more research funds, and more service development (http://www.cdc.gov and http://www.cms.hhs.gov).

Counselors, as case managers, can identify DSI programs and specialists through their state or governor's advisory councils on deafness/blindness. These councils have various titles and may be composed of clients, family members, educators, administrators, rehabilitation specialists, sign language interpreters or teachers, and others who are interested in improving conditions for people of all ages with DSI.

It is hoped that individuals with DSI will have access to their other senses (touch, taste, smell), which can provide environmental clues. For example, the use of touch will be vital for verbal, intellectual, and emotional communication. If clients are interested and motivated, they can begin to write messages on a notepad and receive messages written on their palms with a finger. They might also wish to learn Braille, to use a computer to type messages and to receive various forms of messages (e.g., raised letters), or to use interpreters who are skilled in communicating with people who are deaf and blind.

One excellent, almost vital, resource is a support service provider (SSP). SSPs can give medical assistance; tend to activities in the home; and assist with social interaction, recreational activities, vacations, financial issues, shopping, errands, and other business-related needs. SSPs can also provide help with understanding the spoken word, participating in meetings, using transportation, going to sports events and restaurants, and dealing with emergencies and grooming (e.g., applying makeup; Arizona Governor's Council on Blindness and Visual Impairment, Deaf-Blind Committee, 2011).

Although SSPs can provide a vital function for people with deafness and blindness, some people are not aware of their services. In a survey of 25 individuals with a combination of significant hearing and vision losses, the Arizona Governor's Council on Blindness and Visual Impairment, Deaf-Blind Committee (2011) found that only 67% of the participants used SSP services. Respondents who used SSP services indicated that they were so valuable they would like to have them for additional time (1 to 21 more hours) each week. Counselors, as case managers, can identify and contact SSPs in order to help clients gain access to these important service providers.

Because SSPs have the skills to assist with communication, they can potentially provide a vital link between the counselor and the client. When using an SSP, counselors will need to ask about the appropriate etiquette in their use. For example, counselors should communicate directly with the client (using "I" and "you" statements) instead of speaking directly to the SSP (e.g., "Tell him that I . . ."; "Does he want . . . "). Other resources include sign language interpreters. Some of these specialists may have received training in methods to communicate with people who are both deaf and blind.

Touch is a very important method of communicating with people with DSI. Type of touch is also important. For example, a pat on the cheek or the head can be patronizing, condescending, and de-humanizing, whereas a touch on the hand or arm can be helpful. Furthermore, touch should only be used to the degree to which a client is comfortable with it (Casciani, 2012a; Loe, 2011). As in-dicated in the Chapter 9, counselors will need to obtain individual consultation from other counselors or their professional counseling association regarding this issue. Perhaps because counselors are gener-ally discouraged from touching clients, an alternative can be to work with family members, significant others, and other service providers to consider the importance of touch and the degree to which they feel comfortable using it.

Summary

People who have knowledge about their sensory losses will be more likely to cope with these losses as they age (Kemmet & Brotherson, 2008). Counselors can help individuals and their families develop this knowledge. Because sensory losses can be caused by a number of medical conditions, counselors can advocate for a correct diagnosis. Counselors can also encourage consumers and their significant others to engage in creative problem solving to identify professionals who can provide practical advice about and assistance with their losses. Another very important counselor function is to help consumers and their family members express and work through their feelings associated with sensory losses and eventually come to some degree of acceptance of and adjustment to the situation. In this process, it is not appropriate to assume that reaching acceptance of a loss will be a quick fix; it is also not appropriate for the counselor to minimize the hurt and unpleasantness of the loss or losses (Casciani, 2012a, 2012b). Finally, counselors must learn and practice communication and other strategies that will strengthen their ability to interact with their clients who have sensory losses.

Chapter 9
Maintaining and Managing Interpersonal Relationships

The desire for a sense of belonging seems to be universal and may even be vital to people's well-being. For example, the sense of belonging and concern about family members has been found to have a strong relationship to older people's reasons for living (Gadalla, 2009; Kissane & McLaren, 2006). Furthermore, a survey conducted by AARP (L. L. Fisher, 2010) showed that close ties to friends and family are very important to quality of life. Among individuals age 60 to 69, 96% of males and 97% of females indicated such ties were important, and among those age 70 or older, 100% of males and 99% of females reported the same. Both quantity and quality of social support are important to older people (Berg, Hassing, McClearn, & Johnasson, 2006), and being supported by people who value the older person is likely to contribute to that person's sense of self-esteem, value, psychological well-being, and perhaps even physical performance (Bailis & Chipperfield, 2002; Kim & Nesselroade, 2002).

In contrast, social isolation is associated with major clinical depression and suicidal tendencies (Morrissey & Krahn, 1995). Unfortunately, loneliness may be a somewhat common experience for older people, especially for those who are very old (i.e., centenarians). Among older people, the following conditions have been found to be related to loneliness: depression (J. Golden et al., 2009); tension and apprehension, high systolic blood pressure, and poor physical health (Hawkley et al., 2010); and forgetfulness or confusion (Alzheimer's Disease Education and Referral Center, 2012a, 2012b).

Although staying connected with others contributes to healthy aging, it is sometimes not easy to do so. Situations such as illness, death of significant others or friends, retirement, moves to new locations, transportation issues, and changes in support networks can all limit older people's opportunities to interact with others (Saisan, Smith, et al., 2012). The purpose of this chapter is to focus on a wide range of issues associated with interpersonal connectedness. Broad topics include interpersonal relationships with family, extended family, and friends; lesbian, gay, bisexual, and transgender (LGBT) issues; caregiving (which is typically a family matter); and sexuality/physical intimacy.

Interpersonal Relationships With Family, Extended Family, and Friends

As indicated in Chapter 2, people's cultures may have a strong influence on their views of older people's roles, responsibilities, relationships, and values within their community (Kampfe et al., 2007). For example, one group may believe that taking care of their elders is expected, whereas another group may see this as unnecessary and may even consider it a burden. One group may see elders as community or family leaders, whereas another group may devalue older people. One group may desire to be with their elders, whereas another group may avoid them. One group may see their elders as having wisdom, whereas another group may disregard their opinions. One group may view their elders as the central focus of family activities and decisions, whereas another group may largely ignore older people in activities and decisions. Furthermore, as our society and culture change, so do people's attitudes and practices. What was culturally expected in the past may no longer apply. For example, in 2012, Hmong immigrants, as a group, had lived in Wisconsin for approximately 30 years. Because of their traditions, older people expected to be "taken care of" by their children; however, after moving to the United States, conditions and perspectives changed for the upcoming generation, resulting in disappointment among elders because they were not receiving the support they had expected (Xiong, 2012).

Physical closeness, touch, and hugs are important aspects of interpersonal relationships. Older people, however, may not have the opportunity for such physical closeness because of ageism, loss of loved ones, distance from family, or single status. Touch from family members may be especially important; however, physical contact with older relatives may be uncomfortable for younger ones. Because many older people may be touch deprived, touch can be therapeutic (Casciani, 2012a; Loe, 2011). Counselors can ask family members about their perceptions of the client's need for physical contact and to consider the degree to which they, themselves, feel comfortable with touching, hugging, and kissing older family members. In these discussions, they can be invited to read Loe's (2011) opinions about the important need for touch among older people.

Another important aspect of interpersonal relationship involves one's sense of autonomy. The sense of autonomy is a strong predictor of psychological well-being; therefore, family members and friends need to be mindful and respectful of the need for older people to maintain a balance between support and independence. To gain balance, family members can let their relatives know that they are willing to help but avoid forcing help on them. They can also trust their elders to do things for themselves and make their own decisions when feasible. Some older people may attempt to maintain control of their lives by manipulating those around them, by being stubborn about what they want to do, and perhaps by risking safety in order to be independent. Family members may be frustrated by these behaviors, but counselors can help them understand that these actions may be demonstrations of positive coping or signs that older people are feeling disempowered. In this case, counselors may need to explore the degree to which disempowerment is occurring and work with family members to show them the importance of trusting their older relatives to make decisions for themselves. Furthermore, if family members have begun to speak to their parents or grandparents as if they were children, counselors can discuss the importance of talking adult-to-adult with their older family members. Family members, friends, and caregivers also need to be watchful for others (e.g., health care professionals, service providers, waiters, etc.) who speak "across" older people or disempower them. When this happens, family members can redirect the speaker to their parent or grandparent or can demonstrate respectful behavior (e.g., "Dad, what do you think about that?" "Mom, which menu item looks good?"; Hope Heart Institute, n.d.).

As indicated throughout this book, loss is a common experience among older people, and the multiple losses older people experience are cumulative. It is therefore important for family members and friends to offer support for such losses. Although counselors know the importance of allowing clients to grieve in their own ways (Shallcross, 2012c), it is also important for family members, friends, and other service providers to be aware of this need. Counselors can help significant others understand that being cheerful (e.g., putting on a happy face) when people need to talk about their losses can stifle their abilities to work through their feelings. Rather than trying to change how older people feel about a loss, family members and friends can assist them by respectfully and seriously listening to their thoughts and feelings and by allowing them to fully express themselves (Hope Heart Institute, n.d.).

Older people can have many interpersonal roles. For example, they may be husbands or wives, life partners, daughters or sons, mothers or fathers, grandparents, great-grandparents, great-great-grandparents, aunts or uncles, brothers or sisters, cousins, extended family members, or friends. As older people and their family members or friends age, their roles and relationships may also change. The remainder of this section of the chapter focuses on the following subtopics associated with some of these roles or role changes: marriage, divorce, cohabitation, intergenerational interaction, and extended families and friends. This section also includes a discussion of additional counseling strategies that focus on interpersonal issues.

Marriage

A 2009 report of U.S. citizens who were ages 65 or older indicated that more men (72%) than women (42%) were married and living with their spouses (Administration on Aging, 2009). Marriage is legally defined as a sanctioned union between two people. Because it involves a legal agreement, partners are typically given automatic privileges to share many things, such as income, savings, homes, cars, income tax payments, health care benefits, a last name, and insurance benefits. Husbands and wives also generally inherit their spouse's estate automatically, and they are typically given the power to make decisions about each other's medical care as well as the responsibility for any debts that a spouse may have. Marriage is also defined as an emotional relationship between partners. This aspect of marriage involves intimacy and human interaction and may or may not be legally sanctioned (Whitbourne & Whitbourne, 2011).

Regardless of definitions, a large body of research has shown a positive relationship between marriage and quality of life. Studies have shown that married older adults had lower mortality rates (i.e., 9% to 15%; Manzoli, Villari, Pirone, & Boccia, 2007) and higher degrees of happiness than nonmarried older adults (Wood, Goesling, & Avellar, 2007). Furthermore, L. L. Fisher (2010) found that having a good relationship with a spouse or partner was important to older people. Among those age 60–69, 94% of men and 83% of women indicated that a good relationship with a spouse or partner was important to their quality of life. Among those age 70 or older, 94% of men and 81% of women indicated that this was so. This same group was asked how emotionally satisfying their relationships were with their partners. Responses were similar across ages and gender. Among people age 60–69, 57% of both men and women indicated that their relationships were very to extremely satisfying. Among those age 70 or older, 51% of men and 55% of women indicated the same. Conversely, 15% of men and 17% of women age 70 or older indicated that their relationships were not satisfying at all.

Taken together, these findings indicate that for some older people (especially those who are age 70 or older), there may be a considerable gap between perceived importance of relationships with a spouse or partner and the actual satisfaction with these relationships.

Implications are that counselors may need to focus on interpersonal relationships among partners, especially for clients who are age 70 or older. Additional information about partners is provided later in this chapter under the section Caregiving of Older People and the section Sexuality/Physical Intimacy Among Older Individuals.

Divorce

The U.S. rate of divorce (defined as being currently divorced) has increased among the middle-aged and older population. Among people age 50 and above, the rate doubled from 1990 to 2010 (Brown & Lin, 2013). The divorce rate is much lower for older adults than for middle-aged adults; however, it has also risen over the years. For example, among people age 65 and older, the rate increased from 5% to 10% among men and from 4% to 12% among women from 1980 to 2008 (Manning & Brown, 2011). It must be noted that current marital status is not a measure of a new divorce (i.e., incidence of divorce). For example, many of the people who are currently divorced may have become divorced many years ago.

Approximately one in four of the new divorces in 2010 were among people who were age 50 or older (Brown & Lin, 2013), and these divorces were much more likely to happen among the middle-aged individuals than among older individuals (Amato, 2010; Brown & Lin, 2013). It has been speculated that an increase in the number of new divorces (incidence) will occur for several reasons: the cohort of middle-aged and older people may be more accepting of divorce than the cohorts that came before them (McDermott, Fowler, & Christakis, 2009); many older people may have remarried, and the divorce rate is much higher for people who remarry than for those who have been married to only one partner (Brown & Lin, 2013; Sweeney, 2010); women have developed more economic independence than in the past (Brown & Lin, 2013); marriages are more difficult to maintain in light of the individualism of our society; our society has a belief that people do not need to remain in a relationship that is empty (Wu & Schimmele, 2007); and there are many stressors, such as declining health and retirement, that can cause marital stress (Bair, 2007).

Regarding divorce, there appear to be some differences between men and women. Older women's incidence of divorce is higher than older men's. Among people age 50 or older, the odds of divorce are 12% higher for females than for males. Once divorced, older women are less likely to remarry than older men (Brown & Lin, 2013). These data seem to fit with other discrepancies between men and women with regard to relationships.

Divorce can be either a welcome or unwelcome change. Regardless of one's perspective, however, divorce typically involves a broad range of practical issues regarding finances, housing, and other concerns that can be taxing and time consuming (Whitbourne & Whitbourne,

2011). Furthermore, people who are divorced have been found to have poorer health, more substance abuse problems, more depression, more negative life events, lower levels of psychological well-being, higher rates of mortality, less satisfying sex lives (Amato, 2000), and more physical limitations (Bennett, 2006) than those who are married.

One of the issues associated with divorce involves losing joint friends. This loss can be problematic because during and after a divorce people need friends for support and enjoyment. Although both men and women have this need for friendships, women seem to adapt more easily. For example, the number of friends increases for women after a divorce, but the same is not necessarily true for men (Whitbourne & Whitbourne, 2011).

Perhaps older adults should obtain couple's counseling before deciding on a divorce because divorce has several long-term consequences both on the divorced individuals and on their adult children. These consequences include the following: encountering financial ramifications; no longer experiencing life as they knew it; being more likely to need social support and caregiving from children; having the parent–child relationship suffer; and having decreased interaction with family, especially with fathers (Lin, 2008; Shapiro, 2003). In the divorce process, mediation can result in more positive resolution of issues than when done with attorneys. Mediation involves a cooperative dispute rather than a legal dispute. A longitudinal study comparing mediation versus legal assistance showed that conflict between partners significantly declined for those who participated in mediation (Sbarra & Emery, 2008). This study was not of older people, but it may have relevance to any divorce dispute. Counselors might wish to refer clients to qualified divorce mediators when they are involved in this process, or they might wish to determine whether they, themselves, are eligible to become mediators.

In any case, counselors can help divorced clients process what has happened, review the history of the relationship, and fully express their thoughts and feelings about the event. Counselors can then ask clients to consider the positive aspects of the break-up and/or living alone, evaluate their strengths, identify what they want in the future, make specific plans for the next phase of their lives, and find ways to expand their social relationships (Shallcross, 2012c). Counselors might also address any of the issues mentioned above that seem to be prevalent among divorced individuals.

Cohabitation

While the divorce rate among older individuals is going up, so is opposite-sex cohabitation. Brown, Bulanda, and Lee (2012) reported that cohabitation of people over age 50 increased from 25% in 2000 to 37% in 2010. One of the couples who was interviewed (ages 70 and 66) said that their separate finances made things easier with regard to their independence and their financial decisions about their separate children. Individuals who are considering cohabitation might benefit by engaging in creative problem solving that includes reviewing both the positive and negative aspects of cohabitation as well as a possible break-up in the future.

Intergenerational Interaction

Perhaps some of the most complicated and important relationships are between older people and their children, grandchildren, nieces, nephews, mentees, or other younger friends. Depending upon the interactions among, attitudes toward, and distance from each other, these relationships can involve a wide variety of thoughts, emotions, activities, and outcomes. They can be supporting, gratifying, satisfying, saddening, or disappointing. Older people may find that relationships with younger relatives are the most important and satisfying experiences of their lives. Their younger relatives' support and affection can meet many socialization needs and can be a source of comfort, self-worth, and safety. Furthermore, their younger relatives' successes can be a source of pride (Hoyer & Roodin, 2009; Whitbourne & Whitbourne, 2011).

Adult Child–Parent Relationships
Adult child–parent relationships appear to maintain their importance throughout a lifetime (K. R. Allen, Blieszner, & Roberto, 2000), but variation exists in the way adult children perceive these relationships. Fingerman, Hay, and Birditt (2004) found that 56% of adult children felt close to their parents, 38% were ambivalent about their relationship with their parents, and 6% perceived their relationships as problematic. These findings are important because strong positive attachments between adult children and older parents have been found to have a positive impact on the psychological well-being of both adult children (Perrig-Chiello & Höpflinger, 2005) and older parents (Koropeckyj-Cox, 2002). Furthermore, adult child–parent relationships can be important for older parents' *generativity* (i.e., a developmental task that involves making the world better for future generations; Erikson, 1963). This seems to be particularly true of older women (An & Cooney, 2006). Perhaps positive outcomes exist, in part, because adult child–parent relationships typically involve people helping each other. Although a great deal of information exists regarding caregiving by the adult child, it is important to note that a large body of research has shown that most older parents and their adult children have reciprocal relationships. In other words, parents help children and children help parents (Blieszner, 2006).

Relationship problems can exist between adult children and their older parents. One of these problems involves a *developmental schism*, defined as differing perspectives, differing degrees of a particular perspective, or differing amounts of effort between the adult child and the older parent (Fingerman, 2001). Examples include parents putting more effort than their adult children into positively resolving issues between them, daughters or sons seeking approval of their parents and feeling guilty if they are not meeting their parents' expectations, mothers being more likely to consider their daughters as confidants than daughters consider their mothers as confidants, parents regarding their children as more important to them than their children regard them, and parents being interested in their children's lives and activities but children viewing their parents' interest as being intrusive (Birditt, Rott, & Fingerman, 2009).

Counselors can help older clients consider ways to improve their relationships with their younger relatives or friends. For example, as children become adults, parents might wish to ask of them, "What do you expect of me now as a father?" Children's answers might help clarify their changing parent–child relationships and might give them an opportunity to have a deep discussion about their interactions with each other (Paprocki, 2012). Furthermore, when family members feel that they have lost their loving relationships or when they feel that they never had such a relationship, a life review family group may help them review both positive and negative aspects of their past lives together and might lead to open discussions regarding their current relationships and how these can be improved, strengthened, or resolved.

Grandparenting

Grandparents and grandchildren often provide support and love for each other (Schaie & Willis, 2002). Hoyer and Roodin (2009) indicated that when people become grandparents, they are surprised at how meaningful that aspect of their lives is. Being a grandparent may involve an extension of self and family into the future; a biological renewal; and a sense of fulfillment, companionship, and satisfaction that they did not feel as parents. On the other hand, other older people may perceive the role of grandparent as of little importance and a remote experience (Kivnick, 1983).

Grandparenting can also benefit grandchildren. A recent study indicated that the benefits of maternal grandmother–grandchild interaction included helping children avoid emotional and social problems, improving children's social skills, and softening the grandchild's environment. Higher levels of contact were linked to fewer behavior problems and better social competency, especially among children at risk of behavior problems (M. A. Barnett, Scaramella, Neppl, Ontai, & Conger, 2010).

The phrase "Nana power" can apply to both grandmothers and grandfathers (Adler, 2011). Symbolic roles played by grandparents may include the stabilizer, the caregiver or supporter in times of need, the arbitrator between parent and grandchild, the family historian, and the transmitter of values and traditions (Schaie & Willis, 2002). Grandparents may also provide some, or a major portion of, child care for their grandchildren (Braus, 1995). In the past, grandfathers tended to give advice about jobs, education, finances, and life responsibilities, whereas grandmothers tended to be concerned about family ties and interpersonal issues (Hagestad, 1985). More recently, however, older women and men have held nontraditional work roles throughout their lives; therefore, their roles as grandparents may also have changed.

Older People Taking on Major Family Responsibilities
Older people may take on the major responsibility for the younger children in their families (Braus, 1995). This responsibility can take the form of guardianship and sometimes adoption of grandchildren, nieces, or nephews. This situation typically occurs when the parents are unable to provide a safe environment for their children because of substance abuse or mental health issues, and when a decision (often legal) has been made that the children must not be raised by their birth parents. It has been estimated that 2.5 million grandparents in the United States are involved as what has been termed *kincare givers*; many of the grandchildren who are being cared for have multiple issues, such as disabling conditions and sadness or confusion because they cannot be with their birth parents. Several terms have been used to describe grandparents who are raising their grandchildren (e.g., *aging caregivers*, *kincare givers*, *elderkin*). Another term used in conjunction with this type of family situation is *grandfamilies* (United Cerebral Palsy of Southern Arizona, n.d.).

Counselors should be aware of the positive and negative issues associated with this type of family situation. On the positive side, elder family members have expressed great happiness at having their young relatives live with them and knowing that they are safe and secure. Furthermore, having the responsibility for younger family members can contribute to an elder's sense of personal worth and integrity. On the negative side, raising young children can interrupt the elder's plans for retirement and be a major lifestyle change for everyone. Other problems include the difficult legal process of obtaining guardianship or achieving adoption, concerns about financial support for the children, the need to learn about and interact with educational and service systems available for the children, and problems associated with service providers who may not understand that elders are responsible for decisions about the children. This experience can seem like a new world for older people and can lead to them feeling overwhelmed (United Cerebral Palsy of Southern Arizona, n.d.).

Many of the children in these situation may have special needs because they came from a disruptive family, were born with a disabling condition because of in utero drug damage, and have undergone the trauma of leaving their parents and moving to a new home.

The children may be traumatized, hurting, afraid, angry, lonely, and emotionally wounded. They may want to be with their birth parents and not understand why they cannot be with them. Because of these issues, elders may need to obtain and understand appropriate diagnosis, treatment, and other services for the children (United Cerebral Palsy of Southern Arizona, n.d.). They may also need individual and family counseling.

Associated with these issues is the difficult interaction between the birth parent, children, and elder (often the grandparent). Initially, the decision that a parent is no longer able to provide the children with a safe environment can be very taxing and involve many emotional interactions among everyone involved. It is important for elders/grandparents to help the young children understand the situation in the most positive light. In other words, elders will need to help the young children realize that they are loved and that their parents love them but are unable to take care of them. At the same time, elders may be hurting, angry, and mourning because of the issues associated with their adult children who are the birthparents of their grandchildren (United Cerebral Palsy of Southern Arizona, n.d.).

If people at ages 40 to 75 have adopted children or have become the primary caregivers of young children, they may experience the empty nest (children leaving home) when they are ages 60 to 95. Although these circumstances can be similar to those experienced by younger parents, advanced age may make this transition more difficult (or perhaps easier). It may also be a time when older people are requiring assistance from the younger generation, but because their adopted or foster children are just starting their own adulthood, they may not be able to help. This phenomenon may also occur for older parents whose children were born when they were ages 40 through 50.

Because of the multiple issues that elders and their foster or adopted children can face, it is important for elders to know their resources and to obtain counseling. They need to know where to get financial help, social support, medical support, and emotional support for both themselves and the children they are raising. Fortunately, in some locations, there are programs that are designed specifically for their needs. An example of such a program is the KARE Family Center of Tucson, Arizona, which offers information and referral, guardianship classes, support groups, assistance to kinship families, case management, legal advice, advocacy, senior services, adoption and guardianship training, parenting class referrals, and family–child activities (kares@arizonachildren.org). Counselors can help elders find and interact with these kinds of resources.

Changing Roles and Relationships Among Family Members
The relationships (i.e., affection, contact, roles) between older and younger family members may change as they all age. Silverstein and

Long (1998) found that older grandparents had a higher degree of affection for their grandchildren than did younger grandparents but that the amount of contact with grandchildren decreased as the grandparents aged. Variables that influenced contact between grandparents and grandchildren were closeness/affection between the grandchildren's own parents and the grandparents, contact between grandchildren and their own parents, and reduced health status of the grandparents.

Some older people may feel a deep sense of disappointment that younger family members (adult children, grandchildren, nieces and nephews) find excuses to avoid being with them; never contact them; ignore phone, e-mail, and text messages from them; and generally display behaviors that indicate that they no longer value them. As one of Gloria Goldreich's (2008) characters states, "When children are little, they sit on your lap; when children are older, they sit on your heart" (p. 208), and as Paprocki (2012, p. 66) noted, "As kids grow up, heavily involved fathers can feel abandoned." In these cases, counselors can give older people the opportunity to express their grief for having lost their relationships with these younger people. They might also use life review techniques to support the client's discussions of the past events with the younger generation, to reexperience their positive feelings for these children, and to identify the key ingredients in the relationships they had. Counselors can also use cognitive behavioral techniques to help older people rethink the situation and recognize the need for younger people to move on. One analogy that can be used is the "chrysalis and the butterfly phenomenon." At the chrysalis stage, the young butterfly stays safely in its cocoon, but in order to become an adult, it must go through the difficult process of breaking the chrysalis and flying away. I have found that this analogy sometimes helps older people reframe their own experience. After giving clients sufficient time and support to feel their losses, and after reframing their understanding of the younger generation's need to move on, counselors can use creative problem solving to help them identify other ways to develop new relationships of significant value.

Extended Families and Friends

Older people can gain a great deal from social bonds with people other than their family, particularly if they live far away from, are estranged from, do not have, or do not receive a great deal of support from their families of origin or legal families. Because relationships outside of kinship can be equally or more valuable than relationships with kin, it might be helpful for older people to redefine their idea of family (Loe, 2011). For example, friendships can lead to higher levels of well-being and can even be more important to self-esteem than marital status or income level. Furthermore, friends can act as buffers to stress (Siebert, Mutran, & Reitzes, 2002) and as catalysts for social activity (Lang & Carstensen, 1994).

Additional Counseling Strategies Associated With Interpersonal Interaction

Family members often have regrets about things they wish they had said or done with their deceased elders. Counselors can listen empathetically to their thoughts and feelings and then help them find ways to resolve these through rituals, letters to the deceased person, or visits to their burial sites or special places. Counselors can also invite family members to discuss both the good and the bad memories they have of the person (see Chapter 13). To avoid future regrets, counselors might ask the younger family member the following: "If your mother/father/grandmother/aunt were to die today, what regrets would you have about your relationship with him/her? What would you wish you had done or said when they were alive?" Once younger relatives respond to these questions, counselors can ask them if there is any reason why they cannot do that now, while the older person is still with them.

Counselors, with the use of creative problem solving, can help clients and their families find programs that encourage intergenerational interaction. A senior pass to national parks and monuments allows the cardholder to invite loved ones (friends or family) to enter the area for free as long as they accompany the person owning the pass. Other programs offer the opportunity for older individuals to take the family to dinner in restaurants where children eat free. AARP often provides information about these opportunities.

Counselors can use creative problem solving to help clients find ways to maintain, change, or increase their opportunities for connectedness and socialization. Some possibilities for clients to consider are doing volunteer work with people who share similar interests and passions or joining support groups of people who have experienced similar losses or have comparable physical conditions or needs (Saisan, Smith, et al., 2012). The use of technology is another way to obtain social support or to socialize. Although older people have taken somewhat longer than younger people to use technology, the 2012 Pew Research Center Internet and American Life Project found that more than half of Americans age 65 or older were using the Internet. Over one third of these individuals were actively involved in social networking sites (e.g., Facebook), and more than two thirds were using cell phones, including 13% who were using smartphones. Through these and more current media, older people can keep in touch with family members, old friends, new friends, new ideas, controversial issues, and life events of many people (Rainie, 2012). Skyping may also be an excellent way for older people to stay in touch with their family and friends, especially if they have mobility issues or live long distances from the ones they care about.

Bibliotherapy can be used to work through feelings about interpersonal relationships and to find new ways to interact with others. Likewise, media can contribute to a counselor's awareness and understanding of various issues associated with interpersonal relationships of older people. Novels about family issues include *Open Doors* (Goldreich, 2008); *Two Old Women: An Alaska Legend of Betrayal, Courage, and Survival* (Wallis, 1993); *Wedding Ring* (E. Richards, 2004); *A Month of Summer* (Wingate, 2008); *Keeping Time* (McGlynn, 2010); and *Love All* (Wright, 2013). Movies about multiple-generational issues include *Everybody's Fine* (Gori, Field, & Jones, 2009), *Hanging Up* (L. Davis & Keaton, 2000), *On Golden Pond* (Gilbert & Rydell, 1981), *Trouble With the Curve* (Eastwood & Lorenz, 2012), *Jayne Mansfield's Car* (Kosinski, Rodnyansky, & Thornton, 2012), *Diamonds* (Green & Asher, 1999), *Secondhand Lions* (Kirshner & McCanlies, 2003), *The Iron Lady* (Jones & Lloyd, 2011), and *Nebraska* (Berger, Yerxa, & Payne, 2013). Textbooks such as *Family Ties and Aging* (Connidis, 2010) can also be informative to counselors and clients.

On a systemic level, counselors can encourage nursing homes or senior centers to incorporate children's and family services into their programs (e.g., Head Start, classrooms, day care centers, Sunday schools, Bible schools, etc.). These types of programs may encourage intergenerational interaction that can be helpful to both the client and the children. Often nursing homes invite children to make short visits for special events, but it might be more beneficial for full-scale programs to be adopted that involve ongoing interaction between children and elders (e.g., storytelling, giving cooking lessons, making crafts, reading, playing, gardening). In such programs, elders can act as teachers, mentors, friends, and valuable assets to the children. Bonds of friendship and caring can be developed, and both elders and children can experience the joy of intergenerational fun and learning. An example of such a program can be found at the Grace Living Center, a nursing home in Jenks, Oklahoma, which has added two classrooms to their facility where young children (kindergartners and preschoolers) interact with the residents of the nursing home. Other types of programs that can encourage intergenerational interaction include inviting older people to participate in community programs that serve youth, such as youth shelters, YMCA events, day care centers, and hospital programs.

Lesbian, Gay, Bisexual, and Transgender (LGBT) Issues

To become competent counselors of older LGBT clients, counselors need to be knowledgeable about and sensitive to the issues; have a bias-free perspective of the topic; have skills in working with LGBT issues; be familiar with terminology, community, and resources of older LGBT individuals; and understand that there is a broad array of perceptions, expectations, and judgments about LGBT issues among the LGBT community and their families.

Counselors can begin to develop their knowledge base by reading and assimilating two documents prepared by the Association for Lesbian, Gay, Bisexual, and Transgender Issues in Counseling (ALGBTIC). These two documents are *ALGBTIC Competencies for Counseling With Lesbian, Gay, Bisexual, Queer, Questioning, Intersex and Ally Individuals* (ALGBTIC LGBQQIA Competencies Task Force, 2012) and *ALGBTIC Competencies for Counseling With Transgender Clients* (ALGBTIC Transgender Committee, 2009).

Reading the competencies is not enough. Counselors need additional training, supervision, and consultation from professionals who have proficiency in aging and LGBT issues. They will also need to examine their own perspectives and values regarding this topic to ensure that they can provide an atmosphere that promotes the welfare and dignity of their clients (ALGBTIC LGBQQIA Competencies Task Force, 2012). Methods to improve their competencies can include joining ALGBTIC and/or the World Professional Association of Transgender Health Standards of Care; attending ALGBTIC annual meetings and sessions during the ACA World Conference; subscribing to the *Journal of Homosexuality*; having discussions about important concepts and concerns with LGBT friends and colleagues; reading materials such as those written by Friend (1990), P. A. Robinson (2005), and Dworkin and Pope (2012); obtaining materials from or joining the National Association on HIV Over Fifty (http://www.hivoverfifty.org); and becoming familiar with the APA Task Force on Gender Identity and Gender Variance. It will also be important to keep abreast of the growing knowledge and research associated with the LGBT experience (ALGBTIC LGBQQIA Competencies Task Force, 2012).

Although not specifically stated, all of the 2009 and the 2012 competencies apply to older LGBT individuals. Furthermore, some competencies appear to be more relevant to the older population than others. Of particular importance is the intersection of gender identity with other sociocultural identities, one of which is being an older person. As indicated in Chapter 1 of this book, the older population is one of the most diverse groups in the United States. It is also a group that experiences discrimination in many areas. It is, therefore, probable that older LGBT clients will face multiple forms of discrimination. Furthermore, there is some concern that ageism exists within the LGBT community itself (R. Helling, personal communication, September 23, 2013). Because of these issues, counselors will want to adopt a theoretical orientation that includes social justice and advocacy (ALGBTIC LGBQQIA Competencies Task Force, 2012; Goodman et al., 2004) as well as multicultural (Sue & Sue, 2008), feminist (Worell & Remer, 2003), and strength-based perspectives when working with older clients. Hence, counselors not only work with their clients, but also work to change systems and attitudes within professional and public communities (ALGBTIC LGBQQIA Competencies Task Force, 2012; ALGBTIC Transgender Committee, 2009).

It is also important to recognize that historically mental health professions have pathologized LGBT individuals, resulting in reparative, reorientation, and conversion therapies that involved an attempt to change the sexual and affectional orientation of individuals who were LGBT. Likewise, many professions have been insensitive to, uninformed about, inattentive to, and inadequately trained to provide culturally sensitive services to LGBT clients and their significant others (ALGBTIC LGBQQIA Competencies Task Force, 2012). Because of these situations, people who are currently in the older population are likely to have lived with strong pressures to hide, question, or change their identities. Such pressures will likely have resulted in undue stress, causing many LGBT clients to continue to question or hide their identities. These practices may also have resulted in mistrust of the counseling profession; therefore, clients may test counselors to see how comfortable they are with LGBT issues (Kimmel, 2012). Furthermore, older clients may be hesitant to engage in self-disclosure, "which may compound problems establishing a therapeutic environment" (Thomas, Gillam, & Hard, 2012, p. 71).

To counteract earlier negative experiences of older clients and to establish a therapeutic relationship, counselors can provide empathic listening; can help clients work through the lifelong issues that have been caused by professional and public discrimination; and can recognize, appreciate, and support clients' rich lives, histories, and pride. Counselors can assist clients in appreciating and acknowledging their identities, respect clients' personal choices regarding their identities, and support their efforts to come out at an older age if that is their wish. Counselors can also display or provide LGBT materials in their offices as a demonstration of respect for diversity (ALGBTIC LGBQQIA Competencies Task Force, 2012).

Past negative attitudes toward LGBT individuals may have affected many aspects of their lives. These attitudes may have affected their careers (negative evaluations, limited career options, underemployment, overrepresentation or underrepresentation in certain careers, less opportunity to access financial resources), their past and current views of themselves (e.g., negative self-esteem), and their current lives (ALGBTIC LGBQQIA Competencies Task Force, 2012). Counselors can help older people work through their feelings about some of these issues by reviewing the roadblocks that they faced and overcame (or did not overcome). Counselors can also help older people find ways to believe in and celebrate their own strengths, identities, and positive qualities.

Because older people may be likely to come out as our professional and general populations change their attitudes, these older people may be faced with many developmental issues that are not congruent with their chronological ages. For example, individuals who have recently come out may need to discuss their new identities, which may be multifaceted. Counselors should be aware that this process is normal, be open to exploration of these issues, and validate the new identity or multiple identities. Counselors should also become familiar with coming out identity development models and be fluid rather than linear in their counseling approach (ALGBTIC LGBQQIA Competencies Task Force, 2012).

On the other hand, some older people may remain in the closet indefinitely, especially if they are married and have children and they may privately have relationships with other LGBT individuals. In these cases, their straight marital partner may or may not be aware of their LGBT status. Counselors may need to be open to these relationships and available to both the LGBT individual and the married partner for counseling (R. Helseth, personal communication, September 23, 2013).

One important point is that within the LGBT community, multiple close-knit relations exist. It is therefore important to recognize this probability and to seek appropriate consultation or supervision regarding ethical practices in situations involving more than one client (ALGBTIC LGBQQIA Competencies Task Force, 2012). Another important point is that counselors must not engage in a sort of voyeurism and thus lose the counselor role when discussing sexual behaviors with clients (Kimmel, 2012). If counselors are aware that this situation is occurring, they should seek consultation from a supervisor or a professional who has expertise in this area.

With regard to group work, very little research has been conducted to determine best practices for LGBT groups (e.g., psychotherapy, counseling, task, psychoeducational, family). Groups, however, can provide a powerful process in community development, affirming identity and connection. As indicated earlier, older people may have been subject to past group work that focused on reparative or conversion therapy. Because of this experience, they may mistrust or avoid group work. Counselors will, therefore, need to ensure that they create an LGBT-affirming, nonjudgmental atmosphere during the entire group process, including screening (ALGBTIC LGBQQIA Competencies Task Force, 2012).

As with all issues, language has power and imparts attitudes. Thus, it is very important to use appropriate language that is the least restrictive and most affirmative. It is also important to know that language is fluid and evolving. This means that in one group or at one time, a particular word or phrase may be appropriate, but in another group or time, it may be inappropriate. Furthermore, specific terms may have different meanings for different individuals or groups, and as time progresses and attitudes change, terminology will change (ALGBTIC LGBQQIA Competencies Task Force, 2012). It is, therefore, important to keep up-to-date with appropriate language. Lists of terms and definitions can be found in *ALGBTIC Competencies for Counseling With Transgender Clients* (ALGBTIC Transgender Committee, 2009) and the *ALGBTIC Competencies for Counseling with Lesbian, Gay, Bisexual, Queer, Questioning, Intersex and Ally Individuals* (ALGBTIC LGBQQIA Competencies Task Force, 2012).

Associated with this issue are the terms and pronouns that individual clients wish to use to identify themselves. Because there is wide variety in clients' vocabulary, perspectives, and identities associated with LGBT issues, counselors need to identify, honor, and use the preferred terms desired by the specific client. Doing so will foster empowerment, self-determination, and a trusting relationship (ALGBTIC LGBQQIA Competencies Task Force, 2012; ALGBTIC Transgender Committee, 2009).

An important point made in the 2009 and 2012 competencies for counselors is that just because a client is LGBT, counselors should not assume that the issues they wish to discuss have to do only with this aspect of their lives. Counselors need to focus on the entire individual rather than only on issues associated with gender or affectional identity. This point was also made in Dworkin and Pope's (2012) book regarding counseling older gay men and lesbians. A powerful message of their book is that LGBT clients have similar concerns as the general population, and that counseling strategies that are used with the general population are appropriate for LGBT clients. Another key point is that older LGBT individuals vary widely with regard to many issues, and that counselors should not make assumptions about their clients' perspectives on the basis of their gender identity or age (Kimmel, 2012; Kimmel, Rose, & David, 2006; Thomas et al., 2012).

Transgender Issues

The *Competencies for Counseling With Transgender Clients* refer to the term *transgender* as "an umbrella term used to describe . . . genderqueer people, gender-nonconforming people, transsexuals, cross dressers and so on. People must self-identify as transgender in order for the term to be appropriately used to describe them" (ALGBTIC Transgender Committee, 2009, p. 28).

The competencies include the phrase "across the lifespan" several times, indicating that they apply to people of all ages. Furthermore, many aspects of the competencies apply directly to older individuals. Specifically, they indicate that competent counselors do the following:

A.2. Notice that respective developmental periods throughout the lifespan (e.g., youth, adolescence, elderly) may impact the concerns and process that transgender clients present in counseling.

A.3. Affirm transgender mental and medical health care (e.g., hormone therapies, sexual reassignment surgery, safe and trans-positive general medical
services) through the entire lifespan, not just during the initial assessment
process or during transition . . .

A.5. Identify the gender-normative assumptions present in current lifespan
development theories and address for these biases in assessment and
counseling practices . . .

A.10. Understand how transgender individuals navigate the complexities for self
and others with regard to intimate relationships throughout the lifespan.

A.11. Understand that the typical developmental tasks of transgender seniors
often are complicated or compromised by social isolation and visibility,
medical problems, transgender-related health concerns, family-of-origin
conflicts, and often limited career options . . .

A.12. Recognize that gender identity formation, self-acceptance of transgender
identity, and disclosure of transgender status are complex processes that
are not necessarily permanently resolved and may be experienced repeatedly across one's lifespan . . .

B.5. Recognize, acknowledge, and understand the intersecting identities of
transgender people (e.g., race/ethnicity, ability, class, religion/spiritual
affiliation, age, experiences of trauma) and their accompanying developmental tasks . . . [and]

B.9. Identify transgender-positive resources (e.g., support groups, websites,
brochures) that address multiple identities of transgender people. (ALGBTIC
Transgender Committee, 2009, pp. 6–9)

Counselors also need to recognize that gender identity and expression
will vary from person to person.

Family and Partner Issues for LGBT Clients

When discussing family and partner issues, counselors should be aware
that the terms *affectional orientation* or *affectional relationship* may
be used instead of *sexual orientation* or *sexual relationship*. Affectional orientation involves emotional, physical, spiritual, and mental
bonding predispositions (ALGBTIC LGBQQIA Competencies Task
Force, 2012). The term is intended to recognize the multiple aspects
of relationships and to deemphasize the sexual aspect of identity. It is
thought that these affectional orientations may evolve over a person's
lifetime; therefore, older people may be experiencing this evolution.

Family issues can be very complicated and involve all family members. An in-depth discussion of these issues is beyond the scope of
this chapter, but I offer a few examples of situations that may result
in the need for counseling for the straight family member or for the
LGBT family member.

Family-of-origin difficulties may occur when straight older individuals have younger LGBT family members. This identity may not
be acceptable to the straight older individual and may cause family
tensions, sorrow, and misunderstandings. On the other hand, family
members may be open to this identity and give support to the person
who is LGBT. In other words, straight older individuals with LGBT
progeny, mates, or other relatives can have unexpected multiple

responses to their family member's sexual or affectional preferences; if their responses are negative, they may need counseling to work through their thoughts, feelings, and behaviors regarding their LGBT family member. Likewise, people who are LGBT can benefit from individual or group counseling regarding their family's reaction to them.

Family-of-origin difficulties may also occur when an older person first identifies as LGBT. Some individuals may wait until they are older to come out because they fear their family's response. In this case, heterosexual siblings, parents, children, spouses, and significant others may need support in understanding and working through their responses to this event (Kimmel, 2012). Counselors will need to use their empathetic listening skills to support straight individuals as they deal with their thoughts and feelings about their older family member's identity; make decisions about their relationship with the individual who identifies as LGBT; and examine their own core spiritual, religious, and cultural beliefs that may not be supportive of their family member and may be causing them to have deep negative feelings about the situation (ALGBTIC LGBQQIA Competencies Task Force, 2012). Counselors can do this individually, but they can also provide group counseling among family members to help them express and work through their feelings for each other.

In addition to providing emotional support to straight family members, counselors might help them learn more about LGBT and—if and when they are ready—explore ways that they can be accepting and supportive of their family member who identifies as LGBT. In this process, counselors can provide materials that describe the issues and terminology associated with LGBT. Counselors can also help straight family members deal with any efforts on the part of the non-LGBQQIT (lesbian, gay, bisexual, queer, questioning, intersex, and transgender) community to discredit, disrespect, or avoid straight or LGBT family members (ALGBTIC LGBQQIA Competencies Task Force, 2012).

When older LGBT individuals decide to come out, counselors can use creative problem solving to help them identify strategies for discussing it with their families. Counselors can also help clients work through their thoughts and feelings about family responses to this event. Empathetic listening and support regarding the client's possible sense of loss or rejection is very important. Kimmel (2012) suggested that CBT can be used to help clients rethink the situation in order to avoid a downward spiral into sadness or depression about their family's lack of acceptance. Bibliotherapy can be helpful. The novel *Open Doors* (Goldreich, 2008) describes how one older parent learns to accept and celebrate her child who is gay. The movie *Beginners* (de Pencier et al., 2010) depicts a family's reactions to, and acceptance of, a man who comes out at age 75.

Other issues can arise among families with straight and LGBT members. Kimmel (2012, p. 58) provided a case example of such issues. In this case, a gay man who was married to a woman during his earlier life learned that she was dying. He felt the need to be with her during her illness, and upon her death, he needed to grieve. In other words, there was a need to integrate his past and present lives, and there was a need for family members to allow him to interact with his former wife, if she was open to such interaction. In cases such as this, counselors can assist grievers in a number of ways. They might help them deal with their grief by using empathetic listening and by encouraging them to identify rituals or other activities that will help them work through their feelings. They can invite clients to engage in life review of their relationship with the dying or deceased former partner. They can also invite clients to discuss and work through any feelings they have about the family's allowance or disallowance of the LGBT survivor to be involved in any aspects of their former partner's death. Additional suggestions for counseling individuals who have been excluded from the family grieving process can be found later in this section of the chapter and in Chapter 13.

It is important to recognize that the definition of family may be unique for LGBT clients. Because they are sometimes rejected by their families of origin, they may define their family as people who perform the function of the family but who are not related to them. In other words, they may have a family of choice. Likewise, the individual's "family" may change over time because of the original family's acceptance or rejection of their LGBT family member, same-sex partnerships that change, society's view of same-sex partnerships or marriages, and new laws relating to same-sex marriage. Counselors need to be aware of and honor clients' definitions of their families (ALGBTIC LGBQQIA Competencies Task Force, 2012; ALGBTIC Transgender Committee, 2009). Counselors can also refer clients to the local Services and Advocacy for Gay, Lesbian, Bisexual, and Transgender Elders (SAGE) program, which sometimes helps individuals develop and find "new families" (http://www.sageusa.org).

Kimmel (2012) indicated that when two male partners have sex, they may feel an emotion that could be interpreted as love, but love involves trusting and knowing each other. Kimmel, as a counselor, advises clients to get to know the person before using the word "love." This practice may allow them to avoid hurt feelings if a relationship does not continue. Kimmel also indicated that "most male couples eventually want to explore sex outside their relation-ship and need to work out some sort of mutual agreement that is comfortable for both of them" (Kimmel, 2012, p. 60). Counselors might help them, individually or as a couple, negotiate such an agreement. In the event, however, that one partner engages in an outside relationship without such an agreement, counselors may need to use paraphrasing and reflection, advanced empathy, cognitive behavioral techniques, and problem solving to help that person's partner work through thoughts and feelings about the situation and to decide how to respond.

Another issue experienced by older gay couples is the fear of HIV/AIDS. Kimmel (2012) provided a case study in which an older couple began to avoid sex (especially with others) because of the AIDS epidemic, even though they tested negative for HIV. They had experienced the illness and death of many friends over their lifetime during the epidemic; as a result, sexuality frightened them. Additional information regarding HIV/AIDS can be found in the last section of this chapter.

For same-sex long-term partners who do not marry, there may be concerns about end-of-life planning, wills, power of attorney, health care directives, and living trust documents. There may be outsiders who contest legal documents or decisions regarding disposition of property or health care. For this reason, it is important for couples to understand the laws within their state regarding these issues. They should seek legal advice from an attorney or organization designed to provide such advice.

Access to caregiving support has become a major issue for older LGBT individuals. Because these individuals may fear an unwelcoming or hostile health care provider or may worry that a health care provider will not be familiar with the issues faced by the LGBT community, they may either avoid seeking needed assistance or go back into the closet when they are most vulnerable. In other words, there may be a tendency for older individuals to avoid seeking various services (e.g., residential care or assisted living, home health care) because they are afraid of discrimination. For example, older LGBT adults may be 5 times less likely to seek social services or health care and be twice as likely to live alone than older adults who are heterosexual. Not seeking services can lead to financial difficulties, caregiving issues, and premature institutionalization. Furthermore, going back into the closet can have a multitude of psychological and social implications (SAGE, 2011, 2012).

In addition to this issue, older LGBT individuals typically do not have as much informal caregiving support as their heterosexual counterparts because a large percentage of long-term care in the United States is provided by family members. Older LGBT adults are twice as likely to live by themselves and are 4 times as likely to have no children as their older heterosexual counterparts have. Furthermore, they are often estranged from their younger family members. For these reasons, many older LGBT individuals must rely on their friends, their family of choice, or their partner for caregiving. Up until 2013, federal and state governments had not typically recognized these relationships. Hence, LGBT caregivers and partners were often denied medical decision-making authority, resources, and support that heterosexual partners received (SAGE, 2011). With the advent of the 2013 U.S. Supreme Court decision on same-sex marriages, this situation may be changing; however, counselors and their clients must be vigilant in learning about state and federal laws, court decisions, and regulations.

Death of a Same-Sex Partner

The death of any partner can be emotionally devastating, but when a same-sex partner dies or is dying, there can be other unique complications. End-of-life planning, financial planning, and a will are particularly important in these cases. It is also important to prepare documents that describe who can be responsible for decisions about one's health, life, and death when one partner is ill. The U.S. Supreme Court ruling on June 26, 2013, may make this less of an issue for same-sex partners who are married; however, it is yet to be seen how it will affect unmarried same-sex couples.

Often surviving partners become disenfranchised grievers. They may not be acknowledged by or included in activities of the deceased partner's family and other friends, and they may be shunned or ignored in decisions about such ceremonies or may not even be allowed to attend. It is therefore important that counselors help a bereaved partner to validate the importance of the relationship and to honor his or her grief (Doka, 2002; Meagher, 1989; Sklar & Hartley, 1990). Furthermore, these partners may feel unresolved guilt about a number of issues associated with their deceased partner that may ultimately result in self-punishment or self-recrimination. If this guilt exists, counselors will need to help them let go of the guilt and engage in the internal process of self-forgiveness (Meagher, 1989).

As indicated in Chapter 13, rituals can be very healing. They can act as a transition point for the surviving partner, offer the opportunity to express feelings, provide structure and meaning to the grieving process, and give partners a vehicle to begin to move toward a new identity. Counselors can invite surviving partners who have not been involved in the community ritual to create their own ritual. Doing so might give them the opportunity to engage in planning an activity, grieve openly and legitimately, and write a eulogy of their partner, thus enfranchising themselves as an important person in the deceased's life. Even if the bereaved partner does not create an actual ritual, counselors can invite him or her to describe an imagined funeral or event in which the departed is honored (Doka, 2002; Meagher, 1989; C. A. Walter, 2003).

Survivors can be invited to discuss, in detail, their memories of the deceased partner and their relationship. Doing so in a nonjudgmental and open atmosphere might provide support to survivors who have experienced negative reactions of others, give them the sense that their relationship with the deceased is understood, and help them celebrate and honor their relationship with the deceased. These discussions might also include their feelings about being left out of, or uncomfortable with, family and community rituals and support (C. A. Walter, 2003).

Survivors might also benefit from attending support groups. Such groups can normalize the grief and provide validation and support for those who have been left out of the grieving process or who have not been acknowledged as a grieving partner. Care should be taken in recommending or forming an appropriate group to ensure that group members are open to unmarried partners and nonconventional spouses (C. A. Walter, 2003).

Housing Issues

Thomas et al. (2012) stated that older LGBT individuals may not be comfortable in a straight retirement setting; however, it is not easy to find a gay-friendly retirement community. On the other hand, SAGE (2012) indicated that there are growing numbers of senior housing, retirement communities, and high-end housing options that have been developed to serve LGBT individuals. These options offer many caregiving and community-building services designed to help people feel safe and comfortable. Counselors can use the same strategies described in Chapter 12 to help individuals decide whether they wish to move to such a community, choose a community that fits their needs, and make the transition into the community in an empowering way.

LGBT Resources

Knowledge of resources is an important aspect of counselor competency (ALGBTIC LGBQQIA Competencies Task Force, 2012). Generally, services designed for LGBT people are more likely to be available in urban than rural areas (P. A. Robinson, 2005); therefore, clients who live in rural areas may need additional assistance with referrals to appropriate sources. Following are nationally available resources.

LGBT Aging Center, http://www.lgbtagingcenter.org/resources
National Association on HIV Over Fifty, http://www.hivoverfifty.org
National Center for Transgender Equality (NCTE), http://transequality.org/
National Resource Center on LGBT Aging, http://lgbtagingcenter.org
SAGE (Services and Advocacy for Gay, Lesbian, Bisexual, and Transgender Elders), http://sageusa.org; for the SAGE network of affiliates that provide local services throughout the United States, see http://www.sageusa.org/advocacy/sagenet.cfm
Transgender Aging Network (TAN), http://forge-forward.org/aging/

Caregiving of Older People: Typically a Family Matter

Family support is very important to people, especially when they experience disabling conditions or decreased functional levels (Marinelli & Del Orto, 1999). Family members or significant others are often caregivers for their relatives or friends, and because of this, caregiving involves complicated interpersonal relationships. The term *caregiver* can be used loosely to mean anyone who assists a person with ADLs (Adler, 2012). This situation can involve the caregiver moving into the home of the older person, the older person moving into the home of the caregiver, the older couple (one of whom is the caregiver) living together, and the older person living in one location with the caregiver making regular visits to the home or place of residence. Caregivers can even live some distance away and make regular visits to the person they are caring for.

Caregiving issues vary depending upon the needs or conditions of the older person, the age and gender of the caregiver, previous relationships between the caregiver and the older person, income levels and temperaments of the caregiver and the older individual, skill levels and strengths of the caregiver, other multiple responsibilities of the caregiver, and available resources. Regardless of specific situations, caregiving typically takes a great deal of time, effort, coordination, and planning. Caregivers may, therefore, have troublesome thoughts and feelings about lack of support from others; change in family roles; day-to-day caregiving demands (which can be 24 hours a day); transportation issues; everyday errands; decisions about specialists, treatments, housing, and care needs for their older family member; limitations in their own personal lives; personal financial issues; and profound and unknown changes in their own future. They may be overwhelmed with the combination of the needs and responsibilities associated with their older family member; their own jobs (i.e., paid employment); and their own household, children, mates, or friends. In addition to having these multiple responsibilities and concerns, caregivers are likely to experience many feelings associated with their older relative's or friend's decline in function and that person's need for help. For example, caregivers of persons with dementia typically experience additional stressors such as changes in the older person's memory and personality and the possibility that the person being cared for no longer recognizes the caregiver (e.g., mother does not recognize the daughter).

As a result of these issues, caregivers may experience a combination of sadness, grief, depression, loss, frustration, confusion, anger/ irritability, anxiety, fear, resentment, impatience, guilt, denial, stress, physical strain, disappointment, exhaustion, sleep issues, and health problems (Alzheimer's Disease Education and Referral Center, 2012a, 2012b; American Health Assistance Foundation, 2012b; Hope Heart Institute, n.d.). On the other hand, caregivers who believe they are making a difference and who are heavily engaged in the process may feel content and happy about what they are doing (Goyer, 2013; Sloan Center on Aging and Work, as cited by Abrahms, 2012b).

One variable that seems to ease the burden of caregiving has to do with monetary exchange for their work (Whitbourne & Whitbourne, 2011). This monetary exchange might come in the form of expected inheritance (Caputo, 2002), or it may involve a payback situation in which children want to give care to their parents because their parents provided them with monetary assistance when they were younger (Keefe & Fancey, 2002; Silverstein, Conroy, Wang, Giarruso, & Bengston, 2002). Other strategies for monetary payback for services can include elders paying the caregiver for their time and perhaps including this as a medical expense when submitting taxes, other family members contributing money for the caregiver's time, long-term care insurance policies that might cover home care and pay for caregiver time, and Medicaid pay to family caregivers (if this is available in one's particular state; Goyer, 2013).

Counseling Caregivers

Early in the process, counselors can help caregivers identify the wide range of responsibilities and issues associated with caregiving, examine the degree to which they are prepared to take on this task, and identify resources that they can draw on. Prospective caregivers should consider how the situation might influence the relationship between the caregiver and the older person; the effect that the new situation may have on the caregiver's spouse, children, and others; the home structural changes needed to accommodate the older individual; strategies to ensure privacy of the older person, the caregiver, and his or her other family members; and expected financial, social, and physical contributions from others (Hope Heart Institute, n.d.). One practical and easy-to-read book regarding caregiving is *A Complete Eldercare Planner*, which deals with many of these topics (Loverde, 2009).

Because many caregivers have jobs in addition to being a caregiver, counselors might use creative problem solving to help them determine if their employers offer flex hours, part-time employment, telecommuting, job sharing, shift changes, or employee assistance programs that can help workers deal with caregiving, home health care, or custodial care for relatives. Counselors can also help caregivers discuss strategies for informing their work supervisors of their caregiving responsibilities and the occasional need to deal with an unexpected crisis or late arrival. Counselors, as case managers, might also wish to advocate for state and federal policy to require that workplaces make such accommodations and check with the Department of Labor or the VA to determine whether they can be of assistance (e.g., Family, Medical and Leave Act; Coates, 2012; Goyer, 2013; Hope Heart Institute, n.d.; Rand, 2012).

Because there are often emotional undercurrents associated with caregiving, counselors can provide unconditional positive regard for caregivers and encourage them to express their worries and feelings in a safe environment. As mentioned above, caregivers may have strong feelings about their situations. Having someone with whom they can express these feelings without fear of being judged can help them validate their feelings and begin to find ways of dealing with them. Counselors can encourage caregivers to give themselves credit for doing their best, avoid unrealistic expectations of themselves, and accept that they are not—and cannot be—perfect. Counselors can also help them recognize that they are enhancing the quality of life and dignity of those they are caring for.

Counseling can be done either individually or in a support group in which caregivers can share their concerns and feelings with other caregivers as well as provide valuable strategies and resources for caregiving (Hope Heart Institute, n.d.; University of Arizona Life and Work Connections, 2012). One counseling theory that has been applied to caregivers of older individuals is the Adlerian approach. The DVD *Practical Strategies for Caring for Older Adults: An Adlerian Approach for Understanding and Assisting Aging Loved Ones* (Horton-Parker & Fawcett, 2010) provides case examples and explanations of how many of the principles and practices of this approach can be applied to caregiving (e.g., mistaken beliefs, reinforcement, logical consequences, the need to be valued and to belong). This DVD can be acquired via the ACA website at www.counseling.org/

Counselors, using open- and closed-ended questions and CBT, can help caregivers recognize when it is time to request help from others. Signs of the need for help include decreasing sense of love for the older person, disregarding their own feelings, thinking that they are the only one who is giving care to the older person, thinking that they are not doing enough, and noticing a deterioration of the older person's condition despite a great deal of effort. Personal signs of needing help can include exhaustion, depression, resentment, vulnerability to illnesses, almost never having fun or being happy, feeling overwhelmed, failing to care for oneself (e.g., turning to alcohol or drugs, gaining or losing weight, not exercising, ignoring personal medical issues), being argumentative, feeling selfish when taking care of personal needs, having little time for home life, experiencing a breakdown in other family relationships, having financial issues, and having no time or place to be alone. Work-related signs of needing help include being late for or missing work and having problems focusing on paid work issues (Rand, 2012; Shallcross, 2012c).

When caregivers decide that they need help, counselors can act as case managers to identify and activate the help that is needed. For example, case managers might help find and contact programs that provide low-cost or free assistance with home health or nursing care, housekeeping, yard work, home repairs and maintenance, home-delivered meals, special transportation, medical appointments and needs, pet grooming and walking, and special equipment. Case managers can also work with Medicare, Medicaid, or other government-sponsored programs to determine what types of services they offer for people who remain at home and whether there are situations in which caregivers can be paid for their time. If clients have long-term care insurance, case managers can work with insurance companies to determine the degree to which they can help older individuals in their homes. Case managers can also identify and contact day care programs or senior centers that provide socialization, nursing care, meals, exercise, diet counseling, ADLs training, music or art therapy, and various types of medically related therapy (e.g., speech, physical, occupational; Hope Heart Institute, n.d.). Case managers can learn about these types of programs by contacting local agencies on aging, independent living centers, independent living rehabilitation counselors, or city and state information and referral services.

In addition to finding help with daily needs, case managers can find facilities or programs that can give respite care. Such care involves a temporary move to a nursing home, retirement community, assisted-living facility, local hospice, or some other overnight facility to give both the caregiver and the older person a break from one another. It might also involve the older person's temporary move to another family member's home or a temporary switch of caregivers in the older person's home. This kind of break has been listed as a high priority among caregivers because it gives them time to take care of their own business, to relax, and to regenerate (Hope Heart Institute, n.d.; Shallcross, 2012c).

Case managers can also coordinate paperwork and communications associated with Medicare, Medicaid, or other insurance policies; identify and maintain lists of current support systems or specialists (e.g., pharmacist, lawyer, physician, religious organization, neighbors, friends, in-home helpers); and prepare and maintain lists of important information and documents (e.g., medical ID, Medicare/Medicaid information, emergency contacts, medical bills, home health care policies, advance directives, estate plans, wills, trusts, durable power of attorney, medications). These activities can be extremely time-consuming, irritating, and frustrating. As counselors begin to understand and navigate the various systems, the process becomes easier; however, they should be prepared for long telephone holds, multiple contacts, incomplete or conflicting information, and a sense of frustration with multiple systems. In this process, case managers should avoid engaging in activities that lawyers or financial consultants could better handle.

Communication Between Family Members

In caregiving situations, it is important to have open communication among all significant individuals in the family or extended family. If possible, this communication should include the person who needs the care. Conferences of significant individuals (i.e., those who are most affected, have resources, are most concerned, will be doing the caregiving) may be helpful to all who are involved, both early in the decision-making process and throughout the remainder of the older person's life. Counselors can facilitate these conferences or they can help family members, friends, and the older person prepare for them. Suggestions for such conferences include giving everyone the opportunity to speak openly, identifying and focusing on the most pressing problems, making certain that all information is current and available to all participants, having more than one conference if the situation seems overwhelming, and considering how caregiving will influence the life/lives of the prospective caregiver/caregivers and their families. Such conferences will, it is hoped, encourage each participant to offer what he or she is able to give and do (e.g., time, money, relief, meals) in order to ease the load of the primary caregiver. Because family members and significant others may be located across the country, the family meeting could be done in the form of a conference call, Skype, or some other current method of group communication (Hope Heart Institute, n.d.).

Relationship Between Caregiver and Older Person

The relationship between the caregiver and the older person is very important. Counselors might need to help caregivers understand that caregiving is not a matter of taking control of another person's life. Rather, it is has to do with helping the person deal with a variety of difficult issues. Counselors can also help caregivers realize that there is dignity in inclusion and responsibility. For example, caregivers can ask the older person for assistance with doable tasks, such as folding clothes, helping cook, giving the correct spelling for a word, sorting papers, reading to grandchildren, putting stamps on envelopes, and hand-washing small objects or clothes. The key is to be creative and to ask older people what they think they might be able to help with. It is also important for caregivers to respect the older person's privacy and for the caregiver to have privacy, too. This topic can be discussed between the caregiver and the client to determine house rules to maintain some privacy for all concerned (Hope Heart Institute, n.d.).

Spending quality time together is important for both the caregiver and the person being helped (University of Arizona Life and Work Connections, 2012). As indicated above, however, there are so many caregiver tasks and responsibilities that they may focus only on these tasks, which results in a lower quality of life for both themselves and the person they are caring for. Counselors might ask the caregiver about the quality of the relationship they have with the person they are caring for and ask them to reflect on how their relationship has changed because of the caregiving responsibilities.

Creative problem solving can be used to identify ways to enhance the interpersonal interaction between the caregiver and the person being cared for and to find ways to have fun or enriching experiences together. For example, when my mother was in need of long-term care (both in her home and, at a different time, in a nursing home), she, my sister, and I hired a yoga instructor to give us regular yoga lessons, watched *Dancing With the Stars* together, decorated her room or house for holidays, got silly, did our nails, looked through family albums, had red beers, and sang our favorite songs. We invited Mom's friends, her grandchildren, our husbands, the children of her departed friends, and our childhood friends to come for lunch or dinner (usually prepared by someone else). We also invited relatives who were interested in the family tree to come discuss family history with us, and we invited neighbors and friends for root beer floats. We asked Mom for advice and input on many things and for her help with important tasks (e.g., reading a manuscript to check for readability). Each of these activities was fun and/or enriching, and they all focused on a variety of important social, physical, and emotional needs for all of us.

Although this section focuses on the relationship between the caregiver and the older person, it also applies to the relationships between older people and their family members and friends in general. Counselors can use these same concepts when working on their clients' interpersonal relationships.

Caregivers Taking Care of Themselves

Because caring for oneself is a very important survival strategy, counselors can use creative problem solving to encourage caregivers to find ways to care for themselves. Counselors might start this process by asking the caregivers to identify something they can do for themselves every day for at least 30 minutes. The focus is on how they can make time for simple pleasures (e.g., long bath, lunch with a friend, napping, watching television or a sports event, meditation/relaxation). Counselors can also invite caregivers to consider other ways to take care of themselves by engaging in regular pleasurable exercise, eating appropriately, taking care of their own medical needs, making time for other life-affirming activities with family members and friends, and getting enough sleep. Counselors might also use brainstorming with caregivers regarding efficient use of time and energy. For example, caregivers might consider making same-time appointments for both themselves and the older person for haircuts, massages, dental work, banking, and so forth. This counseling process can end by asking the caregiver to make a commitment to do one or more of these activities. Follow-up on the part of the counselor is important (Hope Heart Institute, n.d.; University of Arizona Life and Work Connections, 2012).

Resources for Family Members and Caregivers

AARP Caregiving Resource Center, http://www.aarp.org/caregiving
American Grandparents Association, http://www.grandparents.com
Caring for Mom, http://www.caringformom.org
Children of Aging Parents (CAPS), http://www.caps4caregiverss.org
or 800-227-7294

Circles of Care: How to Set Up Quality Home Care for Our Elders,
   http://www.shambhala.com
Family Caregiver Alliance (FCA), http://www.caregiver.org or 800-
   445-8106
Health Awareness Center, Inc., 616-343-0770
HELPGUIDE.ORG, http://www.helpguide.orgInternational
International Association of Marriage and Family Counselors, http://
   www.iamfconline.org
National Caregivers Library, http://www.caregiverslibrary.org or
   804-327-1111
National Center for Fathering, Eldercare Online, http://www.ec-online.net
National Family Caregivers Association (NFCA), https://www.caregiver.
   org/national-family-caregivers-association-nfca
Next Step in Care, http://www.nextstepincare.org

Sexuality/Physical Intimacy Among Older Individuals

Sexuality and physical intimacy are important aspects of interpersonal
relationships; however, because counselors are members of the general
society, they may have negative or unfounded attitudes about older
people's sexuality. These attitudes could influence their comfort levels with, openness to, and encouragement of discussing their client's
concerns about sexuality; in addition, it could even affect counselors'
quality of service. Older people have a broad range of attitudes, beliefs,
and practices regarding sexuality; therefore, counselors must remain
open to each of these (J. E. Myers & Schwiebert, 1996). To do this,
counselors need to examine their own attitudes by engaging in individual
reflection; obtaining consultation from colleagues and supervisors;
attending workshops; joining the AARP Health Blog; reading Elder-
sexual.org publications; viewing movies or documentaries; and reading
books, articles, or novels that focus on sexuality among older people.

   In addition to being open to the broad range of sexual attitudes
and practices among older people, counselors should have knowledge
of the topic (J. E. Myers & Schwiebert, 1996). Counselors should
be aware of the statistics associated with sexual practices, the physical and psychological issues associated with sexuality, maintenance
and improvement strategies of sex life, and HIV/AIDs among older
people. This information will help counselors and their clients work
through the complex issues associated with sexuality. It might also
help normalize beliefs or practices that clients have about their own
sexual relationships.

Sexual Practices Among Older People

Several studies have examined older people's sexual practices and attitudes. The Pew Research Center (2009) found that among people
age 65 and older, 79% were sexually active. Another study (Lindau

et al., 2007) indicated that adults age 57 to 85 generally stayed sexually active, but that sexual activity diminished with age (i.e., 73% of people age 57 to 64 years were sexually active vs. 53% of those age 65 to 74 years and only 26% of those age 75 to 85 years).

AARP sponsored a complex survey that focused on sex, romance, and relationships during the past 6 months. Among those age 60 to 69, 68.8% of men and 51% of women reported that they kissed and hugged at least weekly (but 15.8% of men and 38.6% of women had not kissed and hugged in the past 6 months); 49.6% of men and 49.9% of women used sexual touching and caressing at least weekly (but 21.4% of men and 38.6% had not used this in the past 6 months); 24.2% of men and 8.2% of women used self-stimulation at least weekly (but 49.5% of men and 63.3% of women had not used self-stimulation in the past 6 months); 24.4% of men and 23.9% of women engaged in sexual intercourse at least weekly (but 40.3% of men and 54.8% of women had not engaged in this activity in the past 6 months); 11.1% of men and 11.8% of women engaged in oral sex at least weekly (but 69.8% of men and 75.4% of women had not engaged in oral sex in the past 6 months); and 0.7% of men and 3.3% of women engaged in anal sex at least weekly (but 96.6% of men and 94.9% of women had not had anal sex in the past 6 months; L. L. Fisher, 2010).

Among those age 70 and older, 51.4% of men and 32.4% of women engaged in kissing and hugging at least weekly (but 27.0% of men and 59.5% of women had not kissed and hugged in the past 6 months); 32.4% of men and 11.9% of women engaged in sexual touching and caressing at least weekly (but 40.9% of men and 75.9% of women had not done this in the past 6 months); 13.4% of men and 1.0% of women used self-stimulation at least weekly (but 53.5% of men and 81.8% of women had not used self-stimulation during the past 6 months); 14.6% of men and 4.8% of women engaged in sexual intercourse at least weekly (but 59.8% of men and 86.7% of women had not engaged in sexual intercourse in the past 6 months); 2.7% of men and 3.2% of women engaged in oral sex at least weekly (but 83.2% of men and 91.0% of women had not used oral sex in the past 6 months); and none of the men or women engaged in anal sex on a weekly basis, with 98.6% of both men and women not having anal sex in the past 6 months (L. L. Fisher, 2010).

Other writers have found that some older people have indicated that sex is "better than ever" (Howard, 2012b). Perhaps this is because older people may be able to relax and enjoy sex, know each other's bodies (Saltz, 2011), are more comfortable with themselves, have fewer distractions, and have more time for sex than when they were younger (Howard, 2012b). Furthermore, older men may be slower, have better control, be less likely to have premature ejaculations, and be more likely to focus on their partner's needs than younger men (Saltz, 2011; Whitbourne & Whitbourne, 2011).

Physical Issues Associated With Sexuality

With age, both men and women show pronounced decreases in de-hydroepiandrosterone (DHEA), a steroid associated with testosterone and estrogen (i.e., there is a 60% decrease between age 20 and age 80; Feldman et al., 2002). This decrease in DHEA is called *andropause* and will likely result in reduced sexuality. Furthermore, very low levels of DHEA are related to some forms of cancer, dysfunction of the immune system, cardiovascular disease, and obesity. The loss of DHEA is greater in men than in women, although men maintain higher levels of DHEA over the lifetime than women. Prescription drugs are available for low DHEA; however, they have been linked to the risk of prostate cancer and liver problems. Alternatively, physical exercise can compensate for the loss of DHEA (Whitbourne & Whitbourne, 2011).

Lindau et al. (2007) found that older people who had very good to excellent health were sexually active, whereas those in fair to poor health were less sexually active. Approximately half of their respondents, however, indicated that they had at least one "bothersome" problem related to sexual behavior (i.e., 37% of men had erectile difficulties, 43% of women had low desire for sexual behavior, 39% of women had dry vaginal walls, and 34% of women were unable to climax).

Medications can have negative effects on both men's and women's sexuality. Studies have shown prescription drugs (e.g., statins and fibrates, antidepressants, blood pressure medication, benzodiazepines, anticonvulsants, H2 blockers) are linked to sexual dysfunction in as many as one of every four cases of this condition. For this reason, counselors can recommend that their older clients talk with their physicians to determine whether their sexual issues are being caused by their medications before seeking additional treatment for sexual dysfunction. It is also vital for them to talk with their doctors before deciding not to continue to take a prescribed medicine (Neel, 2012).

Physical Issues Specific to Women

Both men and women experience a climacteric as they age. For women, a dramatic change occurs in the 40s and 50s, during which time they experience menopause. This change involves decreased estrogen levels; a thinning, drying, shrinking, and loss of elasticity of vaginal tissues; and decreased secretions of lubricants, which are likely to result in discomfort and pain during intercourse. This pain can certainly be a deterrent to their desire for sexual activity (Hoyer & Roodin, 2009; Schwartz, 2012). The decrease in estrogen can also increase the danger of high blood pressure, weak bones, and cardiovascular disease. Furthermore, older women may experience incontinence, urinary infections (Whitbourne & Whitbourne, 2011), and a decrease in blood flow to the genitals. Although physical problems exist, it should be noted that the clitoris is not typically affected in the aging process and is therefore as sensitive as it has been throughout the woman's life. Because of reduced blood flow to the area, however, longer foreplay may be necessary for stimulation (Schwartz, 2012).

Although a decline in hormones such as progesterone and estrogen in women may result in vaginal dryness and pain during intercourse, there are various prescriptions and OTC lubricants that can be helpful (Howard, 2012b; Schwartz, 2011). For example, women can try estrogen-based creams to "pump up" vaginal tissues, thus reducing or eliminating pain. Consultation with a physician is necessary to ensure that the side effects are understood and that the body is healthy enough for these treatments. For example, women who have had cancer should typically avoid estrogen. Furthermore, a recent study has linked estrogen treatments with dementia (Tokar, 2011). OTC water-based or silicone-based lubricants can also be helpful. Silicone-based lubricants last longer and are smooth. One issue with these lubricants or other drugs is women's resistance to introducing the product into the vagina. It is important to note that even though the lubricants may solve the issue of pain during intercourse, it may take some time for some women to get over their anticipation of this pain (Schwartz, 2011, 2012).

Physical Issues Specific to Men

As indicated above, older men typically have a decline in testosterone (Howard, 2012b). The terms *andropause* or *hypogonadism* are used to refer to the decline of testosterone; however, only about 6% to 10% of men between the ages of 40 to 70 have abnormally low levels of testosterone (Whitbourne & Whitbourne, 2011). Older men may experience erectile dysfunction (ED), defined as the inability to sustain an erection long enough for sexual intercourse. The AARP report mentioned above indicated that 29% of men age 60 to 69 and 48% of men age 70 or older have been diagnosed with this condition. The report also indicated that 38% of men age 60 to 69 and 56% of men age 70 or older are sometimes or never able to get and keep an erection that can be used in sexual intercourse (L. L. Fisher, 2010). These findings are similar to those reported by Whitbourne and Whitbourne (2011), in which 44% of men age 65 or older are likely to have ED. Furthermore, older men may have less intense climaxes, fewer spasms, and less quantity in ejaculation than younger men (Hoyer & Roodin, 2009).

Men who have ED can seek medical advice for treatment (Saltz, 2011). Although certain medications such as sildanefil (e.g., Viagra) can be effective in treating ED, they have potential dangerous side effects or negative relationships with metabolic syndrome, diabetes, hypertension, and obesity (Howard, 2012b; Whitbourne & Whitbourne, 2011). Other noninvasive treatments include a decrease in smoking, an increase in intake of antioxidants (Howard, 2012b), and use of devices to assist with ED. Men may also experience pain during sex if the skin around the penis becomes too tight, if they have herpes, or if they have some other condition. When men experience pain, they should seek a medical opinion (Schwartz, 2012). When discussing the physical issues associated with sexuality, it should be noted that, in spite of these issues, the desire for sexual intimacy continues to be strong (Hoyer & Roodin, 2009).

Psychological Issues and Sexuality

Personal and societal attitudes about sexuality among older people may influence their interest in and enjoyment of sexual activities, therefore the AARP survey included several questions regarding this issue. Responses varied depending upon the kinds of questions asked. When asked if sex becomes less important to people as they age, older men and women provided similar responses. At ages 60 to 69, 45% of men and 44% of women agreed with this statement. At ages 70 and older, 63% of both men and women agreed that sex was less important as people age. Participants were also asked if sexual activity was important to their overall quality of life. Among those ages 60 to 69, 55% of the men and 33% of the women said yes. Among those ages 70 or older, 46% of men and only 12% of the women said yes. When asked if they would be quite happy never having sex again, 5% of the men and 18% of the women ages 60 to 69 said yes as did 15% of the men and 38% of the women ages 70 or older (L. L. Fisher, 2010).

On the other hand, when asked if sex is only for younger people, none of the men and only 3% of the women who were ages 60 to 69, and only 5% of the men and 8% of the women who were ages 70 or older, agreed with this statement. When asked whether having a satisfying sexual relationship was important to their overall quality of life, 84% of the men and 62% of the women age 60 to 69 stated it was important versus 80% of the men and only 39% of the women age 70 or older. Taken together, these responses indicate that there is a broad perspective about sexuality among older people, and that having a sexual relationship and sexual activity is more important to men than to women (L. L. Fisher, 2010).

The U.S. Census Bureau has reported that by age 80 or older, the male-to-female ratio is 38.1% to 61.9%; by age 90, the ratio is 27.8% to 72.2%; and by age 100, the ratio is 17.2% to 82.8% (cited by Chatters & Zalaquett, 2013). In other words, there are many more older women than older men. A possible implication is that older men may have more opportunities to meet and have sexual relationships with women simply by virtue of the larger number of women than men. Perhaps this fact partially explains the AARP finding that older men were significantly more likely to have a regular sex partner than women were, and that by age 70, men were nearly twice as likely to have such a partner as women (L. L. Fisher, 2010).

Some older people may avoid sexual activity because they doubt that their older bodies are alluring or attractive. Schwartz (2011), however, indicated that sex is not just about how one looks, but that perceiving that one's body is less than perfect may interfere with a passionate sex life. Schwartz said that people become aroused by kissing passionately, stroking each other, or appreciating romantic or witty comments rather than by the status of other people's bodies; instead of worrying about how one's older body looks, people should be proud that they are still capable of enjoying sex and giving pleasure to another person. The AARP report indicated that among men, 44% of those age 60 to 69 and 50% of those age 70 or older reported that their current or most recent sexual partner found them to be physically attractive. Among women, 65% of those age 60 to 69 and 57% of those age 70 or older indicated that their partner found them to be so (L. L. Fisher, 2010). When evaluating their partner's attractiveness, 58% of the men who were age 60 to 69 and 51% of those age 70 or older thought their partners were attractive. Among women, 58% of those age 60 to 69 and 48% of those age 70 or older thought their partners were attractive (L. L. Fisher, 2010). Although these findings show that about half (or more) of the respondents indicated that they believed their partners found them attractive and about half of the respondents thought their partners were attractive, the other half did not indicate so. This finding may be an indication that attractiveness is only partially important in a sex partner; however, it may also mean that older people are correct when they express concerns that they may not be attractive to a sex partner.

Another psychological issue may have to do with a woman's reaction to her partner or to sex in general. It is possible that deep psychological issues inhibit some women from enjoying sex and cause them to clench up when having sex. These issues might be associated with their relationship with their partner, or they may have to do with other aspects of their lives (Schwartz, 2012). As indicated in Chapter 6, many older women have experienced long-term violence from their intimate partners (Goenjian et al., 1994) or have experienced rape or childhood sexual or physical abuse (Wilke & Vinton, 2005). These experiences might have a serious impact on women's later perceptions of sex, desire for sex, or pain experienced while having sex. Perhaps the combination of physical pain and psychological issues accounts for L. L. Fisher's (2010) finding that a sizable percentage of older women would prefer never to have sex again. Counselors will need special skills to deal with these women's situations and should seek training and supervision in this area.

Romance is important to sexuality, especially to women. It is also an important aspect of nonsexual interpersonal relationships. Loving words, gifts of flowers, and soft caresses are thought to enhance romance (eldersexual.org, 2012a). A study of a small sample of women who were married after they were age 50 showed that even though they had strong sexual chemistry with their husbands, they had made a shift from sexual intercourse toward other expressions of intimacy, such as companionship, cuddling, and affection (Hurd Clark, 2006).

In response to the AARP questions about keeping romance alive in a relationship, older men and women (from 55% to 69%) made a point to say "I love you" to their partners and to recognize birthdays and anniversaries (women were more likely to do this than men). A smaller proportion (from 18% to 38%) set aside one night or day a week just to enjoy their partner (men age 70 or older were more likely to do this than younger men). Another smaller proportion (19% to 36%) brought each other flowers, presents, or surprises (women ages 60 to 69 were more likely to do this). On the other hand, 18% of the men (ages 60 and over) and approximately 21% of the women (ages 60 and over) responded yes to the item, "Romance? What's that?" (L. L. Fisher, 2010).

When asked if their current or most recent sexual partner was romantic, less than half of older respondents indicated yes (i.e., 40% of men age 60 to 69 and 34% of men age 70 or older; 37% of women age 60 to 69 and 26% of women age 70 or older). When asked if this sexual partner loved them deeply, however, older people gave strongly positive responses (i.e., 68% of men age 60 to 69 and 67% of men age 70 or older indicated that his partner loved him deeply; 72% of women age 60 to 69 and 65% of women age 70 or older indicated that her partner loved her deeply). When asked if the partner was kind and gentle, participants generally indicated that this was so (63% of men age 60–69 and 67% of men age 70 or older; 70% of women age 60–69 and 62% of women age 70 or older; L. L. Fisher, 2010).

On the basis of this broad range of findings, counselors cannot assume their clients will have a particular attitude about sexuality. Counselors will also need to be aware that if an older client has a negative attitude toward sexual activities, he or she may feel uncomfortable about or unwilling to talk about the topic. Following is information that counselors can use when working with older people.

Maintaining or Improving Sex Life

In spite of the various physical, psychological, and attitudinal issues associated with sex and aging, older people can achieve orgasm when they are engaged in sexual activity. The AARP study of sexuality (L. L. Fisher, 2010) found that among people age 60 to 69, 91% of men and 82% of women can achieve an orgasm; among people age 70 or older, 82% of men and 61% of women can do so. Following are a few suggestions that might enhance their sex lives.

Because sex should not be painful, partners should seek medical help to determine the cause and remedy of pain if possible. If they have knee, shoulder, or wrist difficulties, they may no longer be able to have sex in the way they are accustomed to, but they can be creative in finding positions that are comfortable (Schwartz, 2012). Likewise, people with back problems can adjust their position in order to enjoy sex. People who have one or more conditions that create major problems with sexual activity can take more time while love making to achieve sexual readiness, or they can "spoon" or "make out" without penetration (Saltz, 2011). Furthermore, staying fit seems to support an active sexuality; therefore, physical exercise is one of the best ways to keep one's sex life alive (Schwartz, 2011, 2012; Whitbourne & Whitbourne, 2011).

Being together too much may cause irritation or boredom between partners, resulting in a negative effect on their relationship and their sex life. Recommendations for retired persons are to set ground rules and boundaries and to find more time to pursue individual interests. It is speculated that these practices will likely result in couple's enjoyment of their time together as well as their sex life because a stimulating individual life may contribute to a stimulating partnership in which each will have things they can share and talk about. Partners can rekindle old feelings by reminiscing about what first attracted one person to another, pretending to go on a first date, talking about their fantasies, watching a sexy movie together, or simply giving one another a compliment (Saltz, 2011). People in a long-term relationship may also need to identify new and creative ways to engage in sex (Schwartz, 2011). Obviously, some of these strategies might work for one person but not for another, and some might even be repulsive to one or both of the partners. Watching an explicitly sexy movie or training film, for example, might interest one partner but be a big turn off for another partner.

Other Counseling Strategies Regarding Sexuality

After counselors have developed knowledge about and comfort levels with sexuality among the older population, they can use their counseling skills to do individual and couple counseling regarding this area of life. Interpersonal counseling can be an important tool because many of the issues associated with sexuality are vitally linked to interpersonal relationship issues. Creative problem solving and the counselor's knowledge of issues associated with sexuality among older people can also be helpful. With additional training and supervision, counselors might also provide marital therapy weekends or week-long experiences.

Bibliotherapy can be used to challenge attitudes and provide new information about sexuality and intimate relationships, or it can stimulate questions and discussions about the topic. Examples of self-help books are *The Intimate Marriage* (Allender & Longman, 2005), which is a series of books that includes a leader's guide, and *Love With Intention* (Carter & Carter, 2012), which focuses on mindfulness, commitment, honesty, intimacy, integrity, passion, purpose, self-responsibility, and self-empowerment. Self-disclosures by older people such as Betty White may be assistive. Movies that might generate interest in, or conversation about, sexuality among older people include *Hope Springs* (Black, Casady, & Frankel, 2012), *The Best Exotic Marigold Hotel* (Broadbent, Czernin, & Madden, 2011), *Meet the Fockers* (DeNiro, Roach, & Rosenthal, 2004), and *Something's Gotta Give* (Block & Meyers, 2003).

Case Study/Activity Regarding Sexuality

Jane and Bob were married for 50 years, and because of some physical issues, they moved into a long-term care facility that was located outside of their small town among corn fields. They shared a room, but there was no lock on the door; thus, staff could, and did, enter the room at any time. Jane and Bob had always enjoyed having sex but were concerned about the lack of privacy in their new residence. After 2 months of living in this facility, they decided they must find a solution to this issue. They thought it might be fun to take a short walk into the nearby cornfield and have sex. At mid-morning, they proceeded with their plan. Because they had not had sex for 2 months and because they now enjoyed long and slow love-making, they did not make it back to the facility for lunch. The staff became concerned that they were missing and went to search for the couple. In a short time, the staff found Jane and Bob lying in the cornfield having sex. This was so shocking to the staff that the story went around town: "Did you hear that they found Jane and Bob having sex in the cornfield outside the nursing home?"

If you were a counselor or case manager, how would you have handled this situation?

1. What could you have done to help Jane and Bob avoid this occurrence?
2. How could you have interacted with the staff, early on, to avoid this situation?
3. Once Jane and Bob were found in the cornfield, what could you have done?
4. How might you work with the staff regarding privacy for Jane and Bob?
5. How might you work with the staff regarding confidentiality for Jane and Bob?
6. How could you use this incident as a training opportunity for staff of the facility?

HIV/AIDS Among Older Individuals

Acquired Immune Deficiency Syndrome (AIDS) is a disease caused by the Human Immunodeficiency Virus (HIV). Older people have become the fastest growing group of the HIV-positive population. Furthermore, it is speculated that one out of seven newly diagnosed individuals is over age 50. By the year 2017, it is estimated that half of the entire HIV-positive population will be over age 50. These statistics are attributable to a combination of factors: the growth in the population of older people, the longer life span for those who are affected, and the belief that older people do not need protection (e.g., condoms) when having sex. One assumption is that condoms are needed only for birth control, and because older people do not have to worry about pregnancies, they do not need to use protection. Another assumption is that older people are less likely to have the HIV virus than younger people; therefore, there is little need for protected sex. The bottom line, however, is that older people should wear condoms when having sex, especially if they are sexually active with more than one partner (Anft, 2011; eldersexual.org, 2012a).

Open communication about HIV status, testing, and previous sexual relationships is vital for both current partners and couples who are contemplating having sex. Because many older people do not consider the possibility of acquiring HIV/AIDS and because the topic is uncomfortable, they may not speak with their current or new partner about this issue. This silence puts everyone at risk (eldersexual.org, 2012a).

Diagnosis for HIV/AIDS is difficult for older people because many of the symptoms of HIV/AIDS are also symptoms of other age-related conditions. These symptoms include fatigue, mild flu-like symptoms, sleeplessness, weight loss, memory loss, and shingles. Furthermore, many health care providers may not think of older people as being sexually active; therefore, older people are likely to be undiagnosed or to be diagnosed in the later stages of the disease, which results in lower survival rates. It is vital that sexually active older adults request testing for the virus on a regular basis (i.e., about every 6 months or more often if they have been exposed to the virus; eldersexual.org, 2012b).

Once older people acquire HIV/AIDS, they are vulnerable to illness and infections because they have compromised immune systems. Because cells that are vital to the immune system age quickly, a person who is 55 and has HIV/AIDS is likely to have as many chronic conditions as a noninfected person who is 75. Furthermore, older people who have HIV/AIDS experience depression at approximately 5 times greater rates than older people without HIV/AIDS. Counselors working with older people will therefore need to be sensitive to and alert for these possibilities (Anft, 2011; eldersexual.org, 2012a).

Counselors also need to be aware of the dangers of unprotected sex among their older clients, provide information and resources about the topic, discuss the importance of testing with their sexually active clients, and make sure that their clients are aware of the need for open communication with their sexual partners regarding whether or not they have been tested or are infected (eldersexual.org, 2012b). Counselors should also stay up-to-date on new guidelines for prevention and treatment that exist or are being developed for older people and inform their clients of these guidelines and treatments when appropriate (Anft, 2011; Shallcross, 2012c).

Counselors working with clients who have HIV/AIDS must be aware of and follow the *ACA Code of Ethics* regarding reporting this type of condition. The *ACA Code of Ethics* (ACA, 2014, Standard B.2.c.) states,

> When clients disclose that they have a disease commonly known to be both communicable and life threatening, counselors may be justified in disclosing information to identifiable third parties, if parties are known to be at serious and foreseeable risk of contracting the disease. Prior to making a disclosure, counselors assess the intent of clients to inform the third parties about their disease or to engage in any behaviors that may be harmful to an identifiable third party. Counselors adhere to relevant state laws concerning disclosure about disease status.

Resources Associated With HIV/AIDS in the Older Population

AARP, http://www.aarp.org/health/conditions-treatments/info-05-2011/ways-to-get-condoms-and-std-tests.html
AIDS Community Research Initiative of American (ACRIA), http://www.acria.org
Division of AIDS (DAIDS), National Institutes of Health, http://www.niaid.nih.gov/about/organization/daids/Pages/default.aspx
National Conference on HIV/AIDS and Aging, http://www.hivoverfifty.org
New England AIDS Education and Training Center (NEAETC), http://www.neaetc.org/index.php

Summary

Interpersonal relationships are vital to psychological well-being and involve many different kinds of interactions and variables. Counselors need to be informed of the types of relationships that older people have and ways to enhance this aspect of their lives. Because of the strong emotional overlay associated with interpersonal relationships, counselors must be prepared to provide an unconditional and respectful environment in which their clients can express their feelings. Counselors must also have information that can help them understand their clients' issues and that can be used in problem solving about issues that need to be resolved.

Chapter 10
Social Security and Medicare-Related Programs: Sorting Through the Maze

Counselors can play many roles when serving older individuals. One of these complicated and important roles has to do with case management associated with the Social Security Administration (SSA), Medicare, and medical insurance programs. The purpose of this chapter is to provide basic information regarding these programs. Because these programs are extremely complicated, may vary from state to state, and will change over time, this chapter provides general information rather than intricate details.

Social Security Benefits

The SSA is a vast federal government agency that administers Social Security and interacts closely with state governments and other public and private organizations to administer a broad range of programs that are supported through federal legislation. For example, SSA and the Medicare and Medicaid Services systems are closely linked and often interact with one another. The three most basic SSA benefit programs are Social Security benefits, Social Security Disability Income (SSDI) benefits, and Supplemental Security Income (SSI) benefits. Having basic knowledge of these programs is important because each one can have significant implications for older people. The information in this section of the chapter is based on my professional experiences with Social Security, discussions with SSA representatives, a host of SSA publications that are periodically updated, and the Social Security website (http://www.socialsecurity.gov).

Basic Information Regarding Social Security Benefits

At the most basic level, Social Security benefits (often called retirement benefits) involve monthly income (payments) to individuals who qualify for the program. The amount of money in these monthly payments is based on the annual amount of Social Security benefits a person is entitled to. To qualify for Social Security benefits, individuals who were born in 1929 or later must have earned at least 40 Social Security credits while they worked in jobs and paid Social Security taxes (those born before 1929 need fewer credits). Individuals can acquire up to 4 credits for each year that they work, as long as they make a specified amount of income and contribute to Social Security (i.e., Social Security taxes) during that time. To support this process, each year employers match an employee's contribution to Social Security and send taxes and reports of income to the Internal Revenue Service. The Internal Revenue Service sends the SSA a copy of each individual's Wage and Tax Statement (W-2), and SSA maintains a lifelong record of these reported earnings. For this reason, it is very important that names and Social Security numbers are accurately reported on tax forms and on communications with the SSA (SSA, 2011f, 2011g, 2011h, 2011i, 2013).

As indicated in Chapter 1, a large percentage of older people (age 65 or older) receive Social Security benefits (Administration on Aging, 2007). Annual and monthly benefits, however, are different for each person because they are based on the amount of earned income individuals or their spouses have contributed to Social Security and on the age at which they retire. At the time of retirement, the SSA calculates people's average wages for the 35 years in which they earned the most money. This calculation is done to determine both eligibility and the amount of annual benefits a retired worker can receive. An important side note is that Social Security benefits are not typically based on dividends, interest, investment earnings, pensions, annuities, or capital gains. Rather, they are based almost solely on earned income from employment that resulted in contributions to Social Security. It is also important to recognize that age 65 is no longer the age at which individuals are eligible for full Social Security benefits (e.g., those born from 1943 through 1954 do not reach full retirement age until they are 66, and those born after 1959 must be 67; SSA, 2010, 2011c, 2011e, 2011j, 2013).

Individuals who are self-employed, are in the military, do domestic or farm work, or work for a church can also earn Social Security credits and are therefore potentially eligible for Social Security benefits. Special rules and guidelines apply to these situations and are beyond the scope of this chapter. For detailed information about these, counselors and clients can contact the SSA directly (800-772-1213 or TTY 800-325-0778) or obtain publications from SSA such as those referred to in this chapter. These and other updated publications can be found at http://www.socialsecurity.gov/pubs.

Individuals who have worked in certain types of jobs may not be eligible for Social Security benefits or may have lower Social Security benefits (e.g., railroad employees who have worked for more than 10 years with the railroad, most federal employees, some state and local government employees). They may not be eligible because these individuals typically have not paid Social Security taxes and because their places of employment have their own benefits programs. There are factors that can influence whether or not these individuals are eligible for Social Security benefits and the amount of Social Security retirement or disability benefits they will receive. One such factor for government workers with a pension is the Windfall Elimination Provision. A discussion of each of these provisions is beyond the scope of this chapter; however, case managers should be aware of such issues. Additional information can be found at http://www.socialsecurity. gov or http://www.socialsecurity.gov/gpo-wep and in SSA publications and their updates (SSA, 2011h, 2013).

Individuals can start receiving their Social Security retirement benefits at age 62; however, if they do so, they will receive lower annual benefits than if they had waited until reaching full retirement age. Furthermore, applying early for Social Security benefits will negatively influence the annual amount of benefits they will receive when they reach full retirement age, as defined by the SSA. Conversely, people who delay application for Social Security benefits or who request that payments be suspended to later than their full retirement age will receive higher Social Security annual income when they finally begin to receive payments. Chapter 11 provides information regarding the impact of continuing to work after full retirement age.

Special Issues Associated With Being a Spouse or Family Member

When individuals start receiving Social Security income or disability benefits, their family members may also be eligible for payments. Examples of family members who can receive Social Security benefits are as follows: (a) a spouse who is age 62 or older, (b) a spouse who is caring for the beneficiary's child who is disabled or younger than age 16 and receiving Social Security benefits that are based on the worker's record, (c) an unmarried child who is younger than age 18, (d) an unmarried child who is between age 18 and 19 and who is a full-time elementary or secondary student, (e) an unmarried child who is age 18 or older and severely disabled, and (f) a divorced spouse who meets certain criteria. The amount of benefits that a family member will receive depends upon the rules and regulations that exist at the time. It must also be noted that if eligible individuals are married or divorced, and if their spouses or ex-spouses are also eligible for Social Security, they can choose to take their own Social Security benefits or take benefits that are based on their spouse's Social Security benefits, whichever is greater. Each of the above situations must be reviewed by the SSA and meet specific regulations before eligibility can be established (SSA, 2011f).

When people who are eligible for Social Security benefits die, family members may be eligible for survivor's benefits. Survivors can include (a) a widow or widower who has reached a specific age; (b) a disabled widow or widower who has not yet reached a specific age; (c) a widow or widower who is any age and caring for the deceased spouse's child who is younger than age 16 or disabled and receiving Social Security benefits; (d) a divorced spouse under specific conditions; (e) dependent parents who are at least age 62 years and were dependent on the deceased worker for at least half of their support; and (f) certain children, adopted children, and grandchildren. In the case of a surviving spouse, the benefit amount will depend upon the survivor's age and the amount the deceased spouse was entitled to when he or she died (SSA, 2011f, 2013).

As with all other Social Security programs, there are many and varied guidelines associated with family benefits, and these can change over time. Because of the complex nature of rules and regulations, it is important to speak directly with SSA representatives regarding specific situations associated with survivor benefits. These representatives are typically helpful, informative, and truly willing to find the best option for each individual. Case managers can help older people and their families contact these individuals and sort through complex issues associated with their needs.

Social Security Disability Income (SSDI)

SSDI is available to individuals who have a long-term "severe" disability and who have paid Social Security taxes to amass enough credits to be eligible. The number of credits needed depends on how old they are when they acquire a disability and on the amount of credits they have accumulated while working. For example, in 2012, people who became disabled at age 58 needed only 36 credits (9 years of work) to be eligible, whereas people who acquired a disability at age 62 or older needed 40 credits (equivalent of 10 years work).

Disability benefits can be paid to people of all ages who have severe disabilities. People are considered to have a disability if they cannot do work that they did before a medical condition(s) and cannot adjust to other work because of the condition(s). The disability must also last, or be expected to last, for at least one year or result in death. Individuals who meet these criteria can apply online at http://www.socialsecurity.gov, over the telephone, or by appointment with their local SSA office. This initial application process takes an hour or more and requires a great deal of detailed information, such as past and current work and income records; Social Security number; birth or baptismal certificates; names, addresses, and phone number of doctors, hospitals, clinics, and caseworkers; type and dosage of medications; in-depth medical records from all providers; laboratory and test results; a copy of the most recent W-2 form or federal tax form; and information about convictions of crimes, violations of the conditions of parole or probation, and outstanding warrants for arrest (SSA, 2011a). Being prepared for this application is very important; therefore, case managers can help clients assemble this information prior to the process.

Because the application review is complex and intricate, it can take from 3 to 5 months to process. If individuals are currently earning more than a certain amount each month, or if they are not found to have a "severe" disability, their application for SSDI will be denied. This decision can be appealed, and individuals who appeal their cases have the right to be represented by an attorney (SSA, 2011a). Occasionally, local and state programs offer free assistance to those who have been denied. Such services might be available via local centers on independent living or centers for disability law.

If the application or claim for disability benefits is approved, recipients will receive a monthly disability benefit (payment) that is based on average lifetime earnings. Once individuals have received disability payments for 2 full years, they will automatically be eligible for Medicare. Certain members of the recipient's family may also qualify for benefits. These include (a) a spouse who is age 62 or older; (b) a spouse, at any age, who is caring for the recipient's child who is younger than age 16 or who is disabled; (c) an unmarried child who is younger than age 18 or younger than age 19 if in elementary or secondary school full time; or (d) an unmarried child, age 18 or older, who acquired a disability prior to age 22. A divorced spouse may also be eligible for benefits as long as he or she had been married to the recipient for at least 10 years, is not currently married, and is at least age 62 (SSA, 2011a).

Several situations may cause beneficiaries to either lose or receive lower Social Security disability benefits. These situations include (a) receiving other government benefits, (b) improved status of a disability, (c) increased earned income, or (d) incomplete information. Because of strict monitoring of earned income for individuals who are receiving SSDI benefits, there may be a disincentive for recipients to work. Disincentives to work are discussed in Chapter 11 and in the following SSA publications or their updates: *How Workers' Compensation and Other Disability Payments May Affect Your Benefits* (SSA, 2011d), *Government Pension Offset* (SSA, 2011b), and *How We Decide If You Are Still Disabled* (SSA, 2005).

Supplemental Security Income (SSI)

SSI involves payments to people who are age 65 years or older, are disabled or blind, and have low incomes or resources. Eligibility for this benefit is determined by the state or local medical assistance (Medicaid) agency, welfare office, or social services programs for the geographical area in which an individual lives. Once eligibility is established, earned income levels are closely monitored. In other words, people who exceed the earned income limit will not be eligible for or will lose their SSI benefits. For example, in 2011, if people earned more than $1,540 per month, their SSI income would be negatively affected (SSA, 2011i).

Other Resources for Social Security

http://www.aarp.org/about-aarp/events/webinars/?intcmp=DSO-
  SEARCH-AARPSUGG
http://www.ssa.gov

Medical Insurance for Older People

As indicated in Chapter 1, older people are likely to acquire chronic disease and to have one or more disabling conditions; thus, there is a strong likelihood that they will require extensive medical and prescription drug treatment. It is therefore vital that they find appropriate funding sources for their medical needs. The complexity of public and private medical insurance programs, however, can be overwhelming, with multiple types of available insurance policies designed to meet a plethora of different needs. Even individuals who have worked with and understand the system continue to encounter complications and changes in federal legislation, regulations, and rulings as well as annual changes in private supplemental medical insurance policies and practices.

Medical insurance programs present both opportunities and challenges. The opportunities involve the availability of needed medical services. The challenges involve identifying, understanding, enrolling in, affording, monitoring, and utilizing the appropriate programs (Mamboleo & Kampfe, 2009). The purpose of this section of the chapter is to inform counselors of the extreme complexity associated with medical insurance and to offer general information that will help counselors and their clients begin to understand and access these systems. Specific details about the various Medicare programs are not included because of the potential for changes in such programs and because the options are too divergent and vast in number to include here.

Before discussing Medicare, it must be noted that some individuals will have access to insurance programs offered by VA, current or previous employers, or unions (e.g., state or federal retirement systems or private employer plans). In some cases, all medical insurance (i.e., hospital, medical, dental, vision, and prescription drug) are offered by these sources, whereas in other cases, only one or two types of insurance are offered. Occasionally, employers provide retirees with funds to the pay Medicare monthly premiums; however, these sources may cover only one or two aspects of medical insurance (e.g., medical only). Older people may therefore need to use a combination of insurance options (e.g., current or previous employer plan, Medicare or Medicaid, supplemental health insurance programs, the Affordable Care Act programs, and perhaps some new programs associated with new legislation).

Important Basic Terms and Their Definitions

Counselors and clients need to have basic definitions of terms associated with medical insurance policies in order to understand what those policies offer. Following are definitions provided by Medicare (Centers for Medicare and Medicaid Services [CMS], 2014).

Premium: The amount of payment (typically on a monthly basis) that individuals make to Medicare, an insurance company, or a health care plan for insurance coverage.

Deductible: The amount of money individuals pay for health care or prescriptions before an insurance policy begins to pay for the service.

Coinsurance: The amount individuals may be required to pay as their share of the cost for services after they have paid their deductibles. Coinsurance is usually a percentage of the cost of the medical service (e.g., client pays 20%).

Copayment: The amount individuals may be required to pay as their share of the cost of a medical service or supply. A copayment is usually a set amount, rather than a percentage (e.g., $10 or $20 per prescription or doctor's visit).

Out-of-Pocket Costs for Prescription Drugs: This is what clients pay when they fill a prescription for a covered Part D drug (this includes payments for the clients' drugs that are paid by a family member, friend, "extra Help" from Medicare's Coverage Gap Discount Program for Part D, Indian Health Service, AIDS drug assistance programs, and most State Pharmaceutical Assistance Programs [SPAPs]).

Medicare Insurance Programs

Medicare insurance programs are administered by the CMS, U.S. Department of Health and Human Services; they are sometimes referred to as Medicare benefits, and they typically require monthly premium payments. CMS and the SSA work closely together in administering these programs, especially with regard to enrollment and premium payment. For example, the SSA is responsible for determining Medicare eligibility, enrollment and disenrollment into certain Medicare programs, maintaining or changing addresses of individuals on Medicare, and automatically taking certain premiums out of monthly Social Security income (CMS, 2014).

Eligibility guidelines for Medicare are somewhat complicated. Basically, individuals who are U.S. citizens must have a work history in which they have contributed a specified amount of money, per quarter, into the Medicare system for at least 40 quarters (4 quarters per year = 10 years). In other words, individuals who are eligible for Social Security benefits are typically eligible for Medicare, too. There are also many other situations in which individuals are eligible for Medicare. For example, people who have contributed to the Rail Road Retirement Board for at least 10 years will be eligible for Medicare and will enroll through the Rail Road Retirement Board. Other examples of people who are eligible for certain aspects of Medicare (Part A and Part B) are those who were entitled to Social Security disability benefits for 2 years prior to age 65, those who have End-Stage Renal Disease, those who are under age 65 who have certain disabilities, spouses or ex-spouses of people who are eligible for Social Security benefits, and aliens who have been lawfully allowed to work and who have contributed into the Medicare system. Eligible individuals are informed by Medicare that they will automatically be enrolled in basic Medicare at least 3 months prior to enrollment (CMS, 2014).

Enrollment in Medicare is not mandatory; however, individuals who do not enroll in Medicare within a specified time after reaching age 65 will pay a lifetime penalty or surcharge for late enrollment if they choose to enroll at a later time. Enrollees who start Medicare after their initial enrollment period will not be charged this penalty if they can show proof that they had creditable insurance coverage through another source up until the time of Medicare enrollment. It should also be noted that if individuals are not eligible for Medicare benefits, they can pay an additional monthly premium to buy Medicare coverage (CMS, 2014).

Individuals who wish to enroll in Medicare have two basic choices: Original Medicare and Medicare Advantage Plans. Original Medicare is offered directly through Medicare and includes several types of individual insurance policies: Part A (hospital insurance), Part B (medical insurance), Part D (prescription drug coverage purchased privately), and Medigap (Medicare supplemental insurance purchased privately). Medicare pays only a small percentage of medical costs; therefore, recipients will be responsible for the remainder of the costs (thus the need for Medigap insurance). Participants must apply for and pay separate premiums for each "Part" —although Part A often does not typically require a premium—and can enroll in one or all of these, depending upon their needs. Another somewhat different type of Medicare insurance policy involves Medicare Advantage Plans (Part C). These are offered by private insurance companies that have been approved by Medicare and are much like HMO or PPO insurance plans in that they combine the services associated with Part A, Part B, and usually Part D into one insurance policy. Individuals who enroll in Medicare Advantage Plans do not typically need a Medicare Supplement Plan (CMS, 2014). Further discussion of Medicare Advantage Plans is beyond the scope of this chapter.

Original Medicare

Original Medicare is a fee-for-service insurance program managed by Medicare, and as indicated above, is composed of various parts (i.e., Part A, Part B, Part D). The system also administers Medigap, which, as indicated above, is supplemental insurance that helps pay costs that Original Medicare does not pay. Some Original Medicare programs are administered directly by Medicare (i.e., Part A–hospitalization and Part B–medical insurance), and some are offered by private insurance companies (Medigap and Part D–drug coverage). Most Medicare programs require monthly or quarterly premiums to be paid by the recipient, and most involve a late enrollment penalty if individuals do not sign up when they are first eligible. For Medicare Part B, premiums vary according to annual income, with higher premiums for those with higher income levels (based on modified gross income reported on recent tax returns; CMS, 2014).

With Original Medicare, clients have a choice of doctors, hospitals, and other providers that accept Medicare, and they do not need a primary care doctor or referrals to see a specialist as long as the specialist is enrolled as a Medicare provider. To be enrolled as a provider, a doctor or medical service or facility "accepts assignment," which means that they have signed an agreement with Medicare to accept the Medicare-approved fee for covered services. Some doctors, health care providers, and equipment companies have not "accepted assignment." It is, therefore, prudent to determine whether they have done so prior to receiving their services. Clients or their case manager can ask the service provider directly, call Medicare, or visit http://www.medicare.gov/physician or http://www.medicare.gov/supplier.

Clients do not need to file their own insurance claims for any services provided by programs that are Medicare providers. Hospitals, doctors, skilled nursing facilities, home health agencies, and other suppliers are required to file claims for any covered services that they provide, and they cannot charge more than the Medicare-approved fee. Under Part B, clients will be expected to pay a deductible and coinsurance; however, clients are typically not asked to pay these until Medicare has processed a claim and paid its share. Part D also requires that clients pay for part of their drugs in addition to that paid by the insurance company. The formulas for these payments are extremely complicated and often change from year to year (Mamboleo & Kampfe, 2009; CMS, 2014).

I have found that various medical providers have devised ways to charge for additional services or costs for which they request a patient's signature during an office visit—the result is the patient is charged for services that Medicare does not reimburse. For example, a person may go to a general doctor for an annual "wellness visit" because this is a free service to the client (CMS, 2014). While at the doctor's office, the patient may be asked to sign an additional form and then be charged for a "physical examination" that is considered to be over-and-above the wellness visit. Counselors, as case managers, need to make their clients aware of this possibility and help them develop strategies to avoid this situation or be prepared for an invoice for this aspect of the visit.

Special Programs to Assist With Paying for Medical Insurance

In discussions of medical care for older people, it is important to note that provisions of the Affordable Care Act will affect Medicare and that many preventative services will now be covered without coin-surance or a deductible (see http://www.medicare.gov/about-us/affordable-care-act/affordable-care-act.html). Counselors will want to stay abreast of any regulations associated with this and other health care acts. Furthermore, several programs are designed to help individuals with low incomes or low resources with the costs of medical insurance or medical services. Information about these programs is not always consistent, guidelines are complex and change from time to time, and some programs are based on short-term local grants.

Medicaid is perhaps the most commonly used of these programs and is a joint federal and state effort. Medicaid offers several types of programs to help with various aspects of medical insurance, each of which has eligibility criteria. Generally, Medicaid can help pay Medicare costs (usually the Medicare Part B premium as well as the 20% that Medicare does not cover, over the deductible). Furthermore, if individuals are eligible for assistance with paying Medicare Part B premiums, they may automatically qualify for help with paying premiums for their Part D drug prescription plan. Medicaid also offers much more than medical assistance. For example, it can provide help with the costs of housing, food, and transportation (SSA, 2011f).

Medicaid programs are unique to each state and may have different names (e.g., Medi-cal, Medical Assistance). Counselors with clients who need support for their medical insurance payments or for medical treatment should, therefore, encourage clients to contact local and state Medicaid or Social Security offices or their State Health Insurance Assistance Program (SHIP). In addition to helping with questions about Medicaid and other federal programs, these local and state offices may provide information about special local assistance projects.

Other Case-Management Issues Regarding Medicare and Other Medical Insurance

Because Medicare offers a wide variety of opportunities for medical insurance, the system is extraordinarily complicated and is nearly impossible to fully comprehend. Understanding the options, enrolling in programs, meeting appropriate deadlines, making arrangements for appropriate payments, and ultimately utilizing these programs to their fullest can be daunting to clients, family members, and case managers.

Furthermore, because Medicare involves various types of insurance, it is typical for individuals to find themselves with several different insurance policies, all with different payment plans, rules, and regulations. Some of these may be administered directly by Medicare, but many will be offered by private stand-alone insurance companies that have various guidelines and policies. Furthermore, several methods exist for paying premiums for the various Medicare-related insurance policies. For example, people may pay for their insurance by automatic deductions from their Social Security checks, automatic payments from a bank or from credit card companies, or checks using payment coupons. They may also make quarterly versus monthly premium payments. Case managers can help their clients keep track of the complex situation by preparing a chart or grid that includes the following for all of policies held by an individual: type of policy (e.g., primary medical insurance, prescription drug, dental, supplemental insurance), the entity providing the insurance, the amount of premium due each month or quarter, the method of payment for each policy, and contact information. It is also helpful to develop files that contain correspondence from each of these entities.

Resources for Medicare and Medicaid Issues

AARP Benefits QuickLINK, https://www.benefitscheckup.org/aarpkeybenefits—Navigates through local, state, federal, and private/public benefit programs. Includes information on Medicare savings programs; Medicare prescription drug coverage; Medicare RX extra help; State Pharmaceutical Assistance Programs (SPAP); Medicaid for Aged, Blind and Disabled; and the Supplemental Nutrition Assistance Program (SNAP). AARP also offers http://www.aarp.org/medicare, which includes enrollment periods, benefit options, and comparisons of Medicare plans.

Centers for Medicare and Medicaid Services (CMS), 800-633-4227 or TTY 877-486-2048, http://www.medicare.gov

EyeCareAmerica.org—Helps determine whether an older person qualifies for a no-cost comprehensive medical eye examination and up to 1 year of care by a volunteer ophthalmologist

Federally funded health centers—Provide medical and dental care on a sliding scale; visit http://www.findahealthcenter.hrsa.gov

Local dental schools—Visit local dental schools or http://www.nidcr. nih.gov/ for free or low-cost dental care

Medicare, http://www.socialsecurity.gov/pubs

National Council on Aging (NCOA) online screening service, http:// www.BenefitsCheckUp.org

Social Security Administration (SSA), 800-772-1213 or http:// www.socialsecurity.gov/extrahelp

Summary of Case-Management Tips for Medicare and Other Medical Insurance

Because eligibility for many programs is based on a lifetime of work records and Social Security tax payments, it is important that names and Social Security numbers are correct in all correspondence and paperwork, including W-2 forms and applications for and correspondence with the SSA.

Statutes (laws), regulations, and rulings are the official and legal documents that describe medical insurance and medical systems available to older people. Because these can be revised from year to year, it is important to review all new medical insurance laws and guidelines and Medicare plans annually (typically in the fall) and to read all correspondence from Medicare, Social Security, or other medical insurance companies.

Open enrollment dates for Medicare or other health insurance policies may change from year to year; therefore, it is important to be aware of correct enrollment deadlines.

Prior to annual enrollment deadlines, people are barraged with a multitude of advertisements from various medical insurance companies. These communications can lead to a great deal of confusion about what is offered.

Each state has a Medicare-funded SHIP to help consumers make choices and understand their insurance options (especially Medicare, Part D). Specific state SHIP programs can be found at http://www. seniorsresourceguide.com/directories/National/SHIP/, the National Eldercare Locator (800-677-1116), the state insurance commissioner's office, or local senior centers.

Occasionally, companies offering prescription drug coverage will notify participants of an arbitrary switch in their type of plan for the following year. These switches must be reviewed carefully, because they sometimes benefit the company rather than the client. It is probably best to contact a SHIP program each year to identify the most cost-effective policies available for each person.

Occasionally, there can be a breakdown in communication between Medicare and other entities (e.g., Social Security, private insurance companies). This lack of communication can result in inaccurate insurance enrollment status, which can be a serious situation and may involve multiple communications with all parties to ensure that clients are truly enrolled.

Monthly insurance premiums are often paid via deductions from Social Security. It is, therefore, helpful to monitor Social Security deductions to be certain that any Medicare premiums are being paid appropriately. This same concept applies to any other methods of premium payment.

In the event that a case manager needs to communicate with the SSA, Medicare, or an insurance company, it is vital to have official status to do so. Each program or company has its own requirements for such authorization. For Medicare, authorization forms can be obtained by visiting Medicare at http://www.medicare.gov or by calling 800-MEDICARE. Seeking forms online seems to be much faster and more effective than telephone requests for forms.

It is important to be prepared with specific information when communicating with the SSA, Medicare, or insurance companies. At the very least, one must have the correctly spelled name, address, birth date, Social Security number, Medicare number, authorization to speak with these entities, and sometimes specific medical information. Obtaining each of these items can be time consuming and frustrating; therefore, good client records and attention to deadlines can be helpful.

When contacting the SSA, Medicare, and specific insurance companies, it is not uncommon to receive inconsistent information both within each organization and from one organization to another. Follow-up calls and triangulation (i.e., checking more than one resource or calling back to ensure that the information is correct) is useful.

Each year, Medicare publishes a number of information guides. One very useful publication is *Medicare and You*. This publication provides (a) an overview, (b) detailed information, and (c) current contact numbers and websites.

When calling Medicare, it is not uncommon to wait for at least 15 minutes to be served. This is especially true in the early part of the week and month. Callers are given the option of asking for a call back rather than being put on hold without losing their place in line. This call-back system is typically effective and time-saving.

Older people may need the help of a case manager to understand and access benefits associated with retirement and aging (Institute on Rehabilitation Issues, 2009). When considering case management, however, it is important for counselors to remember that many older people have lived lives that involved decision making, adjustment to transitions, resilience, and self-determination (Shallcross, 2012c). Furthermore, counselors may not have the information or expertise to provide case management for many of the financial and benefits issues of older people. It may, therefore, be inappropriate for counselors to conduct case management in these areas.

Chapter 11
Retirement and the Need or Desire to Work

The purpose of this chapter is to discuss various aspects of retirement. Topics addressed include perceptions of retirement and variables that might influence one's response to this event, the degree to which older people need or desire to work, the positive qualities of older workers, the financial impact of working after retirement age, the barriers to employment that exist for older people, the pros and cons of volunteer work, and issues associated with counselors retiring.

In the past, age 65 was considered to be the traditional retirement age, and retirement was viewed as a sedentary time; however, this concept is changing. The cohort that preceded the Baby Boomers has already begun to change the face of retirement with regard to the need and desire to work, the type of housing they prefer, and the lifestyles they are living. Furthermore, Baby Boomers have been accustomed to making things change, challenging authority and norms, and demonstrating resilience. As they reach the traditional retirement age, they may once again challenge the norms regarding retirement (AARP, 2011; Shallcross, 2012c).

Retirement can be viewed in a variety of ways. Some people perceive it as a positive change because it may free them from demanding stressful jobs and give them time to take it easy or to partake in activities that they enjoy (Kim & Moen, 2002). They may see it as a time when they can travel, do things they have always wanted do, and live in a variety of locations. The chapters on housing issues (Chapter 12) and aging well (Chapter 4) give details about various possibilities that can be considered during retirement.

Other people may perceive retirement as an unsettling experience or a negative change that they feel uncertain about, dread, or associate with a loss of vitality. They may, therefore, feel overwhelmed and disoriented as they approach or reach retirement age. They may also grieve the reality that they have fewer years to live and that they are facing other transitions that may not seem positive. Once retired, they may have difficulty adjusting because leaving a job can involve a loss of one's identity, self-worth, and social network. These losses can result in an increased sense of isolation and diminished sense of morale and well-being (Kim & Moen, 2002; Shallcross, 2012c).

Studies (primarily of men) regarding the relationship between psychological well-being and retirement have resulted in mixed findings. Some have shown that retirement is positively related to psychological well-being, some have shown that it is negatively related to psychological well-being, and others have shown no relationship between retirement and psychological well-being (Kim & Moen, 2002).

A number of variables may influence people's psychological responses to retirement. These variables include gender, prior levels of psychological well-being, marital quality, financial state, and postretirement decreases in subjective health and/or personal control. For example, Kim and Moen (2002) found that men who had low morale when still working had greater increases in morale after retirement than those who had high morale when they were working. In contrast, men who had depressive symptoms earlier in retirement reported more depressive symptoms as time progressed. Downward changes in perceived health after retirement were related to decreased psychological well-being for both men and women. Downward changes in marital quality after retirement were related to decreased psychological well-being for women but not for men. Decreased personal control after retirement was the strongest predictor of decreased psychological well-being for both men and women.

Length of time since retirement may influence thoughts and feelings about retirement. Kim and Moen (2002) found that newly retired men had higher levels of psychological well-being and fewer depressive symptoms shortly after their retirement (e.g., within 2 years) than they had when they were working, whereas men who had already been retired for some time showed more depressive symptoms than they had when they were working. Furthermore, newly retired men showed higher morale scores than men who had been retired for some time or men who had not yet retired. These findings may be an indication that for men, the immediate transition into retirement may reduce the worry, overload, and work strain associated with their jobs, thus contributing to their immediate psychological well-being; however, long-term retirement may result in lower psychological well-being. On the other hand, Kim and Moen found no evidence that retirement was related to women's psychological well-being.

Counselors' Considerations When Working With Preretirees and Retirees

Preretirement planning is very important. Riker and Myers's (1989) retirement planning model, as adapted by Thomas, Martin, Alexander, Cooley, and Loague (2003), may be useful in this process. This model includes planning for spiritual growth, intellectual stimulation, social involvement, community involvement, professional involvement, and special issues such as health constraints. Counselors working with preretirees can ask open-ended questions such as, "What will you do with your free time?" "How can you use your knowledge, skills, and interests when you are retired?" and "How do you plan to stay connected with others?"

For partners, planning for retirement is not a one-person issue. Therefore, it is important for them to consider their diverse or mutual desires and needs (Kim & Moen, 2002). Counselors can ask couples to consider the following issues: Are they both ready to retire, or is just one person wanting to retire? If only one person is retiring, how will they handle the new situation/relationship? If both retire, what are their individual dreams about retirement, and what kind of compromises will they need to make? If both retire, how will this affect their income levels and their ability to pay their expenses and do the things they want to do? (J. B. Quinn, 2012).

Often, preretirees and retirees do not have a strong understanding of their projected expenses after retirement. Counselors can, therefore, invite clients to review their anticipated expenses and ask them questions about costs they may not have considered. For example, counselors can ask clients to review, in detail, the costs associated with food; recreation; housing; transportation; travel for pleasure; health care; long-term or assisted care; multiple medical, life, and long-term care insurance premiums; gifts or support for family members; and other financial responsibilities (Braman, 2012; J. B. Quinn, 2012).

Many of these expenses, such as the cost of medical insurance, may seem like new expenses because individuals must pay for these in new ways upon retirement. For example, prior to retirement or prior to a spouse's retirement, the costs of insurance policies may have been automatically withdrawn from their paychecks or partially paid by an employer. After retirement, however, the individual and/or the spouse may be surprised at the costs of various health insurance premiums. Because maintenance of health insurance is critical in retirement, it is vital that clients understand the costs and benefits associated with various policies. For example, it is important to realize that in a marriage or partnership, if one of the retired partners has not yet reached eligibility for Medicare, the cost of private insurance is very high, especially if the partner is age 60 or older (J. B. Quinn, 2012). Retirement and health insurance issues will also be important for older people who still have dependent children or adopted children. They will need to give a great deal of thought to the impact that their retirement will have on insurance and other needs of their children. Counselors can encourage clients to consider these expenses prior to making a decision to retire so that they can determine when to retire and how to prepare for it. Counselors will also want to encourage clients to consider how the Affordable Care Act may ameliorate the issue of affordability of insurance and provide a website address that can provide information about this and other legislation (http://www.healthlawanswers.aarp.org).

In addition to being unaware of their projected expenses after retirement, many people do not have sufficient information about their projected income after retirement (Braman, 2012; J. B. Quinn, 2012), and many do not have sufficient savings to fully retire (S. M. Smith & Kampfe, 2000; Wadsworth et al., 2006). Counselors can, therefore, invite individuals to compare their projected postretirement expenses to their income and assets at retirement (e.g., Social Security, pensions, savings, investments). If clients discover that their estimated postretirement costs will be more their than income, counselors can use creative problem solving to help them consider alternative solutions, such as delaying their retirement (which has many implications); moving to a state with lower taxes; selling a current home and purchasing a smaller one or renting a small apartment; sharing housing with children or friends; taking in a boarder; cutting back on gifts, travel, or optional expenses; or finding other ways to make certain that they have sufficient income (Braman, 2012).

As people begin to think about retiring, they might want to spend a year living on the amount of income they project they will have after retirement. This exercise will give them an opportunity to determine whether they can maintain the kind of lifestyle they want. It can help them consider whether they need to cut back on expenses, find other sources of income in retirement, or postpone retirement in order to save funds for the future and/or to increase the amount of annual benefits they will receive from Social Security (J. B. Quinn, 2012). Counselors can invite preretirees to consider this exercise and to discuss their experiences with the counselor and other professionals. If clients are not willing to do this for one year, they can be invited to do it for one month.

Once clients have retired, it is important for counselors to listen respectfully to any doubts they have about their retirement and to help them work through these. Counselors can ask clients to compare the positives and negatives of their retirement. In this process, counselors should not assume that retirees are finished with new life experiences. Rather, it is important to assume that they can take on new and challenging tasks and projects and tap into their strengths (Shallcross, 2012c).

Need and Desire to Work Beyond the Traditional Retirement Age

As indicated above, the concept of retirement is evolving. Most studies show a trend toward continued work after the traditional retirement age (i.e., age 65). For example, Cahill, Giandrea, and Quinn (2006) found that approximately 60% of their older participants who had a history of career employment continued to work after retirement age. There are two primary reasons for continuing to work: the need to work for additional income and the desire to work for personal reasons.

Need to Work for Income

Financial security is extremely important to older people. On the basis of a survey of AARP members, L. L. Fisher (2010) reported that 99% of men and 98% of women who were ages 60–69 and 100% of men and 99% of women who were ages 70 and older indicated that financial security was important to quality of life. Many people, however, may arrive at retirement age without this security and may, therefore, need to work beyond the traditional retirement age.

Lack of financial security may be attributable to a combination of rising living expenses (AARP, 2003; Bernaccio & Falvo, 2008) and rising health care and prescription drug costs (Finch & Robinson, 2003). It may also be attributable to nonexistent or unstable pensions (Hoyer & Roodin, 2003; Mamboleo & Kampfe, 2009; S. M. Smith & Kampfe, 2000), lack of personal savings (Helman et al., 2006; S. M. Smith & Kampfe, 2000; Wadsworth et al., 2006), lack of survivor benefits (Wadsworth et al., 2006), lack of affordable health insurance (Bernaccio & Falvo, 2008; Maples & Abney, 2006), ineligibility for or low levels of Social Security benefits (Hoyer & Roodin, 2003; Kampfe et al., 2008), and/or ineligibility for or low levels of SSI or SSDI. Even those who have one or more sources of income may find that these are inadequate to meet their financial needs (Hoyer & Roodin, 2003). Furthermore, in the past, people became eligible for Social Security benefits at age 65; however, as indicated in Chapter 9, this eligibility age has increased and will continue to do so. For example, people who were born from 1943 through 1954 will need to wait until age 66 years to be eligible for full benefits (SSA, 2011e).

The need to work for income is expected to be particularly relevant to those who have disabilities, have a minority status, and/or are women because these groups have traditionally experienced job discrimination, low-paying jobs, and sporadic employment and subsequently have less savings. Furthermore, those who have not paid sufficient Social Security taxes during their lifetimes will not be eligible for Social Security, or those who have had low-paying jobs will have a small amount of income from Social Security (Dixon et al., 2003; Wadsworth & Kampfe, 2004). Because the older population is composed of a large percentage of women (Newman & Brach, 2001; S. M. Smith & Kampfe, 2000) and people with minority status (Dixon et al., 2003), it appears that a large segment of this population will be in need of earned income beyond the traditional retirement age.

Desire to Work

Many older people wish to continue to work after the traditional retirement age for personal and interpersonal reasons. With regard to the Baby Boomers, who will turn age 65 between 2011 and 2029, 26% intend to work even though they do not project a need for additional income at retirement age (AARP, 2011).

Older people may work to enhance or maintain their physical, mental, and psychological well-being; social contacts and support; personal growth and learning; identity; sense of order; and enjoyment (AARP, 2003, 2011; Institute on Rehabilitation Issues, 2009; Kampfe, 1994; Kampfe et al., 2008). Some may wish to continue to work in order to maintain their sense of productivity, usefulness, meaningfulness, life purpose, independence/self-efficacy, self-esteem, structure, personal satisfaction, and pride (Bernaccio & Falvo, 2008; Dendinger, Adams, & Jacobson, 2005). Others may wish to continue to work because they do not perceive themselves as being old enough to retire (Wadsworth et al., 2006) or because they wish to share their knowledge with others in their working community (Bernaccio & Falvo, 2008; Dendinger et al., 2005). Finally, some older people may continue to work after the traditional retirement age as a coping mechanism to help them adjust to, or put off, a major psychologically challenging life transition (i.e., leaving the work force and the feelings and meanings attached to work; Dendinger et al., 2005).

Generally then, continuing to work may contribute to people's physical and psychological well-being. For example, researchers at the University of Maryland in 2009 (cited by Murphy, 2013) found that people who continued working on a limited basis after they retired (i.e., semiretirement) had better health and mental health outcomes than those who did not continue to work in some capacity. This finding was particularly true if people remained in their original field rather than trying a new profession.

Because many people may need or wish to work beyond the traditional retirement age, it is not ideal to use chronological age as the primary criterion for ceasing to work. Counselors will want to be aware of this situation and supportive of a client's choice to continue working. Counselors will also want to be respectful of those who intend to retire as soon as they are eligible to do so.

Positive Qualities of Older Workers

Older workers typically have a broad array of work skills and strengths that have been developed over a lifetime. The obvious strengths include maturity, knowledge, experience, and specific skills and expertise. Other positive qualities may include understanding of the work ethic, loyalty to and likelihood of staying with one employer, reliability/dependability, adaptability, resilience, good judgment, ability to work independently, willingness to be involved in projects, openness to variable work schedules, and high productivity. Older workers' performance has been found to be superior to younger workers' performance, and they are less likely to have disabling on-the-job injuries than younger workers. They may have an institutional memory that can be valuable in problem solving and planning, and they may have developed networks with work colleagues and clients that can contribute to company productivity. Furthermore, because of their lifetime of experience, they may be interested in supervising or mentoring younger individuals in the workplace (Borman & Henderson, 2001; Bruyére, Harley, Kampfe, & Wadsworth, 2008; Duncan, 2003; Finch & Robinson, 2003; Institute on Rehabilitation Issues, 2009; Kampfe et al., 2007; Pitt-Catsouphes, Smyer, Matz-Costa, & Kane, 2007; Wadsworth & Kampfe, 2004).

Working Conditions That Older People Want or Need

It is important for counselors to be aware of the types of working conditions that their older clients desire. Older individuals have indicated a desire to work in jobs that provide pension plans, health benefits, and employee-friendly environments where workers' opinions are valued (AARP, 2003). They have also indicated that they would prefer part-time work and flexible working hours. The desire for these working conditions may be due to responsibilities associated with aging spouses, parents, friends, or other family members who require time and attention. For example, older people may be providing caregiving, shopping, or transportation for other older individuals (Institute on Rehabilitation Issues, 2009), and/or they may be caregivers of grandchildren, either on a part-time or full-time basis (Quadagno, 2005). Furthermore, older people may have physical conditions that require rest or that necessitate a considerable amount of time for adjusting to new treatments or for ongoing medical treatment. They may also have one or more disabling conditions that require various accommodations to perform the essential functions of a job (Bruyére et al. 2008; Hoyer & Roodin, 2003; Kampfe et al., 2008; Schonbrun & Kampfe, 2009). From a different perspective, they may want to work part-time because they wish to engage in life-enhancing, relaxing, fun, leisure activities; to do things that they have not had the time to do before; and to have time to spend with their families. In other words, they may wish to achieve a balance between their work and their personal lives (AARP, 2003).

Work conditions that can meet many of the above needs include working fewer hours in the day, working fewer hours in the week, having flexible times at which to start and finish the workday, taking time off for family responsibilities, working from home using telecommuting devices, working at different work sites in the summer and winter (with the same employer), changing the scope or intensity of a job, working only a few months of the year, working as a consultant, engaging in self-employment, cycling in and out of a job, decreasing physical demands, sharing jobs, having occasional breaks from the work station, obtaining ergonomic evaluations, and using adaptive devices (AARP, 2003; Bruyére et al., 2008; Center on Aging and Work/Workplace Flexibility, 2005; Institute on Rehabilitation Issues, 2009; Kampfe et al., 2008; Pitt-Catsouphes et al., 2007). A term used to describe some of these conditions is *bridge employment*, or *phased retirement*, defined as work that occurs after official retirement age but before complete withdrawal from the work force (J. F. Quinn, 1999).

As indicated above, many retirees wish to have fun during their retirement but also need or wish to work. Example of jobs that combine work and leisure can be found in the U.S. Park Services. Jobs with the Park Services entail a broad range of activities, such as working as a receptionist, a gift shop sales person, and a bookkeeper. Workers typically receive a small salary, do part-time work, get free lodging and food, and have special privileges associated with various parks throughout the United States. Other types of resorts typically need seasonal or part-time workers who can fill a wide variety of jobs, such as groundskeeper, room cleaner, bartender, valet, fitness or yoga instructor, golf pro, salesperson, mechanic, and tour guide. More information about these types of jobs and living conditions is provided in Chapter 12 (C. Crandall, personal communication, March 15, 2013).

Other examples of jobs that provide opportunities to combine work and pleasure or travel include transporting vehicles across the United States, transporting people during tourist season, working as a traveling nurse, or being a dance instructor on a cruise line. Tourist-related companies may have seasonal work that meets the need for working and playing simultaneously. For example, Disney theme parks or other resorts may offer part-time jobs that include selling tickets, providing customer service, working concession stands, assisting with performers' wardrobes, and playing the roles of fantasy characters. Another example of seasonal and fun work involves working at spring training camps for Major League Baseball teams (e.g., ushering, selling programs or food, fielding ticket inquiries, driving players and staff to the airport, providing IT support, consulting, marketing).

Counselors can help clients think outside the box by considering options such as these when they express an interest in both working and playing. Many of the above options can provide opportunities for older individuals to remain engaged in work, benefiting from both added income and the social and psychological benefits of employment. The flexibility also provides the opportunity to enjoy other activities or fulfill their responsibilities to family or friends while remaining employed. Counselors can use this information and their creative problem-solving skills to help clients clarify their work and leisure needs, identify jobs and job schedules that meet these needs, consider the pros and cons of each job opportunity, and finally apply for these jobs.

It is important for counselors not to expect that every person will have the same desire to work or desire for certain conditions at work. Fortunately, counselors have been trained to understand their client's worldview rather than to impose their own values and desires on the client. Furthermore, many have been trained to help clients find employment that is consistent with their interests and aptitudes, education level, social skills, physical restrictions and other vocational limitations, general temperament, general qualifications, and other needs and characteristics. Counselors can use their skills in interviewing, paraphrasing, testing, problem solving, and career counseling to help clients clarify their vocational/job needs and find ways to meet these needs.

Positive Financial Impact of Working After Retirement Age

Employment is a key aspect in promoting financial independence and security (Hoyer & Roodin, 2003; McColl, 2002). Working, in combination with various benefits programs, will help older individuals afford lodging, food, health, medical, and other basic needs as well as provide funds for leisure activities that they may have been looking forward to in retirement.

Working after full retirement age can also have a positive impact on Social Security income in several ways. If individuals choose to work after reaching this age, and if they continue to pay Social Security taxes as shown on their W-2 tax forms, this situation may eventually increase, to a small degree, the annual and monthly amount of benefits (income) that they receive from the SSA. This increase in benefits occurs because once each year, the SSA recalculates earnings by adding employment income from the previous year. This recalculation may result in an increased benefit payment (SSA, 2011c).

A second way that working beyond full retirement age can increase the amount of Social Security benefits is for individuals to forgo Social Security income until a later age, which will likely result in higher monthly benefits when they do apply. A note of caution regarding waiting to apply for Social Security benefits beyond the point of eligibility is that, although this action may increase the monthly and annual benefits received, it may over time result in receiving less total income from Social Security (SSA, 2011c).

Working beyond full retirement age can also be of great assistance to individuals who have not achieved the required number of work credits throughout their lives to be eligible for Social Security benefits. As indicated in the chapter on Social Security (Chapter 10), eligibility is established by achieving 40 work credits over a lifetime. If individuals have not reached this number of credits, they can continue to work until they have done so. At that time, the SSA will inform them that they are eligible for benefits (SSA, 2011c).

Working in a job that provides medical benefits and insurance may enhance older people's financial situations. As indicated in Chapter 10, people often have to pay premiums, co-payments, and deductibles for their medical care and medical insurance. If employers offer affordable health insurance, older workers may no longer need to pay Medicare premiums and may therefore have fewer expenses. Again, each situation is unique. Older employees will need to compare the insurance policies offered by the company they work for to the insurance policies offered by Medicare to determine which will provide the greatest benefits and the least amount of expenses.

Working after retirement age may also allow people to continue to contribute to their retirement savings programs and/or help avoid withdrawing funds from these programs (Institute on Rehabilitation Issues, 2009). It is vital that individuals seek advice from appropriate financial specialists regarding this issue because of the changes in the economy and the uniqueness of each type of savings program. Although counselors cannot provide this function, they should be aware of the financial issues that clients are facing and use their listening skills to help clients discuss their options.

Negative Financial Impact of Working After Retirement Age

Employment may have a negative financial impact on some individuals because earned income can influence eligibility for or decrease the benefits associated with a variety of SSA programs. If people apply for Social Security benefits prior to the specified full retirement age and then continue to work for pay, their monthly Social Security check may be decreased depending on the amount of work-related income they are receiving. For example, in 2011, the annual earnings limit for those who had not reached full retirement age was $14,160. For every $2 these individuals earned over $14,160, the SSA deducted $1 from their benefits. If an individual made $24,160 in a year, his or her Social Security benefits would be reduced by $5,000 for that year ($24,160 – $14,160 = $10,000/2 = $5,000). The implication is that clients who are taking Social Security benefits before full retirement age should be aware of the current earned income limit allowed by SSA before they make decisions about continuing to work. On the other hand, if individuals have reached full retirement age, their benefits from Social Security will not be reduced, no matter how much work-related income they earn (SSA, 2011c, 2011f).

If clients are receiving survivors' benefits and they have reached full retirement age, income from work will not affect their benefits. If they have not yet reached full retirement age, however, income from work can negatively affect their survivors' benefits. Because unique rules apply to this type of income, and because guidelines can change over time, clients will need to check with the SSA to clarify the degree to which work will affect these payments (SSA, 2011i).

Working for pay may also negatively affect benefits received from SSI and SSDI. Each of these programs has its own unique rules regarding the amount that can be earned without affecting the amount of payment individuals can receive as benefits. These rules can have a strong negative impact on older people who wish or need to work yet also need the assistance provided by SSI and SSDI. It is important, therefore, for clients to be aware of the impact of earned income on their benefits and to understand exactly how much they can earn from work without affecting these benefits (Kampfe et al., 2008).

In summary, the need to bring in additional funds through work can present a double bind for some individuals who are receiving Social Security retirement benefits, Social Security Disability benefits, Medicaid, and/or SSI because of the limits imposed on savings or income levels necessary to receive benefits from these programs (Institute on Rehabilitation Issues, 2009). In other words, although income from benefit programs are so low that individuals need to work to have an adequate amount of money to live, additional income from working may result in loss of benefits that are helping them survive. This is called a *disincentive to work*, or *work disincentive*.

Because the government is aware of these disincentives to work, it has designed a number of Social Security work incentive programs for individuals with disabilities who are receiving SSDI. These programs include trial work period, extended period of eligibility, expedited reinstatement of benefits, continuation of Medicare for individuals receiving Social Security disability benefits, and work expenses related to disability. A trial work period allows people to test their abilities to work for at least 9 months, during which they can receive their full disability-related Social Security benefits, regardless of how much they earn. The extended period of eligibility involves continuing to work after 9 months without affecting disability-related Social Security benefits, as long as the earnings are not "substantial" (defined differently each year). Expedited reinstatement involves the opportunity to reinstate government Social Security disability benefits that have been discontinued because of substantial income. Reinstatement of Social Security disability benefits can occur when people are no longer able to work within a 5-year period. Continuation of Medicare is offered to individuals who have disabilities but whose Social Security disability benefits have stopped because of their earnings. These individuals can receive free Medicare Part A coverage for an extended period of time after their 9-month period of work. They will also be eligible to continue paying for and receiving Part B Medicare insurance. Work expenses related to disability involve taking into account additional expenses incurred because a person has a disability before determining whether he or she is still eligible for continuation of Social Security disability benefits (SSA, 2011i).

The U.S. government has also initiated a number of guidelines and programs to assist people who are receiving SSI and who wish to work without jeopardizing their SSI benefits. As a reminder, SSI benefits are paid to people who are age 65 or older, disabled, and have low incomes or resources. The amount of SSI payments that people receive is based on their current income from other sources; therefore, when income goes up, SSI payments typically go down. The limits that one can earn are different for each state. Regulations designed to help people who are receiving SSI and who wish to work include (a) expedited reinstatement, (b) work expenses related to one's disability, and (c) a plan to achieve self-support. Some of these regulations are similar to those listed above for SSDI. Expedited reinstatement involves restarting SSI payments for individuals who become unable to work after they have had their SSI payments stopped because of their income levels. Work expenses related to disability involve taking into account disability-related work expenses in determining eligibility for SSI benefits. Plan to achieve self-support involves developing a plan that will help individuals reduce or cease SSI payments. Any earned money that people use to achieve this goal will not be counted when the SSA calculates the amount of SSI payments the individual will receive (SSA, 2011i).

The guidelines associated with these programs are far too complex for counselors and clients, themselves, to understand. Furthermore, guidelines and governmental support for these programs will likely change over time, may be different from state to state, and apply differently to those who have or have not reached full retirement age. Counselors should be aware of the potential negative impact of income from work and encourage consumers to identify resources that can help them determine the amount of earned income they can make without jeopardizing their benefits. For example, counselors can encourage clients to make an appointment or obtain a telephone consultation with their local or national SSA office to discuss the implications that either working or not working will have on their Social Security income and other benefits. After such a consultation, counselors can invite clients to reflect on the information they have received and decide whether they need to make follow-up appointments with SSA to be certain that they are making informed choices about whether work will have a positive or negative impact on their finances.

Barriers to Employment

Many barriers to employment exist for older people. These barriers include the stereotype that older people should naturally disengage from work, legal and historical definitions of retirement age, various types of discrimination, work disincentives mentioned above, and lack of the working conditions that older people desire (Cavanaugh & Blanchard-Fields, 2006; Hoyer & Roodin, 2003; Kampfe et al., 2008; Wadsworth et al., 2006).

As indicated above, age 65 has historically been considered full retirement age. This arbitrary age marker may create an attitudinal barrier to employment for older people. In other words, it may result in questioning the appropriateness of employment for people who are 65 or older and excluding older people from the work force. This arbitrary definition of retirement age may change, however, because of the 2007 revised legal definitions of the ages at which individuals are eligible for Social Security benefits and because of the large number of Baby Boomers who intend to continue working (Kampfe et al., 2008; Wadsworth et al., 2006).

Another barrier to employment might be our society's assumption that older people will have enough funds to retire comfortably. People may believe that Social Security benefits were designed to meet the financial needs of retirees; however, this is not the case. As indicated in Chapter 10, Social Security was designed to supplement other income or savings, and it is only available for those who have contributed at least 40 units to the system earlier in their lives. Employers may also believe that older people have access to many benefits that are not available to younger people or that they have saved enough money to supplement their Social Security income. Those who hold these beliefs may assume that older individuals do not need employment as much as younger individuals do and therefore give priority to younger workers (Institute on Rehabilitation Issues, 2009).

Discrimination in the workplace may be especially relevant for older individuals with disabilities because these people may face two kinds of discrimination (age and disability). People with disabilities, regardless of age, have experienced multiple challenges associated with obtaining employment and with working conditions (Wadsworth, Estrada-Hernandez, Kampfe, & Smith, 2008). For example, the National Organization on Disability (2001) found that among people age 18 through 65, 81% without disabilities were employed, whereas only 32% with disabilities were employed. Another research group found that among people age 60 through 64, 65% of the nondisabled and 28% of the disabled groups were employed (Mitchell et al., 2006).

Once they are employed, people with disabilities receive lower benefits and salaries (U.S. Census Bureau, 2000), lower promotion rates (Bordieri, Drehmer, & Taylor, 1997), and shorter rates of retention (Mueser, Becker, & Wolfe, 2001) than people without disabilities. Because a large percentage of older people have at least one disabling condition, they may be facing at least two types of discrimination (i.e., age and disability).

Other types of discrimination are based on racial/ethnic backgrounds and gender. As noted in Chapter 1, people with minority status and women constitute a large proportion of the older population. Both of these groups have experienced discrimination in employment (Dixon et al., 2003). Furthermore, individuals with minority status have a high incidence of disability (Larkin et al., 2003). Given these circumstances, it can be assumed that many older people may be facing up to four types of work discrimination (i.e., age, disability, racial/ethnic, gender). Several Congressional acts exist that focus on work discrimination of this kind. Examples of these are Title I of the Americans with Disabilities Act (ADA) and the Age Discrimination in Employment Act (ADEA). Title I of the ADA ensures that qualified individuals with disabilities will have equal access to employment (Rubin & Roessler, 2008). The ADEA provides coverage against discrimination for workers of all ages, including those who are age 65 or older (Kramer, 1995). A discussion of these acts is beyond the scope of this book; however, counselors need to be aware that they exist and that they are designed to protect against discrimination in the workplace.

Suggestions for Counselors Who Are Assisting Older People Who Wish to Work

Because many older people may want or need to work, they may benefit from career counseling of various types. As indicated earlier, the older population is a diverse group; therefore, counselors must take into account and respect varied perspectives about employment among older people (S. M. Smith & Kampfe, 2000). Furthermore, counselors can be aware of employers', families', and clients' negative attitudes toward employment for older people to ensure that these attitudes are not creating barriers to employment for their clients. When such negative attitudes exist, counselors can work to dispel them (Kampfe et al., 2008). For example, counselors can inform employers of the positive qualities of older workers, as described above.

Career development can be conceived of as a dynamic, lifelong progression rather than an activity that only occurs in one's younger years. As such, it can be a process that involves a lifetime of engagement in continued assessment, analysis, and synthesis of one's vocational self in the world of work. Thus, career development can continue into older adulthood (Kampfe et al., 2005).

Because older people may have experienced changes in health, functional level, vocational interests, or views about the circumstances under which they wish to work, they may need a career transition plan. Counselors, especially those who have skills in vocational counseling, can assist these older clients with their plans (Kampfe et al., 2008; S. M. Smith & Kampfe, 2000; Wadsworth & Kampfe, 2004). Such planning can involve recognizing, developing, and retaining a vocational skill set that can be transferred across various and successive employment situations (Kampfe et al., 2005).

Assessment is an important aspect of job placement, job development, and other facets of career counseling. Because the older population is a diverse group, it will be important to utilize an individualized and adaptable assessment strategy that accommodates and captures the unique qualities of each person and includes a measure of interests, aptitudes, and cognitive and physical capabilities. Because older people have a lifetime of experiences, assessment should include a detailed history of their past activities and jobs that can be used to identify transferable skills for future employment. As indicated earlier, older individuals may desire certain work conditions (e.g., flexible and fewer hours). It is therefore important for assessment to include an in-depth review of each person's unique needs and desires in addition to their skills and backgrounds. This review will help the counselor and the client focus on jobs that can meet these needs (Kampfe et al., 2005, 2007, 2008). It is also important to be aware of the general issues associated with assessment of older people, as discussed in Chapter 7.

The unique working conditions desired by older people (e.g., flexible work schedules and fewer working hours) can also pose a challenge for the counselor because these conditions may not meet the needs of certain employers. Job development and job placement services may, therefore, be required in many cases. In this process, counselors and their clients can conduct a job trend analysis that includes information about the kinds of companies that are open to and/or enthusiastic about employing older individuals, the kinds of jobs that meet the individual needs of the client, the skills that are required in the available jobs, the work accommodations/flexibility associated with various jobs, and the benefits associated with specific employers (Kampfe et al., 2007, 2008).

Finally, as in every aspect of counseling, it is important that career counseling has the goal of empowering older people to make their own vocational choices. Therefore, counselors will want to ensure that it is the clients, themselves—not the counselors—who are the ones making decisions associated with their desire and need to work (Kampfe et al., 2005).

Employment Resources

Several ACA divisions focus on employment or assessment. These are the American Rehabilitation Counseling Association, the National Career Development Association, the National Employment Counseling Association, and the Association for Assessment in Counseling and Education. Other professional organizations that focus on employment are the National Rehabilitation Association, the National Rehabilitation Counseling Association, and the Career Planning and Adult Development Network (http://www.careernetwork.org). Other resources for career counseling, job placement, job development, or job accommodation are listed below. Many of these function at the state or local levels; therefore, contact numbers or websites may not be provided. Counselors can contact their local hot line or referral service to identify these resources.

Job Accommodation Network, 800-JAN-PECH
Job Opportunities for the Blind, National Federation of the Blind, 410-659-9314
JobSource, National Council on Aging and the Bank of America Charitable Foundation, http://www.ncoajobsource.org/
One-Stop Employment Centers such as One-Stop Career Centers or One-Stop Delivery Systems (state operated)
Rehabilitation Services Administration (RSA) such as Vocational Rehabilitation or Rehabilitation Services (state operated)
Senior Community Service Employment Program (SCSEP), Older American's Act, U.S. Department of Labor (state operated)
U.S. Department of Housing and Urban Development (HUD) projects designed for homeless people willing to live in a shelter and able to work full time (state operated)
U.S. Department of Labor, various specific projects for cultural or racial and aging groups (state operated)
U.S. Department of Veterans Affair's Vocational Rehabilitation and Employment, http://www.benefits.va.gov/vocrehab/
U.S. Equal Employment Opportunity Commission (EEOC) and state civil rights enforcement agencies, http://www.eeoc.gov (and state operated)
Work Incentives Planning and Assistant (WIPA), Social Security Administration, 866-968-7842, https://secure.ssa.gov/apps10/oesp/providers.nsf/bystate

Resource Exploration Activity

Identify three programs that offer vocational services to older people and make an appointment to visit these sites, electronically or in person. Prepare a list of questions prior to making the visit, such as, "What is the purpose of your program?" or "What are the kinds of jobs that older people have found?" If this visit is done as a group, hold a follow-up discussion of the positives and negatives of each program and how the programs can be accessed by older clients who wish to work.

Volunteering

Volunteering can contribute to one's sense of self-worth, strength, identity, and personal satisfaction. These positive attributes are especially relevant when individuals are doing volunteer work that fits their interests, skills, and personality and when volunteers are treated with respect and are recognized for their contributions (National Center for PTSD, 2012; Saisan, Smith, et al., 2012; Shallcross, 2012c).

Volunteering can enhance one's social interactions because it typically involves communication with at least one other person (e.g., the program coordinator) and often entails interaction with groups of people (e.g., staff, consumers, other volunteers; Saisan, Smith, et al., 2012). It can also stimulate social interaction with partners, friends, and family because it offers new and interesting topics to discuss, opens up potential activities that can be shared, and shows that the person is a valuable member of a community (Saltz, 2011).

Volunteering can promote involvement in activities that people love and enjoy but do not wish to (or are not able to) engage in on a full-time basis (L. Robinson & Seagal, 2012). For example, people who love animals (e.g., dogs, wild animals) can volunteer in animal shelters. People who enjoy program development can become involved in various boards or committees that match their professional backgrounds and interests (e.g., drama, business, education). People who love children can find satisfaction in working in shelters or hospital wings that serve children (e.g., rocking babies, playing games).

Each type of volunteering situation will have its unique benefits. For example, serving on a local board for a theater company may entitle an individual to attend special presentations, free of charge; taking tickets at a rock concert or a golf tournament may involve free attendance; picking up a guest speaker for a large-scale writers' workshop may result in meeting exciting authors; serving on a national board may offer the opportunity to travel free to board meetings; or volunteering at a botanical garden may lead to free admission to special events.

On the other hand, volunteering may not be appropriate for or desired by all older people, and counselors should not assume that all clients will benefit from this type of experience (Shallcross, 2012c). Those who are not interested in volunteering may think that they have already made enough contributions in their younger lives, that they currently want to focus on being less responsible, that they want to travel, that they want to play, and that they simply want unrestricted free time.

Downsides of volunteering can include being taken advantage of by the volunteer agency, being asked to do more and more work and to give up valuable free time, getting involved in the politics of the agency, having a poor match between the volunteer and the goals and practices of the agency, having personality conflicts with other volunteers or paid workers, being asked to contribute financially to an organization, losing valuable income because of lack of time to do paid work, and being tied to a schedule that precludes flexibility for other activities. The results of some of these negative issues may be a sense of resentment, hurt, anger, exhaustion, and self-doubt.

If clients indicate that they are interested in doing volunteer work, counselors can help them identify experiences that might meet their needs, personalities, skills, and time commitments and constraints (Shallcross, 2012c). Because it often takes several different volunteer experiences to find the one that fits best, it is important to do a follow-up to ensure that the experience is appropriate for the client. If clients are not happy with their volunteer experience, the counselor can help them realize that an unsuccessful volunteer experience only means that they have not found a good fit; it does not necessarily reflect on the client or the agency in which they have volunteered. It might, however, mean that the client does not wish to engage in volunteering, and he or she should be supported in this decision. The keys are finding the right fit, providing support when things are not working, and not expecting that all individuals wish to be volunteers.

Counselors' Own Retirement

As the American population ages, so does the counselor population. Many counselors are age 65 years or older, and many more will soon reach that traditional retirement age. As this age approaches, counselors may be contemplating their own retirement or may already have retired. The challenge will be to apply the same concepts and practices to themselves as they have used with their clients who were retiring.

Murphy (2013) and Shallcross (2012b) conducted interviews with ACA members (i.e., counselors and counselor educators) who were contemplating retirement or who had recently retired. These interviews form the basis of the following discussion of counselor retirement. Some interviewees indicated that their preretirement lives had been built around their interactions with the counseling community, and that their identities were closely tied to being a counselor or a counselor educator. In other words, counseling was more than a profession. It was deeply connected to nearly every aspect of their lives. Important questions were, "When I retire, how can I define myself?" "What will I do with my time?" "Will I still be creditable?" and "Will my life be purposeful?" Counselors who are contemplating retirement may want to focus on these questions as they make plans for this transition. Because counselors' lives have generally been very meaningful with many connections (e.g., work community, clients, service providers, boards), they will need to use their knowledge, skills, and resources to move into equally meaningful retired lives or perhaps even to identify and enjoy a new identity (i.e., no longer the counselor, counselor educator, or researcher).

As they contemplate and experience retirement, counselors may need to focus on their own needs rather than on other people's needs. Counselors can identify activities that help them maintain their resilience and be intentional about ways to keep learning, having fun, making life meaningful, and staying healthy. They can ask themselves, "What gives me joy?" and then find ways to do this.

As indicated earlier, it is very important to develop a retirement plan long before one retires. It is also important that the plan extends at least 2 to 3 years after retirement. One aspect of retirement planning is to fully understand projected financial needs and resources and to devise ways of saving early and often. It is also important to consider one's partner in the retirement plan and to make sure that he or she understands the implications of the retirement. Employers, Area Agencies on Aging, and other programs are likely to provide preretirement planning services. Attending planning sessions such as these (at any age) can be helpful for three reasons. They can (a) help counselors plan for their own retirement, (b) give counselors the opportunity to experience what it is like to be counseled in this way, and (c) demonstrate a model for counseling their own clients who are contemplating retirement.

Counselors can choose from many options for their retirement. Because counselors have worked with other people at an intimate level and because their identities may be strongly connected with being a counselor, they may wish to find ways to continue to be involved in the counseling community but at a less intense level. For example, instead of having a full-time counseling practice, retirees might change to part-time status, write a mental health column for a newspaper, stay abreast of the counseling publications and research, or serve on boards in counselor-related programs. Counselor educators or researchers can typically continue to function as emeritus faculty, thereby maintaining their professional identity to some degree. They can continue to serve on committees, act as part-time faculty or directors of programs, conduct research, write for publication, teach a course, supervise internships, and act as paid consultants.

Counselors may wish to enjoy their retirement without work-related responsibilities. Some of the positives associated with retirement include being able to move nearer to family members, spend more time with children and grandchildren, wake up whenever one wishes, have more time for self-care and health-related programs, feel rested, travel whenever one wishes, take long walks, spend time in leisure activities with friends, have no work worries or pressures, and have a shorter work-related list of things to do. In spite of these benefits, retirees need to be careful about overextending themselves. For example, common statements are "I don't know how I had time to work" or "I have too much to do." An important strategy is to set and keep boundaries regarding what they were willing to do.

The retirement process involves numerous decisions to be made and a myriad of tasks to be completed. Counselors need to know what has to be done and the paperwork that is required for each task. They will need to understand the guidelines, rules, benefits, and limitations involved in the retirement process and will need to meet important deadlines associated with these. Some of these tasks are further discussed in Chapter 10.

Counselors need to make choices about maintaining or dropping professional association memberships, professional credentials (certification and licensure), and professional insurance; however, they may find that these offer retirement rates. Other practical issues have to do with balancing expenses with income and savings. Even though they may have saved all their lives and contributed to Social Security, there may still be the uncertainty of whether they have saved enough to have a quality lifestyle.

One transition involved in retirement is moving out of the office. Such moves force counselors to physically experience their retirement. It also forces them to decide what to do with old books, journals, awards, and files that they have kept for years. Although some of these are likely to be in electronic format, counselors may still have problems disposing of these because of their own feelings about these objects and difficulties in getting them to recycling centers.

For practicing counselors, there are many client issues that must be considered (ACA, 2014). Counselors must "assist in making appropriate arrangements for the continuation of treatment, when necessary" (Standard A.12.). To accomplish this, they must do the following: "ensure that appropriate clinical and administrative processes are completed and open communication is maintained with both clients and practitioners" (Standard A.11.d.), "prepare a plan for the transfer of clients and the dissemination of records" (Standard C.2.h.), "protect client confidentiality" (Standard B.6.i.), and "obtain written permission from clients to disclose or transfer records to legitimate third parties" (Standard B.6.g.). This transfer of clients should involve obtaining accurate informed consent to transfer case files to new counselors, making arrangements for record accessibility, and being sure that the new counselor will meet the client's needs. The eventuality of termination underscores the need for a well-designed informed consent form during initial meetings with clients. Such forms should include information about closure so that the clients will understand this concept from the very beginning of their counseling process.

Termination or closure of relationships with clients must be carefully considered (Hirsh, 2013), and counselors will need to "provide pretermination counseling and recommend other service providers when necessary" (ACA, 2014, Standard A.11.c.). Because each client will be different, there may be variability in the amount of time and emotional support they will need for a transition to a new counselor; however, it is good practice to start informing clients of the upcoming closure at least 3 or 4 weeks before it takes place. During the last weeks of counseling, counselors can invite the clients to review treatment goals, recognize the growth that has occurred, recognize their strengths, and identify issues they may wish to continue to work on. It will also be important to discuss client concerns about the closure and about restarting with a new counselor. Counselors can obtain consultation regarding closure from other knowledgeable counselors, colleagues, supervisors, or the ACA Ethics and Professional Standards Department (ACA, 2014, Standard I.2.c.), or they can use the ACA services available by e-mailing ethics@counseling.org.

Counselors may need to work through their own closure issues because the counseling relationship is a unique form of intimacy. They may feel some sense that they are abandoning their clients and that their clients need them. These notions can be reframed by considering the probability that clients are strong enough to withstand a change, that a change may be beneficial because a new counselor will offer a new perspective and a new skill set, and that meeting with a new counselor may give the client an opportunity to look at their situation through new eyes.

Summary

Older adults have a variety of perspectives about retirement. Some may wish to use this time to play and enjoy their lives in ways that they had not previously been able to do. Others may want or need to continue to work after the traditional retirement age, either because of the need for additional financial support or because they enjoy working. Counselors need to remain open to these various perspectives as they work with clients who reach traditional retirement age, and they need to use their knowledge and skills to assist clients in planning for and engaging in their retirement experiences. Counselors can also use their knowledge about retirement when they, themselves, are considering this transition.

Chapter 12
Residential Issues for Older People

The purpose of this chapter is to discuss the various issues associated with living arrangements for older people. The chapter includes discussions of things to consider when making a decision about housing, housing options available to older individuals, how to find and select a residential facility, the psychosocial aspects of moving into and living in a residential facility, counselor and family roles as advocates for people living in a residential facility, payment for long-term care housing and/or services, books and movies that might give insight into housing issues for older people, and resources for housing consultation and support. The chapter also focuses on the adjustment process when a person transitions from one living arrangement to another, and it emphasizes client choice and empowerment in the decision-making process.

Most books on counseling would not include a chapter on housing, but for older people and their families, this issue is very important. For example, in a study of older individuals who had recently made residential relocations that involved moves from one level of independence to another level of independence (typically to a level offering less independence and more care), 80% of the participants thought their moves were somewhat to very significant events, 52% thought their moves were stressful, and 43% thought their moves were disruptive (Kampfe, 2002).

Things to Consider When Making a Decision About Housing

Older people have a broad range of desires or needs regarding their places of residence. Some may wish to stay in their original residences (stay at home), others may look forward to a new type of retirement housing, others may need to make housing decisions that consider their need for assistance with daily living and medical conditions, and others may be forced to move because of family or financial pressures. As indicated in Chapter 1, the older population is composed of a wide variety of individuals who were born over a period of at least four decades. The age cohort to which one belongs will have some influence on people's perspectives of the type of housing and lifestyle they wish to have as they age. For example, the oldest old may be accustomed to living in moderation and therefore have a different view than younger-old individuals about what living conditions should entail (Loe, 2011). It has also been speculated that the oldest old, or people from specific cultures, may have expectations that they can move in with their children because in their youth this was a traditional practice. Today's households and lifestyles, however, do not typically allow for this practice; therefore, some older people may feel disappointed, resentful, or abandoned when they are not invited to live with younger family members (Kolker & Winters, 2012; Xiong, 2012). Furthermore, family members who had earlier pledged to their parents that they would never "put them into" a nursing home may feel a sense of guilt when they are not able to invite their relative to live with them (Adler, 2012). Counselors may need to work with both parents and their children as they deal with these types of issues.

Where people live can affect many important aspects of their lives (Loe, 2011). A number of factors need to be considered when choosing optimum housing arrangements. These factors include lifetime patterns of housing choices, current living arrangements, desire for more or less community and social involvement, desire to live alone or with another person (e.g., partner, family member, friend), cultural perspectives of living arrangements, availability of transportation, desired lifestyle and geographical location, and availability of assistance with medical conditions or ADLs. Older individuals also need to consider housing availability, their own openness to existing housing, concerns of family members about housing options and locations, and financial variables (e.g., monthly income, personal savings, outside financial support, long-term care insurance policies, family financial support, Medicare, Medicaid). Because each of these issues can influence people's needs, desires, and/or options, counselors may need to spend a significant amount of time exploring them with clients.

The 4 S Model for Solution-Focused Family Groups—developed by Schlossberg, Waters, and Goodman (1995) and modified by Thomas and Martin (2010)—is designed to provide families with a client-empowering structure for decision making among family members, especially with regard to decisions about residential relocation and support systems. This model involves family meetings during which family members work together to identify resources and problems associated with current living arrangements, advantages and disadvantages of staying in the current home or moving to a new location, and other alternatives if the first choice does not work out. During this process, the counselor acts as the facilitator who seeks input from all family members, fosters cooperation among the group members, and focuses on the client's desires and decisions. The model is designed to encourage the client and family members to make informed decisions, develop workable strategies, and gain a sense of control of the situation (Thomas et al., 2012).

Creative problem solving can be used to support a client's review of possible living options. As a reminder, creative problem solving involves defining the problem or situation, setting goals, identifying alternatives, gathering information, analyzing the alternatives, making a decision, developing a plan, and implementing the plan (Kampfe, 1995; E. B. Waters & Goodman, 1990). Counselors can begin the process by asking individuals to consider each of the issues discussed in the previous paragraphs. Important keys to this process are (a) good listening on the part of the counselor; (b) involvement, input, and decision making on the part of the client; (c) counselor respect of client decisions; and perhaps (d) negotiation with significant others regarding housing decisions. This process offers clients the opportunity to decide for themselves; thus, they gain a sense of personal control over a potentially difficult decision (Kampfe, 1995). This pre-move planning can also help avoid some unexpected aspects of residential relocation, thereby giving the client greater control over the move, itself (Kampfe & Kampfe, 1992).

Housing Options

Individuals who are older have a variety of potential living arrangements from which to choose. Knowing these options can help the client creatively consider the possibilities and become aware of issues associated with each potential living arrangement. The basic options include the following: (a) remaining in one's current residence without assistance, (b) remaining in one's current residence with assistance, (c) residential relocation without the need for assistance, and (d) residential relocation in order to receive assistance.

Remaining in Current Residence Without Assistance

Although there is variability regarding the type of housing older people desire, they will likely wish to remain in their current residences for as long as possible. This situation is called *aging in place*. A survey conducted by AARP found that 93% of the respondents indicated that they wished to remain in their local communities, 89% wanted to stay in their current residence for as long as possible, and 72% wanted to stay in their current homes because of what their community had to offer (Zimmerman, 2011). Another study of people who were forced to move from their homes to a residential facility indicated that this experience was not at all desirable. One participant indicated that death would be preferable to leaving one's home (Cotter et al., 1998).

Many people who wish to stay in their current living situations will not need assistance to do so, particularly if they are newly retired or are in good health. Concerns faced by these individuals may be of a financial nature: uncertainties about continued rent or house payments, house taxes, community dues, house and yard upkeep, and utility bills. Counselors, as case managers, can help clients clarify the costs associated with their current housing and provide a list of programs that can advise clients about financial sources for paying these. Another concern might have to do with safety. This issue can be addressed by asking clients to identify potential neighborhood watch programs, local police contacts, and other night watch neighborhood practices regarding residential security. Clients can be asked to consider obtaining and posting important telephone numbers in strategic locations in the home and purchasing home alarm systems or personal health monitors.

One option for people who wish to continue to live in their current homes or to live independently (such as in an apartment) is the so-called *village movement*. The village movement is based on the notion of neighbors helping neighbors and involves a joint effort of people in a specified geographical area to obtain assistance with chores, transportation, and so forth. To belong to a village, people pay an annual fee that entitles them to services, such as yard work and transportation, and discounted charges from a variety of service providers. Some villages offer a reduced rate for those with low incomes. Typically, the village office (one or two people) acts as a liaison between members, service providers, volunteer organizations, wellness programs, medical facilities, and so forth. The office also encourages mutual assistance by identifying village members who can help each other and by coordinating a member-calling-member program. Additional information can be found at the Village to Village (VtV) Network (http://www.vtvnetwork.org), the Boston Beacon Hill Village (http://www.beaconhillvillaga.org), and AARP (http://www.aarp.org/villagemovement; Thomas, 2011).

Another housing option is to maintain one's current living arrangement for a portion of the year and either rent or purchase a home, apartment, condominium, or mobile home in one or even two locations. Another similar option is to purchase a motor home in which to travel and live for extended periods of time away from one's primary home. The decision to have more than one residence is often based on weather conditions, location of family and friends, or the desire to have extended vacations in the second or third home. Individuals who live part of the year in one location and part of the year in a southern location are typically called *snow birds* and are often associated with a sense of freedom and fun as they move from one location to another.

Problems associated with this lifestyle include ensuring that medical and social support systems exist in each location; obtaining the type of health insurance that will allow people to live in two places; knowing the laws, regulations, and safety practices in the second location; maintaining two households when absent from one of them; having expenses associated with two living arrangements; having the time, money, and stamina to travel from one location to another; having local transportation and services at the second home; keeping track of important documents; making certain that mail, telephone, television, and Internet services are transferrable between the two locations; arranging safe pet transportation; remembering the locations of keys, house and car codes, telephone numbers, and other household items; ensuring the safety of each home and its contents while living in the second home; and achieving some agreement between partners and other family members regarding this arrangement. Counselors can invite clients who are contemplating this type of living arrangement to consider each of these issues. Once individuals have found two or more semipermanent residences, counselors can encourage them to prepare lists of important items to be transported to and from each location, codes or locations of important items and documents in each residence, and a caretaker who can monitor their empty homes.

Another unique way to incorporate people's desires for leisure, travel, and entertainment into their housing decisions is to maintain their original place of residence but live and work seasonally in U.S. National Parks. When working for U.S. Park Services, individuals typically receive free lodging, meal stipends, a minimal salary, a life insurance policy, and some hours of paid time off. Jobs can range from park ranger to sales clerk. Additional information about these opportunities can be found at https://www.usajobs.gov/. Other housing opportunities within the national park system include working for a private park concessionaire, which may offer lodging, a small salary, food, and free trips on days off. Jobs can include food and beverage service, paperwork, and clerking. For further information about these types of opportunities, clients can visit http://www.coolworks.com. Individuals might also be able to obtain housing and work opportunities with associations such as the Grand Canyon Association (a nonprofit association). Individuals can work at the same park from year to year, or they can select different parks in order to experience a variety of environments.

Other positive aspects of these types of housing and work situations are that they typically provide a vacation-like atmosphere, an opportunity to experience national parks in a totally unique way, and a chance to make new friends and experience a family-like relationship with people from all over the world. Workers receive the psychological benefits from work, have a somewhat flexible work schedule, live in a safe and carefully monitored environment, and can sometimes invite friends or family members for short-term, rent-free stays in the park. Many of these positive aspects match the worker needs of older people, as discussed in Chapter 11. The negative aspects of these programs are that they do not provide medical or other benefits; individuals must be committed to staying with their jobs for a specified time; housing is simple and basic; and many parks are located in remote, difficult-to-reach areas, which may result in feelings of confinement, homesickness, or difficulty in obtaining appropriate and timely medical services (C. A. Crandall, personal communication, November 24, 2013). Counselors, therefore, can ask individuals who are contemplating this option to consider both its positive and negative aspects. Prior to making a decision, clients might wish to visit the living quarters and examine a 100-mile radius to see what resources are available.

Remaining in Current Residence With Assistance

According to the U.S. Department of Health and Human Services, many people who are age 65 or older will eventually need some type of assistance, such as help with dressing, bathing, and eating (Kolker & Winters, 2012). Furthermore, older people may need complex assistance with their medical needs. Individuals who wish to stay in their residences but who have assisted living or long-term care needs have a variety of options from which to choose. These options include (a) adding a small house or apartment to the home or on the property in which caregivers can live, free of charge, and receive a salary; (b) hiring one or more caregivers to sleep in a second bedroom; (c) asking or paying a family member to provide some of the ADL services; (d) inviting a family member to live in the home and provide caregiving; or (e) living at home alone with visiting specialists, aides, or outside programs that provide additional services.

Any of these options can include meal delivery by local senior centers or restaurants, medical supply and medication delivery by medical equipment companies or pharmacies, personal care visits for bathing and dressing, home security services, personal emergency response systems, friendly visitor or companion services, and home visits by various specialists or entities (e.g., health care managers, occupational therapists, physical therapists, speech therapists, home health care specialists, visiting skilled care nurses, independent living specialists, assistive technologists, clergy, representatives from local community programs, housekeepers, and respite care providers), many of which may be available through the Older American's Act (National Clearinghouse for Long-Term Care Information, 2012c). For example, occupational therapists can evaluate a home to determine modifications needed to make it accessible and safe (e.g., grab bars, ramps), make a simple change themselves (e.g., remove rugs from floors, switch cabinet doors), evaluate and adjust assistive devices (e.g., wheelchair, walker), and work with residents to help them remain as independent as possible (e.g., by providing training in balance and strength exercises, use of assistive devices, cooking strategies, and bathing strategies). Services that cannot be provided in the home can be made available via community transportation systems or family vehicles that are designed for people with disabilities.

Other services can include adult day facilities that offer activities, meals, companionship, transportation, and some medical care. An example of this kind of program is the Program of All-Inclusive Care for the Elderly (PACE), which is designed for older people who are frail but who do not wish to live in a residential facility. People who qualify for Medicaid are eligible for this free service, and others pay a monthly fee. Another example of a program designed for people who wish to stay in their homes is the Senior Corps, which involves home visits from volunteers who are ages 55 or over. These home visits typically involve friendly visits and companionship rather than assistance of any kind (Adler, 2012).

It is obvious that finding, setting up, coordinating, identifying payment for, and monitoring such a wide variety of home and health services can become very complex, time consuming, and frustrating and can certainly be beyond the older person's or their family members' abilities, knowledge, interests, or time constraints. For this reason, case managers are often a key to setting up and maintaining the system. Although most case managers have been nurses or social workers, it is my belief that counselors (especially those who have expertise in aging issues) could ideally provide this function. If interested in doing so, they might wish to become certified as geriatric care managers (see http://www.caremanager.org/) in addition to being certified counselors.

Case Example of Remaining at Home With Assistance

After approximately one year in a nursing home in a town that was 50 miles away from her home, my mother decided that she wanted to return to her house. The nursing home staff did not think she could live alone and suggested that it would be best for her to continue to live at their facility. My sister and I decided to honor her desire to move back home and made this possible by developing and carrying out a complex plan for caregiving. My mother also worked

at improving her strength and ability to engage in ADLs and gave
us input regarding her desires. We hired a team of aids who spent
the night in her home (in a second bedroom); helped her clean up,
dress, and do her prescribed exercises in the morning; assisted her
with medications; prepared breakfast and an evening snack; watched
television with her in the evening; and helped her transfer between her
walker, wheelchair, and bed or living room lift chair. We redesigned
her home to include a walk-in shower, wider doors, a ramp to the
house, grab bars, and so forth. Her meals were delivered by the local
senior center at noon and a local restaurant in the evenings and on
weekends. Her bills and financial affairs were taken care of by a local
bookkeeper, with our oversight. Her telephones and television were
designed for easy access. She had an alarm system that she wore in
the event that she needed help during the day. She was visited, on a
regular basis, by home health care nurses, a health care coordinator,
oxygen technicians, representatives of the Area Agency on Aging,
occupational therapists (for problem solving regarding the home
and wheelchair), physical therapists (when prescribed), her minister,
and other individuals from various churches and the community. We
purchased a van with an electric lift so that we or the aides could
help her get to medical and other appointments or simply get out of
the house for social events. My sister typically visited her on a daily
basis to be sure that everything was going well and just to enjoy being with Mom. My brother-in-law took care of the yard and house
repairs. Because I lived in another state, I flew home about 4 times a
year and spent from 2 to 5 weeks with her each time, often performing the functions of the aides. Finding and coordinating all of these
services was a tremendous effort on the part of Mom, my sister, and
me. Fortunately, Mom had two long-term care insurance policies,
Medicare, and supplemental policies that allowed us to pay for many
of these services; therefore, it was doable, and it allowed Mom to
live at home for several years before moving to a local nursing home.
This process was very complex, requiring a great deal of knowledge
of systems, coordination, time, oversight, and assistance from individuals who were familiar with the various service systems. If we had
not had case-management skills and had not respected Mom's desire
to stay at home, she might have had to move back into a long-term
care facility much earlier than she eventually did. In situations like
this, outside case managers (i.e., a counselors) would be very helpful.

Residential Relocation Without the Need for Assistance

There are many reasons for people who do not need assistance with
ADLs or long-term care assistance to make a residential relocation
(e.g., desired change of lifestyle, geography, or weather; desire to
live near family members; and necessity to move because of financial
constraints). There are also many residential options for those who do

not need assistance. These options include moving to smaller homes that are less expensive and easier to manage (i.e., downsizing); mobile homes located in year-round RV or trailer camps or on a piece of owned land; resort homes or apartments that offer amenities such as golf membership, swimming, and various social activities; affordable retirement communities that offer educational, recreational, and social activities designed specifically for older people; various types of multigenerational housing that may offer yard maintenance, house insurance, and recreation opportunities; senior co-housing where homeowners live within small supportive communities designed for older people (e.g., pocket neighborhoods or house sharing); rooms for rent in private homes that may include meals; low-income housing offered by various associations such as the VA; small affordable apartments associated with city housing projects; ECHO (elder cottage housing opportunity) housing, which involves living in a small cottage on a friend's or family member's property; a fully equipped portable mini-apartment that can be placed in a backyard of a family member or friend and attached to that person's utilities; and continuing care retirement communities (CCRCs), life care communities, or luxury adult retirement communities, which typically require a lifetime commitment and offer a complete menu of housing options, including independent living in a home or apartment with the opportunity to move into assisted living or skilled care in a hospital-like setting when needed (see below for additional information about CCRCs).

Residential Relocation in Order to Receive Assistance

Many housing options exist for people who need some type of assistance, and there are many different definitions of and types of housing and care options available. Furthermore, there are many national, state, and professional organizational guidelines, standards of care, laws, and best practices regarding residences that provide assistance. It is, therefore, important to understand the definitions and guidelines that are being used in each specific situation. One source of current definitions is the most recent annual publication of *Medicare and You* (CMS, 2014).

Generally, state governments are responsible for setting standards, publishing guidelines, and monitoring residential programs for older people. For example, Arkansas increases Medicaid reimbursement to facilities that provide a "homey" feeling, whereas Rhode Island rates facilities on the basis of the amount of flexibility permitted in residents' routines. Because the states have primary responsibility for guidelines, certification, licensing, and monitoring, counselors can best find information about these topics at the state level (e.g., the Department of Health or the state survey, certification, and licensure agency). Other ways to determine the current certificates, licenses, and regulations associated with institutional living are to contact the local Area Agency on Aging (AAA), the National Consumer Voice for Quality Long-Term Care (http://www.consumervoice.org), or the local or national Aging and Disability Resource Center (ADRC; http://www.adrc-tae.org). Another way to obtain a copy of clients' rights and the various regulations associated with a particular facility is to request this information directly from the institution in which the client is living or will be living. Asking for these will highlight the family's and counselor's recognition of and interest in quality care.

Following are brief explanations of the various types of residences that provide care. It must be remembered that definitions may vary across states and across professions.

Assisted living residences involve apartments or private rooms (usually with personal kitchens or kitchenettes, bedrooms, and bathrooms) allowing for more autonomy than possible in a long-term care facility. Assisted living residences are designed for individuals who can live somewhat independently but who need support services such as personal care assistance or help with some ADLs, meal preparation, laundry, housekeeping, or medications. There are many types of assisted living facilities; however, they all must meet their state regulations for assisted living facilities (Adler, 2012; National Clearinghouse for Long-Term Care Information, 2012b).

CCRCs offer a variety of levels of assistance within one campus. As indicated above, living arrangements can range from independent housing, to assisted living, to long-term care, to nursing care. Residents can live in any of these levels and switch to another level when the need arises. In order to "join" a CCRC, individuals must typically pay a one-time entrance fee and monthly fees thereafter. Fees vary widely from community to community but are generally quite high. Furthermore, fees may change when individuals move to a more intensive care level. The value of this type of housing is that transitions from one level of independence to another do not involve extreme moves from one community to another, and individuals who live in these communities enter them knowing that they may move from one level to another, as needed. Each has its own rules regarding fees, services, departure from the community, and restrictions that may or may not meet the client's needs. These communities must meet the state regulations for the various levels of service that they offer (National Clearinghouse for Long-Term Care Information, 2012a, 2012b).

Long-term care facilities offer a broad range of services that people need over a long period of time. Most long-term care facilities can provide assistance with personal and daily living tasks such as dressing, bathing, using the toilet, transferring from a wheelchair to bed, eating, and dealing with incontinence; some also offer nursing care. Furthermore, long-term care facilities often provide special programming for people with Alzheimer's disease or other forms of dementia

(National Clearinghouse for Long-Term Care Information, 2012b). Long-term care can be obtained from a variety of providers. The type of care offered depends upon the focus and capabilities of each provider and the personal needs of the client. Examples of facilities that provide long-term care are nursing homes, adult foster care programs, board and care homes, assisted living homes, and CCRCs (National Clearinghouse for Long-Term Care Information, 2012a, 2012b).

Nursing homes or skilled nursing facilities provide 24-hour housing, supervision, and a broad range of services (e.g., occupational, physical, and speech therapy) in addition to long-term care services such as nursing care and assistance with ADLs. Individuals may need to stay in these facilities for a short time or a long time, depending upon their needs. Nursing homes must meet state standards in order to provide various services (National Clearinghouse for Long-Term Care Information, 2012b).

Adult foster care homes are family homes in which individuals who need long-term assistance with personal care activities such as eating, bathing, or taking medications can live and receive services. Foster care homes can accommodate one or a small group of individuals and must meet the unique licensure requirements of the state in which they are located (National Clearinghouse for Long-Term Care Information, 2012b).

Board and care homes (e.g., group homes or residential care facilities) typically provide housing and long-term care to a small group of individuals (i.e., six or fewer individuals). These facilities offer personal care, meals, and 24-hour staff assistance. Medical and nursing services are not typically provided, but some homes do offer these services. Residents typically have a choice of shared or private rooms. Board and care homes are required to meet state licensing requirements, which vary greatly from state to state (National Clearinghouse for Long-Term Care Information, 2012b).

Finding and Selecting a Residential Facility

One of the most important aspects of moving into a residential facility is client involvement in the decision of whether and where to move, yet this client involvement often does not happen. In interviews with people who had made recent moves into a residential facility, participants made statements such as, "They must have known I was going to stay; they brought my chair, didn't they?" and "You just know they are going to say 'no' [when discussing one's desire to move back to one's home]" (Cotter et al., 1998).

Finding an appropriate residential facility can be very complex, confusing, and frustrating, so much so that it can be nightmarish for clients and their families and may require several moves before an appropriate match can be found. Even professionals who work with residential facilities on a regular basis find the system of housing options difficult to understand (Adler, 2012). A memoir written by Kane and West (2005) titled *It Shouldn't Be This Way: The Failure of Long-Term Care* will give insight into the obstacles and complexities associated with finding an appropriate facility.

When selecting a residential facility or other type of living arrangement, families, clients, and counselors (as case managers or advocates) can engage in a number of activities. Multiple unscheduled visits to the facility at different times of the day (e.g., morning, mid-day, and night) provide a great deal of information. During these visits, it is important to note if the residents, their clothes, individual rooms, and other areas look and smell clean; the rooms are individualized and contain personal mementoes and furniture; residents are smiling and interacting with each other; the atmosphere is homelike and warm; and residents are being listened to and treated with respect and kindness. It is also helpful to schedule a meeting with the facility director during which the specific needs of the potential new resident can be discussed and inquiries about licenses and accreditations can be made (Adler, 2012; Silverstone & Kandel Hyman, 2008).

Much can be learned from eating meals at the facility. During these visits, prospective residents, case managers, and family members can determine whether people seem to enjoy the meals; the food is nutritious, fresh, tasty, colorful, and served in a timely manner; the dining rooms and staff are pleasant and clean; residents interact with each other; residents have choices of what they eat and where they sit; and residents receive appropriate assistance. It is also helpful to talk to residents, their families, clergy, hospital discharge planners, housekeepers, and other case managers regarding their perspective of the facility. The state agency that licenses these facilities (usually the Department of Health) can also give additional perspectives of the facility (Adler, 2012; Hope Heart Institute, n.d.; Silverstone & Kandel Hyman, 2008).

After these visits, it is very important to ask clients about their reactions to a facility. For example, when my mother needed to choose a residential facility after a hospitalization, she and I had lunch in a variety of locations. She said that some of the facilities were too plush and too luxurious, and that she would not feel comfortable in these. She opted for a less "glamorous" facility but one that was more homelike. If she had not visited several facilities and if I had not listened to her, she would have been uncomfortable with the surroundings that I would have chosen.

It is also important to note the medically related qualities of a facility. These can include whether a physician or physician's assistant is on call or on staff and, if not, the frequency with which they visit the facility. It is also important to know whether there are registered nurses and licensed practical nurses round-the-clock, the number of falls that people have had in the last month, the number of times an outside professional reviews medications, and the noise levels that might interfere with hearing or cause hearing loss (Hope Heart Institute, n.d.; Silverstone & Kandel Hyman, 2008). Nursing homes are ranked by Medicare on the basis of inspections. These rankings can be found at http://www.medicare.gov/nursinghomecompare/ and at http://www.caregiverlist.com/.

Psychosocial Aspects of Moving to an Assisted Living or Long-Term Care Facility

Decisions to move from one level of independence to another are often precipitated by a change in physical or cognitive functional levels (Kampfe, 1999, 2002; W. M. Wheeler, 1996), a recent significant event such as death of a loved one, a physically or mentally disabling condition (temporary or permanent), a burglary, a fall, or a hospitalization. In many cases, the decision to move to such facilities is made for older people by physicians, social workers, and family members (Cotter et al., 1998). In other cases, individuals make the decision to move because of fear of falling, fear of living alone and being vulnerable, fear of being unable to cope, general insecurity and anxiety (Department of Health, Great Britain, 1994), loneliness, lack of support, or depression (I. Allen, Hogg, & Peace, 1992).

Regardless of the reasons for residential relocations into assisted living or long-term care settings, these moves are often highly emotional experiences for older people (Kampfe, 1999) and can involve complex and often difficult transitions that are stressful (Burger, Fraser, Hunt, & Frank, 1996). As indicated above, a study found that a large percentage of people perceived their moves into or within a residential facility to be a significant life event, and about half thought the move was stressful (Kampfe, 2002).

As mentioned in Chapter 6, the cognitive phenomenological theory of psychological stress (Folkman & Lazarus, 1980) indicates that perceptions of an event can influence how one responds to that event. On the basis of this theory, perceptions of a move may influence an individual's psychological well-being. For example, I found that perceived personal control over a residential relocation and perceived personal control over present living arrangements were positively related to life satisfaction (Kampfe, 1999). These findings are of concern because other studies have found that many older people perceive that they have little or no choice or control over decisions regarding their care and that they are not typically asked about their choices regarding housing (e.g., Cotter et al., 1998). This lack of personal control was substantiated by hospital staff, who indicated that discussions about client choice of living arrangements were fragmented, ad hoc, and arose only when the older person brought them up (e.g., Reed, Morgan, & Palmer, 1997).

Counselors can help clients who are considering or making residential relocations by simply doing what counselors do best (i.e., listening empathetically). Counselors can encourage clients to discuss their feelings and to identify ways to gain or regain their internal sense of personal control regarding new living arrangements (Kampfe, 1995, 1999). Counselors can also help clients identify and perhaps reframe their perceptions of their residential relocations in order to find the positive aspects of their new residences. Furthermore, because lower levels of life satisfaction have been found to relate to wishful thinking and avoidance (Kampfe, 1999), counselors can gently challenge clients when they use these strategies and encourage them to find ways to face the issues and do something about them.

Counselors can help families and service providers recognize the potentially stressful nature of a transition from home into a residential facility, and as advocates, counselors can encourage them to give older clients the opportunity to be in charge of (or at least involved in) decisions regarding whether to move, where to move, when to move, and what to do with their old residence and belongings (Hope Heart Institute, n.d.). Perhaps active involvement on the part of the client can be conceptualized on a continuum (Cotter et al., 1998). If they cannot choose whether or not they need to live in an assisted living or long-term care setting, they can be given the opportunity to choose the facility they wish to move into; if they cannot choose the facility, they can choose the type of room they wish to live in; if these choices are not available, they can choose where they wish to have their bed located in the room; if they cannot chose where their bed is located, they can choose what colors they want on their bed; if they cannot choose what colors they want, they can choose what they want hung on their walls. In other words, if certain options are not available to older movers, counselors, family members, and service providers need to find other opportunities for them to have control of their environment (Kampfe, 1999).

During the adaptation to a new nursing home, the following new resident practices were found to be important: reflecting on and maintaining continuity of self, developing familiarity with the home, learning about and adhering to the social conventions of the new residence, adjusting lifelong social behaviors to match the atmosphere of the new home, and learning to manage one's self in a new environment (Reed & Payton, 1996). Counselors can facilitate these practices by helping the client learn about the facility's rules, activities, and physical plant and by encouraging the client to identify ways to maintain lifelong social behaviors and beliefs within the context of the new residence. Counselors may also wish to suggest that the facility design a new client orientation program that incorporates these practices.

Social support is very important when clients move to a new location. Counselors can advocate for movers to have the opportunity to say goodbye to friends and neighbors and to find ways for these people to visit the new residence (Hope Heart Institute, n.d.). For example, counselors can use creative problem solving with the client and family members to develop a plan to encourage social interaction with old friends, community members, family members, and new acquaintances in the new residence.

Psychosocial Aspects of Living in a Long-Term Care Facility

One issue associated with institutional living is the potential lack of opportunities to make personal decisions and the resultant loss of independence (Adler, 2012; Cotter et al., 1998). Because a sense of personal control is vitally important, older people should be given as much opportunity for choice as they wish. Opportunities for choice can include decisions about when to bathe, where to eat, what to eat, what activities to be involved with, and whether or not to keep a light on in the room. Some of these choices may not be possible in a residential facility because of the vast number of tasks that staff must accomplish; however, counselors and family members can remind staff of the importance of autonomy and brainstorm with them regarding the types of personal control that clients can have over their environment (Adler, 2012).

Another issue associated with long-term care is that staff members often do not take the time (or have the time) to really listen to clients. This situation is typically not because they do not care, but rather because they are too busy. Cotter et al. (1998) reported that focus groups of people living in long-term care settings repeatedly indicated that no one listens and that nursing staff do not have time to talk. Examples of statements included the following: "While everybody's nice, nobody's listening"; "One minute you would be talking to them, when you look around, she's gone. She has got to go and do something else for one of the patients . . . most nurses are like that"; "They don't listen, I must listen to them"; "I haven't been consulted about anything"; "Well, it's not suggested to you, it's more thrust upon you"; and "No one is listening to the loss, anger, and bereavement!" Clearly, these staff behaviors can be interpreted to mean that the resident's opinion does not matter.

These residents' statements (a) underscore the importance of having the opportunity to express their feelings in a safe and respectful environment; (b) are perhaps the most compelling reason that counselors should be working in or advocating for persons living in long-term care settings; and (c) are reasons that the counselor's priority should be to listen, really listen, truly listen.

As counselors know, skillful listening is the key to good counseling. Counselors must listen without preconceived notions about the client or the situation. Counselors cannot assume that they know what the person experiences, believes, thinks, or feels. Counselors must listen with their ears, their eyes, their minds, and their hearts. Not only must they hear what the person says verbally, they must also observe the client's eyes, face, hands, and body. Nonverbal cues are often more telling than verbal statements. One technique that can be used is to imagine that a gossamer thread is attached between the client's heart and the counselor's heart and to "listen" to the person through this delicate emotional string as well as through one's mind. This strategy allows the counselor to focus on both thoughts and feelings of the client. It encourages advanced empathy.

Counselors and Families as Advocates: "The Gentle Warriors"

It is vital for individuals who are moving to or living in an institution to have an outside advocate. As indicated above, many times older clients are "placed" into an institution by their physician or family members. In other words, they are not given a choice about moving into a residential facility or about which facility they will move to, or they are placed in a rehabilitation unit within a nursing home but retained without their input when their rehabilitation is completed (Cotter et al., 1998). Common phrases might be "I had to put Mom into a nursing home," "My children put me here," "My doctor put me here," or "We advise that you stay here after your rehabilitation." All of these phrases denote lack of autonomy and possible lack of respect for the desires and potential abilities of the older person. Counselors as advocates can work with families and older people to make certain that their clients are involved in making decisions about their living arrangements and that they are given the opportunity to live as they wish, to the degree possible.

Once a client is living in a residential facility, it is important for the advocate to consider whether the individual is thriving, happy, and comfortable; being treated with respect; being listened to and served on a timely basis; experiencing independence (when desired and possible); being supported in maintaining lifelong identities; being given privacy to attend to personal matters; being recognized for his or her talents and positive qualities; being valued; being assisted, on a timely basis, in using the bathroom; living in a restraint-free environment (chemical or physical); being given appropriate and the minimum amount of medications to be effective; receiving high-quality medical and other necessary services; and being provided an environment in which they can hear and understand friends, visitors, other residents, and service providers. When counselors find that these conditions are not available to the client, they must take steps to change the situation, and they can encourage family members to do this also.

Obviously, the counselor and family members will need to observe the environment and ask questions to obtain information about the conditions in the client's residence. As in selecting a residential facility, one method of observation is to visit the client at different times of the day and to partake of meals or activities with the client to observe the interactions among staff, other residents, and clients.

Counselors can use their listening and observation skills to learn clients' thoughts and feelings about their living conditions and can watch for signs of depression and failure to thrive as well as signs of growth and improved health. During counseling sessions, they might ask clients whether the move has been positive or negative, whether they have control over various activities during the day, whether staff members are responsive to their needs, and whether they feel good or bad about their living situation. Counselors can ask open-ended questions such as, "What do you like best or least about this place?" "If you could change something here, what would it be?" "Who do you especially like/dislike here?" "Do you feel safe here?" and "How much control do you have over your daily schedule?" Obviously, responses to these questions can be paraphrased and certainly empathized with. If the person appears not to be thriving or has many worries or complaints, counselors can follow up with these.

Counselors, clients, and family members need to know that they can ask questions, make requests, make suggestions for change, and monitor activities. They can request medication reviews to ensure that there are no drug interactions, that the dosages are appropriate for the age and size of the client, and that the medications are not causing any cognitive or psychological problems. They can make suggestions for appropriate bathing times and methods, other bathroom concerns, and privacy issues. Other suggestions can be found in Chapter 3 and in the staff training outline regarding dignity versus dehumanization (Kampfe, 1990b). A really helpful book is *Nursing Homes: Getting Good Care There* (Burger et al., 1996), which was published by the National Citizens' Coalition for Nursing Home Reform (now the National Consumer Voice for Quality Long-Term Care). Although the book is no longer in print, it can be purchased on amazon.com.

Counselors, family members, and clients can attend and be active members of residential care planning meetings rather than be passive observers. To do this, they will need to be prepared for such meetings. It is helpful to come with a list of the things that staff members are doing well in addition to things that might be problematic. During such meetings, counselors and/or family members can interact with the staff in a respectful but assertive way and can work with them as a team to creatively identify ways to improve situations for the client (using the expertise of every staff member in the meeting). Clients should be given the option of attending or not attending care plan meetings; if they prefer not to attend, they can suggest issues they would like to have discussed or resolved. In any case, clients should be informed of the team's existence and composition, information being shared, and the purpose of sharing such information. In this process, counselors should ensure that they understand the client's perspective of how, when, and with whom information is to be shared. Counselors should also get permission to work with staff prior to doing so.

As indicated in other chapters, counselors and family members can also advocate for clients by demonstrating respectful behaviors toward them. If a staff member asks the counselor a question about the client's needs, the counselor can turn to the client and ask, "What do you want?" or "What do you need?" If staff members are making decisions for the client that can be made by the client, advocates can indicate that it would be best for the client, himself or herself, to make these decisions. If staff members speak with the client as if he or she was a child, advocates can demonstrate a respectful adult-to-adult interaction with the client. If staff members say "honey" to the client, advocates can ask the client what he or she prefers to be called and do so. If staff members ignore requests for help, advocates can stop any conversation they are having with staff and ask the client what he or she needs.

Older people do not have to feel "stuck" if they are not happy and thriving. As indicated earlier, it is not uncommon for people to try various living arrangements before they find one that is suitable. Counselors can help individuals and their families realize that a particular placement does not need to be permanent, and that it is perfectly appropriate if they wish to try some other option. Contemplating another move might be overwhelming, especially if the first move was protracted, done under stress, unwanted, or in some cases a relief to family members. Furthermore, facility staff might indicate to the older resident or the family that they believe a move will not be good for the person, especially if the contemplated move is to a residence that offers and requires more independence. This warning should not stop the process of exploring options for a new living arrangement. Cotter et al. (1998) indicated that the staff may not believe that returning home is the best option, but allowing this choice might give residents the opportunity to decide whether it was still tenable to be at home and, if not, smooth the path into long-term institutional care. See the earlier case example of a situation in which an older person returned home after one year of living in a long-term care setting.

Payment for Long-Term Care Housing and/or Services

Skilled care and long-term care are expensive. It is important to know that the government does not pay for as much long-term care as people might expect. Medicare, for example, only pays for long-term care if individuals require skilled services or rehabilitation services for a "short period of time" after a 3-day hospitalization (a sort of oxymoron). Other federal programs such as the VA, programs associated with the Older Americans Act, and Medicaid help pay for long-term care; however, each serves only specific populations who are in specific circumstances, and each has its own regulations (National Clearinghouse for Long-Term Care Information, 2012d, 2012e). Additional information regarding government aid can be found at the National Council on Aging (go to https://www.benefitscheckup. org/ for more information).

Residential Relocation Activity

Each residential option is unique, with its own set of advantages and disadvantages. Counselors can encourage individuals to make a list of their needs, identify their options, and then list the positives and negatives associated with each of these. It is often helpful to do this in some written format so that clients can review and revise the lists as they learn more about their needs, desires, and options. Counselors who have a client who is contemplating a move can try the following activity with the client. Or counselors can role play it with another counselor or individual as if they were contemplating future housing needs.

1. List his or her needs, desires, or concerns regarding finances, geographical location, transportation, socialization, privacy, family nearness, family responsibilities, meals, lifestyle, lifetime housing likes and dislikes, cultural perspectives, independence, desired tax rate, affordability, intellectual stimulation, recreation, entertainment, collaboration, help with ADLs, medical or psychological support, safety, availability of jobs, partner's desires, and so forth.
2. List things to avoid in housing, and list constraints.
3. Choose two or more housing options that might fit the needs, desires, and constraints listed above.
4. List the positive and negative aspects of each of these options. This process can help clarify the positives and negatives of available options and can open up new questions and possibilities that had not earlier been considered.
5. Let the list rest for a few days while the client has time to think about these options. If possible go online, make telephone calls, visit with representatives of or individuals who live in these types of settings, and talk with family, friends, and professionals before returning to the list.
6. Return to the list, make revisions and additions, and consider which living situation might be best.
7. Before deciding on an option, make physical visits to these sites to experience and observe how they operate. During the visit, walk or drive around the neighborhood, have a meal, use the facilities, and observe and talk with the residents and staff.

If physical therapy or recreational activities are offered, ask to observe these. In other words, become familiar with the atmosphere and the people who live and work there. (This visit can be done by the counselor, client, and family members.)

8. Discuss your findings with others.
9. Make a tentative decision about a housing choice and contemplate it.
10. Make a housing choice.

Books or Movies Regarding Residential Issues for Older People

Counselors and families of older people can learn much about the factual and emotional aspects of various living arrangements by reading texts and novels or watching films about the topic. Books such as *Home and Identity in Late Life: An International Perspective* (Rowles & Chaudhury, 2005) provide a great deal of useful information for counselors and family members. Excellent novels include *Where the River Turns to Sky* (Kleiner, 1996), *Keeping Time* (McGlynn, 2010), and *Water for Elephants* (Guen, 2006). Excellent movies include *Quartet* (Dwyer, Mackinnon, & Hoffman, 2012) and *The Best Exotic Marigold Hotel* (Broadbent et al., 2011). Many of these focus on the strength and humanity, positive risk taking, and creativity of older people; family issues associated with their elder's living arrangements; housing options that are available; the importance of personal choice; and strategies that can be used when living in a residential facility.

Resources for Housing Consultation and Support

American Association for Homes and Services for the Aging, http://www.aahsa.org or 202-783-2242

Area Agencies on Aging (AAA). To find local AAAs, visit http://www.n4a.org

Assisted Living Facility Comparisons, http://www.medicare.gov

Assisted Living Placement Services. These are local private programs that charge a fee to find assisted living or long-term care facilities. Contact the local Area Agency on Aging.

Assistive technology specialists for home accessibility. Contact the local Area Agency on Aging, State Independent Living Council (SILC).

Commission on Accreditation of Rehabilitation Facilities (CARF) directory of accredited care and service facilities for older individuals, http://www.carf.org or 888-281-6531

Eldercare Locator, a public service website, http://www.eldercare.gov or 800-677-1116

Helpguide.org presents long-term care and housing options for seniors.

Independent Living Centers (ILCs) are stand-alone programs mandated under Title VII of the Rehabilitation Act of 1973. Contact state Independent Living Councils.

Independent Living Rehabilitation (state/federal program). Contact the state Office of Rehabilitation or Vocational Rehabilitation.

Leading Age, http://www.leadingage.org

National Association for Home Care and Hospice, http://www.nahc.org

National Center for Assisted Living (NCAL), http://www.ncal.org or 202-842-4444.

National Clearinghouse for Long -Term Care Information, Administration on Aging, U.S. Department of Health Services, http://longtermcare. gov/ or 202-619-0724.

National Clearinghouse for Long-Term Geriatric Care Managers, http://www.caremanager.org

National Long-Term Care Ombudsman Resource Center, state contacts for ombudsmen, nursing home licensure, http://www. ltombudsman.org or 202-332-2275

Nebraska's Money Follows the Person Project (NMFP), designed to help people who want to move from a nursing home or other facility to an apartment or family home, http://www.dhhs.ne.gov/Money-FollowsThePerson/

A Place for Mom, http://alzheimers.aplaceformom.com

RetirementHomes.com, http://www.retirementhomes.com or 888-544-9124

SeniorDECISION.com. Senior housing or home health care options by state, with consumer reviews and ratings, http://www.seniordecision.com

SNAPforSeniors, http://www.snapforseniors.com or 888-651-7627

State Departments of Health and Social Services give information on respite and support services, financial assistance, facilities, licensing, and regulations.

State Ombudsman Program. Contacts for these can sometimes be obtained from the state Health Care Association or state Assisted Living Association, the long-term care facility itself, the Area Agency on Aging, or the state Department of Health and Human Services.

Summary

People's residences are an important aspect of their lives. A wide array of housing options are available for older people, each having its own unique qualities that may or may not meet the client's needs. Counselors can help clients review their housing needs and identify the options that are available to them. Counselors may act as (a) a sounding board on which clients can express their thoughts and feelings; (b) a facilitator of creative problem solving to help make decisions; (c) a case manager who can help collect and provide information, carry out decisions, and do follow-up; and (d) an advocate to ensure that clients are involved in housing decisions. If clients move into a residential facility that offers ADL or nursing assistance, counselors can help them adjust to this move and act as an advocate, when necessary.

Chapter 13
End of Life, Death and Dying, Grief and Loss

But nobody can heal old age. Because old age is not a disease.
Old age is a part of being born, part of living.
And dying is part of living, too.

—Kleiner, 1996, p. 328

Counselors who work with older people are likely to have clients die or to have clients lose someone they love (Loe, 2011). Thus, counselors must be sure that they have a clear understanding of their own feelings and beliefs about death and dying, that they do not impose these on their clients, and that they have adequate knowledge of and supervised experience with a broad range of end-of-life counseling practices. The purpose of this chapter is to discuss end-of-life issues that older people and their loved ones may face, to suggest interventions and resources that counselors might use in a variety of death-related situations, and to provide information about counselors' own responses to a client's death.

Theories Associated With Death and Mourning

Various theories exist regarding death and mourning. One extensive theory is that of Elizabeth Kübler-Ross (e.g., 1969, 2011; Kübler-Ross & Kessler, 2005). Perhaps the most well known aspects of her work are the five stages of grief (i.e., denial, anger, bargaining, depression, and acceptance). These stages can be applied to one's own impending death, the impending death of a significant other, and the aftermath of a significant other's death. When considering Kübler-Ross's stages, it is important to realize that everyone grieves uniquely, that the stages are not linear, that they are not absolute, and that they are theoretical. Some people may experience one or all of the stages of grief, whereas others may not experience these at all. Furthermore, people may experience the stages in a unique order and may re-experience them. In other words, the stages of grief are one way of conceptualizing a response to a loss such as death rather than an absolute descriptor of grief (Kübler-Ross & Kessler, 2005). For this reason, counselors should not assume that one person's response to death will be the same as another person's response or that everyone will experience the stages of loss.

Grieving is certainly much more complex than described in the confines of Kübler-Ross's stages of grief. Other theories of grief can provide counselors with additional information regarding ways to assist clients who are losing or have lost a loved one to death or who are facing death themselves. Some of the more recent theories have been developed by Worden (2002), Rubin (1999), Neimeyer (1998, 2001), and Klass et al. (1996).

C. A. Walter's (2003) book *The Loss of a Life Partner* gives a synopsis of these theories. According to Walter, Worden indicated that a bereaved individual must go through four tasks in the mourning process. These are "(1) accepting the reality of the loss, (2) working through to the pain and grief, (3) adjusting to an environment in which the deceased is missing, and (4) emotionally relocating the deceased to move on with life" (C. A. Walter, 2003, p. 3).

Rubin offered a two-track/axis model that focuses on disruption, reorganization, and eventually new levels of homeostasis. The first axis involves identifying how an individual naturally functions (e.g., family relationships, somatic concerns, depressive affect, anxiety, self-esteem, meaning structure, investment in tasks) and how this functioning is affected by a loss or upsetting experience. The second axis involves identifying an individual's emotional and cognitive vision of the person who has died as well as issues such as the degree to which the individual is preoccupied with the death, and positive and negative memories of and feelings about the deceased.

Neimeyer indicated that the central process in grieving involves an endeavor to reconstruct world meaning and personal meaning that can help grievers participate in and anticipate important experiences in their lives. He indicated that death can invalidate or validate a person's belief systems, that grief must be viewed in the context of one's understanding (constructing, reconstructing, and maintaining one's sense of self and the world), that grieving should be active rather than passive, that feelings associated with grieving have a function that need to be understood, and that an individual's broad social context is vital in the grieving process.

Klass et al. focused on adaptation and change in the bereaved person's relationship with the deceased individual. They do not support the notion that an individual will achieve closure or that grieving ends. They indicated that grieving may involve negotiating and renegotiating, over time, the meaning of the loss; that individuals will need to identify the things they have lost in the death of a significant other (e.g., a social role); and that even though a significant person has died, the living person continues to have a relationship with the deceased.

Meaning of Death and Variability in the Response to Death

The meaning attributed to death is not universal. Variability exists with regard to belief in an afterlife, the presence of spirits or angels (helpful and nonhelpful), the taboos associated with death, the need to bury personal items with the deceased, the need to move the person out of the home immediately after death, and the extent to which death is viewed as a welcome release from life versus an unwanted end of life. Variability in belief also exists regarding whether or not families and loved ones reunite after death, the deceased member remains as a presence in the lives of the living (either as a positive or negative force), death is a natural or unnatural aspect of life, death happens for a higher purpose, or death is a test of one's faith (Hospice and Palliative Nurses Association, 2009a; Thurlo & Thurlo, 1995). The meaning that one assigns to death depends on a number of variables, including the following: culture, language, religion, spirituality, ethnicity, past experience with death, family beliefs and practices, education, arts, death-related rituals, occupation, and so forth (APA, 2001; Atchley, 2000; Chetnik, 2000; Hospice and Palliative Nurses Association, 2009a; Wadsworth, Harley, et al, 2008; Whitbourne & Whitbourne, 2011).

H. I. Smith (2002) provided overviews of the perspectives, beliefs, practices, mores, and rituals of various religious, cultural, and ethnic groups with regard to death and dying (e.g., Jewish, Amish, Irish, African American, Asian American, Japanese American, Mexican American, Hispanic, Taiwanese, Tibetan, Appalachian, homosexual, military, Buddhist, Muslim, Islamic, and various Christian groups). Reading H. I. Smith's book and others that concentrate on specific cultural groups, counselors can gain some measure of understanding of various perspectives of death and its associated rituals.

Although counselors must recognize that different cultures or groups view death in unique ways, it is also important to understand that not all people from a similar or same culture ascribe to their culture's traditional ways of thinking. In other words, counselors should not assume that because individuals are a part of a particular culture or group, they have the same beliefs and practices as others of that culture or group. Responses to the death or the dying process may also be influenced by the age of the person who is dying or who has died, the survivor's history and experience with death, the circumstances of the death (e.g., protracted, sudden, painful, expected, deliberate, etc.), the earlier relationships between the deceased and the survivor, the degree of guilt associated with the death or the impending death, and so forth (Chetnik, 2000).

The meaning people assign to death will influence their responses to their own death. For those who are dying, variability will exist with regard to their fears or positive expectations, sense of comfort, sense of acceptance, view of what is to come, degree to which they cherish or are dissatisfied with their current lives, their perception of the dying process, and their desire to have more or less control over that process. Some people may believe in and practice passive acceptance of death; some may welcome death; some may accept death as a natural part of life; some may fight or be frightened of death; some may perceive that there is life after death; some may believe that death is the end of their being; some may be confused about the prospect of death; some may discover that their lifelong beliefs of death have changed as death draws near; and some may see that death enhances the meaning, significance, and direction of life and helps them to live fully in the present. Some may wish to die facing the East, some may wish to have ceremonies before their death, some may wish to die alone, some may want their loved ones near, some may wish to die at home, some may prefer to die outside under the trees and sky, and some may prefer to die in a health care facility or a palliative or hospice care program (Minkowski, 1970; C. A. Walter, 2003; Whitbourne & Whitbourne, 2011).

People's responses to death may be influenced by their "typical" responses to loss or crisis. Some may have a pattern of stoicism, some may feel great relief in being able to discuss their feelings, some may find comfort in being with others, some may feel more comfortable being alone, some may use their spirituality or their religious beliefs for support, some may wish not to be asked about their loss or impending loss, and so forth. Perhaps, for this reason, it will be important for counselors to ask their clients to describe their typical way of coping with stressful situations (Chetnik, 2000). This question might help identify effective and noneffective strategies that clients are currently drawing on or that are available to them. Counselors can support the strategies that are working as well as encourage clients to consider other strategies for dealing with death (C. A. Walter, 2003).

As indicated above, there is wide diversity in response to death or to conditions that are associated with impending death. For example, among cancer patients, counselors might encounter wide extremes. On the one hand, people may be fatalistic and accept the diagnosis without looking for information or confronting the condition. They may feel hopeless, helpless, and pessimistic about surviving and may therefore adopt a passive acceptance of their condition in which they are unable to actively cope with or be involved with treatment protocols. Furthermore, they may focus on the past (e.g., reflect backward on their lives) and be future truncated (e.g., avoid dealing with the future or avoid learning more about their condition). One the other hand, people may develop a "fighting spirit" and draw upon their resilience. They may engage in obtaining information about the condition, looking for treatments, and remaining optimistic about the outcome of their condition. These clients are likely to be actively involved in their treatment regimens and make future plans to minimize the effect of cancer on their lifestyles (Livneh, 2013).

Counselors need to be sensitive to all these perspectives, and in cases where a treatment regimen is important to survival, they may ask the client to consider the benefits of such treatments. On the other hand, counselors will want to be open to the passive perspective of death, which may be a realistic view of what is to come. In summary, because there are so many perspectives on death and dying, it is vital that counselors avoid imposing their own values or feelings about death or make assumptions about their clients' perspectives, faith, fears, enthusiasm, dread, rituals, or general experience of death. Counselors will need to understand and respect each person's wishes and do what is necessary to facilitate his or her wishes.

Choice, Autonomy, and Dignity in Death

One theme that may arise as people approach death is the fear of dependency; in addition, many fear loss of control, autonomy, and dignity (APA, 2001; Wadsworth, Harley, et al., 2008). According to Loe (2011), when a dying person is able to actively participate in making decisions, it empowers that person because it emphasizes his or her opportunity to gain control of many aspects of the end of life. This active participation can be approached in individualized, creative, and adaptive ways. If given the opportunity, people can draw upon their lifelong traits of assertiveness, love of life, creativity, resilience, adjustment, and acceptance of the end of life.

During the late 1980s and 1990s, a variety of professions, as well as the federal government and Congress, focused on the concept of empowerment in death. For some people, death with dignity meant having the choice of when to die, dying without extreme pain, controlling their bodies, and making independent decisions. In other words, some people and their families wished to avoid a lengthy and difficult dying process (D. Humphrey, 1991). Dr. Jack Kevorkian and others, such as members of the Hemlock Society, suggested that physician-assisted suicide (PAS) might be appropriate for such individuals. PAS involves the conscious decision of individuals who have a terminal illness to end their lives through euthanasia (lethal dose of medication from an osteopathic or medical physician), rather than dying over a protracted amount of time. Those who support PAS believe that individuals should have the right to make a decision to end their lives via euthanasia in order to relieve suffering and fears associated with a protracted death (Georges et al., 2007; Whitbourne & Whitbourne, 2011).

These early movements regarding empowerment of dying people prompted the medical community to establish practices and guidelines for the terminally ill. For example, in 1997 the American Medical Association published quality of care guidelines for people who are at the end of their lives. The movement also resulted in the passage of a variety of legislative bills regarding dignity and choice in death. Two states enacted laws legalizing PAS (Oregon Death with Dignity Act and Washington Death with Dignity Act; Whitbourne & Whitbourne, 2011); in 1990, Congress passed the Patient Self-Determination Act, which guarantees the right of all competent adults to have control over their health care during serious illness.

The current thought about autonomy and death is that there are many options for people who are dying and that their wishes about how they end their lives should be respected (i.e., death with dignity; Vig, Davenport, & Pearlman, 2002). Adults are now able to write advance directives (ADs) that allow them to make decisions prior to illness about accepting or refusing treatment at the end of their life. ADs are legally binding and must be included in medical records to be certain that the patient's wishes are documented (Hoyer & Roodin, 2009; Whitbourne & Whitbourne, 2011). ADs can include a durable power of attorney for health care and a living will. A durable power of attorney for health care is a document, signed in advance, that identifies a relative, physician, friend, or lawyer who has been given the power to make health care choices for an individual who is no longer able to make such choices. In this case, it is very important that the person listed in this document has had in-depth discussions with the individual and is fully aware of his or her desires regarding health decisions before that individual becomes ill or incapacitated in some way (Hope Heart Institute, n.d.; Hoyer & Roodin, 2009). A living will is a document that ensures that people can decide for themselves, in advance, whether they wish to accept or reject heroic measures to keep them alive when they are very ill or dying. Specifically, the living will is a document in which people specify the conditions under which life-sustaining measures can be given or withheld. Individuals can also request do-not-resuscitate (DNR) orders. DNRs are directives to physicians, hospitals, or nursing homes not to use resuscitation (e.g., open chest massage, cardiopulmonary resuscitation, electric shock) when a person's heart or breath has stopped.

There are a number of concerns about ADs. One of these concerns is that people may think and feel very differently about wanting or not wanting treatment or heroic measures when they are actually ill versus when they signed the directives. In other words, there may be a disconnect between what they projected they would want and what they actually want at the time of severe illness. Another concern is that AD paperwork might not be transferred from one institution to another (e.g., from a hospital to a nursing home or vice versa); therefore, the person's wishes may not be known at the second facility. Other concerns involve the potential for age-biased medical treatment and lack of medical training regarding end-of-life and withdrawal-of-life-support decisions. Another concern is that family members may not have been consulted with or advised about these directives and may, therefore, be unable to understand or unwilling to support them. They may also strongly object to withholding treatment, even if they are aware of an AD to do so. Likewise, if a physician believes that a treatment outcome will result in life, he or she may not be willing to withhold that treatment (Choice in Dying, 2006; Hoyer & Roodin, 2009).

Because of these concerns, it is important that end-of-life issues be discussed early and openly among the client, health care providers, family, and person(s) listed as decision makers for the client. It is also important that copies of ADs be given to family members, primary-care physicians, nursing homes, hospices, hospitals, attorneys, and perhaps friends (Hope Heart Institute, n.d.; Hospice and Palliative Nurses Association, 2009b). Counselors can encourage clients to discuss their wishes with significant others and to provide copies of ADs to the appropriate people. It might also be important for counselors to act as facilitators of these conversations and to keep a copy of such ADs in their client files.

Other choices have to do with day-to-day treatment of people who are ill. For example, people can make decisions about whether to receive hospice or not. If they choose hospice, they can choose whether they wish to receive this service at home or in a care unit of some type. They can make choices about having a permanently implanted infusion line for continuously needed medications such as morphine or having a feeding tube (Munday, Dale, & Murray, 2007). Unfortunately, this opportunity for choice is not always available because people who are dying may be so ill that they are unable to express their wishes (Whitbourne & Whitbourne, 2011).

Counselors must be cautioned that although our Western culture has generally emphasized the need for and right of independence and autonomy, these needs and rights are not universally accepted or practiced. As indicated in Chapter 2, many people have a collectivistic perspective that involves shared family or group decisions in all aspects of life (Reese, Melton, & Ciaravino, 2004; Wadsworth, Harley, et al., 2008). In this case, it will be important to ensure that significant others, healers, and other professionals are included in end-of-life decisions. This inclusion may be especially true for the older population because it is a widely diverse group.

Palliative Care and Hospice

Counselors should have a working knowledge of palliative care and hospice programs. Palliative care and hospice are based on the premise that people have the right to die pain free and with dignity, and that the families of people who are dying should be given support in this process. The goals for palliative and hospice care are, therefore, to ease pain, relieve symptoms, enhance the quality of life, and respect the decisions and choices of the client. One important aspect of palliative care and hospice is that pain can be managed through medications in all settings, and that medical personnel, family members, and those in pain can advocate for expert pain relief. Another focus is on caring for, not curing, a person with an illness or condition that is expected to lead to death (National Hospice and Palliative Care Organization, 2012a, 2012c).

Palliative care applies to people in the earlier stages of the disease process and involves services that enhance their comfort. Palliative care is expected to segue into hospice care as the illness or disease progresses. Hospice can be provided in hospitals, long-term care settings, and free-standing hospice centers, but it is most often provided in the client's home. Family members, therefore, typically provide much of the care. For this reason, family members will likely need support and coaching (National Hospice and Palliative Care Organization, 2012a; Whitbourne & Whitbourne, 2011).

Hospice involves an interdisciplinary team effort. The team is typically composed of a personal physician, a hospice physician, home health aides, nurses, social workers or counselors, clergy, trained volunteers, and various therapists, as needed. The team develops a plan that is specific to the individual's needs for symptom control and pain management. In addition to managing symptoms and pain, the team provides spiritual and emotional support to the individual and family members, drugs, equipment, medical supplies, special services such as physical therapy, short-term inpatient care when caregivers need respite from responsibilities or when the symptoms or pain are too difficult to manage in the home, and bereavement counseling and care for surviving friends and family members (National Hospice and Palliative Care Organization, 2012a).

Hospice is covered by most insurance plans, such as Medicaid, Medicare, HMOs, and other plans (National Hospice and Palliative Care Organization, 2012a); however, there is some concern that hospice may not be universally available in nursing homes because of inconsistent reimbursement regulations and reimbursement structures. In other words, when people are discharged from hospitals under the Medicare skilled nursing benefit for end-of-life care, they do not seem to be receiving the benefits of hospice care in addition to skilled nursing care, resulting in little or no access to high-quality end-of-life care and/or failure to follow the client's end-of-life wishes (National Hospice and Palliative Care Organization, 2012b). Case managers and advocates may need to be watchful for these potential lapses in accessibility to program benefits.

Complementary Therapies for Those Who Are Dying

According to the Hospice and Palliative Nurses Association (2009a), nondrug symptom management therapies (complementary therapies) may improve the quality of life, help relieve discomfort, lessen suffering, and manage symptoms of persons who are dying. They may promote a sense of well-being and relaxation, help relieve tension and stress, promote healing, and facilitate a sense of balance between body, mind, and spirit. These complementary therapies are recommended only in combination with, not in place of, medical care. Examples of complementary therapies are acupressure, acupuncture, reiki, reflexology, massage, pet therapy, music therapy, art therapy, and aromatherapy. Counselors or the hospice team can inform individuals and their families of these therapies, help them evaluate the potential benefits associated with them, identify local programs and specialists who offer these, and facilitate their selection. Counselors may also have skills associated with such therapies and include these in their practices.

Spirituality and Dying

The approach of one's own death or the loss of a loved one through death brings individuals face to face with their spiritual and religious beliefs (Lynch, 1998). This process may give people comfort, strengthen their faith, or cause them to question their faith. In the latter case, they may be faced with spiritual distress (i.e., disruption of a person's value and belief system). Although spiritual distress is commonly experienced by individuals with terminal illness, it may be expressed in different ways. Signs of spiritual distress include seeking spiritual help, having a fear of falling asleep at night or other fears, questioning one's belief system, experiencing anger toward a higher power, questioning the meaning of life, feeling a sense of emptiness or loss of direction, feeling abandoned by a higher power, questioning the meaning of suffering, and/or having other physical symptoms. Counselors and caregivers will want to be alert to these complaints as well as out-of-character behaviors, symptoms that are getting worse, sudden rejection or neglect of earlier beliefs or practices, possible side effects of medications, talk about suicide, lack of caring about life in general, and lack of caring about oneself (APA, 2001; Hospice and Palliative Nurses Association, 2009c; Wadsworth, Harley, et al., 2008). Counselors can help by providing deep listening, referring clients to counselors who have been trained in spiritual counseling, or contacting a spiritual leader who the client is interested in seeing. One organization that focuses on these issues is the Association for Spiritual, Ethical, and Religious Values in Counseling, a division of the ACA.

For many people, prayer is viewed as very important in times of grief and loss (T. Walter, 1999). It may also be important in the dying process. Whether or not to include prayer in a counseling session is a complex question. A wide variety of opinions about prayer and religion are expressed in various books and articles written for counselors and other helping professions. Opinions vary depending upon the philosophy, professional association, professional identity, clinical practice, place of employment, and personal religious affiliation of the counselor (H. I. Smith, 2002). As with all issues, the important point is to provide a respectful, nonjudgmental atmosphere in which an individual can express himself or herself. If a client wants to pray, it would seem that counselors can use their good listening skills (regardless of their own beliefs) to sit quietly as the person prays. It is possible that by doing so, counselors will learn a great deal about the person's perspective of death and loss. They can use paraphrasing, clarification, and reflection of the thoughts and feelings that have been expressed by the client during prayer. As in all cases in which deep personal issues are involved, counselors must refrain from judging, directing, or imposing their own values on clients who wish to pray (ACA, 2014, Standard A.4.b.). Likewise, counselors who believe that prayer is valuable in their own lives should not impose this activity on their clients.

Diallo (2013) found that people preferred counselors who were knowledgeable about their religion or spirituality over counselors who had the same religious background but were not knowledgeable about the religion. Counselors can, therefore, take steps to learn about and understand various religious and spiritual beliefs and practices associated with death and mourning. To do this, they can read books, attend ceremonies and rituals, watch movies, and request consultation from spiritual and religious leaders. This quest for understanding of various cultural perspectives of death and mourning might help counselors be open to, and comfortable with, their client's thoughts, feelings, and actions associated with death.

Anxiety and Dying

At the time of approaching death (of oneself or a loved one), individuals will likely experience anxiety. This emotional response may also occur for loved ones after a death. Symptoms of anxiety are shaking, tension, sweating, fear, worry, confusion, sleeplessness, disturbing dreams, rapid heartbeat or breathing, inability to relax or be comfortable, and problems with concentration or paying attention. Suggested strategies for those with anxiety are to take appropriate prescribed medications, get involved with activities that have helped with anxiety in the past, write down feelings and thoughts, get treatment for any physical problems that can cause anxiety, keep the environment as calm as possible, engage in relaxation practices (e.g., taking medication, getting a massage, practicing yoga, using deep breathing, listening to music), perhaps limit visitors, count backwards from 100 to 0, exercise (e.g., swim, go for a walk), avoid alcoholic beverages or caffeine, reach out to others for support, provide support to others, and take things one step at a time (APA, 2001; Hospice and Palliative Nurses Association, 2011; Wadsworth, Harley, et al., 2008). Other methods for assisting people with anxiety are provided in Chapter 2.

The Hospice and Palliative Nurses Association (2009c) provides suggestions for family members to help their dying loved ones who are in distress. Many of these suggestions can be used by counselors, including the following: being "present" without having to "do something"; providing a relaxing, calm setting; treating the person with respect and dignity; avoiding saying, "I know how you feel"; avoiding "helping" while providing support; facilitating client contact with other family and friends; listening and reminiscing; being willing to discuss spiritual issues; finding ways to honor and maintain desired lifestyles and rituals; enjoying the time that is left together to make memories; and contacting the hospice or palliative team to ask questions. Other suggestions that might help the client are listening to music or devotional tapes (when appropriate) and working on a project.

Communicating With People Who Are Dying

As might be expected, there are some fundamental aspects of communicating with people who are dying. Unfortunately, family members, friends, and health care providers may have difficulty communicating with and listening to a dying person. They may distance themselves from the person, resulting in isolation at a time when communication is important; they may speak of the person in the third person rather than use the person's name; they may not believe that the condition is terminal and still be hoping for recovery; and they may treat the condition rather than the person (Foster, 2007; Rando, 2000; Wadsworth, Harley, et al., 2008). This phenomenon has been called *social death*, and it may happen long before the actual death (Foster, 2007).

Final conversations with a dying friend or family member are very important to both those who are dying and survivors. Discussion themes can include the effects that the loved one has had on the survivor, the enduring love that exists between the person who is dying and the survivor, the importance and maintenance of the relationship, a validation of spiritual or religious beliefs, and resolution of problems within the relationship (i.e., forgiveness or unfinished business; Hoyer & Roodin, 2009; Wadsworth, Harley, et al., 2008). During the dying process, counselors can encourage family members and the dying person to focus on these issues; later, counselors can discuss these issues with survivors.

Because communication is important at death and because many family members and care providers may not be comfortable communicating with the dying person, counselors can provide a vital service at this time. When working with a client who is dying, it is important to place the dying person first; to respect his or her beliefs, feelings, and wishes; to listen without judging or imposing one's values; and to remain supportive and calm (Hoyer & Roodin, 2009). Openness to a dying person's thoughts and feelings and encouragement for family members to communicate openly can help ensure that the dying person's wishes are honored (Engelberg, Patrick, & Curtis, 2005). This openness is also thought to help dying people focus on four important domains: social, spiritual, psychological, and physical (Corr, Nabe, & Corr, 2000). The social domain involves the maintenance of attachment to others; the psychological domain involves issues associated with security, quality of life, and independence; the spiritual domain involves meaning, hope, transcendence, and connectedness; and the physical domain involves minimizing physical discomfort or pain (Hoyer & Roodin, 2009). Good listening and family support can also help the individual engage in the "hard work" of dying. This hard work can include controlling and managing their disease and pain; establishing a legacy; finding a system of security, safety, and support; and searching for meaning (Coyle, 2006).

Counselors who are working with clients who are dying should be aware of the signs that a person is near death. These signs may include sleeping more; speaking to people who are not physically in the room; withdrawing from communication; talking about taking a trip or going on a journey; eating or drinking less; having swallowing problems; turning blue around the nose, mouth, fingers, or toes; having cool legs, arms, or hands; having less pain or needing less pain medication; hearing less well; having blurred vision; breathing differently (e.g., long breaks between breaths followed by deep, quick breaths; sounding congested); losing control of bowel movements and urination; moaning; and becoming confused (Hospice and Palliative Nurses Association, 2012).

When a person is near death, hospice team members, nurses, counselors, family members, and friends can stay close (unless the person has earlier expressed a desire to die alone), turn on a fan or open a window if the person is having problems breathing, maintain a sense of calmness in the room, softly play favorite music, keep a light on in the room if that has been important to the person, identify oneself when talking or coming into the room, talk to the person, say important things that need to be said (the person may be able to hear even though he or she cannot respond), write down the things that the person says to be used later for personal comfort, ensure that medications are given (e.g., medcations for agitation, moist breathing, restlessness, anxiety, or pain), place a cool cloth on the forehead (if the person is hot or feverish), dampen the individual's mouth with a damp cloth or sponge, reposition the client for comfort, include members of the family who wish to or are willing to be involved, and allow the individual to sleep as much as desired (Hospice and Palliative Nurses Association, 2012). It will also be important to include any spiritual, religious, or cultural practices and to avoid any taboos that the person or family practices or believes in.

Grief, Bereavement, and Mourning of Those Who Have Lost a Significant Other

Counselors need to be aware of the manifestations of grief and provide support for people who experience them. In other words, counselors should be cognizant of the potential thoughts, feelings, behaviors, and physiological reactions associated with grief and bereavement. Counselors should also recognize that there is wide variation in response to grief. Grievers can experience headaches and dizziness, muscle aches, dry mouth, exhaustion, weakness, tightness in the chest and throat, breathlessness, digestive disturbances, and feelings of emptiness. They may experience confusion, difficulty with concentration, impairments in attention and memory, preoccupation with the person who has died, and hallucinations. They may feel sadness, depression, anxiety, helplessness, numbness, fearfulness, ambivalence, shame, yearning, and anger (toward family, a higher power, health care providers, the person who has died, or themselves). They may sleep less or sleep more, change eating habits, cry, sigh frequently, dream of the deceased, be overly active and busy, or withdraw from activities. They may become susceptible to physical illness because their immune systems may be compromised, or they may be at risk of accidents. Many of these symptoms may last approximately one year and then subside (Hospice and Palliative Nurses Association, 2009a; Whitbourne & Whitbourne, 2011).

The important point is that grief is a normal response to loss, and individuals will experience this emotional reaction in their own unique ways. In other words, there is no right or wrong way to grieve (Hospice and Palliative Nurses Association, 2009a), and counselors should keep this in the forefront when counseling people who have a loved one who is dying or has died.

Whereas grief has to do with feelings and thoughts about death and dying, mourning is considered to be an outward expression of grief that may include rituals (Hospice and Palliative Nurses Association, 2009a, 2009b). Rituals can be as simple as having a favorite drink that one has previously shared with a deceased person to as complex as full-out prescribed rituals practiced by one's culture or faith. According to some grief specialists, rituals may be important in maintaining and interacting with the memory of a deceased loved one, especially soon after that person has died. Furthermore, some rituals offer the opportunity to celebrate a person's life and can be helpful to those left behind (e.g., initial intense mourning and prayer, the funeral, rituals to help the deceased person pass to the next world, anniversary rituals or prayers for the deceased; Rando, 1984).

As with grief, mourning and rituals are influenced by the meaning one has assigned to death, resulting in a wide variety of rituals. It is important for counselors to know that individuals from various cultural, ethnic, religious, or racial groups may have unique practices, rules, mores, traditions, and customs associated with dying, death, and mourning (Wadsworth, Harley, et al., 2008). This wide variety may be particularly true among the older population because it is a highly diverse group. For example, people from various cultures feel and think differently about viewing or avoiding the body, attending funerals, holding specific ceremonies (e.g., dances, wakes), attending the burial, visiting or avoiding the burial spot, entering the home of the deceased (e.g., avoiding the house, knocking a hole in the wall, boarding up the house, feeling close to the loved one in the house), collecting important possessions of the deceased for burial, and dispensing with property of the deceased (Hospice and Palliative Nurses Association, 2009a; Thurlo & Thurlo, 1995; Wadsworth, Harley, et al., 2008). Because of this variability, counselors cannot assume that any one ritual or mourning activity will be appropriate for every individual. For example, if clients have strong beliefs that they need to avoid going to places where one has died, avoid talking about loved ones who have died, avoid burial grounds, and so forth, counselors would err in encouraging the client to do these things.

In some cases, rituals do not meet the needs of individuals for a variety of reasons. These reasons can include the following: a mismatch between the mourner's spirituality and the ritual; the arrival of a mourner who had not been a part of the family or friendship circle because of past negative circumstances; an unexpected display of grief by a mourner; a physical response of a mourner, such as fainting; or a botched ritual in which the minister, healer, or leader did not understand the intent of the event or know the individual who had died. Counselors may find that these types of ritual-related experiences need to be worked through and reframed. Counselors can ask grieving clients to describe their thoughts, actions, and feelings about the ritual and can help them discuss any negative aspects of the ritual or service that they experienced. They can also invite them to discuss the positive aspects of the ritual or service and how it is helping them grieve (H. I. Smith, 2002).

Another potentially emotionally charged issue is the situation in which survivors have chosen not to, or were unable to, partake in a ritual (e.g., too busy, did not want to, was out of town, was excluded, did not know about it, did not have the money to get there or fund the ritual). People who did not attend a ritual may have regrets. They may feel lack of closure, lack of balance, anger with those who did attend, and guilt for not attending. Counselors can ask them about their thoughts and feelings associated with not attending and allow them to explore these in depth. Counselors might ask whether they were able to express their grief in their own ways; if not, counselors can ask whether there are other rituals or things they can do to express their loss or honor the deceased person. These other rituals or practices can take any form and can be designed by the client. Examples include lighting a candle; meeting with friends of the deceased; going for a walk in the mountains, grasslands, or city; or using some traditional ritual (H. I. Smith, 2002). If the client decides to partake in such a ritual or practice, the experience can be discussed at a subsequent counseling session. All this is said with the caveat that the counselor should not impose his or her own views regarding grieving and the importance of or type of rituals.

Death of a Spouse or Partner

The death of a spouse or partner can be one of the most stressful events a person can experience. In the case of older adults, this death may mean the loss of a significant relationship that has lasted 45 years or more. As indicated earlier, people respond to the death of a significant person in a variety of ways, yet the literature has indicated that widows and widowers typically have symptoms of anxiety and depression and have increased rates of mortality after the loss (referred to as the *widowhood effect*). This widowhood effect is more common among men and may be associated with poorer health practices, increased use of alcohol, and loss of intimacy (M. Stroebe, Schut, & Stroebe, 2007).

Other literature has shown that variation clearly exists among spousal survivors. Bonanno et al. (2002) found five patterns of bereavement over an 18-month period after widowhood. They labeled these as resilience, improvement during bereavement, common grief, chronic depression, and chronic grief. They indicated that widowed individuals display a wide range of grief responses, and that it is not appropriate to expect widows and widowers to respond in a particular way.

Various factors can ease the response to a partner's death. For example, if the death was the result of a protracted disease that put a great deal of burden and stress on the surviving spouse or if the loved one had a difficult death involving pain, sorrow, fear, lack of autonomy, disappointment, lack of dignity, and so forth, the grief the partner feels about this death may be assuaged. In these cases, the surviving spouse may feel relief and a decrease of depression and stress after the spouse dies (Bonanno, Wortman, & Nesse, 2004). The pre-illness relationship might also have an effect on the survivor's response to the death of a spouse. For example, a surviving partner of a loving and supportive relationship may respond differently than a surviving partner who has not been happy in the relationship.

Role Identity and Socialization Changes

When a person loses a partner, it is an emotional loss, but there are also other important transitions having to do with identity, role, and socialization (M. Stroebe, Schut, & Boerner, 2010; C. A. Walter, 2003). In other words, survivors change from being a mate to being a single person. On the basis of these changes, bereaved widows and widowers will likely need to develop a new sense of self and identity as an individual (e.g., changing from "we" to "I"; C. A. Walter, 2003). Hence, it might be important for counselors to help bereaved clients discuss the loss of any of their previous social rolls and to facilitate the exploration of new social roles and identities they may wish to, or need to, assume (Lopata, 1996; Rando, 1984; C. A. Walter, 2003). This process may involve identifying their needs as a single person, finding ways to meet these needs, and renegotiating their relationship with the deceased partner (Campbell & Silverman,1996).

Surviving mates may have socialized only with people who were friends of the couple and may therefore lose or feel uncomfortable with their old social network. They may be faced with redefining and/ or being uncomfortable with their old friendships and may need to develop new friendships. Because they may have filled a particular and narrow social role, they may not have developed skills needed to function fully in new social roles as a single person. Not having these social skills may result in a low sense of self-esteem and difficulty in expanding their social contacts. Counselors may, therefore, need to help clients identify the skills they already have, invite them to consider developing new skills, and help them find ways to do this (Lund, Caserta, & Dimond, 1993, C. A. Walter, 2003). For example, Lund et al. (1993) found that 58% of the survivors in their study indicated that they felt better about themselves after developing new skills.

Counselors can also help survivors identify the roles, identities, lifestyles, and friendships that have remained consistent despite the loss of a partner. Doing so can help them recognize the continuity of their lives and give them a sense of security that they may think they have lost (Rando, 1984). Counselors might ask, "What is your role at work, in your neighborhood, in your church, etc.?" or "How are your relationships with other people, such as your grandchildren, children, friends, neighbors, parishioners, and club members?" In addition to helping clients discover that there is, indeed, some continuity in their lives, these questions may also identify problem areas that need to be addressed.

On the basis of the issues discussed above, survivors may need to consider ways of enhancing their social contacts. Counselors can support their efforts to maintain previously valued relationships, work through their disappointments in or loss of old "couple" friends, and form new relationships. Counselors can also refer clients to self-help support groups for widows or widowers who might also need new friends and acquaintances. These groups can be found in community or family services agencies, religion-based organizations, hospice programs, and agencies on aging (C. A. Walter, 2003).

Another situation that seems to soften the loss of a partner is having supportive children (Li, Liang, Toler, & Gu, 2005). Counselors may, therefore, need to help surviving partners maintain positive and appropriate relationships with their children or with their partner's children. Relationships with children can be complex and involve feelings that range from strong emotional attachment to strong emotional separation. Counselors can invite clients to review both positive and negative aspects of their relationships with their children (C. A. Walter, 2003) and brainstorm ways to maintain or improve these relationships. See Chapter 9 for additional information about family relationships.

Tasks Associated With Being a New Widow or Widower

Surviving partners and significant others are typically left with many tasks that need to be completed after they have lost a loved one. Tasks associated with the death itself can include making plans and paying for services, memorials, rituals, and burial for the deceased; paying hospital and other bills associated with the deceased's health care; settling accounts with long-term care facilities; returning and disposing of medical equipment; obtaining or finding copies of birth and death certificates, wills, trusts, and insurance policies; working with insurance companies to ensure that all accounts are closed appropriately; writing thank you notes; meeting with a lawyer regarding wills and any legal and inheritance tax issues; and sorting through and making decisions about the decedent's personal property. Other important tasks may include finding and organizing paperwork or documents that the deceased maintained (e.g., bank accounts, savings accounts, investment accounts, pensions, deeds to property, business/partnership information, written agreements or contracts) and meeting with private or public representatives who can assist in understanding, transferring, continuing, or closing these. In many of these cases, the survivor may not be familiar with necessary processes or may not even know that they exist (M. Stroebe et al., 2010; C. A. Walter, 2003).

Secondary consequences of loss of a partner include the potential need for the newly widowed to take on new responsibilities that the partner always took care of (e.g., doing yard work; taking care of financial planning and bookkeeping; grocery shopping and cooking; performing household chores; maintaining upkeep on cars, appliances, and the house; communicating with outsiders; driving; scheduling various appointments; using the computer; keeping up connections with family; celebrating holidays; buying gifts for the kids; taking care of grandchildren; and washing and repairing one's own clothes). New or ongoing tasks might include determining and keeping track of the regular payments of rent, house and car installments, house and car insurance, property and car taxes, homeowner's dues, loans, credit card or other bills, state and federal taxes, state and federal programs, and a vast number of complex health insurance and life insurance policies. Survivors will also need to keep track of their income types and amounts (e.g., Social Security, special programs, interest income, farm or business income, pensions). Other tasks might include keeping track of and scheduling home upkeep or improvement and consulting with home accessibility specialists, hospice for bereavement counseling, home health care services, Meals on Wheels, and so forth (M. Stroebe et al., 2010; W. Stroebe, Schut, & Stroebe, 2005; C. A. Walter, 2003). Clearly, taking on all these responsibilities at a time when one is experiencing grief can be very difficult.

If the tasks are too complicated, too numerous, or too overwhelming for clients and surviving family members are unable to take on these responsibilities, counselors—as case managers—can help develop plans to complete the tasks, carry out these plans, or identify resources that can do so. An important case-management strategy is to consolidate all the tasks that need to be done in table form. Sometimes multiple tables are required (i.e., one for each kind of task). The tables can include columns listing the tasks; names and contact information of people, companies, or organizations that require payments; names and contact information for entities that can assist with the task; the costs or income associated with each task; and deadlines and dates associated with each task. These kinds of tables are extremely helpful to case managers, older people, family members, or other consultants.

Survivors may also need to consider whether their living arrangements are appropriate for their new roles, responsibilities, desires, needs, and income. Some clients may wish to remain in their current living arrangements, whereas others may need to move in order to receive support from and/or social interaction with family members, friends, or service providers (M. Stroebe et al., 2010; C. A. Walter, 2003). Counselors can facilitate a review of clients' living arrangements to ensure that their environments are meeting their needs. Information regarding housing options can be found in Chapter 12.

Death of Other Family Members and Friends

It is, perhaps, normal to expect that older people will lose parents, siblings, and friends to death. Although these events are considered normative (i.e., age-appropriate; Whitbourne & Whitbourne, 2011), they can be extremely difficult. Furthermore, the compilation of many of these types of losses can be devastating. Because of the normative nature of this kind of loss, there is the possibility that older people's grief may not be acknowledged by others or by themselves. In these cases, counselors can be available to discuss these losses and to help clients work through their grieving process. Counselors may also wish to form a support group of people who have lost close friends, parents, or siblings (or refer a client to such a group). These groups can help individuals who have been mourning separately or whose grief has not been acknowledged by others (Sklar & Hartley, 1990).

Conversely, it has been speculated that when one's friends or family members die, there may be a tendency to develop or strengthen relationships with other friends and relatives (Roberto & Stanis, 1994). Counselors might help grievers identify who these people are and find ways to connect with them.

Older people will also be more likely than younger people to lose a child or grandchild to death because older people's children and grandchildren will be older themselves. For example, a 90-year-old parent may have a 70-year-old child and a 50-year-old grandchild. The death of a child can be devastating, and it often leads to intense grieving that may involve long-lasting feelings of guilt and depression as well as health problems (Rogers, Floyd, Seltzer, Greenberg, & Hong, 2008). The intense mourning can be attributable to many factors—including the expectation that parents die before their children—and the loss of a child may mean the loss of a primary support person (McKiernan, 1996).

The death of a grandchild can also be devastating to older people. This anguish can be attributable to the expectation that this child would outlive them, but it is also attributable to the loss of someone precious in their lives. As with losing a child, grandparents may feel guilt for being alive when their grandchild is not (Fry, 1997). These responses may be particularly intense when the grandparents were involved in raising their grandchild (J. R. Allen, Whittlesey, Pfefferbaum, & Ondersma, 1999).

Practices that seem to help people through the loss of a child or grandchild include focusing on a sense of meaning and purpose in life, continuing to feel connected with the deceased child, connecting with other people (I. Wheeler, 2001), supporting other family members, and becoming involved in community projects that are associated, in some way, with the reason for the death of the child or grandchild (J. R. Allen et al., 1999).

Additional Counseling Strategies to Assist Survivors in the Healing Process

A key issue in the counseling process is the relationship between the counselor and the client (Rando, 1984; Raphael, Middleton, Martinek, & Misso, 1993; Worden, 2002). Giving comfort as well as accepting and encouraging expressions of grief and other emotions are central to this relationship. A nonjudgmental atmosphere, where clients are taken seriously and are shown respect, allows them to fully express their feelings about death and about the relationships they had with the deceased. This atmosphere requires that counselors be empathetic, sensitive, gentle, and fully present in the counseling session (Lazarus, 1971; C. A. Walter, 2003). Extended discussions of counseling strategies that can be used for loss and grief are provided by K. M. Humphrey (2009).

Expressing and Working Through Feelings

Inherent among many of the interventions and stages mentioned in this chapter is the importance of working through feelings associated with a death. Counselors can provide a safe atmosphere in which clients can express feelings of all types (e.g., anger, sorrow, fear, happiness, relief) and help them realize that it is possible to have all of these seemingly unrelated feelings about the same issue (Rando, 1984; C. A. Walter, 2003). To do this, the counselors, themselves, need to be comfortable with the wide variety of emotions that might exist and how they are expressed.

When training new counselor trainees, I have found that many are not comfortable when a client begins to cry. Because crying is often very important in working through a loss, counselors need to examine their own thoughts, feelings, and internal dialogues about crying. For example, when a client begins to cry, some ineffective thoughts a counselor may have might be, "Oh no!" "Now what am I going to do?" "How can I take the pain away?" "This is really uncomfortable for me." "What can I say to stop him from crying?" or "How can I fix this?" More appropriate internal dialogue might be "Good, he is finally able to cry," "She's making progress," "This is a good sign; she is in touch with her feelings," "I need to sit quietly and let him cry for a while," "I need to show her that it is OK and even good for her to show her feelings," and "I need to honor her feelings." When a client begins to cry, counselors might simply sit quietly, watch the client, provide a tissue box, and let the person cry. Counselors might also say to the client, "It's OK to cry," "Take as much time as you need," or "Stay with the feeling."

As indicated earlier in this chapter, another feeling associated with death may be anger (e.g., anger toward themselves, toward the medical community, toward the person who is dying or who has died, or toward a spiritual being). Therefore, it is important to have a safe environment in which this feeling can be expressed. Because clients may be uncomfortable with their own anger, counselors may need to relabel this feeling before the client can deal with it (Rando, 1984). The counselor's own comfort level with anger will either hinder or encourage the client's ability and opportunity to express this feeling.

If counselors realize that anger may be expected and normal, they can relax with it and encourage angry people to express their feelings.

Zinker (1994) has suggested that it is important for counselors to stay with the process, to avoid pushing outcomes, to respect the client's thoughts and feelings, and to recognize the "usefulness and even the beauty of the way others express their mourning and sense of loss" (p. 262). Relaxing into this attitude can help the counselor provide a solid ground on which clients can also be comfortable in expressing their grief.

Exploring the Circumstances of the Death and the Current Situation

Exploration of a death, itself, can help clients identify and talk about aspects of a loss that they may not have previously resolved or even recognized. Exploration can include reviewing the circumstance associated with the death, the trauma that was experienced, the social and personal responses to the loss, and the reality of the loss (Chetnik, 2000; C. A. Walter, 2003). To help clients reflect on the circumstances of the death, itself, counselors can ask questions such as, "How did his/her death happen/occur?" "Describe that day/night." and "Tell me what happened."

Telling and Retelling Their Story Versus "Getting on With One's Life"

Losing a partner, family member, or friend eventually requires having to "get on with one's life." Although this is an important task, society often expects this to occur before people have had the opportunity to grieve, which can result in them being forced to get on with it before they are ready (C. A. Walter, 2003). The need to tell and retell their story and to talk about a loss is thought to be very important (Carverhill, 1997; Neimeyer, 1998). This fact is not a new concept for counselors. Counselors realize that it is often necessary for individuals to discuss and rediscuss . . . and rediscuss . . . an actual event itself, their evolving versions of or thoughts about an event, and their changing feelings associated with it. This rediscussion of an event (e.g., death), over time, can help clients rethink their own views of the situation, work through their feelings, and adjust to their new and evolving lives and perspectives of their losses or impending losses. In addition to being totally present when listening to clients' concerns, counselors can make referrals to support groups that focus on grief so that clients will have sufficient time to discuss their losses with others who also need such time (C. A. Walter, 2003).

Although it is important to give clients the time to grieve, there is also concern that individuals may become stuck with their loss or engage in unhealthy grieving. Response to the loss of a loved one may, therefore, need to be monitored over time. If mourners increase their use of drugs or alcohol, have thoughts of self-harm or suicide, become socially isolated, experience an unplanned change in body weight, or experience persistent intense grief for months after the death, they will likely need additional intervention or assistance in working through their grief (Hospice and Palliative Nurses Association, 2009a). This precaution does not mean that it is unhealthy to remain attached to the deceased for the remainder of one's life. Although some theorists think that grief that lasts for longer than a year is abnormal, others think that it is appropriate to maintain the departed as an active mental presence, and that keeping possessions of the departed is normal (Whitbourne & Whitbourne, 2011).

Continued Relationship With the Deceased Versus Healthy New Relationships

As indicated above, it is appropriate for survivors to retain some type of relationship with the deceased individual (e.g., keeping memories alive and continuing to relate to the person). Perhaps reminiscence can be used to promote positive memories rather than death-defying thoughts (i.e., behaving as if he or she is not dead). To help clients discuss, analyze, and understand the history of their relationship with the deceased, counselors can say the following, "Tell me about her/him," and "What were the positive and negative aspects of your relationship?" Discussions of past events and feelings can be helpful in retaining some of the old connections with the loved one and can allow the relationship to change from one in which the deceased person was physically present to one in which the memories of the person are maintained (Rando, 1984). The goal is to give up old connections with the deceased and to use the memories of that person to improve the mourner's current functioning (Rando, 1984; Raphael et al., 1993; Worden, 2002).

On the other hand, it is important that individuals be challenged when they focus only on the past, excluding current and future significant relationships. In this case, the reminiscence or rumination may become pathological, nonproductive, or result in being stuck in the past (O'Leary, Alday, & Ickovics, 1998; Rando, 1984). If this situation occurs, individuals can be helped to avoid focusing on their relationship with the deceased (especially if it was negative) and encouraged to begin to focus on present and future relationships (Livneh, 2013; Nolen-Hoeksema & Larson, 1999). Furthermore, counselors can encourage clients to use the death of a loved one to facilitate the search for life meaning and to look toward a positive future. Essentially, this concept has to do with resilience. The hope is that individuals who have sustained a traumatic event will go beyond survival and recovery and begin to thrive and grow because of the experience (O'Leary et al., 1998).

Offer Suggestions With Caution

Counselors can offer suggestions to grievers by describing strategies that have worked for other people, but because the healing process is unique for each individual, it is very important not to force suggestions onto clients. Some thoughts or practices that were not discussed earlier include the following: giving themselves permission to grieve, getting plenty of rest, getting exercise, eating a healthy diet, reminiscing by putting together a memory book or talking with others, getting information about grieving, keeping a journal about their thoughts and feelings, avoiding making changes in their lives too quickly, and eventually creating a "new normal" way of life (Hospice and Palliative Nurses Association, 2009a).

Extra Support During Holidays

Survivors may need additional support during the holidays. Issues may include an accentuation of grief or a dread of the holidays; in addition, other family members or friends may be uncertain about what to do for the bereaved. Because of these issues, counselors may need to offer bereavement counseling prior to and during the holidays and/or check with local hospices to determine whether they offer special programs designed to help the bereaved during these times. There is no right or wrong way to experience the holidays; therefore, counselors can support clients' decisions about how to deal with them. Counselors might also want to identify which aspects of the holidays are most difficult (e.g., religious services, social gatherings, cooking, cleaning, decorating, shopping, mailing cards) and use creative problem solving to find ways to deal with these (National Hospice and Palliative Care Organization, 2012d).

Counselors might also work with family members and friends to identify things that can be done for the bereaved. Examples of things that others can do include helping decorate or shop for the holiday, helping with card preparation, inviting survivors to holiday events or appropriate religious ceremonies, letting them know that they are thinking of them, and donating money or a gift in memory of the deceased. In offering any of these, friends and family will need to be prepared to discover that the bereaved may not wish to do or receive any of these. Perhaps it is most important for friends and family to honor the grief experience and to spend time just listening rather than being conversational. A key point is that friends and family should not be afraid of saying or doing the wrong thing when they make the effort to show that they care (National Hospice and Palliative Care Organization, 2012d).

Group Work and Support Groups

As indicated above, friends, family members, and society may wish for the grieving person to get on with it, or they, themselves, may feel uncomfortable talking about grief (C. Walter, 1997). They may divert conversations about the deceased, try to make things better, avoid talking about sadness and intense grief, discourage crying, or even stay away from the grieving person. For these reasons, bereavement support groups can be very helpful. Because of the focus of these groups, participants can be given time and permission to grieve among others who are also grieving. Support groups for people who are grieving can have several goals. These goals include helping people express their pain among others who have a deep understanding of a similar loss, counteracting social isolation that can occur with a bereaved person, providing information about the changes that participants are experiencing or will experience, and providing comfort and relief to grieving participants (C. Walter, 1997; C. A. Walter, 2003).

Counselors can act as facilitators or leaders of these groups. Examples of topics for discussion include the change from being a couple to being a single person, the change from being the child to being the elder in the family, the kinds of guilt or other feelings that clients might be experiencing, the pressure from others to stop grieving or expressing grief, the difference between being lonely and alone, strategies that have worked for each of group member in a variety of situations, discussions and expressions of grief, and plans for the future.

Men may sometimes be reluctant to join bereavement groups because they may not want to talk about their feelings (Chetnik, 2000). Counselors may, therefore, want to reframe the purpose of the group, focusing on mutual storytelling in which participants tell each other about the events connected with the death of a partner and the aftermath of the experience (Carverhill, 1997). It might also be helpful to hold group meetings in settings that are comfortable for men. For example, counselors might invite a group of men on an excursion (e.g., a one-day fishing trip) to honor their deceased partners or loved ones (T. Golden & Miller, 1998).

Bibliotherapy

Counselors can invite clients to read texts, novels, or autobiographies or to see movies that focus on death and then ask them to discuss their thoughts and feelings about these. These materials may give new insights, open new topics, help resolve a specific issue, and so forth. Again, it is important for the counselor to have read or viewed these resources before suggesting that their clients use them.

Texts that focus on death and dying are *Friendgrief* (H. I. Smith, 2002), *Aging Our Way: Lessons for Living From 85 and Beyond* (Loe, 2011), *The Loss of a Life Partner* (C. A. Walter, 2003), and *Men Don't Cry . . . Women Do: Transcending Stereotypes of Grief* (T. Martin & Doka, 2000). Novels that focus on death and grieving include *Sarah's Key* (de Rosnay, 2007), *Mr. Ives' Christmas* (Hijuelos, 1995), *One Mountain Away* (E. Richards, 2012), *The Summons* (Grisham, 2002),

Open Doors (Goldreich, 2008), *Where the River Turns to Sky* (Kleiner, 1996), and *Keeping Time* (McGlynn, 2010). Autobiographies, memoirs, or thought pieces that might be helpful include *Celebrating the Coyote* (B. Waters, 1999), *A Bittersweet Season: Caring for Our Parents and for Ourselves* (Gross, 2012), and *On My Own at 107: Reflections of Life Without Bessie* (Delany & Hearth, 1997). Movies that focus on death and dying include *Everybody's Fine* (Gori et al., 2009), *Hanging Up* (Ephron, Ephron, & Keaton, 2000), *Get Low* (Zanuck, Gundlach, & Schneider, 2009), *On Golden Pond* (Gilbert & Rydell, 1981), *Secondhand Lions* (Kirschner & McCanlies, 2003), and *Whose Life Is It Anyway?* (Bachman & Badham, 1981).

ACA Code of Ethics

Many aspects of the *ACA Code of Ethics* relate closely to the issues of death and mourning. These are listed below.

A.4.a. Counselors act to avoid harming their clients . . . and to minimize or to remedy unavoidable or unanticipated harm.

A.4.b. Counselors are aware of—and avoid imposing—their own values, attitudes, beliefs, and behaviors. Counselors respect the diversity of clients . . . and seek training in areas in which they are at risk of imposing their values onto clients, especially when the counselor's values are inconsistent with the client's goals . . .

B.2.a. The general requirement that counselors keep information confidential does not apply when disclosure is required to protect clients or identified others from serious and foreseeable harm or when legal requirements demand that confidential information must be revealed. Counselors consult with other professionals when in doubt as to the validity of an exception. Additional considerations apply when addressing end-of-life issues.

B.2.b. Counselors who provide services to terminally ill individuals who are considering hastening their own deaths have the option to maintain confidentiality, depending on applicable laws and the specific circumstances of the situation and after seeking consultation or supervision from appropriate professional and legal parties . . .

B.3.f. Counselors protect the confidentiality of deceased clients, consistent with legal requirements and the documented preferences of the client . . .

C.2.b. Counselors practice in specialty areas new to them only after appropriate education, training, and supervised experience. While developing skills in new specialty areas, counselors take steps to ensure the competence of their work and protect others from possible harm . . .

I.1.c. If ethical responsibilities conflict with the law, regulations, and/or other governing legal authority, counselors make known their commitment to the *ACA Code of Ethics* and take steps to resolve the conflict. If the conflict cannot be resolved by this approach, counselors, acting in the best interest of the client, may adhere to the requirements of the law, regulations, and/or other governing legal authority . . .

I.2.c. When uncertain about whether a particular situation or course of action may be in violation of the *ACA Code of Ethics*, counselors consult with other counselors who are knowledgeable about ethics and the *ACA Code of Ethics*, with colleagues, or with appropriate authorities, such as the ACA Ethics and Professional Standards Department. (ACA, 2014)

Perceptions of Death and Mourning

Counselors must be mindful that because there are many perspectives about death and dying, it is vital not to impose their own beliefs or make assumptions about their clients' experiences of death. In some instances, counselors may find that certain beliefs and rituals about death and mourning are very difficult to personally understand or accept and may therefore perceive clients' comments or beliefs as aberrant. In other words, the client's perspective about death may be so different from the counselor's perspective that the counselor may misjudge the client and take inappropriate action.

To avoid imposing their own values about death and dying—and to provide a nonbiased, culturally sensitive environment—counselors need to be aware of and understand their own beliefs, values, hopes, practices, rituals, and feelings regarding death and mourning. By attending training sessions on death and dying or values clarification, obtaining individual or group counseling, and seeking supervision in this area, counselors can develop a personal understanding of their own view of death (J. E. Myers & Shannonhouse, 2013; Wadsworth, Harley, et al., 2008).

It will also be helpful for counselors to join groups that focus on, or have expertise in, death and mourning. Counselors might wish to join the ACA's Grief and Bereavement Interest Network or the Association of Death and Dying in Counseling (http://www.adec.org). Counselors might also wish to receive additional training on death and dying and seek certification in thanatology (i.e., death, dying, bereavement; see http://www.adec.org).

Case Study/Activity

Five years prior to my father's death in 1996, my parents gave me a book titled the *Final Exit* by Derek Humphrey (1991). I knew this was a significant gift/message because they knew how I felt about the sacredness of all life (e.g., I save ants from pools of water and carry cockroaches and scorpions outside instead of killing them). After reading the book and thinking about the topic, I invited Mr. Humphrey to discuss assisted suicide and the right to choose during a panel at the first national conference of the Association for Adult Development and Aging (held in 1993). The panel was composed of counselors/leaders with widely varying opinions (i.e., strongly opposed to the concept of assisted suicide because of their own religious beliefs; supported the concept of assisted suicide when a person is near death or suffering physical pain; did not know what to think). We asked the audience to consider whether counselors had clear guidance in this type of situation. In other words, we asked the audience to consider what aspects of the *ACA Code of Ethics* applied to this situation. Later, I and two colleagues gave additional presentations about this topic (e.g., Burlew, Kampfe, & Capuzzi, 1996).

Two months prior to my father's death in 1996, the medical procedures that he endured caused a great deal of pain, and he was told that he had a terminal illness. I was with him in the hospital, and after the pain subsided, he looked over at me and said, "I wish I had read that book a little more carefully," referring to *The Final Exit*. I was struck with fear and dread but promised that I would help him if he decided that he wanted assisted suicide. There is no way to describe the anguish that this projected promise gave me. I could not conceive of helping him end his life, yet I had told him I would. I literally felt a dark cloud over my head.

I did not follow through with my promise because Dad seemed to be improving. Because he seemed to feel better, and probably because I was unable to accept that he was dying, I flew back to Tucson to return to work. A week later, I received a call from my mother saying that he had sustained a serious heart attack at that very moment and was dying. I felt some relief because I knew he would want to go, and I felt guilty because I did not follow through with my promise.

I tell this story because it has direct and important implications for counselors. This situation was one in which I would have benefited very much from speaking with a counselor to share my mixed feelings, sort through my options, and feel less alone in my anguish. However, at the time, the *ACA Code of Ethics* required that counselors report any contemplated harm to another person, and there were no guidelines regarding assisted suicide. I therefore chose not to speak to a counselor about this.

Some questions to ask of yourself or your group are as follows:

1. If I had come to you, what would you, as a counselor, have done?
2. How does the current *ACA Code of Ethics* apply to this situation?
3. Does anything need to be added to the *ACA Code of Ethics* to help in this situation?
4. What are the legal implications of this situation?
5. What are your own beliefs about assisted suicide, and how would these influence your ability to help me?
6. How would hospice have been of benefit to my father, my family, and to me?
7. How would calling ACA for assistance in applying the *Code of Ethics* to this situation help you, as the counselor?

8. Would you need to do additional exploration with me and my father to determine whether he was, in fact, terminally ill?
9. Would it be helpful to contact an attorney who specializes in risk management regarding this situation?

Counselor Self-Care

Because counselors of older people may become deeply involved with their clients' end-of-life and grieving issues, they may feel the effects of loss themselves. These experiences can put counselors and other helpers at risk for physical and psychological stress, stress-related disorders, burn-out, and lack of closure—all of which might affect their subsequent objectivity and work proficiency (Everall & Paulson, 2004; NSW Institute of Psychiatry and Centre for Mental Health, 2000; Saari & Silver, 2005; Wadsworth, Harley, et al., 2008). Constant exposure to death and dying might also result in a sort of distancing from the feelings associated with loss (Weinstein, 2008) and might therefore result in reduced ability to empathize with clients regarding this topic.

Because of potential burnout or stress-related disorders, counselors will need to "engage in self-care activities to maintain and promote their own emotional, physical, mental, and spiritual well-being" (ACA, 2014, Section C, Introduction). Resources for general emotional support are friends, family, and support groups. Professional resources are hospice services, counselors or therapists, peers and coworkers, supervisors, counselor self-care networks, and religious or spiritual advisors, all of whom should recognize the need for confidentiality regarding the counselor's concerns. Other resources for counselor self-care include a program guide that has a meditation audio that can be used each day to practice relaxation strategies (Segal et al., 2013); the *Stressbuster Relaxation Exercise, Vol. 1* (Erford, n.d.); and the University of Buffalo School of Social Work Self-Care Kit (http://www.socialwork.buffalo.edu/students/self-care). These supports should be in place at all times in the event that counselors need them at any point in the process of counseling individuals regarding end-of-life issues and/or the death of a client (Everall & Paulson, 2004; NSW Institute of Psychiatry and Centre for Mental Health, 2000; Saari & Silver, 2005; Wadsworth, Harley, et al., 2008).

Like all other individuals, counselors experience personal stressors in addition to the stressors associated with their clients. Counselors can deal with these various stressors through reflection and self-exploration, either with a counselor, a group, or formalized exercises. Counselors might also seek balance between work and other aspects of their lives. For example, engaging in home and community activities that are personally satisfying and uplifting might provide counselors with the positive energy to continue to function in both their work and their personal lives. Identifying one's personal passion and finding ways to support and express this passion can be helpful, and, as indicated throughout this book, seeking social support and engaging in physical exercise are health-promoting behaviors.

Activity

1. Make a list of your personal passions, things that give you joy, or activities that are uplifting (e.g., dancing, singing, building something, golfing, swimming, hiking).
2. Chose one or more of these, and commit to doing them at least once a day, week, or month, depending upon your preference.
3. Tell friends or family members of your intentions, and ask whether you can report back to them each week, or ask whether they want to be involved with you in the activities.
4. Write your commitment down on a card or sticky note, and put this in a place where you see it on a regular basis, or ask your computer or phone to remind you.
5. Write your commitment down and place it in an envelope that is stamped and addressed to you. Ask a friend to send it to you in about one month.

Resources on Death and Dying

Caring Bridge, http://www.caringbridge.org/
Caring Connections, http://www.caringinfo.org
Center to Advance Palliative Care, http://www.capc.org/
Hospice and Palliative Nurses Association, http://www.hpna.org/
National Association for Home Care and Hospice, http://www.nahc. org or 202-547-7424
National Hospice and Palliative Care Organization, http://www. nhpco.org or 703-837-1500
Next Step in Care: United Hospital Fund, http://www.nextstepincare. org/
Palliative Care Leadership Centers, http://www.capc.org/
Palliative Dementia Care Resources, http://www.pdcronline.org

Summary

Older people are likely to experience the death of one or more significant others and most certainly will be facing their own deaths. Variation exists regarding people's views of death and mourning; therefore, counselors will need to be open to a broad range of perspectives of death and mourning. To do this, they must be aware of their own perspectives of death and mourning and be knowledgeable about this topic. Because people who are dying or who have lost a significant person in their life may need to talk about their loss, counselors can provide a vital service: simply using their empathetic listening skills.

Counselors can also use a variety of strategies to help people who are dying, their families, and mourners face the transition and to work through the issues associated with this transition.

References

AARP. (2003). *Workforce trends: Staying ahead of the curve 2003: The AARP Working in Retirement Study executive summary.* Retrieved from http://www.aarp.org/money/careers/employerresourcecenter/trends/a2004-08-02-curve2003.html

AARP. (2010). *Driver safety program participant handbook.* Washington, DC: Author.

AARP. (2011). *Baby Boomers envision what's next. Research and strategic analysis integrated value and strategy.* Retrieved from http://www.aarp.org/work/retirement-planning/info-06-2991/boomers-envision-retirement

AARP. (2012a, April). The healing paws of pets. *AARP Bulletin, 53,* 4.

AARP. (2012b, July/August). 99 great ways to save. *AARP Bulletin, 53,* 21–28.

Abrahms, S. (2012a, July/August). Caregiving: Alternative treatment for dementia. A comfort-and-joy approach. *AARP Bulletin, 53,* 14.

Abrahms, S. (2012b, November). Caring for the caregiver. *AARP Bulletin, 53,* pp. 14, 16–18.

Abrahms, S. (2013, May). Need a ride? *AARP Bulletin, 54,* 28–30.

Abrams, R., Lachs, M., McAvay, G., Koehane, D., & Bruce, M. (2002). Predictors of self-neglect in community dwelling elders. *American Journal of Psychiatry, 159,* 1724–1730.

Acierno, R., Hernandez-Tejada, M., Mussy, W., & Steve, K. (2009). *Prevalence and correlates of emotional, physical, sexual, and financial abuse and potential neglect in the United States: The National Elder Mistreatment Study* (NCJ Publication No. 2264456). Washington, DC: U.S. Department of Justice.

Adams, P. F., & Benson, V. (1992). *Current estimates from the National Health Interview Survey, 1991* (DHHS Publication No. [PHS] 93-1512, Vital and Health Statistics, Series 10, No. 184). Retrieved from http://www.cdc.gov/nchs/data/series/sr_10/sr10_184.pdf

Adler, T. (2011, March/April). Nana Power: How grandparents can help kids stay out of trouble. *AARP: The Magazine, 54*, 55.

Adler, T. (2012, June/July). Your loved one's next move. *AARP: The Magazine, 55*, 51–52.

Administration on Aging. (2007). *A profile of older Americans: 2007.* Retrieved from http://www.aoa.gov/prof/statistics/profile/2007/2007profile.com

Administration on Aging. (2009). *A profile of older Americans: 2009.* Retrieved from http://www.aoa.gov/AoARoot/Aging_Statistics/Profile/2009/8.aspx

Agee, E. M., Freedman, V. A., & Cornman, J. C. (2005). Reconsidering substitution in long-term care. When does assistive technology take the place of personal care? *Journal of Gerontology, 60*, 272–280.

Agility. (n.d.). *Physical therapy for balance problems* [Brochure]. Tucson, AZ: Author.

Aging America. (1991). *Aging America trends and projections.* Retrieved from http://catalog.hathitrust.org/Record/011334539

Agnvall, E. (2012, July/August). Battling belly fat. *AARP Bulletin, 53*, pp. 8, 10, 13.

Ahmad, M., & Lachs, M. (2002). Elder abuse and neglect: What physicians can do and should do. *Cleveland Clinic Journal of Medicine, 69*, 801–808.

Alberts, J., & Dunton, G. F. (2008). The role of temporal orientation in reactive and proactive illness management. *Psychology and Health, 23*, 175–193.

Aldredge, D. (2000). *Spirituality, healing and medicine: Return to the silence.* London, England: Jessica Kingsley.

ALGBTIC LGBQQIA Competencies Task Force. (2012). *Association for Lesbian, Gay, Bisexual, and Transgender Issues in Counseling (ALGBTIC) competencies for counseling with lesbian, gay, bisexual, queer, questioning, intersex and ally individuals.* Retrieved from http://www.counseling.org/docs/competencies/algbtic-competencies-for-counseling-lgbqqia-individuals.pdf?sfvrsn=6

ALGBTIC Transgender Committee. (2009). *Association for Lesbian, Gay, Bisexual, and Transgender Issues in Counseling (ALGBTIC) competencies for counseling with transgender clients.* Retrieved from http://www.counseling.org/docs/competencies/algbtic_competencies.pdf?sfvrsn=3

Allen, I., Hogg, D., & Peace, S. (1992). *Elderly people: Choice, participation and satisfaction.* London, England: Policy Studies Institute.

Allen, J. R., Whittlesey, S., Pfefferbaum, B., & Ondersma, M. L. (1999). Community and coping of mothers and grandmothers of children killed in a human-caused disaster. *Psychiatric Annals, 29*, 85–91.

Allen, K. R., Blieszner, R., & Roberto, K. A. (2000). Families in the middle and later years: A review and critique of research in the 1990s. *Journal of Marriage and Family, 62,* 911–926.

Allender, D. B., & Longman, T., III. (2005). *The intimate marriage series.* Westmont, IL: InterVarsity Press.

Alzheimer's Disease Education and Referral Center. (2012a). *Alzheimer's disease fact sheet.* Retrieved from http://www.nia.nig.gov/pprint/alzheimers/publication/alzheimers-disease-fact-sheet

Alzheimer's Disease Education and Referral Center. (2012b). *Alzheimer's topics.* Retrieved from http://www.nia.nih.gov/alzheimers/topics/

Alzheimer's Disease Health Center. (2011). *Alzheimer's disease may be misdiagnosed.* Retrieved from http://www.webmd.com/alzheimers/news/20110223/alzheimers-disease-may-be-misdiagnosed

Amato, P. R. (2000). The consequences of divorce for adults and children. *Journal of Marriage and Family, 62,* 511–521.

Amato, P. R. (2010). Research on divorce: Continuing trends and new developments. *Journal of Marriage and Family, 72,* 650–666.

American Academy of Ophthalmology. (2002). *Macular degeneration.* San Francisco, CA: Author.

American Counseling Association. (2014). *ACA code of ethics.* Alexandria, VA: Author.

American Geriatrics Society. (2005). Drug treatment. *Aging in the know.* Retrieved from http://www.healthinaging.org/agingintheknow/chapters_tiral.asp?ch=6

American Health Assistance Foundation. (2012a). *Alzheimer's disease.* Retrieved from http://www.ahaf.org/alzheimers.html

American Health Assistance Foundation. (2012b). *Caregiving.* Retrieved from http://www.ahaf.org/alzheimers/livingwith/caregiving.html

American Health Assistance Foundation. (2012c). *Diagnosis of Alzheimer's disease.* Retrieved from http://www.ahaf.org/alzheimers/about/diagnosis

American Health Assistance Foundation. (2012d). *Glaucoma.* Retrieved from http://www.ahaf.org/glaucoma.html

American Health Assistance Foundation. (2012e). *Macular degeneration.* Retrieved from http://www.ahaf.org/macular.html

American Psychiatric Association. (2013). *Diagnostic and statistical manual of mental disorders* (5th ed.). Washington, DC: Author.

American Psychological Association. (1998). *Older adults' health and age-related changes: Reality versus myth.* Retrieved from http://www.apadiv20.phhp.ufl.edu/

American Psychological Association. (2001). *End-of-life issues and care: The role of psychology in end-of-life decisions and quality of care issues.* Retrieved from http://www.apa.org/pi/eol/role/html

An, J. S., & Cooney, T. M. (2006). Psychological well-being in mid to late life: The role of generativity development and parent–child relationships across the lifespan. *International Journal of Behavioral Development, 30,* 410–421.

Anetzberger, G. J., Korbin, J. E., & Austin, C. (1994). Alcoholism and elder abuse. *Journal of Interpersonal Violence, 9,* 184–193.

Anft, M. (2011, July/August). AIDS at 30: Three decades after its emergence, AIDS has a new face: People over 50. *AARP: The Magazine, 54,* 67–71.

Angus, J., & Reeve, P. (2006). Ageism: A threat to "aging well" in the 21st century. *The Journal of Applied Gerontology, 25,* 137–152.

Anubhiti, D. (2008). Future oriented thinking and well-being in diabetic patients. *Journal of Indian Psychology, 26,* 22–30.

Arizona Department of Economic Security. (n.d.). *Help stop adult abuse, neglect, and exploitation* [Brochure]. Tucson, AZ: Author.

Arizona Governor's Council on Blindness and Visual Impairment, Deaf-Blind Committee. (2011). *Summary response to the SSP survey.* Tucson, AZ: Author.

Armstrong, M. J. (2001). Ethnic minority women as they age. In J. D. Garner & S. O. Mercer (Eds.), *Women as they age* (pp. 97–114). Binghamton, NY: Haworth Press.

Association for Spiritual, Ethical, and Religious Values. (2009, May). *Competencies for addressing spiritual and religious issues in counseling.* Alexandria, VA: Author.

Atchley, R. C. (2000). *Social forces and aging* (9th ed.). Belmont, CA: Wadsworth/Thomson Learning.

Atlanta Long-Term Care Ombudsman Program. (2000). *The silenced voice speaks out: A study of abuse and neglect of nursing home residents.* Atlanta, GA: Atlanta Legal Aid Society.

Bachmann, L. P. (Producer), & Badham, J. (Director). (1981). *Whose life is it anyway?* [Motion picture]. United States: Metro-Goldwin-Mayer (MGM).

Bailis, D. S., & Chipperfield, J. G. (2002). Compensating for losses in perceived personal control over health: A role for collective self-esteem in healthy aging. *Journals of Gerontology: Series B. Psychological Sciences and Social Sciences, 57,* 531–539.

Bair, D. (2007). *Calling it quits: Late-life divorce and starting over.* New York, NY: Random House.

Barnett, M. A., Scaramella, L. V., Neppl, T. K., Ontai, L., & Conger, R. D. (2010). Grandmother involvement as a protective factor in early social adjustment. *Journal of Family Psychology, 24,* 635–645.

Barnett, O., Miller-Perrin, C. L., & Perrin, R. D. (2011). *Family violence across the lifespan: An introduction* (3rd ed.). Thousand Oaks, CA: Sage.

Barnow, S., Linden, M., & Freyberger, H. J. (2004). The relation between suicidal feelings and mental disorders in the elderly: Results from the Berlin Aging Study (BASE). *Psychological Medicine, 34,* 741–746.

Bellini, J. (2002). Correlates of multicultural counseling competencies of vocational rehabilitation counselors. *Rehabilitation Counseling Bulletin, 45,* 66–75.

Bennett, K. M. (2006). Does marital status and marital status change predict physical health in older adults? *Psychological Medicine, 36,* 1313–1320.

Benshoff, J. J., Koch, D. S., & Harrawood, L. K. (2003). Substance abuse and the elderly: Unique issues and concerns. *Journal of Rehabilitation, 69,* 43–48.

Berg, A. I., Hassing, L. B., McClearn, G. E., & Johansson, B. (2006). What matters for life satisfaction in the oldest-old? *Aging and Mental Health, 10,* 257–264.

Berger, A., & Yerxa, R. (Producers), & Payne, A. (Director). (2013). *Nebraska* [Motion picture]. United States: Paramount.

Bernaccio, C., & Falvo, D. (2008, February). *A pilot study of older workers with disabilities age 50–59 in Alamance, NC.* Presentation at the National Training Conference of the National Council on Rehabilitation Education, San Antonio, TX.

Bernstein, D. A., Borkovec, T. D., & Hazlett-Stevens, H. (2000). *New directions in progressive relaxation training: A guidebook for helping professionals.* Westport, CT: Praeger.

Bhide, M. (2011a, March/April). Eat this, stay sharp. *AARP: The Magazine, 54,* 20.

Bhide, M. (2011b, July/August). Vine-ripened wonder: This wholesome powerhouse may even keep diabetes at bay. *AARP: The Magazine, 54,* 21.

Birditt, K. S., Rott, L. M., & Fingerman, K. L. (2009). "If you can't say anything nice, don't say anything at all": Coping with interpersonal tensions in the parent–child relationship during adulthood. *Journal of Family Psychology, 23,* 769–778.

Black, T., & Casady, G. (Producers), & Frankel, D. (Director). (2012). *Hope springs* [Motion picture]. United States: Columbia Pictures.

Blancato, R., & Donahue, S. (2012). *One year anniversary of the Elder Justice Act: March 23rd marks the one year anniversary of the Elder Justice Act (the FJA).* Retrieved from http://www.elderjusticecoalition.com/

Blieszner, R. (2006). A lifetime of caring: Dimensions and dynamics in late-life close relationships. *Personal Relationships, 13,* 1–18.

Block, B. A. (Producer), & Meyers, N. (Director). (2003). *Something's gotta give* [Motion picture]. USA: Columbia Pictures and Warner Brothers.

Bonanno, G. A., Wortman, C. B., Lehman, D. R., Tweed, R. G., Haring, M., Sonnega, J., . . . Nesse, R. M. (2002). Resilience to loss and chronic grief: A prospective study from preloss to 18-months postloss. *Journal of Personality and Social Psychology, 83,* 1150–1164.

Bonanno, G. A., Wortman, C. B., & Nesse, R. M. (2004). Prospective patterns of resilience and maladjustment during widowhood. *Psychology and Aging, 19,* 260–271.

Bordieri, J. E., Drehmer, D. E., & Taylor, D. W. (1997). Work life for employees with disabilities: Recommendations for promotion. *Rehabilitation Counseling Bulletin, 40,* 181–192.

Borman, C. A., & Henderson, P. G. (2001). The career/longevity connection. *Adultspan Journal, 3,* 71–76.

Braman, P. (2012, May/June). Is retirement realistic? Plan ahead to ensure the good life through your golden years. *Highroads, 17,* 14.

Brandl, B., & Cook-Daniels, L. (2002). *Domestic abuse in later life.* Retrieved from http://www.vawnet.org/applied-research-papers/print-document.php?doc_id=376

Branfield, M., & Xiong, M. (2012, May). Cultivating a social justice orientation. *Counseling Today, 54,* 18–19.

Braus, P. (1995, April). The baby boom at mid-decade. *American Demographics, 17*(4), 40–45.

Brehm, M. A., & Kampfe, C. M. (1998). Creative dance improvisation: Fostering creative expression, group cooperation, and multiple intelligences. In *China–U.S. Conference on Education: Beijing, People's Republic of China* (pp. 15–22). Greensboro, NC: ERIC/CASS. Retrieved from ERIC database. (ED425401)

Brehm, M. A., & McNett, L. (2008). *Creative dance for learning: The kinesthetic link.* New York, NY: McGraw Hill.

Brennan, M., Horowitz, A., & Sue, Y. P. (2005). Dual sensory loss and its impact on everyday competence. *Gerontologist, 45,* 337–346.

Breslin, M. J., & Lewis, C. (2008). Theoretical models of the nature of prayer and health: A review. *Mental Health, Religion & Culture, 11,* 9–21.

Briggs, W. (2006). The mental health problems and needs of older people following lower-limb amputation. *Reviews in Clinical Gerontology, 16,* 155–163.

Broadbent, G., & Czernin, P. (Producers), & Madden, J. (Director). (2011). *The best exotic marigold hotel* [Motion picture]. United Kingdom: 20th Century Fox.

Bromley, S. M. (2000). Smell and taste disorders: A primary care approach. *American Family Physician, 62,* 427–436.

Brooks, F., & McHenry, B. (2009). *A contemporary approach to substance abuse and addiction counseling: A counselor's guide to application and understanding.* Alexandria, VA: American Counseling Association.

Brown, S. L., Bulanda, J. R., & Lee, G. R. (2012). Transitions in and out of cohabitation in later life. *Journal of Marriage and the Family, 74,* 774–793.

Brown, S. L., & Lin, I.-F. (2013, March). *The gray divorce revolution: Rising divorce among middle-aged and older adults, 1990–2010* (Working Paper Series). Bowling Green, OH: National Center for Family and Marriage Research, Bowling Green University.

Bruyére, S. M., Harley, D. A., Kampfe, C. M., & Wadsworth, J. S. (2008). Key concepts and techniques for an aging population. In M. Stebnicki & I. Marini (Eds.), *The professional counselors' desk reference* (pp. 477–485). New York, NY: Springer.

Budd, K. (2012, June/July). New adventures, new risks, new you! *AARP: The Magazine, 55,* 56–59.

Bulman, P. (2010, April). Elder abuse emerges from the shadows of public consciousness. *NIJ Journal, 265,* 4–7.

Burger, S. G., Fraser, V., Hunt, S., & Frank, B. (1996). *Nursing homes: Getting good care there.* San Luis Obispo, CA: Impact.

Burgess, A. W., Dowdell, E., & Prentky, R. (2000). Sexual abuse of nursing home residents. *Journal of Psychosocial Nursing, 38,* 11–18.

Burlew, L. D., Kampfe, C. M., & Capuzzi, D. (1996, April). *Right to die decision and victimization: Dilemmas in counseling the older adult.* Presentation at the 1996 ACA World Conference, Pittsburgh, PA.

Butterfield, S. (2007). *A new look at the elderly and how to care for them.* Retrieved from the American College of Physicians website: http://www.acprinternist.org/archives/2007

Cahill, K. E., Giandrea, M. D., & Quinn, J. F. (2006). Retirement patterns from career employment. *The Gerontologist, 46,* 514–523.

Calkins, E., Bult, C., Wagner, E., & Pacala, J. T. (1999). *New ways to care for older people: Building systems based on evidence.* New York, NY: Springer.

Campbell, S., & Silverman, P. (1996). *Widower: When men are left alone.* Amityville, NY: Baywood.

Capella-McDonnall, M. E. (2005). The effects of single and dual sensory loss on symptoms of depression in the elderly. *International Journal of Geriatric Psychiatry, 20,* 855–861.

Caputo, R. K. (2002). Adult daughters as parental caregivers: Rational actors versus rational agents. *Journal of Family and Economic Issues, 23,* 27–50.

Carter, P. L., & Carter, D. J. (2012). *Love with intention.* Omaha, NE: Carter Counseling Center.

Carverhill, P. (1997). Bereaved men: How therapists can help. *Psychotherapy in Private Practice, 16,* 1–20.

Casciani, J. (2012a). *Sensory loss in older adults—Taste, smell & touch—Behavioral approaches for caregivers.* Retrieved from the EzineArticles website: http://ezinearticles.com/?Sensory-Loss-in-Older-Adults---Taste,-Smell-and-Touch---Behavioral-Approaches-for-Caregivers&id=1099819

Casciani, J. (2012b). *Sensory loss in older adults: Vision–behavioral approaches for caregivers.* Retrieved from the EzineArticles website: http://ezinearticles.com/?Sensory-Loss-in-Older-Adults---Vision---Behavioral-Approaches-For-Caregivers&id=1288952

Cashwell, C. S., & Young, J. S. (2011). *Integrating spirituality and religion into counseling: A guide to competent practice* (2nd ed.). Alexandria, VA: American Counseling Association.

Cavanaugh, J. C., & Blanchard-Fields, F. (2006). *Adult development and aging* (5th ed.). Belmont, CA: Wadsworth/Thomson Learning.

Center for Disability Law. (2012, Winter). Deaf, hard of hearing and visually impaired Arizonans now have additional access to movie theaters. *Advocate,* pp. 1, 4.

Center for Healthy Aging, National Council on Aging. (2012). *Improve health*. Retrieved from http://www.ncoa.org/improve-health/center-for-healthyaging

Center on Aging and Work/Workplace Flexibility. (2005). *Flexibility*. Chestnut Hill, MA: Boston College.

Centers for Disease Control and Prevention. (2007). *Trends in health and aging*. Retrieved from http://www.cdc.gov/nchs/agingact.htm

Centers for Disease Control and Prevention. (2010). *Web-based Injury Statistics Query and Reporting System (WISQARS)*. Retrieved from http://www.cdc.gov/ncipc/wisqars

Centers for Disease Control and Prevention. (2012). *Physical activity*. Retrieved from http://www.cdc.gov/physicalactivity/everyone/guidelines/olderadults.html

Centers for Medicare and Medicaid Services. (2014). *Medicare and you*. Available from Medicare website: http://www.medicare.gov

Chatters, S., & Zalaquett, C. (2013, June). Dispelling the myths of aging. *Counseling Today, 55*, pp. 47–48, 50–51.

Chernof, B. (2011, November 1). Hiding in plain sight: Seeing the person beyond the patient. *Perspectives on Aging With Dignity*. Retrieved from http://www.thescanfoundation.org/hiding-plain-sight-seeing-person-beyond-patient

Chetnik, N. (2000). Reaching bereaved men requires innovation. *The Forum, 6*(5), 1–16.

Chia, E. M., Mitchell, P., Rochtchina, E., Foran, S., Golding, M., & Wang, J. (2006). Association between vision and hearing impairments and their combined effects on quality of life. *Archives of Ophthalmology, 124*, 1465–1470.

Choate, L. H. (2008). *Girls' and women's wellness: Contemporary counseling issues and interventions*. Alexandria, VA: American Counseling Association.

Choice in Dying. (2006). *A living will*. Retrieved from the Right to Die (formerly Society for the Right to Die) website:, http://www.choices.org

Clara, I. P., & Huynh, C. (2003). Four short-form linear equation estimates of Wechsler Adult Intelligence Scale III IQs in an elderly sample. *Measurement and Evaluation in Counseling and Development, 36*, 251–262.

Coates, T. F. (2012, November). Caregivers and bias. *AARP Bulletin, 53*, 8.

Cohn, H. (Producer), & Capra, F. (Director). (1939). *Mr. Smith goes to Washington* [Motion picture]. United States: Columbia Pictures.

Colliver, J. D., Compton, W. M., Gfroerer, J. C., & Condon, T. (2006). Projecting drug use among aging Baby Boomers in 2020. *Annuals of Epidemiology, 16*, 257–265.

Connidis, I. A. (2010). *Family ties and aging* (2nd ed.). Thousand Oaks, CA: Pine Forge Press.

Conwell, Y., Duberstein, P. R., & Caine, E. D. (2002). Risk factors of suicide in later life. *Biological Psychiatry, 52,* 193–204.

Cook, J. M. (2001). Post-traumatic stress disorder in older adults. *PTSD Research Quarterly, 12,* 1–7.

Corey, G., Haynes, R., Moulton, P., & Muratori, M. (2010). *Clinical supervision in the helping professions: A practical guide* (2nd ed.). Alexandria, VA: American Counseling Association.

Corr, C. A., Nabe, C. M., & Corr, D. M. (2000). *Death and dying, life and living* (3rd ed.). Belmont, CA: Wadsworth.

Cotter, A., Meyer, J., & Roberts, S. (1998). Humanity or bureaucracy? The transition from hospital to long-term continuing institutional care. *Nursing Times Research, 3,* 247–256.

Coyle, N. (2006). The hard work of living in the face of death. *Journal of Pain and Symptom Management, 32,* 266–274.

Crawford, K., & Walker, J. (2004). *Social work with older people.* Exeter, United Kingdom: Learning Matters.

Cress, C. J. (2007). *Handbook of geriatric care management* (2nd ed.). Burlington, MA: Jones & Bartlett.

Daniel-Burke, R. (2012, November). Working with the American Indian population. *Counseling Today, 55,* 14–15.

Davidson, S. (2011, March/April). Hot to trot: A horse-loving great-grandmother takes the reins. *AARP: The Magazine, 54,* 52–53.

Davis, L. (Producer), & Keaton, D. (Director). (2000). *Hanging up* [Motion picture]. United States: Columbia Pictures.

Davis, S. (1998). Development of the profession of horticultural therapy. In S. P. Simson & M. C. Straus (Eds.), *Horticulture as therapy: Principles and practices* (pp. 3–18). New York, NY: The Food Products Press.

de Rosnay, T. (2007). *Sarah's key.* New York, NY: St. Martin's Press.

Deacon, A. (2008). Income, health, and well-being from around the world: Evidence from the Gallup World Poll. *Journal of Economic Perspectives, 22,* 53–72.

Deggs-White, S., & Myers, J. E. (2006). Transitions, wellness, and life satisfaction: Implications for counseling midlife women. *Journal of Mental Health Counseling, 28,* 133–150.

Delany, S. L., & Delany E., with Hearth, A. H. (1993). *Having our say: The Delany sisters' first 100 years.* New York, NY: Kodansha America.

Delany, S. L., & Hearth, A. H. (1997). *On my own at 107: Reflections of life without Bessie.* San Francisco, CA: Harper.

DeLoria, D. (1981). *Dancers of the third age* [Photograph]. Liz Lerman Dance Exchange, Washington, DC.

Dendinger, V. M., Adams, G. A., & Jacobson, J. D. (2005). Reasons for working and their relationship to retirement attitudes, job satisfaction and occupational self-efficiency of bridge employees. *International Journal of Aging and Human Development, 61,* 21–35.

DeNiro, R. (Producer), Roach, R. (Producer & Director), & Rosenthal, J. (Producer). (2004). *Meet the Fockers* [Motion Picture]. United States: Universal Pictures.

Denn, R., & Park, J. M. (2012, June/July). Eat healthy for less. *AARP: The Magazine, 55*, pp. 24, 25–26, 31.

Department of Health, Great Britain. (1994). *Implementing caring for people: The F factor; Reasons why some older people choose residential care.* London, England: Author.

de Pencier, M., Knudsen, L., Urgang, L., VanHoy, J., & Vanech, E. (Producers), & Mills, M. (Director). (2010). *Beginners* [Motion picture], United States: Olympus.

Depp, C. A., & Jeste, D. V. (2006). Definitions and predictors of successful aging: A comprehensive review of larger quantitative studies. *American Journal of Geriatric Psychiatry, 14*, 6–20.

Devino, R., Petrucci, V., & Snider, E. (2004). *Aging and employment: Trends in health insurance, pension plans, Social Security, individual savings and their effects on retirement planning.* Retrieved from http://scholar.googleusercontent.com/scholar?q=cache:bmy3U XYhZLAJ:scholar.google.co

DeVivo, M. J. (2004). Aging with a neurodisability: Morbidity and life expectancy issues. *NeuroRehabilitation, 19*, 1–2.

Diallo, A. (2013). Client's willingness to incorporate religion or spirituality in counseling: A brief report. *Rehabilitation Counseling Bulletin, 56*, 120–122.

Dillon, C. F., Gu, Q., Hoffman, H. J., & Chia-Wen, K. (2010, April 7). *Vision, hearing, balance, and sensory impairment in Americans aged 70 years and over: United States, 1999–2006* (NCHS Data Brief, U.S. Centers for Disease Control and Prevention, No. 31). Retrieved from http://www.cdc.gov/nchs/data/databriefs/db31.htm

Disharoon, S. (Producer), & Burke, J. C. E. (Director). (2004). *Aurora borealis* [Motion picture]. United States: Angel City Pictures.

Dixon, C. G., Richard, M., & Rollins, C. W. (2003). Contemporary issues facing aging Americans: Implications for rehabilitation and mental health counseling. *Journal of Rehabilitation, 69*, 5–12.

Doka, K. J. (2002). The role of ritual in treatment of disenfranchised grief. In K. J. Doka (Ed.), *Disenfranchised grief: New directions, challenges, and strategies for practice* (pp. 135–147). Champaign, IL: Research Press.

Douglas, M. (Producer), & Schepisi, F. (Director). (2003). *It runs in the family* [Motion picture]. United States: Metro-Goldwyn-Mayer.

Doyle, R. H., Dixon, C. G., & Moore, C. L. (2003). Expanding rehabilitation services to meet the legal needs of aging Americans. *Journal of Rehabilitation, 69*, 49–54.

Duberstein, P. R., & Conwell, Y. (2000). Suicide. In S. K. Whitbourne (Ed.), *Psychopathology in later life* (pp. 245–276). New York, NY: Wiley.

Duncan, C. (2003). Assessing anti-ageism routes to older worker re-engagement. *Work, Employment, and Society, 17,* 101–120.

Dworkin, S. H., & Pope, M. (Eds.). (2012). *Casebook for counseling lesbian, gay, bisexual, and transgender persons and their families.* Alexandria, VA: American Counseling Association.

Dwyer, F., & Mackinnon, S. (Producers), & Hoffman, D. (Director). (2012). *Quartet* [Motion picture]. Great Britain: BBC Films.

Dyer, C. B., Connolly, M., & McFeeley, P. (2003). The clinical and medical forensics of elder abuse and neglect. In R. J. Bonnie & R. B. Wallace (Eds.), *Elder maltreatment: Abuse, neglect, and exploitation in an aging America* (pp. 303–338). Washington, DC: National Academy Press.

Eastwood, C. (Producer), & Lorenz, R. (Producer & Director). (2012). *Trouble with the curve* [Motion picture]. United States: Warner Brothers.

Edmondson, R., & Kondratowitz, H. J. (2009). *Valuing older people: A humanist approach to ageing.* Bristol, England: Policy Press.

Edwards, J. D., Delahunt, P. B., & Mahncke, H. W. (2009). Cognitive speed of processing training delay driving cessation. *Journal of Gerontology: Medical Sciences, 64,* 1262–1267.

Egoyan, A., & Mankoff, D. (Producers), & Polley, S. (Director). (2007). *Away from her* [Motion picture]. United States: The Film Farm/Foundry Films/Pulling Focus Pictures.

eldersexual.org. (2012a). *Eldersexually responsible: Prevention and testing over 50.* Retrieved from http://www.eldersexual.org/sex/index.html

eldersexual.org. (2012b). *Testing and diagnosis: Every sexually active person needs to know.* Retrieved from http://www.eldersexual.org/responsible/index.html

Engelberg, R. A., Patrick, P. L., & Curtis, R. J. (2005). Correspondence between patients' preference and surrogates' understanding for dying and death. *Journal of Pain and Symptom Management, 30,* 498–509.

Ephron, D., & Ephron, N. (Producers), & Keaton, D. (Director). (2000). *Hanging up* [Motion picture]. United States: Columbia Pictures.

Erford, B. (n.d.). *Stressbuster relaxation exercise* [CD]. Alexandria, VA: American Counseling Association.

Erikson, E. H. (1963). *Childhood and society* (2nd ed.). New York, NY: Norton.

Erikson, E. H. (1982). *The life cycle completed: A review.* New York, NY: Norton.

Erwin, K. T. (2013). *Group techniques for aging adults* (2nd ed.). New York, NY: Routledge.

Etaugh, C. A., & Bridges, J. D. (2004). *The psychology of women: A lifestyle perspective.* Boston, MA: Pearson Education.

Everall, R. D., & Paulson, B. L. (2004). Burnout and secondary traumatic stress: Impact on ethical behavior. *Canadian Journal of Counseling, 38,* 25–35.

Federal Interagency Forum on Aging. (2006). *2006 older America update: Key indicators of wellness.* Retrieved from http://agingstats. gov/agingstatsdotnet/Main_Site/Data/Data_2006.aspx

Feldman, H. A., Longcope, C., Derby, C. A., Johannes, C. B., Araujo, A. B., Coviello, A. D., . . . McKinlay, J. B. (2002). Age trends in the level of serum testosterone and other hormones in middle-aged men: Longitudinal results from the Massachusetts Male Aging Study. *Journal of Clinical Endocrinology and Metabolism, 87,* 589–598.

Finch, J., & Robinson, M. (2003). Aging and late-onset disability: Addressing workplace accommodation. *Journal of Rehabilitation, 69,* 38–42.

Fingerman, K. L. (2001). *Aging mothers and their adult daughters: A study in mixed emotions.* New York, NY: Springer.

Fingerman, K. L., Hay, E. L., & Birditt, K. S. (2004). The best of ties, the worst of ties: Close, problematic, and ambivalent social relationships. *Journal of Marriage and Family, 66,* 702–808.

Fisher, L. L. (2010). *Sex, romance, and relationships: AARP survey of midlife and older adults.* Washington, DC: AARP.

Fisher, M. A. (2011, July/August). What to do when your doctor doesn't know. *AARP: The Magazine, 54,* pp. 61–63, 86.

Folkman, S., & Lazarus, R. S. (1980). An analysis of coping in a middle-aged community sample. *Journal of Health and Social Behavior, 21,* 219–239.

Folkman, S., Lazarus, R., Dunkel-Schetter, C., DeLongis, A., & Gruen, R. (1986). Dynamics of a stressful encounter: Cognitive appraisal, coping and encounter outcomes. *Journal of Personality and Social Psychology, 50,* 992–1003.

Fonda, J. (2011). *Prime time: Love, health, sex, fitness, friendship, spirit: Making the most of all of your life.* New York, NY: Random House.

Foster, E. (2007). *Communicating at the end of life: Finding magic in the mundane.* Mahwah, NJ: Erlbaum.

Fox, R., & Rudin, S. (Producers), & Eyre, R. (Director). (2001). *Iris* [Motion picture]. Great Britain: BBC.

Fraser, A. (2006). Psychological therapies in the treatment of abused adults. *Journal of Adult Protection, 8,* 31–38.

Freedman, V. A., Martin, L. G., & Schoeni, R. F. (2002). Recent trends in disability and functioning among older adults in the United States: A systematic review. *Journal of the American Medical Association, 288,* 3137–3147.

Fried, L. P., & Guralnik, J. M. (1997). Disability in older adults: Evidence regarding significance, etiology, and risk. *Journal of the American Geriatric Society, 45,* 92–100.

Friend, R. (1990). Older lesbian and gay people: A theory of successful aging. *Journal of Homosexuality, 4,* 99–118.

Frueh, B. C., Buckley, T. C., Cusack, K. J., Kimble, M. O., Grubaugh, A. L., Turner, S. M., & Keane, T. M. (2004). Cognitive–behavioral treatment for PTSD among people with severe mental illness: A proposed treatment model. *Journal of Psychiatric Practice, 10,* 26–38.

Fry, P. S. (1997). Grandparent's reactions to the death of a grandchild: An exploratory factor analytic study. *Omega: Journal of Death and Dying, 35,* 119–140.

Furr, R. S., & Carroll, J. J. (2003). Critical incidents in student counselor development. *Journal of Counseling & Development, 81,* 483–489.

Gadalla, T. M. (2009). Sense of mastery, social support, and health in elderly Canadians. *Journal of Aging and Health, 21,* 581–595.

Gant, N. D., & Kampfe, C. M. (1997). Psychosocial challenges faced by persons with Meniere's disease. *Journal of Applied Rehabilitation Counseling, 28,* 40–49.

Genova, L. (2009). *Still Alice: A novel.* New York, NY: Pocket Books.

Genova, L. (2011). *Left neglected.* New York, NY: Gallery Books.

Georges, J. J., Onwuteaka-Philipsen, B. D., Muller, M. T., Van Der Wal, G., Van Der Heide, A., & Van Der Maas, P. J. (2007). Relatives' perspective on the terminally ill patients who died after euthanasia or physician-assisted suicide: A retrospective cross-sectional interview study in the Netherlands. *Death Studies, 31,* 1–15.

Gibson, F. (1992). Reminiscence groupwork with older people. *Groupwork, 5,* 28–40.

Gilbert, B. (Producer), & Rydell, M. (Director). (1981). *On Golden Pond* [Motion picture]. United States: Universal Studios.

Glicken, M. D. (2005). *Improving the effectiveness of the helping professions: An evidence based approach to practice.* Thousand Oaks, CA: Sage.

Goenjian, A. K., Najarian, L. M., Pynoos, R. S., Steinberg, A. M., Monoukian, G., Tavosian, A., & Fairbanks, L. A. (1994). Posttraumatic stress disorder in elderly and younger adults after the 1988 earthquake in Armenia. *American Journal of Psychiatry, 151,* 895–901.

Golden, J., Conroy, R. M., Bruce, I., Denihan, A., Greene E., Kirby, M., . . . Lawlor, B. A. (2009). Loneliness, social support networks, mood and wellbeing in community-dwelling elderly. *International Journal of Geriatric Psychiatry, 24,* 694–700.

Golden, T., & Miller, J. (1998). *When a man faces grief: A man you know is grieving.* Fort Wayne, IN: Willowgreen Press.

Goldreich, G. (2008). *Open doors.* Toronto, Ontario, Canada: MIRA Books.

Gomberg, E. L. (1995). Older alcoholics: Entry into treatment. In T. Beresford & E. Gomberg (Eds.), *Alcohol and aging* (pp. 169–185). New York, NY: Oxford, University Press.

Gomez, V., Krings, F., Bangerter, A., & Grob, A. (2009). The influence of personality and life events on subjective well-being from a life span perspective. *Journal of Research in Personality, 43,* 345–354.

Goodman, L. A., Liang, B., Helms, J. E., Latta, R. E., Sparks, E., & Weintraub, S. R. (2004). Training counseling psychologists as social change agents: Feminist and multicultural principles in action. *The Counseling Psychologist, 32,* 793–837.

Gordon, P., Feldman, D., Tantillo, J., & Perrone, K. (2004). Attitudes regarding interpersonal relationships with people with mental illness and mental retardation. *Journal of Rehabilitation, 70,* 50–56.

Gori, V., & Field, T. (Producers), & Jones, K. (Director). (2009). *Everybody's fine* [Motion picture]. United States: Miramax Films.

Goyer, A. (2013, November). A crisis around every corner. *AARP Bulletin, 54,* pp. 14, 16, 18.

Green, P. (Producer), & Asher, J. (Director). (1999). *Diamonds* [Motion picture], Germany: Cinerenta Medienbeteiligungs KG.

Grisham, J. (2002). *The summons.* New York, NY: Bantam Dell.

Gross, J (2012). *A bittersweet season: Caring for our parents and ourselves.* New York, NY: Vintage.

Guen, S. (2006). *Water for elephants.* Chapel Hill, NC: Algonquin Books.

Gurwitz, J. H., & Avorn, J. (1991). The ambiguous relation between aging and adverse drug reactions. *Annals of Internal Medicine, 114,* 952–965.

Haaga, J. (2011). *Just how many Baby Boomers are there?* Retrieved from the Population Reference Bureau website: http://www.prb.org/Publications/Articles/2002/JustHowManyBaby-BoomersAreThere.aspx

Hagestad, G. O. (1985). Continuity and connectedness. In V. L. Bengston & J. Robertson (Eds.), *Grandparenthood* (Vol. 74, pp. 31–48). Thousand Oaks, CA: Sage.

Haller, R. (1998). Vocational, social, and therapeutic programs in horticulture. In S. P. Simson & M. C. Straus (Eds.), *Horticulture as therapy: Principles and practices* (pp. 43–68). New York, NY: The Food Products Press.

Hamilton, J. M., Kives, K. D., Micevski, V., & Grace, S. L. (2003). Time perspective and health-promoting behavior in a cardiac rehabilitation population. *Behavioral Medicine, 28,* 132–139.

Harley, D. A. (2005). African Americans and indigenous counseling. In D. A. Harley & J. M. Dillard (Eds.), *Contemporary mental health issues among African Americans* (pp. 293–306). Alexandria, VA: American Counseling Association.

Harley, D. A., Jolivette, K., McCormick, K., & Tice, K. (2002). Race, class, and gender: A constellation of positionalities with implications for counseling. *Journal of Multicultural Counseling and Development, 30,* 216–238.

Harris, L., & Johnson, M. (Producers), & Cassavetes, N. (Director). (2004). *The notebook* [Motion picture]. United States: New Line Cinema.

Haslanger, K. (2012, September 11). As fall approaches, a checklist to keep family elders steady on their feet. *Huff Post.* Retrieved from http://www.huffingtonpost.com/katheryn-haslanger/elderly-falls

Hawes, C. (2003). Elder abuse in residential long-term care settings: What is known and what information is needed? In R. J. Bonnie & R. B. Wallace (Eds.), *Elder maltreatment: Abuse, neglect, and exploitation in an aging America* (pp. 446–500). Washington, DC: National Academy Press.

Hawes, C., Blevins, D., & Shanley, L. (2001). *Preventing abuse and neglect in nursing homes: The role of the nurse aide registries* (Report to the Centers for Medicare and Medicaid Services [formerly HCFA]). College Station, TX: School of Rural Public Health, Texas A&M University System Health Science Center.

Hawkley, L. C., Thisted, R. A., Masi, C. M., & Cacioppo, J. T. (2010). Loneliness predicts increased blood pressure: 5-year cross-lagged analyses in middle-aged and older adults. *Psychology and Aging, 25,* 132–141.

Healthways SilverSneakers Fitness Program. (2012). *Remember why you joined* [Brochure/mailed communication].

Helman, R., Copeland, C., & VanDerhei, J. (2006). *Will more of us be working forever? The 2006 Retirement Confidence Survey.* Washington, DC: Employee Benefit Research Institute.

Hendrick, B. (2011) *Alzheimer's disease may be misdiagnosed.* Retrieved from http://www.webmd.com/alzheimers/news/20110223/alzheimers-disease-may-be-misdiagnosed

Higgins, A. B., & Follette, V. M. (2002). Frequency and impact of interpersonal trauma in older women. *Journal of Clinical Geropsychology, 8,* 215–226.

Highroads. (2012, November/December). Rev up for older driver safety awareness week. *Highroads,* p. 14.

Hijuelos, O. (1995) *Mr. Ives' Christmas.* New York, NY: Harper Collins.

Hinrichsen, G. A. (1999). Interpersonal psychotherapy for late-life depression. In M. Duffy (Ed.), *Handbook of counseling and psychotherapy with older adults* (pp. 470–486). New York, NY: Wiley.

Hirsh, S. (2013, June). Terminating clients: A challenge without end. *Counseling Today, 55,* 12–13.

Hoenig, H., Nusbaum, N., & Brummel-Smith, K. (1997). Geriatric rehabilitation: State of the art. *Journal of the American Geriatric Society, 45,* 1371–1381.

Hogg, J., Lucchino, R., Wang, K., & Janicki, M. (2001). Healthy aging—Adults with intellectual disabilities: Ageing and social policy. *Journal of Applied Research in Intellectual Disabilities, 14,* 229–255.

Holahan, C. K., & Chapman, J. R. (2002). Longitudinal predictors of proactive goals and activity participation at age 80. *Journals of Gerontology: Series B. Psychological Sciences and Social Sciences, 57,* 418–425.

Holman, E. A., & Silver, R. C. (1998). Getting "stuck" in the past: Temporal orientation and coping with trauma. *Journal of Personality and Social Psychology, 74,* 1146–1163.

Hope Heart Institute. (n.d.). *Caregiving: Practical tips to help you help others.* Seattle, WA: Hope Publications.

Hope, T., Carey, T. A., & Westheimer, E. (Producers), & Jenkins, T. (Director). (2007). *The Savages* [Motion picture]. United States: 20th Century Fox Searchlight Pictures.

Hope, T., & Schamus, J. (Producers), & Holofcener, N. (Director). (1996). *Walking and talking* [Motion picture]. Germany: Pandora Filmproduktion.

Horton-Parker, R. J., & Fawcett, R. C. (2010). *Practical strategies for caring for older adults: An Adlerian approach for understanding and assisting aging loved ones* [DVD]. Columbus, OH: Old Dominion University.

Hospice and Palliative Nurses Association. (2009a). *Patient/family teaching sheet: Complementary therapies.* Retrieved from http://www.hpna.org/PicViiew.aspx?ID=490

Hospice and Palliative Nurses Association. (2009b). *Patient/family teaching sheet: Grief and mourning.* Retrieved from http://www.HPNA.org/PicView.aspx?ID=322

Hospice and Palliative Nurses Association. (2009c). *Patient/family teaching sheet: Spiritual distress.* Retrieved from http://www.hpna.org/PicView.aspx?ID=54

Hospice and Palliative Nurses Association. (2011). *Patient/family teaching sheet: Managing anxiety/uneasy feelings.* Retrieved from http://www.hpna.org/PicView.aspx?ID=43

Hospice and Palliative Nurses Association. (2012). *Patient/family teaching sheet: Final days.* Retrieved from http://www.hpna.org/PicView.aspx?ID=40

Howard, B. (2011b, May/June). Pain killers in your kitchen. *AARP: The Magazine, 54,* 46–48.

Howard, B. (2012a, June/July). Watch your meds. *AARP: The Magazine, 55,* 20–22.

Howard, B. (2012b, October/November). What to expect in your 60s. *AARP: The Magazine, 55,* 56–61.

Hoyer, W. J., & Roodin, P. A. (2003). *Adult development and aging* (5th ed.). New York, NY: McGraw-Hill.

Hoyer, W. J., & Roodin, P. A. (2009). *Adult development and aging* (6th ed.). New York, NY: McGraw-Hill.

Hummel, T., Landis, B. N., & Hüttenbrink, K.-B. (2011). Smell and taste disorders. *GMS Current Topics in Otorhinolaryngology Head Neck Surgery, 10.* doi:10.3205/cto000077

Humphrey, D. (1991). *Final exit: The practicalities of self-deliverance and assisted suicide for the dying.* Eugene, OR: The Hemlock Society.

Humphrey, K. M. (2009). *Counseling strategies for loss and grief.* Alexandria, VA: American Counseling Association.

Hurd Clark, L. (2006). Older women and sexuality: Experiences in marital relationships across the life course. *Canadian Journal of Aging, 25,* 129–140.

Hynes, A. L., & Wedl, L. C. (1990). Bibliotherapy: An interactive process in counseling older persons. *Journal of Mental Health Counseling, 12,* 288–302.

Ianzito, C. (2011, July/August). The new 'aahs' at spas. *AARP: The Magazine, 54,* 15.

Institute on Rehabilitation Issues. (2009). *The aging workforce.* Hot Springs: University of Arkansas.

Ivers, N. N., & Veach, L. J. (2012, December). Alcohol screening and brief counseling interventions for trauma unit patients. *Counseling Today, 55,* 38–41.

Iverson, K. M., Dick, A., McLaughlin, K. A., Smith, B. N., Bell, M. E., Gerber, M. R., . . . Mitchell, K. (2013). Exposure to interpersonal violence and its associations with psychiatric morbidity in a U.S. national sample: A gender comparison. *Psychology of Violence, 3,* 273–287.

Jacobs, C. (2004). Spirituality and end-of-life care practice. In J. Berzoff & P. R. Silverman (Eds.), *Living with dying: A handbook for end-of-life healthcare practitioners* (pp. 188–205). New York, NY: Columbia University Press.

Jang, S. N., Choi, Y. J., & Kim, D. H. (2009). Association of socioeconomic status with successful ageing: Differences in the components of successful ageing. *Journal of Biosocial Science, 41,* 207–219.

Jansen, A. S. P., Nguyen, X. V., Karpitskiy, V., Mettenleiter, T. C., & Loewy, A. D. (1995, October 27). Central command neurons of the sympathetic nervous system: Basis of the fight-or-flight response. *Science, 270,* 644–646.

Jernigan, K. (Ed.). (1996). *Old dogs and new tricks.* Baltimore, MD: National Federation of the Blind.

Johnson, P. R. (2010, February). *Psychotropic drugs and aging.* Paper presented at the 2010 Behavioral Health and Older Adults Conference, Pima Council on Aging, Tucson, AZ.

Johnson, P. R. (2011). *A behavioral approach to management of neuroleptic-induced tardive dyskinesia: Progressive relaxation training.* (Doctoral dissertation). ProQuest. UMI Dissertation Publishing.

Jones, D. (Producer), & Lloyd, P. (Director). (2011). *The iron lady* [Motion picture]. United Kingdom: The Weinstein Company/YUK Films, Pathe Film4 & UK Film Council.

Kaiser, A. P., Wachen, J. S., Potter, C., Moye, J., & Davison, E. (2013). *Posttraumatic stress symptoms among older adults: A review.* Retrieved from the U.S. Department of Veterans Affairs website: http://www.ptsd.va.gov/professional/treatment/older/ptsd_symptoms_older_adults.asp

Kampfe, C. M. (1990a). Communicating with persons who are deaf: Some practical suggestions for rehabilitation specialists. *Journal of Rehabilitation, 556,* 41–45.

Kampfe, C. M. (1990b, March). *Dignity versus dehumanization in long-term care settings for older persons: A training outline.* Poster presented at the annual convention of the American Association of Counseling and Development, Cincinnati, OH. Retrieved from ERIC database. (ED317917)

Kampfe, C. M. (1994). Vocational rehabilitation and the older population. *Southwest Journal on Aging, 9,* 65–69.

Kampfe, C. M. (1995). Empowerment in residential relocation and long-term care settings. In K. Chandras (Ed.), *Handbook on counseling adolescents, adults, and older people* (pp. 42–53). Alexandria, VA: ACES Adult Development, Aging and Counseling Interest Network, Association for Counselor Education and Supervision.

Kampfe, C. M. (1999). Residential relocation of people who are older: Relationships among life satisfaction, perceptions, coping strategies, and other variables. *Adultspan Journal, 1,* 91–124. doi:10.1002/j.2161-0029.1999.tb00085.x

Kampfe, C. M. (2002). Older adults' perceptions of residential relocation. *Journal of Humanistic Counseling, Education and Development, 41,* 103–113.

Kampfe, C. M. (2003, March). *Parallels between creative dance and creative counseling.* Paper presented at the World Conference of the ACA, Anaheim, CA.

Kampfe, C. M. (2009). Functional and psychosocial aspects of late onset hearing loss. In C. A. Marshall, E. Kendall, R. M. S. Gover, & M. Banks (Eds.), *Disabilities: Insights from across fields and around the world. The experience, definitions, causes, and consequences* (Vol. 1., pp. 143–156). Westport, CT: Praeger Press.

Kampfe, C., Brehm, M. A., Pohanic, N., & Grayson, J. (1998–1999). The use of dance improvisation to foster creative expression, group cooperation, and curricular learning. In *Proceedings of the 1998–1999 Dean's Forum, the College of Education* (pp. 25–29). Tucson: University of Arizona.

Kampfe, C. M., & Dennis, D. J. (2000). Counseling for diversity: Application of the House Model of Social Stress. *Journal of Applied Rehabilitation Counseling, 31,* 20–32.

Kampfe, C. M., Harley, D. A., Wadsworth, J. S., & Smith S. M. (2007). Methods and materials for infusing aging issues into the rehabilitation curriculum. *Rehabilitation Education, 21,* 107–115.

Kampfe, C. M., & Kampfe, R. L. (1992). Coping strategies used by older upper-middle-class persons making residential relocations. *Arizona Counseling Journal, 17,* 3–9.

Kampfe, C. M., & Mitchell, M. M. (1991). Relationships among coping strategies and selected variables in clinical internships. *Rehabilitation Education, 5,* 29–41.

Kampfe, C. M., & Smith, S. M. (1997). Older persons' psychological reactions to presbycusis. *Southwest Journal of Aging, 13,* 53–59.

Kampfe, C. M., & Smith, S. M. (1998). Intrapersonal aspects of hearing loss in persons who are older. *Journal of Rehabilitation, 64,* 24–28.

Kampfe, C. M., & Smith, S. M. (1999). Late-onset hearing loss: Strategies for effective counseling. *Adultspan Journal, 1,* 32–49.

Kampfe, C. M., Wadsworth, J. S., Mamboleo, G. I., & Schonbrun, S. L. (2008). Aging, disability, and employment. *Work: A Journal of Prevention, Assessment, and Rehabilitation, 31,* 337–344.

Kampfe, C. M., Wadsworth, J. S., Smith, S. M., & Harley, D. A. (2005). The infusion of aging issues in the rehabilitation curriculum: A review of the literature. *Rehabilitation Education, 19,* 225–233.

Kane, R. L., & West, J. C. (2005). *It shouldn't be this way: The failure of long-term care.* Nashville, TN: Vanderbilt University Press.

Kaneda, K., Rycroft, M. B. Z., & Williams, J. (Producers), & Williams, J. (Director). (2001). *Firefly dreams* [Motion picture]. Japan: Orfeo Films International.

Kaplan, M., Goldberg, L., & Peyser, M. (Producers), & Lynn, J. (Director). (1992). *The distinguished gentleman* [Motion picture]. United States: Hollywood Pictures.

Keefe, J. M., & Fancey, P. J. (2002). Work and eldercare: Reciprocity between older mothers and their employed daughters. *Canadian Journal of Aging, 21,* 229–241.

Kelley, S. D. M. (2003). Prevalent mental health disorders in the aging population: Issues of comorbidity and functional disability. *Journal of Rehabilitation, 69,* 19–25.

Kemmet, D., & Brotherson, S. (2008). *Making sense of sensory losses as we age—Childhood, adulthood, elderhood?* Retrieved from North Dakota State University and the U.S. Department of Agriculture's website: http://www.ag.ndsu.edu/pubs/yf/famsci/fs1378.pdf

Kenyon, G., Ruth, J. E., & Mader, W. (1999). Elements of a narrative gerontology. In V. L. Bengston & K. W. Schaie (Eds.), *Handbook of theories of aging* (pp. 40–58). New York, NY: Springer.

Kerson, T. S. (2001). Social work practice with women as they age. In J. D. Garner & S. O. Mercer (Eds.), *Women as they age* (pp. 69–84). Binghamton, NY: Hawthorn Press.

Kim, J., & Moen, P. (2002). Retirement transition, gender, and psychological wellbeing: A life-course, ecological model. *Journals of Gerontology: Series G. Psychological Sciences and Social Sciences, 57,* 212–222. doi:10.1093/geronb/57.3.P212

Kim, J. E., & Nesselroade, J. R. (2002). Relationships among social support, self-concept, and wellbeing of older adults: A study of process using dynamic factor models. *International Journal of Behavioral Development, 27,* 49–63.

Kimmel, D. (2012). Counseling older gay men. In S. H. Dworkin & M. Pope (Eds.), *Casebook for counseling lesbian, gay, bisexual, and transgender persons and their families* (pp. 53–62). Alexandria, VA: American Counseling Association.

Kimmel, D., Rose, T., & David, S. (Eds.). (2006). *Lesbian, gay, bisexual, and transgender aging: Research and clinical perspectives.* New York, NY: Columbia University Press.

Kirschner, D. (Producer), & McCanlies, T. (Director). (2003). *Secondhand lions* [Motion picture]. United States: David Kirschner Productions.

Kissane, M., & McLaren, S. (2006). Sense of belonging as a predictor of reasons for living in older adults. *Death Studies, 30,* 243–258.

Kivnick, H. Q. (1983). Dimensions of grandparenthood meaning: Deductive conceptualization and empirical derivation. *Journal of Personality and Social Psychology, 44,* 1056–1068.

Klass, D., Silverman, P. R., & Nickman, S. L. (Eds.). (1996). *Continuing bonds: New understandings of grief.* Philadelphia, PA: Taylor & Francis.

Kleiner, G. (1996). *Where the river turns to sky.* New York, NY: Avon Books.

Klemmack, D. L., Roff, L. L., Parker, M. W., Koenig, H. G., Sawyer, P., & Allman, R. M. (2007). A cluster analysis typology of religiousness/spirituality among older adults. *Research on Aging, 29,* 163–183.

Kolker, C., & Winters, D. (2012, June/July). Leaving home. *AARP: The Magazine, 55,* pp. 49–50, 53, 69.

Koo, E. Y. (2008a). *Cataracts.* San Bruno, CA: The Staywell Company.

Koo, E. Y. (2008b). *Glaucoma.* San Bruno, CA: The Staywell Company.

Koropeckyj-Cox, T. (2002). Beyond parental status: Psychological well-being in middle and old age. *Journal of Marriage and Family, 64,* 957–971.

Kosinski, G., & Rodnyansky, A. (Producers), & Thornton, B. B. (Director). (2012). *Jayne Mansfield's car* [Motion picture]. Russia: AR Films Media Corporation.

Kramer, N. (1995, April). Employee benefits for older workers. *Monthly Labor Review,* pp. 21–27.

Kübler-Ross, E. (1969). *On death and dying.* New York, NY: McMillan.

Kübler-Ross, E. (2011). *Living with death and dying: How to communicate with the terminally ill.* New York, NY: Touchstone.

Kübler-Ross, E., & Kessler, D. (2005). *On grief and grieving: Finding the meaning of grief through the five stages of loss* (4th ed.). New York, NY: Simon & Schuster.

Kwan, S. (2003, June 13). Underfunding of private pension plans. *FRBSF Economic Letter.* Retrieved from Federal Reserve Bank of San Francisco's website: http://www.frbsf.org/publications/economics/letter/2003/el2003-16.html

Lachs, M. S., Williams, C., O'Brien, S., Hurst, L., & Horwitz, R. (1997). Risk factors for reported elder abuse and neglect: A nine-year observational cohort study. *Gerontologist, 37,* 469–474.

Lam, B. L., Lee, D. J., Gomez-Marin, O., Zheng, D. D., & Caban, A. J. (2006). Concurrent visual and hearing impairment and risk of mortality: The National Health Interview Survey. *Archives of Ophthalmology, 124,* 95–101.

Lamb, G. S. (2005). Case management for older adults. In F. Chan, M. J. Leahy, & J. L. Saunders (Eds.), *Case management for rehabilitation health professionals* (2nd ed., Vol. 2., pp. 227–246). Osage Beach, MO: Aspen Professional Services.

Lang, F. R., & Carstensen, L. L. (1994). Close emotional relationships in late life: Further support for proactive aging in the social domain. *Psychology and Aging, 9,* 315–324.

Larkin, V. M., Alston, R. J., Middleton, R. A., & Wilson, K. B. (2003). Underrepresented ethnically and racially diverse aging populations with disabilities: Trends and recommendations. *Journal of Rehabilitation, 69,* 26–31.

Laumann, E. O., Leitsch, S. A., & Waite, L. J. (2008). Elder mistreatment in the United States: Prevalence estimates from a nationally representative study. *Journals of Gerontology: Series B. Psychological Sciences and Social Sciences, 63,* S248–S254.

Lawson, D. M. (2013). *Family violence: Explanations and evidence-based clinical practice.* Alexandria, VA: American Counseling Association.

Lazarus, A. A. (1971). *Behavior therapy and beyond.* New York, NY: McGraw Hill.

Lee, C. C. (Ed.). (2007). *Counseling for social justice* (2nd ed.). Alexandria, VA: American Counseling Association.

Lehembre, M. R. (2012). [Review of the book *Aging our way: Lessons for living from 85 and beyond,* by Meika Loe]. *Adultspan Journal, 11,* 55–58.

Lewis, A. N. (2008). Vocational rehabilitation in the 21st century: Skills professionals need for systems success. *Work: A Journal of Prevention, Assessment, and Rehabilitation, 31,* 345–356.

Lewis, A. N., Cooper, R. A., Seelman, K. D., Cooper, R., & Schein, R. M. (2012). Assistive technology in rehabilitation: Improving impact through policy. *Rehabilitation Education, 26,* 19–32.

Lewis, J. A., Arnold, M. S., House, R., & Toporek, R. L. (2002). *ACA advocacy competencies.* Retrieved from http://www.counseling.org/Resources/Competencies/Advocacy_Competencies.pdf

Li, L., Liang, J., Toler, A., & Gu, S. (2005). Widowhood and depressive symptoms among older Chinese: Do gender and source of support make a difference? *Social Science and Medicine, 60,* 637–647.

Lin, I.-F. (2008). Consequences of parental divorce for adult children's support of their frail parents. *Journal of Marriage and Family, 70,* 113–128.

Lindau, S. T., Schumm, L. P., Laumann, E. O., Levinson, W., O'Muircheartaigh, C. A., & Waite, L. J. (2007). A national study of sexuality and health among older adults in the U.S. *New England Journal of Medicine, 357,* 762–764.

Lindauer, M. S. (1998). Artists, art, and arts activities: What do they tell us about aging? In C. Adams-Price (Ed.), *Creativity and successful aging: Theoretical and empirical approaches* (pp. 237–250). New York, NY: Springer.

Liu, I. C., & Chiu, C. H. (2009). Case-control study of suicide attempts in the elderly. *International Psychogeriatrics, 21,* 896–902.

Livneh, H. (2013). The concept of time in rehabilitation and psychosocial adaptation to chronic illness and disability: Part II. *Rehabilitation Counseling Bulletin, 56,* 71–84.

Livneh, H., & Martz, E. (2007). Reactions to diabetes and their relationship to time orientation. *International Journal of Rehabilitation Research, 30,* 127–136.

Loe, M. (2011). *Aging our way: Lessons for living from 85 and beyond.* New York, NY: Oxford University Press.

Longshore, D., Grills, C., Annon, K., & Grady, R. (1998). Promoting recovery from drug abuse: An Africentric intervention. *Journal of Black Studies, 28,* 319–332.

Lopata, H. (1996). *Current widowhood: Myths and realities.* Thousand Oaks, CA: Sage.

Loverde, J. (2009). *A complete eldercare planner: Where to start, which questions to ask, and how to find help* (2nd ed.). New York, NY: Three Rivers Press.

Lubart, T. I., & Sternberg, R. J. (1998). Life span creativity: An investment theory approach. In C. Adams-Price (Ed.), *Creativity and successful aging: Theoretical and empirical approaches* (pp. 21–41). New York, NY: Springer.

Lund, D. A., Caserta, M. S., & Dimond, M. F. (1993). The course of spousal bereavement in later life. In M. Stroebe & W. Stroebe (Eds.), *Handbook of bereavement: Theory, research, and intervention* (pp. 240–254). New York, NY: Cambridge University Press.

Lupsakko, T., Mantyjarvi, M., Kautiainen, H., & Sulkava, R. (2002). Combined hearing and visual impairment and depression in a population aged 75 years and older. *International Journal of Geriatric Psychiatry, 17,* 808–813.

Lynch, T. (1998). *The undertaking: Life studies from the dismal trade.* London, England: Vintage Books.

Mamboleo, G. I., & Kampfe, C. M. (2009). Medicare prescription drug coverage for older Americans: Implications for rehabilitation counselors. *Rehabilitation Counselors and Educators Journal, 3,* 30–37.

Manning, W. D., & Brown, S. L. (2011). The demography of unions among older American, 1980–present: A family change approach. In R. A. Settersten Jr. & J. L. Angel (Eds.), *Handbook of sociology of aging* (pp. 193–210). New York, NY: Springer.

Manzoli, L., Villari, P., Pirone, G., & Boccia, A. (2007). Marital status and mortality in the elderly: A systematic review and meta-analysis. *Social Science & Medicine, 64,* 77–94.

Maples, M. F., & Abney, P. C. (2006). Baby Boomers mature and gerontological counseling comes of age. *Journal of Counseling & Development, 84,* 3–9.

Marinelli, R. P., & Del Orto, E. E. (Eds.). (1999). *The psychological and social impact of disability.* New York, NY: Springer.

Martin, B. (2006). *Fight or flight.* Retrieved from http://psychcentral.com/lib/fight-or-flight/00030

Martin, P., Hagberg, B., & Poon, L. W. (1997). Predictors of loneliness in centenarians. *Journal of Cross-Cultural Gerontology, 12,* 203–224.

Martin, T., & Doka, K. (2000). *Men don't cry ... Women do: Transcending stereotypes of grief.* Philadelphia, PA: Brunner/Mazel.

Martz, S. H. (1992). *If I had my life to live over I would pick more daisies.* Watsonville, CA: Papier-Mache Press.

McCarthy, T. J., & Light, J. (2005). Attitudes toward individuals who use augmentative and alternative communication: Research review. *Augmentative and Alternative Communication, 21,* 4–55.

McColl, M. A. (2002). Occupation in stressful times. *American Journal of Occupational Therapy, 56,* 350–353.

McDermott, R., Fowler, J. H., & Christakis, N. A. (2009). *Breaking up is hard to do, unless everyone else is doing it too: Social network effects on divorce in a longitudinal sample followed for 32 years.* Retrieved from Social Science Research Network website: http://ssrn.com/abstract=1490708

McGlothlin, J. M. (2008). *Developing clinical skills in suicide assessment, prevention, and treatment.* Alexandria, VA: American Counseling Association.

McGlynn, S. (2010). *Keeping time.* New York, NY: Crown.

McKiernan, F. (1996). Bereavement and attitudes toward death. In R. T. Woods (Ed.), *Handbook of the clinical psychology of ageing* (pp. 159–182). Chichester, England: Wiley.

Meagher, D. (1989). The counselor and the disenfranchised griever. In K. J. Doka (Ed.), *Disenfranchised grief: Recognizing hidden sorrow* (pp. 313–333). New York, NY: Lexington Books.

Mettler, B. (1989). *Materials of dance: A creative art activity.* Tucson, AZ: Tucson Creative Dance Center.

Meyer, I. H. (2003). Prejudice, social stress, and mental health in lesbian, gay and bisexual populations: Conceptual issues and research evidence. *Psychological Bulletin, 129,* 674–697.

Middleton R. A. (2005). Mental health challenges of African American elders: Issues, interventions, and cultural considerations. In D. A. Harley & J. M. Dillard (Eds.), *Contemporary mental health issues among African Americans* (pp. 75–90). Alexandria, VA: American Counseling Association.

Miller, M. D., Cornes, C., Frank, E., Ehrenpreis, L., Silberman, R., Schlernitzauer, M. A., . . . Reynolds, C. F. (2001). Interpersonal psychotherapy for late-life depression. *Journal of Psychotherapy Practice and Research, 10,* 231–238.

Minkowski, E. (1970). *Lived time phenomenological and psychopathological studies.* Evanston, IL: Northwestern University.

Mitchell, J. M., Adkins, R. H., & Kemp, B. J. (2006). The effects of aging on employment of people with and without disabilities. *Rehabilitation Counseling Bulletin, 49,* 157–165.

Molinari, V. (1999). Using reminiscence and life review as natural therapeutic strategies in group therapy. In M. Duffy (Ed.), *Handbook of counseling and psychotherapy with older adults* (pp. 154–165). New York, NY: Wiley.

Monroe, N. K. (2012). It's not all guns and PTSD: Counseling with a cultural lens. *Counseling Today, 55,* 52–55.

Moore, S. F., Kampfe, C. M., Schonbrun, S., Moore, E., McAllan, L., Smith, S. M., & Sales, A. P. (2008). Cultural immersion on the Navajo Nation: Developing multicultural competence. *Rehabilitation Counselors and Educators Journal, 2,* 28–34.

Morrissey, M., & Krahn, G. (1995). ACA helps draft resolutions for White House Mini-Conference on Mental Health and Aging. *Counseling Today, 37,* 6.

Mroczek, D. K., & Kolarz, C. M. (1998). The effect of age on positive and negative affect: A developmental perspective on happiness. *Journal of Personality and Social Psychology, 75,* 1333–1349.

Mroczek, D. K., & Spiro, A., III. (2005). Change in life satisfaction during adulthood: Findings from Veterans Affairs Normative Aging Study. *Journal of Personality and Social Psychology, 88,* 189–202.

Mueser, K. T., Becker, D. R., & Wolfe, R. (2001). Supported employment, job preferences, job tenure and satisfaction. *Journal of Mental Health, 10,* 411–417.

Mugoya, G., & Kampfe, C. M. (2010). Reducing the use of PRN medication in in-patient psychiatric hospitals. *The Rehabilitation Professional, 18,* 141–148.

Munday, D., Dale, J., & Murray, S. (2007). Choice and place of death: Individual preferences, uncertainty, and the availability of care. *Journal of the Royal Society of Medicine, 100,* 211–215.

Munnell, A. H., Golub-Sass, F., & Webb, A. (2007, January). *What moves the national retirement risk index? A look back and an update* (Issue Brief No. 7-1). Chestnut Hill, MA: Center for Retirement Research at Boston College.

Murphy, S. N. (2013, April). Life without an alarm clock. *Counseling Today, 55,* pp. 40–44, 47.

Myers, J. E. (1990). *Empowerment for later life.* Ann Arbor, MI: ERIC Counseling and Personnel Services Clearinghouse.

Myers, J. E. (1999). Adjusting to role loss and leisure in later life. In M. Duffy (Ed.), *Handbook of counseling and psychotherapy with older adults* (pp. 41–56). New York, NY: Wiley.

Myers, J. E., & Degges-White, S. (2007). Aging well in an upscale retirement community: The relationship among perceived stress, mattering, and wellness. *Adultspan Journal, 6,* 96–110.

Myers, J. E., & Harper, M. C. (2004). Evidence-based effective practices with older adults. *Journal of Counseling & Development, 82,* 207–218.

Myers, J. E., & Schwiebert, V. L. (1996). *Competencies for gerontological counseling.* Alexandria, VA: American Counseling Association.

Myers, J. E., & Shannonhouse, L. R. (2013). Combating ageism: Advocacy for older persons. In C. C. Lee (Ed.), *Multicultural issues in counseling: New approaches to diversity* (4th ed., pp. 151–170). Alexandria, VA: American Counseling Association.

Myers, K. (2013, August). Effective treatment of military clients. *Counseling Today, 56,* 62–66.

Myers, M. A. (2012). *Hearing loss and depression.* Retrieved from the EzineArticles website: http://eizinearticles.com/?Hearing-Loss-and-Depression&id=6081657

Nahmiash, E., & Reis, M. (2000). Most successful intervention strategies for abused older adults. *Journal of Elder Abuse & Neglect, 12,* 53–70.

National Center for Health Statistics. (1990, March). *Health, United States, 1989* (DHHS Publication No. [PHS] 90–1232). Washington, DC: Department of Health and Human Services.

National Center for PTSD. (2007a). *PTSD treatment programs in the U.S. Department of Veterans Affairs.* Retrieved from the U.S. Department of Veterans Affairs website: http://www.ptsd.va.gov/public/pages/va-ptsd-treatment-programs.asp

National Center for PTSD. (2007b). *Treatment of PTSD.* Retrieved from the U.S. Department of Veterans Affairs website: http://www.ptsd.va.gov/public/pages/treatment-ptsd.asp

National Center for PTSD. (2011a). *Other common problems.* Retrieved from the U.S. Department of Veterans Affairs website: http://www.ptsd.va.gov/public/pages/fslist-other_common_problems.asp

National Center for PTSD. (2011b). *Understanding PTSD treatment.* Retrieved from the U.S. Department of Veterans Affairs website: http://www.ptsd.va.gov/public/treatment/therapy-med/Understanding-TX.asp

National Center for PTSD. (2012). *Aging veterans and posttraumatic stress symptoms.* Retrieved from the U.S. Department of Veterans Affairs website: http://www.ptsd.va.gov/public/pages/ptsd-older-vets.asp

National Center on Elder Abuse. (2005). *Elder abuse prevalence and incidence: Fact sheet.* Washington, DC: Author.

National Center on Elder Abuse. (2012). *Major types of elder abuse.* Retrieved from http://www.ncea.aoa.gov/Main_Site/FAQ/Basics/Types_Of_Aabuse.aspx

National Clearinghouse for Long-Term Care Information. (2012a). *Continuing care retirement communities (CCRCs).* Retrieved from http://www.longtermcare.gov/Main_Site/Paying/Private_Financing/Saving_LTC/CCRC.aspx

National Clearinghouse for Long-Term Care Information. (2012b). *Facility based services.* Retrieved from http://www.longtermcare.gov/Main_Site/Understanding/Services/Facility_Based_Services.aspx

National Clearinghouse for Long-Term Care Information. (2012c). *Older Americans Act Programs.* Retrieved from http://www.longtermcare.gov/Main_Site/Paying/Public_Programs/OAA.aspx

National Clearinghouse for Long-Term Care Information. (2012d). *Veterans Affairs LTC benefits.* Retrieved from http://www.longtermcare.gov/Main_Site/Paying/Public_Programs/Vererans.aspx

< removed>

National Clearinghouse for Long-Term Care Information. (2012e). *Who pays for LTC services?* Retrieved from http://www.longtermcare. gov/Main_Site/Paying/Costs/Who_Pays.aspx

National Council on Aging. (2012). *Healthy aging programs: Secrets to success.* Retrieved from http://www.ncoa.org/national-institute-of-senior-centers/nisc-news/healthy-aging-programs.html

National Federation of the Blind. (n.d.). *Straightforward answers about blindness.* Baltimore, MD: Author.

National Federation of the Blind. (2011a). *Do you know a blind person?* Baltimore, MD: Author.

National Federation of the Blind. (2011b). *Independence market.* Baltimore, MD: Author.

National Hospice and Palliative Care Organization. (2012a). *About hospice and palliative care.* Retrieved from http://www.nhpco.org/i4a/pages/Index.cfm?pageid=4648

National Hospice and Palliative Care Organization. (2012b). *End-of-life care in nursing homes lacking.* Retrieved from http://www.nhpco.org/i4a/pages/index.cfm?pageID=6716

National Hospice and Palliative Care Organization. (2012c). *LIVE—Without pain campaign helps people advocate for relief.* Retrieved from http://www.nhpco.org/i4a/pages/index.cfm?pageID=6619

National Hospice and Palliative Care Organization. (2012d). *Twelve tips to help a grieving loved one during the holidays.* Retrieved from http://www.nhpco.org/i4a/pages/index.cfm?pageID=6835

National Institute on Alcohol Abuse and Alcoholism. (2013). Alcohol and aging. *Alcohol Alert.* Retrieved from http://www.alcoholism.about.com/library/naa40.htm

National Institute on Deafness and Other Communication Disorders. (2008). *Statistics about hearing disorders, ear infections, and deafness.* Retrieved from http://www.nided.nig.gov/health/statistics/hearing.asp

National Organization of the Senior Blind. (2006). *So you don't see as well as you used to.* Baltimore, MD: National Federation of the Blind.

National Organization on Disability. (2001). *Employment facts about people with disabilities in the United States.* Retrieved from http://www.nod.org/index.cfm?fuseaction=page.viewPage&pageID=1430&nodeID=1&FeatureID=38&redirected=1&CFID=27507339&CFTOKEN=82689433

National Stroke Association. (2012a). *African-Americans and stroke.* Retrieved from http://www.stroke.org/site/PageServer?pagename=aamer

National Stroke Association. (2012b). *Recovery.* Retrieved from http://www.stroke.org/site/PageServer?pagename=recov

National Stroke Association. (2012c). *What is stroke?* Retrieved from http://www.stroke.org/site/PageServer?pagename=stroke

Neel, A. B. (2012, April 25). *7 meds that can wreck your sex life.* Retrieved from http://www.aarp.org/health/drugs-supplements/ info-04-2012/medications-that-can-cause-sexual-dysfunction.html

Neimeyer, R. (1998). *Lessons of loss: A guide to coping.* New York, NY: McGraw-Hill.

Neimeyer, R. (2001). *Meaning reconstruction and the experience of loss.* Washington, DC: American Psychological Association.

Nelson, H. R. (2004). *Senior spirituality: Awakening your spiritual potential.* St. Louis, MO: Chalice Press.

Newall, G., & Eisner, M. (Producers), & Warburton, T. (Director). (2002). I'm just a bill. On *School house rock!* [DVD]. United States: Disney Studios Home Entertainment.

Newman, A. B., & Brach, J. S. (2001). Gender gap in longevity and disability in older persons. *Epidemiology Review, 23,* 343–350.

Niederhoffer, G., Bisbee, S., Bisbee J. K., & Accord, L. (Producers), & Schreier, J. (Director). (2012). *Robot and Frank* [Motion picture]. United States: Samuel Goldwin Films & Stage Films.

Nolen-Hoeksema, S., & Larson, J. (1999). *Coping with loss.* Mahwah, NJ: Erlbaum.

Nordqvist, C. (2012, September 28). Benzodiazepine for insomnia or anxiety raises dementia risk among elderly. *Medical News Today.* Retrieved from http://www.medicalnewstoday.com/ articles/250794.php

Nourhashemi, F., Andrieu, S., Gillette-Guyonnet, S., Vellas, B., Albarede, J. L., & Grandjean, H. (2001). Instrumental activities of daily living as a potential marker of frailty. *Journals of Gerontology: Series A. Biological Sciences and Medical Sciences, 56,* M448–M453.

NSW Institute of Psychiatry and Centre for Mental Health. (2000). *Disaster mental health recovery handbook.* (2000). North Sydney, New South Wales, Australia: Author.

O'Leary, V. E., Alday, C. S., & Ickovics, J. R. (1998). Models of life change and posttraumatic growth. In R. G. Tedeschi, C. L. Park, & L. G. Calhoun (Eds.), *Posttraumatic growth: Positive changes in the aftermath of crisis* (pp. 127–151). Mahwah, NJ: Erlbaum.

O'Neill, L. M. (n.d.). Financial exploitation: Risk factors and warning signs. *Pima [Tucson, AZ] Council on Aging Never Too Late Newsletter.* Copy in Charlene M. Kampfe's possession.

O'Neill, L. M., & Vermeal, R. K. (2013, July). Elder abuse: Clinician reporting. *Arizona Geriatrics Society Journal, 18,* 25–26.

Osgood, N. (1985). *Suicide in the elderly.* Rockville, MD: Aspen Systems.

Owens, G. P., Baker, D. G., Kasckow, J., Ciesla, J. A., & Mohamed, S. (2005). Review of assessment and treatment of PTSD among elderly American armed forces veterans. *International Journal of Geriatric Psychiatry, 20,* 1118–1130.

Papalia, D. E., Sterns, H. L., Feldman, R. D., & Camp, C. J. (2003). *Adult development and aging* (2nd ed.). New York, NY: McGraw Hill.

Paprocki, R. (2012, June/July). Who needs Dad? *AARP: The Magazine, 55*, pp. 62, 66.

Pennar, K. (2012a, June 26). A firm diagnosis of frailty. *The New York Times*, p. D4.

Pennar, K. (2012b, June 26). Unafraid of aging [Interview with Linda P. Fried, geriatrician and dean of the Mailman School of Public Health, Columbia University]. *The New York Times*, pp. D1, D4.

Perrig-Chiello, P., & Höpflinger, R. (2005). Aging parents and their middle-aged children: Demographic and psychosocial challenges. *European Journal of Aging, 2*, 183–191.

Pew Research Center. (2009). *Growing old in America: Expectations vs. reality*. Retrieved from http://pewresearch.org/pubs/1269/aging-survey-expectations-versus-reality

Pillemer, K. A., & Bachman-Prehn, R. (1991). Helping and hurting: Predictors of maltreatment of patients in nursing homes. *Research on Aging, 13*, 74–95.

Pitkala, K. H., Laurila, J. V., Strandberg, T. E., & Tilvis, R. S. (2004). Behavioral symptoms and the administration of psychotropic drugs to aged patients with dementia in nursing homes and in acute geriatric wards. *International Psychogeriatrics, 16*, 66–74.

Pitt-Catsouphes, M., Smyer, M., Matz-Costa, C., & Kane, K. (2007). Summary report of the National Study of Business Strategy and Workforce Development. In *Research highlights* (No. 4). Chestnut Hill, MA: Center on Aging and Work/Workplace Flexibility, Boston College.

Pleis, J. R., Benson, V., & Schiller, J. S. (2003). *Summary of health statistics for U.S. adults: National Health Interview Survey, 2000* (National Center for Health Statistics, Vital Health Statistics Series 10, No. 215) . Retrieved from http://www.cdc.gov/nchs/data/series/sr_10/sr10/215.pdf

Ploeg, J., Fear, J., Hutchinson, B., MacMillan, H., & Bolan, G. (2009). A systematic review of interventions for elder abuse. *Journal of Elder Abuse & Neglect, 21*, 187–210.

Powers, P. W. (2013). *A guide to vocational assessment* (5th ed.). New York, NY: Pro-Ed.

Qato, D. M., Alexander, G. C., Conti, R. M., Johnson, M., Schumm, P., & Lindau, S. T. (2008). Use of prescription and over-the-counter medications and dietary supplements among older adults in the United States. *Journal of the American Medical Association, 300*, 2867–2878.

Quadagno, J. (2005). *Aging and the life course: An introduction to social gerontology* (3rd ed.). New York, NY: McGraw/Hill.

Quinn, J. B. (2012, November). Retirement for two. *AARP Bulletin, 53*, 31–32.

Quinn, J. F. (1999). *Retirement patterns and bridge jobs in the 1990s* (EBRI Issue Brief No. 206). Washington, DC: Employee Benefits Research Institute.

Rainie, L. (2012, November). Seniors' moment in a digital world. *AARP Bulletin, 53,* 36.

Rand, A. B. (2012, November). Caregiving's challenge and reward. *AARP Bulletin, 53,* 25.

Rando, T. (1984). *Grief, dying and death: Clinical interventions for caregivers.* Champagne, IL: Research Press.

Rando, T. A. (Ed.). (2000). *Clinical dimensions of anticipatory mourning: Theory and practice in working with the dying, their loved ones, and their caregivers.* Champaign, IL: Research Press.

Raphael, B., Middleton, W., Martinek, N., & Misso, V. (1993). *Counseling and therapy of the bereaved.* In W. Stroebe, M. Stroebe, & R. Hansson (Eds.), *Handbook of bereavement: Theory, research, and intervention* (pp. 427–453). New York, NY: Cambridge University Press.

Rasmusson, D. X., Rebok, G. W., Bylsma, F. W., & Brandt, J. (1999). Effects of three types of memory training in normal elderly. *Aging, Neuropsychology, and Cognition, 6,* 56–66.

Ratts, M. J., & Hutchins, A. M. (2009). ACA Advocacy Competencies: Social justice advocacy at the client/student level. *Journal of Counseling & Development, 87,* 269–275.

Ratts, M. J., & Pedersen, P. B. (2014). *Counseling for multiculturalism and social justice: Integration, theory, and application* (4th ed.). Arlington, VA: American Counseling Association.

Ratts, M. J., Toporek, R. L., & Lewis, J. A. (Eds.). (2010). *ACA Advocacy Competencies: A social justice framework.* Alexandria, VA: American Counseling Association.

Reed, J., Morgan, D., & Palmer, A. (1997). *Discharging older people from hospital to care homes—Implications for nursing care. Project summary.* Newcastle, England: University of Northumbria.

Reed, J., & Payton, V. R. (1996). *Working to create continuity: Older people managing the move to the care home setting* (Report No. 76). Newcastle upon Tyne, England: Center for Health Services Research, University of Newcastle upon Tyne.

Reese, D. J., Melton, E., & Ciaravino, K. (2004). Programmatic barriers to providing culturally competent end-of-life-care. *American Journal of Hospice and Palliative Medicine, 21,* 357–364.

Reid, C. R., & Kampfe, C. M. (2000). Multicultural issues. In A. Sales (Ed.), *Substance abuse and counseling* (pp. 215–246). Greensboro, NC: ERIC.

Reis, M., & Nahmiash, D. (1995). Validation of Caregiver Abuse Screen (CASE). *Canadian Journal of Aging, 14,* 45–60.

Research Notebook. (2007, January/February). Disability among older Americans continues significant decline. *FDA Consumer Magazine, 41,* 7.

Reyes-Ortiz, C. A. (2006). Spirituality, disability and chronic illness. *Southern Medical Journal, 99,* 1172–1173.

Reynolds, G. (2011, March/April). Super athletes: Older competitors are defying the laws of science and aging. *AARP: The Magazine, 54,* pp. 42–44, 64.

Richards, E. (2004). *Wedding ring.* Toronto, Ontario, Canada: MIRA Books.

Richards, E. (2012). *One mountain away.* Toronto, Ontario, Canada: MIRA Books.

Richards, P., & Bergin, A. E. (2005). *A spiritual strategy for counseling and psychotherapy* (2nd ed.). Washington, DC: American Psychological Association.

Richardson, V. E. (2001). Mental health of elderly women. In J. D. Garner & S. O. Mercer (Eds.), *Women as they age* (pp. 85–96). Binghamton, NY: Haworth Press.

Riker, H. C., & Myers, J. E. (1989). *Retirement counseling: A handbook for action.* New York, NY: Hemisphere.

Riordan, R. J., & Beggs, M. S. (1988). Some critical differences between self-help and therapy groups. *Journal of Specialists in Group Work, 13,* 24–29.

Roberto, K. A., & Stanis, P. I. (1994). Reactions of older women to the death of the close friends. *Omega: Journal of Death and Dying, 29,* 17–27.

Robins, R. W., & Trzesniewski, K. H. (2005). Self-esteem development across the lifespan. *Current Directions in Psychological Science, 14,* 158–162.

Robinson, L., Boose, G., & Segal, R. (2013, January). *Insomnia in older adults.* Retrieved from http://www.helpguide.org

Robinson, L., & Segal, J. (2012). *The therapeutic & health benefits of pets.* Retrieved from http://www.helpguide.org/life/pets.htm

Robinson, P. A. (2005). *Queer wars: The new gay right and its critics.* Chicago, IL: University of Chicago Press.

Rodriguez, V. J., Glover-Graf, N. M., & Blanco, E. L. (2013). Conversations with God: Prayer and bargaining in adjustment to disability. *Rehabilitation Counseling Bulletin, 56,* 215–228.

Rogers, C. H., Floyd, F. J., Seltzer, M. M., Greenberg, J., & Hong, J. (2008). Long-term effects of the death of a child on parents' adjustment in midlife. *Journal of Family Psychology, 22,* 203–211.

Rostad, B., Deeg, D. J. H., & Schei, B. (2009). Socioeconomic inequalities in health in older women. *European Journal of Ageing, 6,* 39–47.

Rothschild, M., & Kampfe, C. M. (1997). Issues associated with late onset deafness. *JADARA: Journal for Professionals Networking for Excellence in Service Delivery with Individuals Who Are Deaf and Hard of Hearing, 31,* 1–16.

Rowan, R. (2011). *Never too late: A 90-year-old's pursuit of a whirlwind life.* Guilford, CT: Lyons Press.

Rowe, J. W., & Kahn, R. L. (1998). *Successful aging.* New York, NY: Pantheon Books.

Rowles, G. D., & Chaudhury, H. (Eds.). (2005). *Home and identity in late life: International perspective.* New York, NY: Springer.

Rubin, S. (1999). The two-track model of bereavement: Overview, retrospect, and prospects. *Death Studies, 23,* 681–714.

Rubin, S. E., & Roessler, R. T. (2008). *Foundations of the vocational rehabilitation process* (6th ed.). Austin, TX: Pro-Ed.

Rudner, R. (2008). *I still have it: I just can't remember where I put it: Confessions of a fifty something.* New York, NY: Three Rivers Press.

Rybash, J. M., Roodin, P. A., & Hoyer, W. J. (1995). *Adult development and aging* (3rd ed.). Dubuque, IA: WCB Brown & Benchmark.

Ryff, C. D. (1989). In the eyes of the beholder: Views of psychological wellbeing. *Psychology and Aging, 4,* 195–210.

Saari, S., & Silver, A. (2005). *A bolt from the blue: Coping with disasters and acute traumas.* London, England: Jessica Kingsley.

Saisan, J., Segal, J., Smith, M., & Robinson, L. (2012). *Gambling addiction and problem gambling.* Retrieved from http://71.6.131.182/mental/gambling_addiction.htm

Saisan, J., Smith, M., Segal, J., & White, M. (2012). *Staying healthy as you age.* Retrieved from http://www.helpguide.org /articles/aging-well/staying-healthy-as-you-age.htm

Saisan, J., White, M., & Robinson, L. (2012). *Senior driving: Safety tips, warning signs, and knowing when to stop.* Retrieved from http://71.6.131.182/elder/senior_citizen_driving.htm

Sales, A. (2007). *Rehabilitation counseling: An empowerment perspective.* Austin, TX: Pro-Ed.

Salizar, C. F. (Ed.). (2009). *Group work experts share their favorite multicultural activities: A guide to diversity-competent choosing, planning, conducting, and processing.* Alexandria, VA: Association for Specialists in Group Work.

Salman, J. (2009). Old, young do not see eye to eye in widening generation gap. *The Florida Times-Union.* Retrieved from http://jacksonville.com/news/metro/2009-06-30/story/old_young_dont_see_eye_to_eye_in_widening_generation_gap

Saltz, G. (2011, March/April). Rekindling the flame. *AARP: The Magazine, 54,* 54–55.

Saucier, M. G. (2004). Midlife and beyond: Issues for aging women. *Journal of Counseling & Development, 82,* 420–425.

Sbarra, D. A., & Emery, R. E. (2008). Deeper into divorce: Using actor–partner analyses to explore systemic difference in co-parenting conflict following custody dispute resolution. *Journal of Family Psychology, 22,* 144–152.

Schade, C. P., Jones, E. R., Jr., & Wittlin, B. J. (1998). A ten-year review of the validity and clinical utility of depression screening. *Psychiatric Services, 49,* 55–61.

Schaie, K. W., & Willis, S. L. (2002). *Adult development and aging* (5th ed.). Upper Saddle River, NJ: Prentice Hall.

Schiamberg, L. B., Oehmke, J., Zhang, Z., Barboza, G. E., Griffore, R. J., Von Heydrick, L., . . . Mastin, T. (2012). Physical abuse of older adults in nursing homes: A random sample survey of adults with an elderly family member in a nursing home. *Journal of Elder Abuse & Neglect, 24,* 65–83.

Schlossberg, N. K., Waters, E. B., & Goodman, J. (1995). *Counseling adults in transition* (2nd ed.). New York, NY: Springer.

Schonbrun, S. L., & Kampfe, C. M. (2009). Work life expectancy of older individuals: Implications for vocational professionals. *Journal of Forensic Vocational Analysis, 12,* 17–23.

Schwartz, P. (2011, May 9). *5 myths about sex and aging.* Retrieved from http://www.aarp.org/relationships/love-sex/info-05-2001/sex-myths.print.html

Schwartz, P. (2012, October). *What to do when sex is painful.* Retrieved from http://www.aarp.org/home-family/sex-intimacy/info-10-2012/what-to-do-when-sex-is-painful

Scurfield, R. M., & Platoni, K. T. (Eds.). (2013). *Healing war trauma: A handbook for creative approaches.* New York, NY: Routledge.

Segal, J., Smith, M., & Robinson, L. (2013). *Bring your life into balance.* Retrieved from http://www.helpguide.org/toolkit/emotional_health.htm

Services and Advocacy for Gay, Lesbian, Bisexual, and Transgender Elders. (2011). *National Resource Center on LGB Aging unveils essential LGBT caregiving resources.* Retrieved from http://www.sageusa.org/newsevents/release.cfm?ID=37

Services and Advocacy for Gay, Lesbian, Bisexual, and Transgender Elders. (2012). *About us.* Retrieved from http://www.sageusa.org/about/

Shafer, M., Glotzer, L., Zuker, J., & Gluck, W. (Producers), & Gluck, W. (Director). (2011). *Friends with benefits* [Motion picture]. United States: Castlerock Entertainment/Zucker/Olive Bridge Entertainment.

Shallcross, L. (2012a, November). Eyes wide open: Recognizing depression in clients, especially among those who are often "invisible." *Counseling Today, 55,* 30–39.

Shallcross, L. (2012b, January). Making your next move. *Counseling Today, 54,* 28–36.

Shallcross, L. (2012c, April). Not content to 'ride off into the sunset': Counselors say that the Baby Boomer generation is challenging traditional beliefs about what it means to age. *Counseling Today, 54,* 40–44.

Shannonhouse, L., & Myers, J. (in press). International perspective on and advocacy against ageism. In C. Lee (Ed.), *Counseling for social justice* (3rd ed.). Alexandria, VA: American Counseling Association.

Shapiro, A. (2003). Later-life divorce and parent–adult child contact and proximity: A longitudinal analysis. *Journal of Family Issues, 24,* 264–285.

Shmotkin, D., & Eyal, N. (2003). Psychological time in later life: Implications for counseling. *Journal of Counseling & Development, 81,* 259–267.

Shumway-Cook, A., Brauer, S., & Woollacott, M. (2000). Predicting the probability for falls in community-dwelling older adults using the Timed Up & Go Test. *Physical Therapy, 80,* 896–903.

Siebert, D. C., Mutran, E. J., & Reitzes, D. C. (2002). Friendship and social support: The importance of role identity to aging adults. *Social Work, 44,* 522–533.

Silverstein, M., Conroy, S. J., Wang, H., Giarruso, R., & Bengston, V. L. (2002). Reciprocity in parent–child relations over the adult life course. *Journals of Gerontology: Series B. Psychological Sciences and Social Sciences, 57,* S3–S13.

Silverstein, M., & Long, J. D. (1998). Trajectories of grandparents' perceived solidarity with adult grandchildren: A growth curve analysis over 23 years. *Journal of Marriage and the Family, 60,* 912–928.

Silverstone, B., & Kandel Hyman, H. (2008). *You and your aging parent: A family guide to emotional, social, health, and financial problems* (4th ed.). New York, NY: Oxford University Press.

Simonton, D. K. (1989). The swan song phenomenon: Last works effects for 172 classical composers. *Psychology and Aging, 4,* 42–47.

Sklar, F., & Hartley, S. (1990). Close friends as survivors. *Omega: Journal of Death and Dying, 22,* 103–112.

Smith, H. I. (2002). *Friendgrief: An absence called presence.* Amityville, NY: Baywood.

Smith, M., Robinson, L., & Segal, R. (2012). *Memory loss and aging: Causes, treatment, and help for memory problems.* Retrieved from http://www.helpguide.org/life/prevent_memory_loss.htm

Smith, S. L., Bennett, L. W., & Wilson, R. H. (2008) Prevalence and characteristics of dual sensory impairment (hearing and vision) in a veteran population. *Journal of Rehabilitation Research and Development, 45,* 597–610.

Smith, S. M., & Kampfe, C. M. (1996). Creating a user-friendly counseling office environment for older persons with hearing impairments. *Arizona Counseling Journal, 21,* 21–26.

Smith, S. M., & Kampfe, C. M. (1997). Interpersonal relationship implications of hearing loss in persons who are older. *Journal of Rehabilitation, 63,* 15–21.

Smith, S. M., & Kampfe, C. M. (2000). Characteristics of diversity and aging: Implications for assessment. *Journal of Rehabilitation Counseling, 31,* 33–39.

Social Security Administration. (2005). *How we decide if you are still disabled* (SSA Pub. No. 05-10053). Available from http://www.ssa.gov/pubs/EN-05-10053.pdf

Social Security Administration. (2010). *If you are self-employed* (SSA Publication No. 05-10022). Available from http://www.ssa.gov/pubs/EN-05-10022.pdf

Social Security Administration. (2011a). *Disability benefits* (SSA Publication No. 05-10029). Available from http://www.ssa.gov/pubs/EN-05-10029.pdf

Social Security Administration. (2011b). *Government pension offset* (SSA Publication No. 05-10007). Available from http://www.ssa.gov/pubs/EN-05-10007.pdf

Social Security Administration. (2011c). *How work affects your benefits* (SSA Publication No. 05-10069). Available from http://www.ssa.gov/pubs/EN-05-10069.pdf

Social Security Administration. (2011d). *How workers' compensation and other disability payments may affect your benefits* (SSA Publication No. 05-10018). Available from http://www.ssa.gov/pubs/EN-05-10018.pdf

Social Security Administration. (2011e). *Understanding the benefits.* (SSA Publication No. 05-10024). Available from http://www.ssa.gov/pubs/EN-05-10024.pdf

Social Security Administration. (2011f). *What every woman should know* (SSA Publication No. 05-10127). Available from http://www.ssa.gov/pubs/EN-05-10127.pdf

Social Security Administration. (2011g). *What you need to know when you get retirement or survivors benefits* (SSA Publication No. 05-10077). Available from http://www.ssa.gov/pubs/EN-05-10077.pdf

Social Security Administration. (2011h). *Windfall elimination provision* (SSA Publication No. 05-10045). Available from http://www.ssa.gov/pubs/EN-05-10045.pdf

Social Security Administration. (2011i). *Working while disabled—How we can help* (SSA Publication No. 05-10095). Available from http://www.ssa.gov/pubs/EN-05-10095.pdf

Social Security Administration. (2011j). *Your retirement benefit: How it is figured* (SSA Publication No. 05-10070). Available from http://www.ssa.gov/pubs/EN-05-10070.pdf

Social Security Administration. (2013). *How you earn credits* (SSA Publication No. 05-10072). Available from http://www.ssa.gov/pubs/EN-05-10072.pdf

Stanley, M. A., & Averill, P. M. (1999). Strategies for treating generalized anxiety in the elderly. In M. Duffy (Ed.), *Handbook of counseling and psychotherapy with older* adults (pp. 511–525). New York, NY: Wiley.

Stevens, P., & Smith, R. (2000). *Substance abuse counseling: Theory and practice* (2nd ed.). Upper Saddle River, NJ: Prentice Hall.

Stroebe, M., Schut, H., & Boerner, K. (2010). Continuing bonds in adaptation to bereavement: Toward theoretical integration. *Clinical Psychology Review, 30,* 259–268.

Stroebe, M., Schut, H., & Stroebe, W. (2007). Health outcomes of bereavement. *Lancet, 370,* 1960–1973.

Stroebe, W., Schut, H., & Stroebe, M. (2005). Grief work, disclosure and counseling: Do they help the bereaved? *Clinical Psychology Review, 25,* 395–414.

Sturges, J. E. (2012). *Resiliency: How to thrive during changing times.* Tucson, AZ: UA Lifework Connections.

Sue, D. W. (2010). *Microaggressions in everyday life: Race, gender, and sexual orientation.* Hoboken, NJ: Wiley.

Sue, D. W., Capodilupo, C. M., Torino, G. C., Bucceri, J. M., Holder, M. B., Nadal, K. L., & Esquilin, M. (2007). Racial microaggression in everyday life: Implications for clinical practice. *American Psychologist, 2,* 271–286.

Sue, D. W., & Sue, D. (2008). *Counseling the culturally different: Theory and practice* (5th ed.). New York, NY: Wiley.

Summers, R. W., & Hoffman, A. M. (2006). *Elder abuse: A public health perspective.* Washington, DC: American Public Health Association.

Sweeney, M. M. (2010). Remarriage and stepfamilies: Strategic sites for family scholarship in the 21st century. *Journal of Marriage and Family, 72,* 667–684.

Swett, E. A., & Bishop, M. (2003). Mental health and the aging population: Implications for rehabilitation counselors. *Journal of Rehabilitation, 69,* 13–18.

Teaster, P. B., Dugar, T. A., Mendiondo, M. S., Abner, E. L., Cecil, K. A., & Otto, J. M. (2006). *The 2004 survey of state adult protection services: Abuse of adults 60 years of age and older.* Washington, DC: National Center on Elder Abuse.

Teaster, P. B., Nerenberg, L., & Stansbury, K. L. (2003) A national look at elder abuse multidisciplinary teams. *Journal of Elder Abuse and Neglect, 5,* 91–107.

Terrell, K., Heard, K., & Miller, D. (2006). Prescribing to older ED patients. *American Journal of Emergency Medicine, 24,* 468–478.

Thomas, M. (2011, May/June). Home sweet home. *AARP: The Magazine, 54,* pp. 42–45, 67.

Thomas, M. C., Gillam, S. L., & Hard, P. F. (2012). Counseling older lesbians: The case of Pat and Salene. In S. H. Dworkin & M. Pope (Eds.), *Casebook for counseling lesbian, gay, bisexual, and transgender persons and their families* (pp. 63–72). Alexandria, VA: American Counseling Association.

Thomas, M. C., & Martin, V. (2010). Group work: Elderly people and their caregivers. In D. Capuzzi, D. R. Gross, & M. D. Stauffer (Eds.), *Introduction to group work* (5th ed., pp. 505–526). Denver, CO: Love.

Thomas, M. C., Martin, V., Alexander, J. J., Cooley, F. R., & Loague, A. M. (2003). Using new attitudes and technology to change the developmental counseling focus for older populations. *Counseling and Human Development, 35,* 1–8.

Thorp, S. R., Sones, H. M., & Cook, J. M. (2011). Posttraumatic stress disorder among older adults. In K. H. Soroco & S. Lauderdale (Eds.), *Cognitive behavior therapy with older adults: Innovations across care settings* (pp. 189–218). New York, NY: Springer.

Thurlo, A., & Thurlo, D. (1995). *Blackening song.* New York, NY: Forge.

Tick, E. (2005). *War and the soul.* New York, NY: Quest Books.

Tjaden, P., & Thoennes, N. (2000, November). *Full report of the prevalence, incidence and consequences of violence against women: Findings from the National Violence Against Women Survey.* Washington, DC: National Institute of Justice/NCJRS.

Tokar, S. (2011). *Estrogen therapy's link with dementia risk depends on the age when taken study finds.* Retrieved from University of California San Francisco website: http://www.ucsf.edu/news/2011/02/8458/estrogen-therapys-link-dementia-risk-depends-age-when-taken-study-finds

Trouillet, R., Gana, K., Lourel, M., & Fort, I. (2009). Predictive value of age for coping: The role of self-efficacy, social support satisfaction and perceived stress. *Aging and Mental Health, 13,* 357–366.

United Cerebral Palsy of Southern Arizona. (n.d.). *Grandfamilies: Kincare givers of southern Arizona: The second time around* [DVD]. Tucson, AZ: Author.

University of Arizona Life and Work Connections. (2012). *Tips for caregivers* [Brochure], pp. 9–12.

Uriri, J. T., & Thatcher-Winger, R. (1995). Health risk appraisal and the older adult. *Journal of Gerontological Nursing, 21,* 25–31.

U.S. Census Bureau. (2000). *U.S. Census data.* Washington, DC: Author.

U.S. Census Bureau. (2006). *Facts for features: Special edition, Oldest Baby Boomers turn 60.* Retrieved from http://www. census.gov/Press-Release/www/releases/archives/facts_for_ features_special_editions/006105.html

U.S. Department of Health and Human Services. (2001). *Psychotropic drug use in nursing homes* (OEI Publication No. 02-00-00490). Retrieved from http://oig.hhs.gov/oei/reports/oei-02-00-00490.pdf

U.S. Department of Health and Human Services. (2007). *National strategy for suicide prevention.* Retrieved from http://mentalhealth. samhsa.gov/suicideprevention/elderly.asp

van Zelst, W. H., de Beurs, E., Beekman, A. T., Deeg, D. J., & van Dyck, R. (2003). Prevalence and risk factors of posttraumatic stress disorder in older adults. *Psychotherapy and Psychosomatics, 72,* 333–342.

Verbrugge, L. M., & Jette, A. M. (1994). The disablement process. *Social Science and Medicine, 38,* 1–14.

Verde, M. (Producer), & Kay, T. (Producer & Director). (2011). *There is a bridge* [Documentary]. United States: TMK Productions. DVD available for purchase at http://www.memorybridge.org/dvd.php

Vig, E. K., Davenport, N. A., & Pearlman, R. A. (2002). Good deaths, bad deaths, and preferences for the end of life: A qualitative study of geriatric outpatients. *Journal of the American Geriatrics Society, 50,* 1541–1548.

Wadsworth, J. S., Estrada-Hernandez, N., Kampfe, C. M., & Smith, S. M. (2008). Economic outcome of employment for older participants in Rehabilitation Services funded by the Rehabilitation Services Administration. *Rehabilitation Counseling Bulletin, 52,* 107–117.

Wadsworth, J., Harley, D., Smith, S. M., & Kampfe, C. M. (2008). Infusing end-of-life issues into the rehabilitation counselor education curriculum. *Rehabilitation Education, 22,* 113–124.

Wadsworth, J., & Kampfe, C. M. (2004). The characteristics of senior applicants of vocational rehabilitation services. *Rehabilitation Counseling Bulletin, 47,* 104–111.

Wadsworth, J. S., Smith, S. M., & Kampfe, C. M. (2006). The use of age 65 as a data management strategy in rehabilitation research. *Rehabilitation Education, 20,* 213–220.

Waller, P. F. (1998). Alcohol, aging, and driving. In E. S. L. Gomberg, A. M. Hegedus, & R. A. Zucker (Eds.), *Alcohol problems and aging* (NIAA Research Monograph No. 33, NIH Publication No 98-4163). Bethesda, MD: National Institute on Alcohol Abuse and Alcoholism.

Wallis, V. (1993). *Two old women: An Alaska legend of betrayal, courage, and survival.* Fairbanks, AK: Epicenter Press.

Walter, C. (1997). Support groups for widows and widowers. In G. Grief & P. Ephross (Eds.), *Group work with populations at risk* (pp. 69–83). New York, NY: Oxford University Press.

Walter, C. A. (2003). *The loss of a life partner: Narratives of the bereaved.* New York, NY: Columbia University Press.

Walter, T. (1999). *On bereavement: The culture of grief.* Birkshire, England: Open University Press/McGraw-Hill Education.

Waters, B. (1999). *Celebrating the coyote.* Denver, CO: DIVINA.

Waters, E. B., & Goodman, J. (1990). *Empowering older adults: Practical strategies for counselors.* San Francisco, CA: Jossey-Bass.

Watson, N., Roulstone, A., & Thomas, C. (Eds.). (2012). *Routledge handbook on disability studies.* Routledge, NY: Routledge Handbooks.

Wechsler, D. (1995). *Wechler Adult Intelligence Scale.* New York, NY: Psychological Corporation.

Weinstein, J. (2008). *Working with loss, death, and bereavement: A guide for social workers.* Los Angeles, CA: Sage.

Weintraub, A., & Ashley, M. J. (2004). Traumatic brain injury: Aging and related neuromedical issues. In M. J. Ashley (Ed.), *Rehabilitation treatment and case management* (2nd ed., pp. 273–301). Boca Raton, FL: CRC Press.

Werngren-Elgstrolm, M., Carlsson, G., & Iwarsson, S. (2009). A 10-year follow-up study on subjective well-being and relationships to person–environment (P-E) fit and activity of daily living (ADL) dependence of older Swedish adults. *Archives of Gerontology and Geriatrics, 49,* e16–e22.

Wheeler, I. (2001). Parental bereavement: The crisis of meaning. *Death Studies, 25,* 52–66.

Wheeler, W. M. (1996). *Elderly residential experience: The evolution of places as residence.* New York, NY: Garland.

Whitbourne, S. K., & Sherry, M. S. (1991). Subjective perceptions of the life span in chronic mental patients. *International Journal of Aging and Human Development, 33,* 65–73.

Whitbourne, S. K., Sneed, J. R., & Skultety, K. M. (2002). Identity processes in adulthood: Theoretical and methodological challenges. *Identity, 2,* 29–45.

Whitbourne, S. K., & Whitbourne, S. B. (2011) *Adult development and aging: Biopsychosocial perspectives* (4th ed.). Hoboken, NJ: Wiley.

Whitley, P. (Producer), & Kroeker, A. (Director). (1989). *Age old friends* [Motion picture]. United States: Central Independent Television.

Whitmer, R. A., Karter, A. J., Yaffe, K., Quesenberry, C. P., & Selby, J. V. (2009). Hypoglycemic episodes and risk of dementia in older patients with Type 2 diabetes mellitus. *Journal of the American Medical Association, 301,* 1565–1572.

Wickremaratchi, M. M., & Llewelyn, J. G. (2006). Effects of ageing on touch. *Postgraduate Medical Journal, 82,* 301–304.

Wiglesworth, A., Mosqueda, L., Mulnard, R., Liao, S., Gibbs, S., & Fitzgerald, W. (2010). Screening for abuse and neglect of people with dementia. *Journal of the American Geriatric Society, 58,* 493–500.

Wilke, D. J., & Vinton, L. (2005). The nature and impact of domestic violence across age cohorts. *Affilia, 20,* 316–328.

Williams, J. M., Ballard, M. B., & Alessi, H. (2005). Aging and alcohol abuse: Increasing counselor awareness. *Adultspan Journal, 4,* 7–18.

Williamson, G. M., & Shaffer, D. R. (2001). Caregiver loss and quality of care provided: Pre-illness relationship makes a difference. In J. H. Harvey & E. D. Miller (Eds.), *Loss and trauma: General and close relationship perspectives* (pp. 307–330). Philadelphia, PA: Brunner/Mazel.

Wilson, R. S., Beck, T. L., Bieneas, J. L., & Bennett, D. A. (2007). Terminal cognitive decline: Accelerated loss of cognitive functioning the last years of life. *Psychosomatic Medicine, 69,* 131–137.

Wingate, L. (2008). *A month of summer.* New York, NY: Penguin.

Wolf, R. S., & Pillemer, K. (1989). *Helping elderly victims: The reality of elder abuse.* New York, NY: Columbia University Press.

Wood, R. G., Goesling, B., & Avellar, S. (2007). *The effects of marriage on health: A synthesis of recent research evidence* (DHHS Report No. 233-02-0086). Retrieved from http://aspe.hhs.gov/hsp/07/marriageonhealth/report.pdf

Worden, J. (2002). *Grief counseling and grief therapy: A handbook for the mental health practitioner* (3rd ed.). New York, NY: Springer.

Worell, J., & Remer, P. (2003). *Feminist perspectives in therapy: Empowering diverse women.* New York, NY: Wiley.

Wright, C. (2013). *Love all.* New York, NY: Henry Holt.

Wu, Z., & Schimmele, C. M. (2007). Uncoupling in late life. *Generations, 31,* 41–46.

Xiong, Y. (2012). Care for Hmong elderly caught between cultures. *Wasau Daily Herald.* Retrieved from http://www.wausaudailyherald.com/article/20120423/WDH0402/204230322/Care-Hmong

Yalisove, D. (2010). *Developing clinical skills for substance abuse counseling.* Alexandria, VA: American Counseling Association.

Zaentz, S., & Douglas, M. (Producers), & Forman, M. (Director). (1975). *One flew over the cuckoo's nest* [Motion picture]. United States: United Artists/Fantasy Films.

Zanuck, D., & Gundlach, D. (Producers), & Schneider, A. (Director). (2009). *Get low* [Motion picture]. United States: Sony Pictures.

Zimmerman, H. (2011, May/June). What I'd really like to do. *AARP: The Magazine, 54,* 64.

Zinker, J. (1994). *In search of good form.* San Francisco, CA: Jossey-Bass.

Index

B

Baby Boomers
as agents of change, 9, 225
geriatrician shortage and, 13
overall health and life expectancy
of, 71–72
retirement savings of, 127
statistics on, 2–3
Balance in aging, 77, 90, 154, 162
Bathroom breaks during counseling, 74
Beck, T. L., 88
Beginners (film), 189
Behavioral relaxation, 29
Bennett, D. A., 88
Benson, V., 101
Benzodiazepine, 112, 115
Bereavement. *See also* Grief and mourning
patterns of, 283
support groups, 291–292
Berries and brain health, 61
The Best Exotic Marigold Hotel (film), 208
Bias
in assessments, 34–35, 118
in counseling, 18, 183, 188
in death/grief perceptions, 294
Bibliotherapy and media use, 23–24
to combat ageism, 67–68
dementia and Alzheimer's, 81, 86–87
as depression treatment, 108
grief counseling and, 292–293
interpersonal relationships and, 183
LGBT clients and, 189
residential issues and, 266
sexuality and, 207–208
vision loss and, 149–150
Bieneas, J. L., 88
Biofeedback, 29, 104
Biological age, as classification system, 2
Bionics, 35
Birditt, K. S., 177
Bisexuality. *See* Lesbian, gay, bisexual,
and transgender (LGBT) clients
Blanchard-Fields, F., 51
Blindness. *See* Vision loss and blindness
Blood pressure, 29, 171
Board and care homes, 257
Bonanno, G. A., 283
Books and publishing. *See* Media
Boston Beacon Hill Village, 250
Braille, 148, 168
Brain health, 58, 59–61, 79–83, 88. *See
also* Strokes
Brainstem strokes, 90–91
Brainstorming
with caregivers, 199

as client advocacy strategy, 45
as coping strategy, 56
on driving issues, 136
on enjoyable activities, 67
in grief counseling, 285
on healthy eating, 61
on needed services, 161, 162
problem solving via, 22–23
Brandt, J., 60
Brehm, M. A., 31
Brennan, M., 167
Bridge employment/phased
retirement, 232
Bridges, J. D., 104
Brief Abuse Screening for the Elderly, 131
Brief psychodynamic psychotherapy, 117
Brooks, F., 119
Brown, S. L., 176
Bulanda, J. R., 176
Burger, S. G., 263
Bylsma, F. W., 60

C

CACREP (Council for Accreditation of
Counseling and Related Educational
Programs), 11–12, 21
CAGE (Cutting down, annoyance,
guilt, and eye opening), 118
Cahill, K. E., 229
Cancer patients, 272–273
Cardiac health, 26, 58, 61
Career counseling and development,
34, 238–241. *See also* Retirement and
work decisions
Caregivers and caregiving, 193–199
case management and, 196–197
communication between family
members, 197–198
counseling caregivers, 195–197
dementia and, 86–87
elder abuse and, 46, 128–129, 131
emotional and physical difficulties
of, 194, 196
LGBT clients and, 190
medications and, 97–98
monetary payback for, 194–195
progressive relaxation and, 30
relationship with aging person,
198–199
resources, 199–200
self-care for, 199
stroke recovery and, 91–92
CarFit evaluations, 134–135
Cars and car accidents. *See* Driving
and transportation issues

Menopause, 202–203
Mental activities, 60
Mental health issues, 101–124
  alcoholism, 119–122
  anxiety and stress, 102–104
  assessment activity for counselors,
    118–119
  depression, 104–108
  physical activity and, 58
  prevalence of disorders, 101
  psychiatric conditions, 122–123
  PTSD, 113–117
  resources, 124
  sleep issues, 111–113
  substance abuse and addictions,
    117–122
  suicide, 108–111
  types of professionals, 13
Metabolism, aging effects on, 73
Mettler, B., 31
Meyer, J., 83
Michigan Alcohol Screening Test
  (MAST), 118
Microaggressions, 18
Military culture, 138–139. *See also* Veterans issues
Minorities. *See* Diversity
Minority Stress Model, 18
Misdiagnoses
  Alzheimer's disease and dementia,
    80, 82
  counselors as patient advocates, 99
  HIV/AIDS, 209
  mental health disorders, 103, 105
  multisensory loss, 167
  pharmacy consultations, 98
  PTSD, 114
  substance abuse, 118
Mistreatment, client advocacy and,
  44–45
Mobility aids, 35
Moen, P., 226
Monroe, N. K., 139
A Month of Summer (Wingate), 73, 91
Mourning. *See* Grief and mourning
Mr. Smith Goes to Washington (film), 41
Multicultural issues in counseling,
  16–21. *See also* Diversity
  addiction counseling, 122
  avoiding cultural bias, 18
  case study, 19–21
  communication and cultural
    awareness of, 17
  cultural self-awareness activity for
    counselors, 19
  death and responses to, 271–272

individualism vs. collectivism, 18
military culture and veterans,
  137–139
religion and spirituality and, 63
social norms and, 16
Multiple group connections, 18
Multiple losses and transitions, 82, 119,
  121, 125–126, 173
Multisensory loss in older people,
  167–169
Murphy, S. N., 242
Muscle mass, decrease in, 74
Music. *See* Dance and music therapies
Music therapy, 277
Myers, J. E., 7, 16, 53, 227
Myers, K., 139

N

Nahmiash, E., 132
"Nana power," grandparenting and,
  178–179
Nanotechnology, 35
National Alliance on Mental Illness, 104
National Association on HIV Over
  Fifty, 184
National Center for Health Statistics,
  71
National Center on Elder Abuse, 128
National Citizens' Coalition for Nursing Home Reform, 263
National Consumer Voice for Quality
  Long-Term Care, 256, 263
National Council on Aging's Center
  for Healthy Aging, 59
National Council on Alcoholism Criteria for Diagnosis of Alcoholism, 118
National Federation of the Blind, 148
National Hospice and Palliative Care
  Organization (NHPCO), 141
National Household Travel Survey, 132
National Institute on Deafness and
  Other Communication Disorders
  (NIDCD), 161
National Organization of the Senior
  Blind, 150
National Organization on Disability,
  237
National parks, 182, 232, 251
Native Americans. *See also* Diversity
  cultural competency (case study),
    19–21
  religion and spirituality and, 63
  suicide risk and, 109
Negative attitudes toward older
  people, 5–8. *See also* Ageism

www.ingramcontent.com/pod-product-compliance
Lightning Source LLC
Chambersburg PA
CBHW060023030426
42334CB00019B/2150